D1432621

James McHenry, Forgotten Federalist

E S T. 75 1 9 3 8
YEARS
THE UNIVERSITY OF GEORGIA PRESS 2013

Studies in the Legal History of the South

EDITED BY PAUL FINKELMAN AND TIMOTHY S. HUEBNER

This series explores the ways in which law has affected the development of the southern United States and in turn the ways the history of the South has affected the development of American law. Volumes in the series focus on a specific aspect of the law, such as slave law or civil rights legislation, or on a broader topic of historical significance to the development of the legal system in the region, such as issues of constitutional history and of law and society, comparative analyses with other legal systems, and biographical studies of influential southern jurists and lawyers.

James McHenry, Forgotten Federalist

KAREN E. ROBBINS

The University of Georgia Press
Athens and London

Parts of chapters 4 and 5 were originally published in different form as "Ambition Rewarded: James McHenry's Entry into Post-Revolutionary Maryland Politics" in the *Maryland Historical Magazine*, Summer 1998. Chapter 11 was originally published in different form as "Power among the Powerless: Domestic Resistance by Free and Slave Women in the McHenry Family of the New Republic" in the *Journal of the Early Republic* 23 (2003). Part of chapter 20 was published in different form as "'Domestic Bagatelles': Servants, Generations and Gender in the McHenry Family of the Early Republic" in the *Maryland Historical Magazine*, Spring 2009.

© 2013 by the University of Georgia Press

Athens, Georgia 30602

www.ugapress.org

All rights reserved

Set in Minion Pro by Graphic Composition, Inc., Bogart, GA

Manufactured by Thomson Shore, Inc.

The paper in this book meets the guidelines for
permanence and durability of the Committee on
Production Guidelines for Book Longevity of the
Council on Library Resources.

Printed in the United States of America

17   16   15   14   13   C   5   4   3   2   1

Library of Congress Cataloging-in-Publication Data

Robbins, Karen E.

James McHenry, forgotten federalist / Karen E. Robbins.

    pages   cm

Includes bibliographical references and index.

ISBN 978-0-8203-4563-5 (hardcover : alk. paper)—ISBN 0-8203-4563-6 (hardcover : alk. paper)

1. McHenry, James, 1753–1815. 2. United States—Politics and government—1789–1816.

3. Statesmen—United States—Biography. I. Title.

E302.6.M12R63 2013

973.3092—dc23

[B]

2013014439

British Library Cataloging-in-Publication Data available

For my parents, Colonel Thomas L. and Mrs. Evelyn M. Robbins,
who first inspired my love of history.

For my husband, Daniel L. Tate, whose encouragement has never wavered.

For my son, Daniel L. Tate IV, whose support is never-ending.

Contents

Acknowledgments

I OWE MANY A DEBT of gratitude. It must be said, however, that meeting Paul Finkelman proved an important day for me. Little did either of us know that his trip years ago to lecture for teachers and academics in western New York would wind up with his helping to publish this book. Paul Finkelman is not only President William McKinley Distinguished Professor of Law and Public Policy and Senior Fellow at the Government Law Center at Albany Law School, but he also co-edits the series on Studies in the Legal History of the South at the University of Georgia Press, in which this book is published. He was pleased to hear that I had been writing a biography of James McHenry, who had attended the Constitutional Convention, and Professor Finkelman indicated that such a book should be published. Then he gave me his card. When the time came, he brought it to the attention of his co-editors and proceeded to give it a meticulous reading with an extremely valuable critique that helped me improve the book enormously. This was in addition to the comments and constructive criticism of two other anonymous reviewers. So I am most grateful to him for taking such an interest in my work.

I also appreciate the support of the two other editors of the series, Nancy Grayson (former executive editor, University of Georgia Press) and Timothy Huebner (L. Palmer Brown Professor of Interdisciplinary Humanities at Rhodes College). Nancy Grayson especially helped, patiently taking the time to shepherd my project through the process of getting the book accepted by the press. As she has recently retired, her assistant editor Beth Snead has graciously guided me since, exhibiting an unfailing good nature in response to my many questions. John Joerschke (project editor at the University of Georgia Press) then took up my case and kindly directed the book to its publication, while Kay Kodner, copyeditor, helped immensely to improve the grammar and style of the book. The professionalism of the people at the University of Georgia Press is to be admired.

Another scholar, T. Stephen Whitman, whom I was fortunate to meet at a weeklong seminar hosted by the Gilder Lehrman Institute of American History and who taught at Mount St. Mary's University in Maryland, gave the manuscript a thorough and thoughtful perusal. His careful reading helped to give the book much greater clarity.

Thanks also go to the *Journal of the Early Republic* and *Maryland Historical Magazine* for permitting me to include in this book, in revised form, articles that I first published through their presses. Andrea Ashby, library technician at the Independence National Historical Park, gathered together many of the photographic images for me, which are published with that organization's permission.

I would also like to express my thanks to Saint Bonaventure University. Theresa Shaffer, head reference and interlibrary loan librarian at the university, is every scholar's dream. No document is too difficult for her to find. If it is not readily found, she considers this a challenge to be met. The university also provided a Keenan Grant for research in Maryland, and Dean Wolfgang Natter has supplied funds for photographic materials in this book. In addition, the History Department, especially my chair Professor Phillip Payne, has always found words of encouragement for this project.

My son, Daniel L. Tate IV, has never failed to encourage my work, understanding my need to write this book. No one, however, can best my husband, Daniel L. Tate, for listening to endless issues regarding McHenry, reading countless drafts, and always supporting me in every way that I needed.

To all I wish to express my thanks.

James McHenry, Forgotten Federalist

Introduction

JAMES MCHENRY'S LIFE unfolds in stories. Writ large, the tale is of a man who tried to live his life honorably and make a difference. But this bigger narrative emerges from smaller ones that reveal important American—and human—themes.

Initially, McHenry was a young immigrant looking for opportunity. He was ambitious for a new and better life, and in this sense he was a man on the make. But McHenry was after more than just a comfortable living; he wanted to rise in status, to become a gentleman, and to live by the gentleman's code of honor. It certainly helped that his family arrived from northern Ireland with some property, enough to begin a dry goods importing business in the growing town of Baltimore. But that was only the beginning.

McHenry also participated in his generation's defining event—the American Revolution. McHenry climbed from the lowest rank of surgeon's mate to serve on General George Washington's staff, making contacts that opened doors for a future in politics, first at the state and then at the national level. Equally important, James got to prove his manhood as citizen-soldier, offering his life in service and possible sacrifice to the republic. His younger brother John was not so fortunate, as someone needed to stay in Baltimore to take care of their aging father and the mercantile business. John's unhappiness over being left out of the Revolution led him to excessive behavior that ultimately killed him.

The Revolution, of course, was an outgrowth of the Enlightenment, from which comes another theme. Enlightenment ideals led James McHenry to embrace fairly advanced views regarding the equality of men and women, as well as of the races, even if he was unable to live up to them fully. Benjamin Banneker, African American mathematician, requested and received

1

from McHenry a laudatory introduction to Banneker's almanac. Despite this, McHenry compromised for his convenience and chose to own domestic slaves. The slaves' attempts to negotiate for their freedom become an important part of this story. In addition, although a youthful McHenry insisted upon the intellectual equality of men and women, the middle-aged McHenry thought his young daughter ought to be educated religiously, in order to learn to submit to her future husband. Two equal partners in a household, he thought, would only lead to conflict.

Legal scholars will be particularly interested in McHenry's role at the Constitutional Convention. His journals are a valuable source of information. Considered by some to be second only to James Madison's, they would have been a treasure trove had he not been called away to nurse his seriously ill brother. When he returned, McHenry tried to influence the Constitution in small ways that had big results. He and General Charles Cotesworth Pinckney of South Carolina urged the equal treatment of ports within the United States, which helped to ensure that free trade would prosper domestically. McHenry was also interested in forbidding ex post facto clauses that allowed people to be prosecuted for acts that were legal when they were committed. He had fought such laws in Maryland, but the records show that Elbridge Gerry of Massachusetts actually made the motion for such a ban, with McHenry seconding it. Gerry's biographer, however, gives no indication that he was interested in this issue at all; he does not even mention that Gerry made the motion. It is likely, then, that McHenry and Gerry met, coincidentally or not, and agreed that Gerry would make a motion prohibiting ex post facto laws to be seconded by McHenry. In any event, McHenry's foresight helped put this clause in the Constitution.

For those interested in the political history of the first administrations, a new perspective emerges with this study of McHenry's tenure as secretary of war under George Washington and John Adams. Rather than an all-too-easy generalization that a monolithic Hamiltonian wing existed during the Adams administration, a close look at McHenry reveals a more complex dynamic among these men. This has been partially unearthed by Richard Kohn's studies of the military establishment, Howard Mattsson-Bozé's treatment of McHenry's term as secretary of war, Stephen G. Kurtz's book about John Adams's presidency, Gerard Clarfield's biography of Timothy Pickering, and James Edward Bland's assessment of the Wolcotts of Connecticut (no modern biography exists). Washington remains a high-minded Cincinnatus, but one who is impatient and a little too concerned about his reputation. Adams, ever the patriot, is nonetheless too suspicious, and many of his later actions are best explained by a shrewd attempt to build a following that could reelect him in 1800. Alexander Hamilton is always brilliant but also underhanded. His propensity for poison-pen letters has been noted recently in Nancy Isenberg's biography of Aaron Burr. Self-righteous describes Timothy Pickering, who was apparently incapable of realizing that being right (and he was sometimes terribly wrong) is not the same as being wise. Oliver Wolcott surfaces as a charming hypocrite, complaining to former secretary of the treasury Alexander Hamilton about McHenry even while he intentionally stymied the War Department.

What role generally did Hamilton play in this? Certainly, McHenry, Pickering, and Wolcott respected Hamilton; consulted him when a need arose; and supported him when they felt it necessary. But none of them—not even his protégé Wolcott (after Wolcott had mastered the Treasury office)—in any consistent way placed Hamilton's views ahead of their own. Although each would sometimes support Hamilton or his ideas, often at different times and in varying ways, there evidently was no Hamiltonian cabal within Adams's cabinet, despite the president's suspicions. In any event, if there was one, McHenry was certainly not a part of it. This, then, was the circle of men who surrounded James McHenry, and the relationships among all of them certainly do confirm the personal, honor-oriented, and often unstable nature of partisan politics in the early republic illuminated by Joanne B. Freeman's book *Affairs of Honor: National Politics in the New Republic*.

There is also a supposition among historians that McHenry, Pickering, and Wolcott (who generally agreed with Hamilton's views) worked together *to override* the views of the president whom they were serving. If this were true, it would indeed be troubling. Although incorrect, it is understandable that both Adams and historians would make this mistake, as the three men did unite and threaten to resign at the beginning of Adams's term should the president choose to send James Madison as a peace delegate to France. This was indeed a heavy-handed attempt to prevail, yet in reality Adams held the cards. He could have accepted their proffered resignations, which he chose not to do. But this is an unusual instance of these three cabinet officers working together—the other occasions happened because Adams had left the capital. The cabinet had met in this way in the rare circumstance of George Washington's absence, and so they continued this pattern during Adams's prolonged absences. As Adams grew testier with them over time, this pattern became a way of providing legitimacy to individual actions, which McHenry especially desired. But the charge of working to override Adams simply does not stand up with regard to McHenry. The charge does apply to Pickering, as will become evident in this book (he surreptitiously worked with senators to undermine an appointment of Adams's, for example), and perhaps to Wolcott (although study would need to be done to establish this), but such behavior was not resorted to by McHenry.

A close look at the politics and men involved in the administration actually helps to revive McHenry's reputation, which took a beating in his day and which historians have often accepted. Each of the reasons historians have used to dismiss McHenry as incompetent, however, turns out to have been the result of completely different factors and not his incapacity. It all started with Hamilton's poison-pen letters to Washington, Pickering, and Wolcott. Hamilton's design was to force McHenry's compliance in what amounted to a Hamiltonian running of the War Department, what Mattsson-Bozé called "Hamilton's Campaign to Take Over."[1] When McHenry refused to knuckle under, Hamilton used his poison-pen technique. He began to write letters critical of McHenry to others, the most important one being to Washington, which hit its mark. Washington at that moment believed that McHenry had done very little regarding the New Army, and temporarily he agreed with Hamilton. Historians have generally left the matter there, paying no attention to the fact that when Washington complained to McHenry, the latter sent a careful accounting of all that he had accomplished or set in motion, and Washington, chagrined, then indicated his satisfaction with McHenry's work. The final, damning point seems to be Adams's request for McHenry's resignation. But few historians have paid attention to the overall context, which involved Adams trying to create his own political base of voters and distance himself from the unpopular New Army to do so. Hence, when the president asked for McHenry's resignation, Adams's guilt over harming the secretary of war's reputation caused him to lash out over the secretary's incompetence. In Adams's ensuing calmer moments, knowing he had wronged McHenry, he allowed the record to reflect that he had not been dissatisfied with McHenry's work, integrity, or capacity. After all, Adams knew that he had repeatedly expressed satisfaction with McHenry's work and that he had also, hoping to avoid war and its expense, personally prevented McHenry from accomplishing his main job—that of raising the New Army. In sum, each of the criticisms of McHenry's competence from Hamilton, Washington, and Adams turns out to be unsound.

Not, then, the incompetent some have thought him, McHenry was instead intelligent, hardworking, honorable, and devoted to Washington, if sometimes overwhelmed by duties Congress refused to lighten. Indeed, McHenry successfully established a regimental framework for the army that would last for much of the nineteenth century, gave important support to the Jay Treaty, oversaw the negotiation of a peace in the Old Southwest, and suppressed Fries' Rebellion in a decisive yet moderate fashion. McHenry was also, however, too easily deceived by Hamilton, Pickering, and Wolcott. One wonders just how convincing their duplicity was, and how much McHenry knew. Of course they were discreet, but McHenry was also overworked—and perhaps he simply did not want to know what these men he considered friends were really up to. He sometimes disapproved of what he learned.

The final story is about McHenry's relationship with Baltimore's most important garrison at the entrance to its harbor, Fort McHenry. He had been a part of the city's defense since the Revolution, and while secretary of war the fortress had been named for him. In the critical battle for Baltimore during the War of 1812, Fort McHenry survived over 1,500 shells fired in its direction. McHenry, like Francis Scott Key, watched the battle from a distance. Paralyzed and in pain, he anxiously turned this battle over to his son and the next generation. But from his bedroom window McHenry surely saw the rockets burst, felt the ground shake, and hailed the flag that inspired Key to write the "Star-Spangled Banner." After this victory, Baltimore and the country were able to carry on with a sense of pride and a new beginning.

Taken together, these stories and more mark the life of a good and honorable man.

PART ONE

Becoming an American

ONE "Of a Persevering Temper"

James McHenry

IT WAS TIME FOR a change. In 1771 James McHenry faced a situation shaped both by domestic events and by history itself. McHenry certainly hoped that his health would improve with rest in a more wholesome setting. James was young, born in Ballymena (near Belfast), County Antrim, probably on November 16, 1753, and so was only sixteen, about to turn seventeen. His family insisted that he had worn himself out, studying too long and sleeping too little, leaving his body weak and in need of recuperation. It could not have helped that his only sister Anna had died that year at the age of twenty, possibly of typhus.[1] Her death and his own illness gave him the determination to retrieve what he could of his well-being in the colonies.

But why did McHenry choose the colonies? A trans-Atlantic voyage from northern Ireland to British North America was far more dangerous than a trip to the spas of Germany or the milder climate of the Mediterranean. Of course, one took risks traveling anywhere—Roman malaria and Barbary pirates posed their own perils. Those destinations, however, did not offer the opportunities found in the colonies. Ambition prodded him to consider the colonies rather than Europe—the family's recent dealings with mortality left him resolved to make the most of his life, and the colonies offered a new start. He was in good company. Many Scots-Irish viewed British North America with hope, if not envy. Such was the case, for example, with "William Drennan, then a young medical student at Edinburgh, [who] enthusiastically sympathized with the Americans. To him America was 'the promised land [he] would wish to view before [he] died,' as well as the place he intended to emigrate to should he fail an examination." For most of the eighteenth century, the Scots-Irish flooded the American colonies in search of that Promised Land. So the journey McHenry now made involved a path well worn by his people; he could count on being received by other Scots-Irish Presbyterians, perhaps especially because he was among the lucky few with some property and a solid start to an education.[2]

In the colonies he might also be able to rise above the limited future northern Ireland, his homeland, offered him. Ireland should have been more hospitable. Most of the Irish Presbyterians had been "transplanted" from Scotland in the seventeenth century, some as early as 1607. The emigration had been encouraged by King James I, a Scotsman who had hoped to tie the Emerald Isle to England by bonds of loyalty to him. Given large parcels of land, the Scots-Irish built castles, established their own schools, and settled towns like McHenry's, Ballymena, on the River Braid in County Antrim and located about twenty-three miles northwest of Belfast.[3]

But history was not on their side. James I had died leaving the Scots-Irish Presbyterians as "dissenters" in a land dominated by the English and their established Anglican church. Anglicans were, nonetheless, a minority and felt themselves politically and socially threatened by both the Catholic majority and the Presbyterians. So the Anglican Irish Parliament not only retained many of the previous centuries' oppressive laws, it created more.[4]

Soon the persecution began. The government barred Trinity College to Presbyterians and imprisoned members of the denomination wholesale. Then, on October 23, 1641, Ireland's desperately suppressed Catholics rebelled, massacring thousands of Protestant colonists. Those not killed in the initial uprising wandered the countryside and most either starved or froze to death. Eight years later, Cromwell invaded and subjugated the island, temporarily banishing the Presbyterians of Down and Antrim to Munster because they would not sign the "Engagement" oath promising fidelity to the government.[5]

Oppression continued through the 1660s. Presbyterian services and schools were forbidden, and the law now required tutors, College Fellows, and the clergy to conform to the Anglican Book of Common Prayer. Magistrates had to take the Anglican sacrament or swear never to attempt a change in church and state. The Test Act (1673) embodied all of this, requiring that all officeholders swear allegiance to England and her established church; this continued well into the eighteenth century.[6]

While the persecution had diminished in the eighteenth century, Presbyterians still could not hold many governmental offices, for "[t]o many leading Anglicans the Presbyterians presented a greater threat to their church than the Catholics, thus explaining the great reluctance of the Irish Commons to repeal the Test Act." By the late 1760s, when the Irish Parliament refused England's request that it augment the army and provide the kingdom additional revenue, Britain dissolved the assembly. Ireland seethed. Secret societies grew among Ulster's "Presbyterian peasants and farmers" over the taking of farmland for pasture. And now, in 1771, business was having an uncertain year. Although the linen trade prospered, general fears for the future resurfaced with the imposition of yet another large rent increase.[7]

Unable to attend Trinity College because of his religion, McHenry had few educational choices within Ireland beyond the academy level. He could not be an officeholder without renouncing his religion, but he might have followed in his father's footsteps and become a merchant. However, he never showed much interest in business beyond trying to ensure a comfortable standard of living. With his love of poetry and his real ability with prose, he might have made an able printer—but that craft was also a business and something for which he seems to have shown no interest. He might also have become a doctor—a choice he later made—but as a Presbyterian that required education abroad, probably in Scotland, which was admittedly not far away.[8] If he was going to leave Ireland, though, it was not to be for other parts of Europe.

The opportunities in the colonies combined with a healthier environment to provide a stark contrast to life in northern Ireland. McHenry's sadness over his sister's death gave way to determination, a pronounced personal characteristic. He admitted, "When [the] matter is of any consequence I am slow in planning, because generally of a persevering temper in [the] execution; or w[ha]t. some may please to call it, obstinate in pursuing w[ha]t. I have once taken into my head."[9]

He chose to leave for Philadelphia.

The City of Brotherly Love was the most important and cosmopolitan in British North America. Philadelphia kept its wharves in good repair as business depended on it, and most of the streets were lighted, paved, and lined with trees and sidewalks. Along them stood the red brick buildings demanded by the city's fire code. Daily newspapers, fifty booksellers, and at least five libraries flourished. Even theater held its own, notwithstanding Presbyterian and Quaker opposition. Despite this general prosperity and a construction boom, anywhere from one-quarter to one-third of Philadelphians had grown poor, causing city Quakers to erect a new almshouse.[10]

McHenry's host in Philadelphia was Captain William Allison. Welcoming the young man into his home, Allison could not know their futures would connect inseparably. The Philadelphian could only see before him an attractive young man with brown hair and blue eyes and of average height.[11]

For his part, the Captain's early years are shrouded in mystery (down to the reason for his title), but he first shows up in 1756 tax records already ranked and valued at twenty pounds. Assuming that he had then recently reached his majority, he should have been in his mid-thirties when James arrived, or roughly twice the young man's age.[12]

Allison's was a story of upward mobility that surely impressed a young man like McHenry who was looking for a future. The Captain, a Scots-Irish immigrant himself, had become a merchant, done well, and joined the First Presbyterian Church. By December 18, 1759, it "was proposed that Mess.[rs] W[m.] Allison and David Caldwall [sic] should be members of this [Seating] Committee [of the Congregation]."[13] Allison and David Caldwell became good friends and remained on the committee together for the next three years.

They might well have become friends anyway, for Caldwell's wife was the Captain's cousin. Caldwell had, in fact, met and married Grace Allison in Ireland before emigrating to the colonies.[14]

The couple had three children—John, Elizabeth, and one on the way in the fall of 1762. But David Caldwell never saw this third child, for his will was publicly registered on October 7. There is no record as to how and why he died, but Grace gave birth to Margaret (Peggy) Caldwell the next day.

Fortunately, David Caldwell had also been a successful merchant, leaving Grace quite comfortable. After the customary settling of his debts, he expected her widow's third to be worth far more than £2,000 in Pennsylvania currency. Caldwell named Captain Allison executor.[15]

A year and suitable mourning period later, on December 17, 1763, Captain William Allison married his widowed cousin. By the time young McHenry arrived on the scene eight years later, Grace had borne William three children—Mary, William, and Elizabeth (Grace's first Elizabeth had died). So when James moved in there were already five children ranging in age from around two to twelve. But James was fondest of the oldest girl— shy, brunette, nine-year-old Peggy Caldwell, whom he instructed in penmanship.[16]

McHenry obviously liked what he found, for he soon appealed to his family in Ireland to immigrate, but not to Philadelphia. McHenry's father was a merchant, and although Philadelphia was a thriving city in which new merchants could and did compete, bankruptcies were common (they had reached their peak in 1767), and the city had been glutted with the dry goods in which McHenry's father dealt. Although Philadelphia prospered, her merchants were concerned about their commercial future. Hard currency had been draining from the colony to England, and the problem of credit reached crisis proportions by 1772, resulting in increased unemployment while poor harvests added to inflation.[17] An immigrant merchant family would do well to look elsewhere.

Instead they looked toward Baltimore, where the Reverend Patrick Allison, a relative of McHenry's host, had recently accepted a post. It was a young town with a growing economy and a sizable Scots-Irish Presbyterian community. Baltimore's future looked promising.

It was the perfect place for the McHenrys. Encouraged by their son's enthusiasm, James's parents Daniel and Agnes brought with them his younger brother John and, by the following year, set up a dry goods business in Baltimore. No longer alone in the colonies, James and his family now called Maryland home.

McHenry at this point faced the matter of his future. By now he knew that it was possible not only to succeed financially but also to rise socially. If James was careful he could become a "gentleman." In Ireland, such a move would have been extremely difficult. While the status of "gentleman" had become somewhat more accessible in the British Isles, most still associated the title with the aristocracy. But in the colonies the path was more open.[18]

Still, there were rules a gentleman was expected to live by. He distinguished himself from the "common sort" in his dress, manners, and learning. A gentleman generally, though not always, possessed sufficient wealth that he did not need to work, but if he did, only a few occupations were open to him—medicine, law, or the ministry. Trade was out of the question. Lastly, honor was crucial, and by the late eighteenth century colonials expected a man to earn it.[19]

Becoming a gentleman would, therefore, require hard work, and McHenry's first step was to attend to an education that had been cut short by poor health. All gentlemen shared a basic familiarity with both the classics and the most important ideas of the day. It gave them an ease in company garnered from a learned confidence in their knowledge and abilities. McHenry soon found himself attracted to an institution in Delaware called the "Newark Academy." A Pennsylvania newspaper emphasized that the academy was not located in a large city: "The noise and tumult of such places are unfriendly to study, they are dangerous to the morals of youth." So the founders had chosen a small and wholesome village "about 40 miles from Philadelphia . . . on the borders of Maryland." All Protestants would be accepted and the prices kept low to encourage the enrollment of local farmers' children.[20]

Newark Academy, then, was all that McHenry needed. Founded in Pennsylvania in 1743 by Francis Alison (no relation to the Allisons) and relocated to Delaware in 1767, the "Academy had taught such [accomplished] men as George Read, Thomas McKean, and Charles Thomson." It possessed a good reputation because of a rigorous curriculum. Since the founders planned to evolve into a college, the school demanded more than the language program of an ordinary academy. Newark's program also required training in "every branch of liberal arts and science." This included "'logic, Mathematics, natural and moral philosophy,'" the latter emphasizing not merely ethics but also the political science of the age.[21] That meant that McHenry and his schoolmates studied enlightenment philosophy, including natural law and the rights of man.

McHenry thrived physically and educationally during his time at Newark Academy, which allowed him to finish his preprofessional education. There could now be no question as to his qualifications for advanced training. From here James could become anything he wished: doctor, lawyer, or minister—there were no restrictions.

With no limits, however, a choice now had to be made. There was no living to be made through his first love, poetry, though he was one of the few active writers of verse in the British American colonies, giving him at least a minor place in early American literature. Although he imitated the trends of eighteenth-century poetry, he also "wove details based on first-hand observation of nature in America—the mocking-bird, the rattlesnake, the Alleghany wilderness with its wolves and bears and blazed trails."[22]

He loved to take country walks, when he would sit somewhere in the open and compose verses, often betraying a youthful reverie about love and "maids with aprons full of peaches."

I have read of Cam's fair rill,
Shady Windsor, Cooper's hill,
And of London, where is seen, (and of London where I ween)

Stars, and garters, and the queen; (all antiquity is seen)
And can spell of every stram
That to music owes its name.

Let the curious visit those,
With, thee, New-Ark, I'll repose,
Shun a city's circling life,
Study nature, but not strife.[23]

The habit of going out on a walk to write would stay with him, and he could not understand those who feared the solitude. It gave him the chance to reflect, and the results of his walks could be memorable. Many important decisions were made on such walks. Perhaps one helped him to choose a career: medicine.

Medicine must have resonated with McHenry at a number of levels. Grief over his sister's death and the experience of his own infirmities surely fed not only his desire to make something of himself but also his respect for healers. McHenry could help others, support himself, and perhaps further his own ambition to become a gentleman. All of this was now possible because of the difficult choices McHenry had made—to leave Ireland and to convince his family to immigrate. His perseverance on this course unlocked his future.

TWO "The Commencement of
Our Independence"

Dr. Benjamin Rush

RETURNING TO PHILADELPHIA in 1772, McHenry appren-
ticed himself to Dr. Benjamin Rush. McHenry's work with him proved vital,
as Rush was in the process of making a name for himself as a doctor and
patriot. Although little written by McHenry during this period survives,
enough is known about Rush, their shared religion, and Philadelphia that
much can be reconstructed. They were both young. McHenry turned nineteen that year, but Rush was only twenty-six and had set up his medical
practice a mere three years earlier; before that, he had been acquiring his
own medical education. For five and a half years the teenaged Rush had
studied with the locally respected Dr. John Redman. Then, like many of the
best colonial doctors, Rush had sailed for Scotland to study at the extremely
prestigious Edinburgh Medical School. After two years there, he further
honed his skills by observing medicine in the larger hospitals of London,
becoming friends with Benjamin Franklin in the process.[1]

Rush came home headstrong and full of his Scottish mentor's ideas. As
McHenry learned, Rush strongly advocated bleeding. Dr. William Cullen of
Edinburgh had taught "that the nervous system is the source of life, and that
disease is due to failure of its regulatory powers." A healthy body existed as a
"balanced" system that fever threw out of gear. Some fevers caused "general
debility" and chills, which indicated low energy and required "restorative
drugs, drinks and diet." At other times, fever led to heated fits that one tried
to reduce through "bleeding, purging and low diet. The adage 'stuff a cold
and starve a fever' is strictly [true] according to Cullen."[2]

Perhaps fortunately for the larger community, the rest of Philadelphia's
doctors followed the ideas of the Leyden school. Less theoretical and more
observational than Edinburgh, the Leyden school recommended the mild use

of drugs and a diet aimed at the individual's symptoms. They bled seldom and more moderately. Though no more theoretically accurate, the Leyden school's treatments were milder and less harmful.[3] Convinced of the superiority of Dr. Cullen's system, however, Rush pitted himself against the other doctors in Philadelphia and destroyed what chances he might have had for their sponsorship.

Without a patron in Philadelphia's elite society, Rush courted the Presbyterian denomination in which he and McHenry had been raised. It did some good. "I was once sent for to see a respectable Scotch sea captain in Southwark," Rush wrote. "[H]e told me that . . . he had made choice of me as physician because he had once witnessed my decent behaviour in . . . the Revd. Dr. Allison's [First Presbyterian] Church." Moreover, "his recommendations brought me several families in his neighbourhood."[4]

McHenry and Rush were both members of this Scots-Irish Presbyterian community, though the denomination could prove difficult for members to maneuver. Pennsylvania's famous toleration of different religions had led to intense competition both between and within the denominations themselves, especially during the Great Awakening revival decades earlier. Presbyterians split into the Old Side, which emphasized the need for an educated ministry, and the New Side, which desired an inspired ministry with a personal relationship to God. The two sides even established separate schools to train their ministry. By 1758 the split supposedly had been mended, but tensions survived.[5] At the time of McHenry's arrival in Philadelphia the Presbyterian congregations could still be distinguished by their Great Awakening leanings.

Theological divisions, however, were not new to McHenry, for Presbyterians in Ireland had split into four groups, not two, which had still managed a kind of cooperation.[6] On this side of the Atlantic McHenry befriended both.

For his part, Rush had soon concluded that his New Side Presbyterian sect was "too small and too much divided to afford me much support . . . it was [also] the object of the jealousy, or hatred of the two Societies, viz. the Quakers and Episcopalians, who possessed between them the greatest part of the wealth and influence of the city." Another way to mitigate financial stresses was to take on paying apprentices. Rush began with only two, but when McHenry joined the number had grown to seven.[7]

Unless their families lived nearby, apprentices like McHenry lived with the doctor (Rush housed them in a nearby barn) who taught them for an

average of three years, with the students available at all times for any medical situation. McHenry would have helped run the pharmacy, kept the
books, and attended lectures, including Rush's on chemistry at the medical school at the new University of Pennsylvania. Spending so much time at
the school, McHenry became a "bosom friend" to James Dunlap, who ran
the apothecary for the University Hospital.[8] Otherwise, apprentices studied
when they were not helping the doctor during his morning office hours and
on his rounds in the afternoons. Here McHenry learned about a Philadelphia he might otherwise have ignored: it was also a city of the poor.

It was ultimately among the poor that Rush established his practice, and
among whom the apprentices like McHenry moved. These were the patients no doctor really wanted since their need was far greater than their
ability to pay. "My shop," Rush recalled, "was crowded with the poor in the
morning and at meal times, and nearly every street and alley in the city was
visited by me everyday. There are few old huts now standing in the ancient
parts of the city in which I have not attended sick people." It was not easy for
Rush or his students. "Often have I ascended the upper story of these huts
by a ladder, and many hundred times have been obliged to rest my weary
limbs upon the bedside of the sick (from the want of chairs)," Rush wrote,
"where I was sure I risqued not only taking their disease but being infected
by vermin. More than once did I suffer from the latter."[9] Eventually, Rush's
faithfulness in treating this group brought him the attention of the city at
large, as well as better-paying patients.

McHenry's apprenticeship was political as well as medical. Indeed, the
events of the next few years radicalized and mobilized large segments of the
Philadelphia community, and McHenry, along with the Rush household,
became intimately involved.

Until now, the Irishman had been able to view from a distance the growing trouble between the colonies and England. But Philadelphia's streets
were rife with discontent over Britain's varied attempts to collect colonial
revenue to help pay off the debt incurred during the French and Indian
War, which had ended in 1763. The Sugar and Stamp Acts of the mid-1760s
had alarmed many colonists who feared that the Empire planned to impose
taxes despite a lack of representation in Parliament. The Stamp Act caused
particular concern. This act required colonists to pay for a stamp on a host
of paper products ranging from legal documents to newspapers and alma-
nacs. Colonists thought this eviscerated one of an Englishman's most basic

rights: to have a voice in the taxes he paid. Britain, however, maintained that Parliament had the right to determine whom, what, and where it could tax. Some, like George Grenville, "first lord of the treasury and chancellor of the exchequer," thought the colonies possessed virtual representation, that is, representation by the other members of Parliament. Colonists did not agree, however, and began to actively resist the Stamp Act. As the law actually raised very little money, they began to fear that something else was at work—that the power to tax was being extended and would provide a dangerous precedent that might ultimately destroy their freedom. Many now suspected that the British ministry, which was behind the Stamp Act, was plotting against colonial liberties and forcing the colonists to rebel. "[A]ll colonists, regardless of rank, disapproved of the act." Between July and December 1765, the decision to resist had been made, and a plan for that resistance had been created. Colonists ostracized men who sold the stamps, enforced the nonimportation of British goods, and created both the Sons of Liberty and the Stamp Act Congress. Resistance had not been easy, but it had laid a foundation for future actions. Colonists were also pleased, for after all the turmoil, they had succeeded—the Stamp Act was repealed.[10]

Unfortunately, it was soon replaced by the Townshend Acts (1767), which imposed customs duties on items like lead, glass, and tea that appeared as thinly disguised taxes. To make matters worse, the imposts were also to be collected by men who were believed to be corrupt, foreigners, or both. In protest, colonists revived nonimportation, ostracism, and the Sons of Liberty. The Massachusetts House of Representatives complained of the duties in a circular letter to the other colonies, and, when it refused to recant as ordered by the British, the assembly was shut down. Though only fifteen at the time and still in Ireland, McHenry surely had seen the parallel, as in that same year, 1768, the British also dissolved the Irish Parliament. This happened because the assembly refused to increase the Irish Army from 12,000 to 15,000 men, an action the Irish took both because they preferred the use of militia within Ireland and to prevent the British from more easily keeping troops in the colonies. Some Irish argued "that the chains being forged for America were first to be fitted in Ireland." To colonial eyes, both Massachusetts and Ireland had lost their representative governments as a result of standing up for their rights. Then, to punish Massachusetts, British troops had occupied Boston. Almost inevitably, clashes between British soldiers and citizens turned deadly when five fell in the bloody snow in March 1770 in what came to be known as the Boston Massacre. The city mourned and a tense lull ensued. Finally, the British withdrew the hated Townshend duties except for that upon tea—but wary colonists noted the exception. As trouble persisted, colonial attitudes toward Britain changed for the worse. By now, many colonists believed that appeals to both Parliament and the British Ministry (their cabinet) had not worked and that resistance had been required. But resistance had not been easy, for the bonds of family, language, religion, and education tied colonists to England; indeed, a number of colonists had been sent to England for their educations. Nonetheless, in terms of government connections, and despite the enormous social and cultural links, only the king remained as the political tie that bound the colonies to the Empire.[11]

Now, in 1773, Benjamin Rush belonged to a group of patriots who helped organize resistance to a new act giving the East India Company a monopoly over tea (with the only remaining Townshend duty) imported to the colonies. McHenry and the other apprentices must have known when a committee of twelve decided to isolate the Quaker firm of James and Drinker that had been privileged to sell the tea; the firm soon agreed to desist. Then the patriots barraged the city with essays decrying the Tea Act and the monopoly it created.[12] It was patriots in Philadelphia and New York who had first condemned the Tea Act; seeing their success, Boston patriots followed their lead. In fact, the Boston patriots' lack of conviction in imposing nonimportation embarrassed their leaders. The city soon made up for this, however. Because Massachusetts' Governor Thomas Hutchinson would not allow the tea to leave Boston before payment of the despised taxes, the Sons of Liberty disguised themselves as Indians and hosted the Boston Tea Party, turning the harbor brown with soggy tea leaves. Down in Philadelphia, after word of the Boston Tea Party had arrived, Captain Ayres of the *Polly* (which carried the unwanted cargo) agreed to leave his ship downriver and personally assess the mood in Philadelphia. Eight thousand citizens opposed to the landing of the tea convinced Ayres that he ought to return to England.[13]

McHenry, now familiar with the byways of Philadelphia, found political excitement in every corner. Newspapers, coffeehouses, and taverns overflowed with information. Class lines blurred as the city became politicized and religious denominational rivalry came to an uneasy truce.

Important patriot leaders now frequented the Rush household, and McHenry and the other apprentices could hardly have avoided meeting them. John Dickinson, a wealthy Quaker merchant and writer of the famous patriot essay "Letters from a Farmer in Pennsylvania," became a friend to

Rush. Charles Thomson (a graduate of Newark Academy like McHenry who later became secretary for the Continental Congress), Thomas Mifflin, and George Clymer admitted Rush into their confidence, and many other members of the First Continental Congress, like Patrick Henry, became Rush's patients. At Thomas Mifflin's Rush met George Washington and Charles Lee. John and Samuel Adams became good friends, dining frequently with Rush and advocating republicanism to all within earshot, McHenry among them.[14]

In the meantime, Britain decided to punish Boston for the Tea Party with a set of Coercive Acts. Britain not only shut down the port but also gave Massachusetts a new and very hierarchical government to replace their previously more democratic form. Other colonies balked; if one government could be so easily transformed, what was to prevent the same from happening elsewhere? In protest, Philadelphia joined other cities in a call for a Continental Congress.[15]

Rush, McHenry, and the other apprentices helped the cause by gleaning popular sentiment from patients that they duly reported to the patriot leaders. In this way they ferreted out and addressed lower- and middle-class concerns that might otherwise have hindered the growing movement.[16]

Both McHenry and Rush had been prepared for revolutionary ideology by many things, not the least of which was their Presbyterian background. It was not just the social community that mattered to them, nor the source of patients, but the religion itself. This background informed everything Rush became involved in. Above all, it affected his choice of medicine, which he practiced because he felt spiritually unworthy of the ministry.[17] Everything McHenry heard from his teacher was somehow, somewhere, grounded or based in theology.

Indeed, most Philadelphia Presbyterians embraced the Revolution because resistance flowed easily from their shared theology. The world functioned in an orderly way according to God's laws. The natural rights of the Enlightenment were among them, and the most important natural right was liberty. The civil contract protected this liberty and assisted men in conforming to the laws of God and the state. In a commonwealth of freedom, virtue (both public spirit and brotherly love) might blossom. Citizens would elect honorable legislatures that would pass enlightened laws that the executive would enforce and the judiciary would support.[18]

The acts of Great Britain threatened this entire conception of the political/moral order. As many Presbyterians saw it, Great Britain meant to force Americans into slavery and away from their Christian freedom into an "'unparalleled System of Tyranny.'" "If civil rights were given up, then religious rights would be endangered."[19] Presbyterian ministers argued that it was their Christian duty to rebel.

In fact, through 1773 one found patriots mainly outside the colony's traditional power groups. Patriots thus tended to be Presbyterians, Baptists, and younger Anglican merchants. But in 1774 a conservative counterreaction followed the city's radical response to the Tea Act. To prevent losing their following, radicals decided to recruit a more balanced representation of Philadelphia's differing denominations and classes. With this shift in thinking, patriots transformed a polarizing situation into a potentially unifying one.[20]

Everywhere McHenry looked, people were becoming radicalized. Presbyterians around him were active; the middle-class mechanic and artisan classes were mobilizing; the more educated publicized their arguments; and all classes were now invited to join the radical cause. Each of these arguments and events blended well with McHenry's education in Enlightenment theory, his Christian faith, and his Scots-Irish hatred of England. All of these factors surrounding him in Philadelphia created a young man very receptive to the radical cause.

In the midst of this political conflict, his mother died. She had been ill for months, and during most of the time James had been unaware of her condition. As late as May, James knew only that she had a disorder, and, alarmed, he begged his brother not only to tender "every form of filial affection" to her but also to write James a more complete account. It was, however, no use. The McHenry men buried her in Baltimore in August 1774, their personal pain for a moment transcending the political turmoil that surrounded them.[21]

But in less than a year the colonies' decision to resist transformed into the resolution to fight. Simultaneously, British General Thomas Gage received orders to take "decisive action." On April 19, 1775, he sent men to Concord, Massachusetts by way of the Lexington Road; Concord was a patriot arsenal and the Provincial Congress had been holding meetings there. Shots were fired on the Lexington village green and eight colonials died with nine wounded. The Minute Men of Lexington, Concord, and the towns between there and Boston defended their communities. More men died—a total of fifty Americans and sixty-five British. The war was on. The countryside swelled with volunteers, and the news spread to other colonies with lightning speed. Rush wrote, "[T]he battle of Lexington gave a new tone to my feelings . . . I considered the seperation [sic] of the colonies from Great Britain as inevitable. The first gun that was fired at an American cut the cord that had tied the two countries together. It was the signal for the commencement of our independence."[22]

McHenry agreed. For on July 29, 1775, shortly after Washington headed for Massachusetts to command the newly forming army, McHenry drew up an informal will. It was critical work; he was "about to set off for the head Quarters in new England, to serve as a volunteer, or Surgeon, in the American Army . . . to defend the liberties of Americans and mankind, against the enemies of both." It was also dangerous work: "I therefore, re-sign the disposal of myself and soul, in all sincerity and lowly reverence to their first giver."[23] He left his share of the family business to his father and his brother, and "for my good and worthy patron" Captain William Allison, he left a book by "'Beattie on the nature and immutability of truth' . . . as a slender memorial of my gratitude and friendship." As if uttering a prayer, James ended with "Amen." He was deliberate in taking this act, just as he had been deliberate in deciding to leave Ireland, finish his education, and become a physician.

But there was something more. Over the past four years James McHenry had apprenticed himself to becoming an American. The colonies offered him opportunities and a freedom unknown in Ireland. He had committed to this country, his new home, accepting the patriotic cause. To the Revo-lution he now brought a solid education, medical training, ideals, ambition, and a firmness of resolve to see it through. Caught in the whirl of revolu-tionary Philadelphia, James McHenry transformed from a young man in need of a change to a young man about to help in making a revolution. Full of youthful idealism, McHenry went to war.

THREE "The Events of War
Are Uncontroulable"

James McHenry

SURVEYING THE TENTED FIELDS of Cambridge, Massachu-
setts, in the summer of 1775, McHenry saw the rudiments of what was still a
young army. In fact, its commander-in-chief, General George Washington,
had only recently been elected by Congress to the position and had arrived
on July 2, so he was merely beginning to make his imprint.[1] The Continental
Hospital was even newer than the army. "Continental Hospital" did not refer
to a medical building but instead was a term Congress used for what one
might call a "medical corps." It functioned as a pyramid presided over by a
director-general, with four surgeons, twenty surgeon's mates, nurses, apoth-
ecaries, and storekeepers comprising the rest of the subordinate hierarchy.[2]
    McHenry served first as a surgeon's mate, the lowest position a doctor
could hold.[3] Fortunately, the camp at Cambridge was relatively healthy. Because of a lull in the fighting, most of the medicine McHenry practiced that
fall was preventive. To avoid malnutrition, the army planted gardens and
built company kitchens. Moreover, because many soldiers bathed only when
ordered, doctors established regular washing days for both clothing and the
body. The soldiers dug outhouses, and hefty fines or even courts-martial
faced country boys who refused to use them. The soldiers did not always
obey, however, and the camps were often filthy.[4]
    Despite such measures, patients crowded the hospitals by November.
"The principal diseases were autumnal remittents, typhoid fever and camp
dysentery." These were serious, as throughout the course of the war two men
died of disease for every man killed in combat. Everyone especially dreaded
smallpox, but inoculation remained experimental and against army policy.
Fearing the pox more than the policy, however, many soldiers (and some
surgeons) disobeyed orders and inoculated each other, sometimes causing

deaths and the further spread of the disease. Washington reconsidered his policy in early 1777, as many of his soldiers now came through Philadelphia where the disease was common. He decided to have them inoculated and quarantined there before joining the army. Congress's medical committee, chaired by Benjamin Rush, approved the procedure.[5]

Once a man was sick, McHenry could actually do very little. He would attempt to restore the body's system to balance through bleeding and purging, which, of course, actually reduced the body's ability to fight off the disease. If, however, the immune system rallied, McHenry's nursing care could be a genuine aid to the patient.

While McHenry practiced medicine, in early November a somber Congress learned that George III had refused their request, known as the Olive Branch Petition, that the monarch help find a way to avoid conflict and had instead declared the colonies to be in rebellion. In so doing, the king had made peaceful reconciliation all but impossible. With this rejection, colonists believed George III had breached his coronation oath. He was no longer acting as an impartial and just king, but was choosing sides. For numerous colonists this was the last straw, leading many to consider independence. It was a difficult choice, and, to make matters worse, neither side gained a clear military advantage. The patriot victory at Great Bridge, Virginia, was offset by Benedict Arnold's defeat at Quebec. The cause found new energy, however, on January 9, 1776, when Thomas Paine published "Common Sense," calling for independence. His essay, emphasizing as it did a readily understood, straightforward, and compelling logic, helped win countless converts to the patriot cause. The timing was excellent, for spring was near and warmer weather would mean a need for new recruits.[6]

Even James's younger brother John considered signing up. He had felt restless for some time, and he wrote James of the three options he thought lay before him. He could join the army and the Revolution; he could return to Ireland with an eye to improving trade with mercantile houses in Great Britain; and, of course, he could remain in Baltimore tending to their trading house and aging father.

James, however, still smarted from the loss of their sister and mother. He was not eager to "damp [John's] military ardor" for the Revolution, but he believed "that one out of our little family was its full share." James reminded John that he was effectively "hea[d of the] family," and that James and their father Daniel greatly "depend on your management and prudence. . . . [Our] capital cannot be much diminished."[7]

On the other hand, James did not believe John should return to Ireland to build up trading connections. Until the war was over, such efforts would be worthless and even dangerous. "We can hardly suppose a reconciliation between Eng[land and] America. Both are too far engaged to recede. [Our] terms of accommodation would be too humiliating to the false dignity of Britain, and theirs too ignominious for the sons of freedom. Strength must decide the present dispute." Indeed, James thought, "it would be foolishness in the extreme to accept [less] than absolute independency."[8] As for John's own independence, James hoped his brother would remain in Baltimore— and he did.

British General Sir William Howe, on the other hand, evacuated Boston upon realizing that the Americans had fortified that city's heights. Howe had initially considered attacking Washington's troops, but then remembered Bunker Hill. The battle had been fought before the Virginian took command, and the British had taken "the ground all the way to Charleston Neck." But if it was a victory, it was a pyrrhic one: the British counted 228 dead and 828 wounded, while the Americans lost 140 with 271 wounded. Howe had no wish to risk repeating the losses of that June day. Then, when Louis XVI secretly sent one million livres' worth of munitions to America, military activity accelerated. A number of advisers had persuaded the French king that surreptitious aid to the Americans would hurt the British without entangling France in the Revolution. The arms provided a much-needed boost for the American cause. Unhappily, however, Benedict Arnold now marched an expedition from Massachusetts to Quebec, a distance of 350 miles that took forty-five days, during which time he lost 300 of 975 men to death, sickness, and desertion. The city, moreover, proved impregnable, forcing Arnold to withdraw.[9]

As the military expanded operations, the Hospital Department did the same. The expansion began even before the new director-general, Dr. John Morgan, replaced Dr. Benjamin Church, who had been caught in treasonous correspondence with the British. On September 14, 1775, Congress had created the Northern Hospital to service the northern army and appointed Dr. Samuel Stringer as its director. In reality, Congress merely recognized a fait accompli; Dr. Stringer had already set up a basic service and procured medicines on the basis of General Philip Schuyler's promise of future congressional recognition.[10]

By the spring of 1776, Dr. Stringer begged for surgeons and mates, and Director-General Morgan placed the matter in the hands of Dr. Jonathan

Potts, inadvertently starting a turf war that involved McHenry. Morgan knew that Potts had applied to Congress for a commission, but he did not realize that Potts had applied for the position of director of the Hospital in Canada, where he had heard a hospital would be established. Congress had welcomed Potts on board in the Canadian Department, yet added that his appointment was not to "supersede Dr. Stringer."[11] Potts assumed that Stringer would be in charge up to the Canadian border but that he, Potts, would be director in Canada proper. At the same time Morgan tried to assist by sending as many qualified men and supplies north as necessary. This was McHenry's chance.[12]

Having served as mate for a year, McHenry felt frustrated and hungry for advancement. His training and service certainly warranted a higher status than mate. So Morgan obliged by promoting him to surgeon and assigning him to serve under Dr. Potts in the Northern Department. Elated and rested after a week's liberty, Dr. McHenry traveled to Philadelphia to apply to Congress for men and supplies. The Northern Hospital needed everything— medicines, blankets, bandages, and tools. Lives would certainly depend on whatever success he had. So McHenry returned to Philadelphia, and found it exhilarated by news of the Declaration of Independence. Although at war for a year, until this document became official the colonies (now states) could have argued they still willingly remained within the British Empire. The Declaration changed that. With its stated grievances against the British people and Parliament, and most especially the nineteen charges against the king, all ties between the colonies and Britain were now sundered. The United States had declared itself into existence.[13]

While attending to his procurement task, Dr. McHenry met Dr. Stringer. Stringer had grown anxious when Potts arrived in the Northern Department, since Congress had certainly been very unclear about who would command where, and Stringer had put too much work into the Northern Hospital to like seeing it slip through his fingers. Stringer should have welcomed Dr. Potts's services, but he was insecure about his command. He left his patients and his post at the Northern Hospital, ostensibly to procure supplies in Philadelphia, a task ordinarily delegated to a responsible subordinate. But a subordinate could not be trusted to petition Congress for a clarification of his appointment. On August 20, 1776, Congress gave Stringer what he wanted, at least partially. They assured him that he alone was director of the Hospital in the Northern Department, but he still answered to Director-General Morgan. He could, however, hire his own staff.

The very next day, August 21, Stringer decided to make a show of independence from the director-general. He relieved Dr. James McHenry, who had been Morgan's appointee. In a state of shock McHenry wrote Potts from New York: "I feel the full force of my disappointment and lament that I cannot join you—except my Commission be recognized by Dr. Stringer; this I have no hope of."[14] Thus, having served the American cause for a year, McHenry found himself without a place. It was, in fact, extremely poor treatment, especially since Stringer needed staff and McHenry had certainly proven himself. Rather than quit in disgust he appealed to Congress.

Congress, now aware of having inadvertently placed McHenry in this embarrassing situation, sought to make up for it. They declared "[t]hat Congress have a proper sense of the Merit and Service of Dr. McHenry," and that he should receive "the First Vacancy that shall happen of a Surgeon's Berth in any of the said Hospitals." On August 27 Congressman Benjamin Rush, concerned about his protégé, sent a copy of this resolution to McHenry, assuring him hyperbolically that "Congress does you as much Honor as if they had made you a Director of a Hospital."[15] Surely it helped that McHenry had met so many congressmen while an apprentice. Rush and Congress did not want McHenry to quit the service and clearly tried to mollify him.

Dr. McHenry was indeed pleased: his promotion to surgeon now effectively came from Congress rather than the medical department. It did not rectify all, but it did publicly acknowledge his merit. In fact, it proved that the changes he had been making in his life had been effective—that this revolutionary society acknowledged him as a gentleman of talent and worth. It also taught him about congressional power. After his recent disappointment, this was certainly gratifying. Moreover, on behalf of Congress, Rush instructed McHenry to inform all the directors, including Stringer, of his priority to a surgeon's berth.

The next available position was not with Stringer, but in New York as surgeon to Colonel Robert Magaw's Fifth Pennsylvania Battalion. Precisely when McHenry joined the battalion is unclear, for he could hardly have received Rush's letter until August 28, 1776. Yet accounts show he later received pay as regimental surgeon beginning August 10.[16] Probably McHenry did not join Colonel Magaw until at least August 30, for events moved too swiftly.

After Howe's withdrawal from Boston, both he and Washington moved their forces south to New York.[17] On August 22 skirmishing began on Long

Island, where Magaw's battalion was stationed. By August 29 Washington decided to evacuate to Manhattan. The troops withdrew under the protection of five units specially picked for their discipline and reliable leaders; Colonel Magaw's Fifth Pennsylvania Battalion was one. Only after all the other Americans had withdrawn did these five units board boats to Manhattan.

Manhattan's defense posed a formidable challenge because the Americans lacked a fleet to patrol the island's surrounding bays and rivers. Instead, they had to rely on inadequate land defense. To prevent British ships from freely roaming the waterways, the Americans erected Fort Lee on the New Jersey shore while Fort Washington stood across the river on Manhattan. The idea was to bombard British ships from both sides and to protect the obstacles that the Americans had placed in the river. The forts were also part of a larger scheme. Washington hoped to prevent the British from landing north of the American forces, which would cut off the Americans' only line of retreat to the mainland above the island.

But once the British started moving to the northeast of Manhattan around Throg's Neck, Washington realized he could not hold the island. On October 16 he abandoned his headquarters on Harlem Heights for White Plains on the mainland, leaving about 3,000 men at Fort Washington. McHenry, along with Colonel Magaw's battalion, remained at the Manhattan fort.

The British moved against White Plains on October 28—and took the town. At this point Howe decided to pursue Washington no further, but chose instead to exert total control over Manhattan and give himself clear land-lines of supply and communication.

Washington had anticipated this, and wanted to abandon Fort Washington, letting the British have the entire island. He now thought the fort, a mere pentagonal earthwork on a bluff rising 230 feet high, unable to withstand a serious British attack. If defense was useless, abandonment made sense.

However, Washington hesitated to make a final decision for two reasons. First, the Continental Congress had ordered him to keep the fort if at all possible. Second, Generals Nathanael Greene, Israel Putnam, and Colonel Robert Magaw, the fort's commander, all insisted that the fort would hold against attack. So the commander-in-chief deferred to their counsel and delayed his decision. On November 12 Washington again discussed the question with General Greene, and two days later they both visited the fort. They did so again on November 16, and before they reached the Manhattan shore they could both see and hear that the outworks were under attack. Deciding to let Magaw do the commanding, they returned to the Jersey shore.

But as the American lines fell back to the fort itself, it became apparent to everyone that Magaw could not hold on. They were, in fact, "sitting ducks."[18] Magaw tried to stall by offering to negotiate, but the British, actually Germans under Colonel Johann Rall, refused to deal and at length General Wilhelm von Knuyphausen threatened to renew the attack. Magaw commanded a small fort, overcrowded and with no source of water. If the British began firing, the number of casualties would be enormous. Seeing no other choice, Colonel Magaw surrendered shortly before he received Washington's orders to hold the fort until night and then evacuate. This debacle boded ill for the American cause. And while Colonel Magaw's work was over, Dr. McHenry's had just begun. Of the nearly 3,000 Americans captured, 54 had been killed and 100 were wounded. At dawn McHenry began to tend the wounded and dying.

There were numerous gunshot wounds. Generally, doctors tried to extract the ball. But if it did not remove easily they would leave it for fear of increasing the risk of infection or doing more damage with too much probing. After cleaning, the wound was generally left open to allow for drainage. Bandages were applied loosely for the same reason. Because the disinfectant qualities of alcohol were discovered during the Revolution, few doctors knew of it at this time. Even worse, doctors often treated profusely bleeding wounds with further intentional bloodletting. Bayonet wounds were treated much the same way. Fractures were another matter. Too often the fracture was both compound and infected, and despite disagreement over proper procedure, many doctors amputated. McHenry spent that first day cleaning, suturing, bandaging, amputating, and preparing patients for transport down to the city.[19]

But New York was in no condition to receive 3,000 prisoners. Two months before there had been a tremendous fire that destroyed close to 300 buildings. Since housing was already in short supply and both civilians and occupying forces crowded what there was, no decent accommodations were available for American prisoners—well, wounded, or dying.

Nevertheless, McHenry tried to keep up his spirits. Five days after the fall of Fort Washington he wrote Benjamin Rush in Philadelphia. Having thought the Americans would abandon the fort, McHenry had expected to see Rush before this. "But the events of war are uncontroulable [sic] and have taught me of how little avail the wisdom and hardihood of a few [Washington] are against the councils and courage of the many [Greene, Putnam, and Magaw]." At this point McHenry felt comforted by a sense of "kindly resignation" toward his imprisonment.[20]

He was, after all, an officer and was free to roam the city. He also had private lodgings with Colonels Magaw, Miles, and others. And he did have his health, unlike Colonel Magaw who had a fever from which he would recover.

Most enlisted men did not fare as well. The British did provide separate quarters for the sick and wounded, but their medical care varied greatly. Those wounded Americans in a different part of the city, cared for by a Dr. Oliver, did tolerably well. Americans injured in McHenry's vicinity received a minimally acceptable level of care while a Dr. Antil was in charge. But toward the end of November, Antil left New York; thereupon the British replaced him with a man they believed to be an American doctor, Louis Debute.

Debute was not, however, a doctor with the American forces. Instead, "he was notorious for crimes, and had been pillor[i]ed some time before [the American forces under Washington] evacuated N. York."[21] Once Debute took charge of the American wounded in McHenry's sector, their health took an immediate turn for the worse.

Yet McHenry found this out only through persistence, for Debute refused to allow American doctors to see the wounded. McHenry, however, attempted repeatedly to gain access to those patients and was let in only once when the guard, perhaps fooled by his brogue, mistook him for a British physician. He wrote both General Howe and British Chief Surgeon Jonathan Mallet of the deplorable conditions. The prisoners lacked beds and bedding, McHenry said. He also described "the almost total want of fire, in consequence of which several of their limbs had mortified," but equally serious was "their want of nurses and tenders to give cleanliness to the place and prepare and give them their drink and nourishment at proper times." At this point Dr. Mallet assured McHenry that the British had given Debute provisions. Since the British consistently maintained that Debute was adequately supplied, it became evident that Debute had sold the provisions for personal profit. Mallet invited McHenry to take over.

McHenry agreed on two conditions. First, Debute would have to be removed from the scene entirely. McHenry knew the man to be an unscrupulous, self-interested fraud with no legitimate claim to being there. He was indirectly killing American soldiers, and any genuine doctor would be tainted by association with him. Indeed, it was McHenry's duty to do everything in his power to get rid of the man, and by agreeing to take personal responsibility for the Americans' medical care he might be able to accomplish it.

But McHenry could not care for the soldiers by himself, and his second condition was that he be provided some nurses or tenders. The British, however, would not agree to these conditions and "Debute was suffered to carry on his inhumanities and deceptions." His dismissal happened only after a fellow American officer insisted that Debute had, in his presence, "given one of [the sick] a blow with his stick, in consequence of which the man died 15 minutes after." For six weeks the ill had been suffering under this man, dehydrated and in extreme cold. "Exclamations for drink and food, from such as had strength left to speak—the groans of the dying— the looks of the dead that lay mixed with the living—and the insufferable impurity of the house," McHenry lamented, "made up altogether a scene more affecting and horrid than the carnage of a field of battle wherein no quarter is given."[22]

At this point McHenry determined that the only real help he could provide the sick was to get them out of New York. He applied to General Howe for permission to remove the prisoners, and under the circumstances Howe agreed.

On January 27, 1777, McHenry signed the official parole form, promising "that I will not bear Arms, nor do, or say any thing contrary to the Interest of his Majesty."[23] Four days later he was in Hydes Town, New Jersey, in charge of twenty-five sick men. But try as he might, he could not save them all. He reported to General Washington that six had died on the way, though he believed the rest would survive if the weather would only improve.

McHenry probably took the Pennsylvania soldiers to Philadelphia; he claimed to come from there on the parole form. He was also assigned to a Pennsylvania battalion, and so he was in Philadelphia in June. Now he only needed the formality of being exchanged for a British prisoner to return to the army.

Philadelphia was also not far from the American army, which McHenry expected to rejoin before long. After the fall of Fort Washington, the American army had retreated all the way across New Jersey to Philadelphia, though they did not stay there long. At this point General Washington made some brilliant moves. These not only salvaged his reputation but proved to be important morale boosters for the Americans. On Christmas night Washington famously crossed the Delaware River and led his men in a surprise early morning assault against the Hessian garrison in Trenton commanded by Colonel Johann Rall. These were the same Hessians who had taken Fort Washington, but this time they themselves were taken captive or killed like Colonel Rall, who was hit, carried into a church, and laid on a bench where he died. It was a decisive victory, after which the elated but exhausted Americans retreated back across the river. But a council of his officers agreed with Washington that they should return to New Jersey, crossing the river once more. Then, on January 2, the Americans won a second battle of Trenton against British General Lord Charles Cornwallis. That night, partially to avoid fighting Cornwallis head-on in the morning, Washington again took the initiative and chose a different battlefield, marching his men to Princeton and winning yet again. Momentarily victorious, Washington set up headquarters in the hills around Morristown.[24] The war now settled into something of a lull.

McHenry's relationship with his brother, however, became alarmingly worse. The trouble came at the end of May when John traveled north from Baltimore to Philadelphia, presumably both to see his brother and to engage in trade. James then became fully aware of just how unhappy John was.[25]

John had duly taken his brother's advice and had remained at Baltimore in charge of the family business. It was, however, difficult for him not to join the war effort: military service was an action that defined a generation of American men. Patriots like James participated in a sort of rage militaire that erupted at the beginning of the war, an enthusiasm for the conflict and attendant sacrifices that was later referred to as the "Spirit of '76." It bonded them profoundly. True citizens, true men, joined the cause. Only slaves would submit to the rule of another; men were self-ruled. Hence one's participation in the war did not merely show a person's political ideals; it also proved one's manhood. So James not only served in the war but also was served by the war on a number of levels: he could simultaneously prove himself the citizen-soldier worthy of the republic he would help to found, assure his future in that nation, and demonstrate his masculinity.

Acting as "head of a family" would have probably been desirable to John in peacetime. It was certainly a loaded term and no coincidence that James had used this language in his earlier letter to John. Generally it referred to a married man with a home, wife, and dependents who was expected to manage an orderly household that pleased those within, hence satisfying society's expectations. James instead emphasized the need for someone to manage the family's finances. The business and capital required attention. "Some people," namely James and their father, depended upon John to make certain their resources were sufficient. This, of course, meant that James looked for John to be the provider.[26]

Taking care of one's immediate relatives in this manner was, after all, the predominant male role and not doing so would have been denounced a moral and masculine failing. Another man might have been pleased to tend to the home during war. John, however, became desperately unhappy; there could be no martial glory, no proof of his willingness to offer the ultimate self-sacrifice. He would never be the citizen-soldier. John could not participate in his generation's test of manhood.

Instead, John consoled himself with prostitutes and drinking binges. By the time James saw him in Philadelphia, John was in poor shape. John's behavior ran counter to all of the values James held, all of the choices he himself had made in life. And so, near the end of May, James, as elder brother and friend, reproached John for his conduct. Naturally, John did not take kindly to his brother's admonitions, and he counterattacked with some criticisms of his own. It was he, John, who had been left to care for the family business alone. James had gone off to become a doctor and yet did not hesitate to continue receiving material support from home based on his third's share in the business. James, John asserted, was not so much concerned about John as he was with his own fortune.

Stunned by John's retorts, James wrote John a letter the next morning. "Your late conduct . . . could not fail of throwing a man of delicate feelings into the deepest distress." James was both "estranged and deeply insulted." He had "ruminated since yesterday evening upon my conduct towards you, and I find that my crime consisted only in sincerity." There was now but one solution. "[Y]our conduct puts it any longer beyond my power to hold it [my fortune] any longer consistent with my feelings and principles of action." In short, James would surrender his rights to one-third of the family business. He would not have John consider him a parasite.

In James's letter, there was also more lecturing as to John's present manner of life, with Christian admonitions that whatever joy one found on earth must "not deprive us of it hereafter." James's religion was a matter he took most seriously; it was quite personal, comprised of a fundamental belief in a constantly provident God. Religion, moreover, served as a guiding force for James, making clear his path through life, and serving as a profound source of comfort during times of trouble.

In contrast, John's debaucheries and "animal appetites" threatened both his soul and a legacy of "disease and a large fund of the most bitter reflections." James may not have said so, but an important component of manhood involved the capacity for self-discipline and the control of one's sexual desires. Married men, after all, were not permitted to engage in adultery. John, of course, was single and young and should have been considering leaving bachelorhood for marriage. Most people in Massachusetts generally thought that "bachelors would either remain celibate and 'fry in the Grease of their own Sexuality' or be 'whoremongers' and engage in out-of-wedlock sexual intimacy." Indeed, John had chosen the latter and he had chosen badly.[27]

In confronting his brother, James believed he was only doing his solemn duty: "Did I openly acquiesce in a constant round of unlawful experiments I should be undeserving the eldership in brotherhood." Nonetheless, he concluded, "[t]he road to my heart is still easy . . . you have only to pursue virtue."

James visited his brother shortly after noon that day. Since they continued to correspond, it may be presumed that there was a reconciliation of sorts. John did not let James give up his portion of the business, while James gave further reassurances that he was motivated only by fraternal concern. Perhaps John even promised to mend his ways. The worst, at least, was over.

In June 1777, James wrote another painful letter, this time to General Washington. It seems that discussions of prisoner exchanges had raised a dispute as to how many prisoners the British possessed; Howe, moreover, claimed that wounded American prisoners had been treated with as much care as if they had been British. Furious, McHenry could not let these claims go unanswered and described the scandalous conditions in New York.[28]

Washington replied from Morristown on July 5. "I never doubted, but that the Treatment of our prisoners in the Hands of the Enemy was such as could not be justified either upon the principles of Humanity or the practice of War."[29] Washington was thus persuaded that he ought not to return all of the prisoners General Howe claimed. Washington added that McHenry's own exchange was overdue, inasmuch as a British physician, Dr. Sanden, had already been returned.

McHenry in fact was not exchanged for over a year, and in the interim he returned home to Baltimore. He was not there long before he and John traveled together south to Edenton, North Carolina, on business. But James disliked the people and the trip gave him little pleasure. The men were "itinerants, . . . shipwrecked sailors, unfortunate adventurers" and the women were so shy it was "intollerably [sic] disgusting to a stranger." This description of Edenton's women is especially ironic, as they had surely overcome their "shyness" four years earlier when fifty-one of them signed a very public agreement supporting Congress. Loyalist cartoonists lampooned them. Presumably, however, McHenry never met any of these particular ladies. Instead, he went home and remained on parole until March of the following year and had much time to reflect on his experience in the war.[30]

It had been anything but pleasant. Even without the inhumanity and corruption he witnessed while a prisoner, a military doctor's life was difficult and had few rewards. Salaries were very low—only $25 a month in 1775—and doctors had to provide their own clothing on that salary until 1779. Physicians slept with the soldiers, often in tents or fields. Because they were constantly in the presence of disease, more doctors died in their proportion than officers of the line. Furthermore, "the surgeon had no real military rank and was not regarded as an officer. Often the surgeons were dismayed to learn that the rank and file would not accept them as friends or companions."[31]

While he was on parole, McHenry's attitude regarding the role he wanted to play in the war transformed. He remained committed to the struggle and would continue to serve as a doctor if necessary. McHenry knew medicine to be good and useful work, but it had also left him restless, disturbed by the unrelenting needs of the sick and the collusion of the British. Now he desired a more purely military role; he was eager to fight the enemy himself. In this field he might make more of a difference. It was also a time-honored way of advancement, and just might be a path to glory. When General Washington wrote Dr. McHenry in March 1778 that he had been exchanged, McHenry happily reported for duty at Valley Forge, making his new preference for a military position known.[32]

Such positions were hard to find, however, so he served as senior surgeon at the Flying Camp, something of a mobile surgical unit, until a suitable military post could be found.[33] At the end of the Valley Forge winter, McHenry presided over a hut that by regulation was "fifteen feet wide, twenty-five feet long, and at least nine feet high . . . covered with boards or shingles, without any dirt. A window . . . on each side and a chimney at one end."[34] By April the hospitals were fighting typhus and the death rate was alarming. Shortages and appalling conditions led men to hide their illness, as "going to a hospital was too often a one-way trip."[35]

In the meantime, McHenry had attracted Washington's attention. They had surely met years before through Benjamin Rush, and McHenry's report of prisoner conditions in New York had merited a personal answer from the general. McHenry's desire for a military position now meshed with Washington's need for aides, who were generally young gentlemen, educated and ambitious, a combination not easily found. This certainly described the young doctor, however, so by May 15 he accepted the position of unpaid assistant secretary to General Washington. It was not a true military post, but might lead to one.

That same day he requested his father's blessing for his service in this voluntary position, which he could leave if his father insisted. The fact that he had clearly accepted the post while telling his father that he was merely considering it, however, suggests that he knew his father would agree, but needed to feel consulted. His father's reply must have been positive but does not survive, although young McHenry's appeal to his father does.

I do not forget the tenderness of our parting, your last injunctions, nor my promise to avoid all places of danger not strictly connected with the duties of my profession. It is the observation of those which prevents me from entering into a post of some danger till I can obtain your approbation. The post in contemplation is one not only of the most honourable but the most flattering to a young man of any military views; or who wishes to be distinguished by the first in the military line. The idea of my being of use in my present station I trust will not be a reason with you why I should not change it for one more agreeable to my wishes. But I must not influence you in a matter which your own feelings must determine. I would only just beg to observe that those who believe in a superintending God can have little to fear from a change of situation. We are all under his eye, and under his particular providence, whether in the walks of private employment, or amidst the hurry and confusion of war and battle. We cannot die without his knowledge, nor live without his protection.

It now rests upon you to say what I shall do.[36]

FOUR "I Gave Up Soft Beds"

James McHenry

MCHENRY BEGAN HIS SERVICE to Washington with a sense of optimism. After all, he admired the general, almost everyone did, and now he could contribute to the war in a martial rather than medical capacity.

When McHenry joined Washington's staff he found that the Virginian had surrounded himself with the most talented young men available, for he sorely needed letter writers, couriers, and, during battle, quick military assistance. He referred to these young men as his "Family," and engaged them because Congress had authorized two categories of assistance. On the one hand, the general had been permitted an unlimited number of aides-de-camp who were clearly military officers, given the rank, pay, and rations of lieutenant colonels.[1] Generally these men did whatever the moment required.

There was, on the other hand, a secretarial category that was not military and carried no rank. As assistant secretary, this was McHenry's new position. These men generally lived the life of an aide-de-camp, yet they were expected to do so without military credit. Indeed, McHenry lived much like any other "gentleman officer." He had "a body servant; he shipped around a lot of personal baggage with the army; he preferred to ride a horse rather than march; whenever he could, he dined at taverns rather than field messes." Furthermore, the lack of rank posed little problem; anyone connected with Washington basked in his reflected glow. This was a very good start for a young man of "military views."[2]

Furthermore, McHenry fully appreciated the honor done him. The general was, after all, quite particular about those he invited into his Family. They had to be devoted to the cause, educated, and possess common sense and an easy temper. Moreover, they could not request consideration for the post; this was a relationship the general initiated. The position was quite "flattering," McHenry admitted, because of its exclusive character.[3]

In his desire for recognition and acknowledgment, McHenry mirrored the other young officers around him. True, these men were patriots, but a number of them also sought military glory and could be quite sensitive over matters of honor. Some served in hopes of an even more important military appointment, ideally a command. After all, other members of Washington's Family had advanced to leading military positions, even to quartermaster general.[4] Certainly handling the general's correspondence with Congress, governors, and other generals provided a personal visibility otherwise not easily obtained.

McHenry joined Headquarters when it needed new blood. The previous year had been difficult for Washington and his men, losing at Philadelphia and Germantown. The men had fought bravely, but Germantown's battle plan had been quite complicated and fog had helped to create confusion. To make political matters worse for Washington, the general's rival, Horatio Gates, had won an important victory at Saratoga, preventing the British from separating New England from the rest of the country. An entire British army had surrendered, and while this was of inestimable benefit for the cause, Washington's successes paled in comparison. It had also been a desperate winter at Valley Forge. The shortage of food and clothing led men to sell what few garments they had for provisions. The desperate men lived for some time on firecakes (a flat patty made of flour and water) and water. Maddeningly, it was not the dearth of food that was the problem, but the inability to get that sustenance to the men; there were insufficient wagons, drivers, and money allotted to hire civilians to do the job. According to Robert Middlekauff,

> [p]ork which had been purchased in New Jersey remained there to spoil for lack of wagons. In Pennsylvania, private contractors shipped flour to New England, where prices were better, while Washington's soldiers had short rations. And a number of farmers around Philadelphia preferred to sell to the British in the city, who had hard cash, than to accept Washington's promises of payment.

None of this was helped by disorganization within the Quartermaster Department, which Congress restructured later in the year. When Washington, who had tried to keep the difficulties secret, finally requested extraordinary aid from the state officials, they provided substantial assistance and expressed indignation that the army had been unable to take care of it-self.[5] Furthermore, during the winter, Washington and his staff had come to believe that an Irish officer named Thomas Conway had participated in a stillborn cabal to oust Washington from his command. In fact, Congress remained supportive of the general.

But important changes had occurred. Surviving the winter bonded the men in a pride reflective of the army's growing professionalism. The French had also become more significant, with Americans secretly receiving arms from Pierre-Augustine Caron de Beaumarchais just weeks before the battle of Saratoga in the fall of 1777. Critically, in February 1778 Benjamin Franklin and his colleagues negotiated an official Franco-American alliance (at least partially as a result of the American victory at Saratoga) that would supply even more essential money and men. Then in March, Friedrich Wilhelm August Heinrich Ferdinand, Baron von Steuben, implemented a rigorous field drill that improved discipline at all levels. And with spring, a new military season arrived.[6]

Beginning May 15, 1778, the Family eased McHenry into his responsibilities slowly, giving him time to learn the job. "James McHenry Esquire is appointed an Assistant Secretary to the Commander in Chief & is to be respected and obeyed as such." On the next day, McHenry wrote his first letter for Washington, a short and perfunctory paragraph to Governor Patrick Henry of Virginia. McHenry's tasks involved transforming the general's written or oral instructions into a letter and submitting it to Washington for changes. The corrected letter was then copied and sent to the recipient, with Headquarters retaining the draft as Washington's copy. The trick was not merely to convey the substance of Washington's notes, but also his intent. By the end of the year, McHenry was the principal correspondent with Major General Philemon Dickinson and Brigadier General Charles Scott.[7]

As McHenry got to know his work, he also got to know the men at Headquarters. There was, of course, George Washington, whom he had probably met in Philadelphia when he was Benjamin Rush's apprentice. Tall, square-jawed, and imposing, almost twenty years older than McHenry and stiffly formal, the general demanded as much from himself as he did from his Family—which made working under him at once both easy and difficult.

Then there was Robert Hanson Harrison, McHenry's immediate superior, who had served as secretary to Washington since 1775. He was also Washington's neighbor, attorney, and old friend, who hailed from Maryland but practiced law in Alexandria, Virginia. Tench Tilghman's position was, at this point, even less defined than McHenry's. Beginning as a company captain, in August 1776 he volunteered to serve on Washington's staff without rank or pay, and hence without position. His personal and familial connections would assist McHenry in Maryland. Richard Kidder Meade had served since March 1777, and had previously been lieutenant colonel of a Virginia regiment that was subsumed into the Continental army. John Laurens, a volunteer extra aide from South Carolina, was also there. He was probably the best "connected" of the aides, since his father was a South Carolina delegate to Congress and at this time also president of that body.[8]

The final aide, and the one with whom McHenry developed a long-lasting friendship, was Alexander Hamilton. Hamilton was born, Broadus Mitchell believes, in 1755, the illegitimate son of James Hamilton and Rachel Lavien in the British West Indies. A few years after his father abandoned them, Rachel died, leaving the young Alexander to the care of relatives. He eventually worked for a merchant firm that he helped manage before some wealthy local patrons sent him to King's College in New York. Brighter than most men, he possessed angled features, blue eyes, and sandy hair. When the Revolution began, Hamilton was available and eager, soon becoming an artillery captain and an aide-de-camp to Washington. He and Laurens were also close.[9]

Despite their obvious differences, McHenry and Hamilton also had much in common. They were both young, as was most of the Family—McHenry and Hamilton were in their mid-twenties. Both were outsiders, immigrants from elsewhere within the British Empire in search of opportunity. Also, both had immediately embraced the full meaning of the Revolution. These factors created a fast friendship between McHenry and Hamilton. Soon they had given each other nicknames they used the rest of their lives—"Mac" and "Ham."

In a few weeks, McHenry learned the ropes. Then on June 9, 1778, with Major General Nathanael Greene as his witness, James McHenry formally renounced allegiance to George III and promised to defend the United States as George Washington's assistant secretary.[10] He was now a full member of the Family at the epicenter of the American army. Everyone, including McHenry's father, approved of James's new position.

Headquarters pondered what strategy the new British commander Sir Henry Clinton would employ.[11] The British might make a bold move before the Franco-American alliance cemented itself. If so, Clinton would attack—somewhere. Or perhaps the British would decide not to fight both the French and the Americans, and instead await a negotiated settlement either in Philadelphia or another area of British strength. All eyes were on Clinton, and Headquarters buzzed with anticipation.

Soon signs suggested that Clinton intended to evacuate Philadelphia. Ships sailed down the Delaware loaded with equipment, apparently destined for New York. McHenry and the other aides implored every officer for any piece of intelligence. They could not know that Clinton had learned he would receive no reinforcements and that he had been ordered to New York minus 8,000 men who were sent to Florida and the West Indies. The Americans only knew that they needed to be ready. Washington directed Colonel Elisha Sheldon to "proceed immediately to . . . the command of Gen[era]l Gates," and Colonel Stephen Moylan to put "your cavalry in the best condi[t]ion for acting." They needed to prepare to fight. The ultimate targets would be Georgia and the Carolinas.[12]

What would the British do with their American prisoners? Washington quickly tried to assemble negotiators. McHenry urged Elias Boudinot, ex–commissary general of prisoners, to come posthaste for it would be far easier to retrieve prisoners from Philadelphia now than after the British had moved them. As Boudinot did not come in time, Washington ordered Hamilton, via McHenry, to meet with the British commissioner and arrange prisoner exchanges, under the assurance that he would back Hamilton's decisions.[13]

In addition, Washington wanted more information about Clinton. Giving Lafayette a division to reconnoiter the Philadelphia area would provide the young marquis with field experience and get Washington additional intelligence. Accordingly, Lafayette moved his men to a location called "Barren Hill" located between Valley Forge and Philadelphia. Unfortunately his outpost security failed and he received only last-minute word that the British were hemming him in against the Schuylkill River. Recovering quickly, Lafayette escaped through adroit maneuvering and brisk marching.[14]

Finally, by June 18 the British moved for New York, with Washington's army following. But the bad weather held them both up and the British delayed a little too long at Monmouth Court House.[15]

The battle of Monmouth Court House should have been a far more significant American victory than it was. Blame for this fell squarely on English-born General Charles Lee, who had earlier in his career served in the British and then the Polish armies, and his troublesome idea that the American army should never meet the British on a formal field of battle.[16] The American army, he thought, was simply no match. Lee would have fought a type of guerrilla war.

But that day Washington wanted to inflict a blow on the enemy's rear-guard as it headed for New York. The American army was to cut off the British rear and subdue it. Despite misgivings, Washington offered his senior officer Lee the command. At first Lee refused it, thinking the tactic a foolish maneuver, but when the young Lafayette accepted, Lee's pride led him to take the command.[17]

The British began moving about 5:00 a.m. McHenry, the newest of the Family, must have been disappointed to be sent behind the lines with Washington's maps and correspondence, but along the way he ran across General Lee advancing to meet the British. Hoping to be of more service, McHenry asked Lee if he could take a message to Washington. The enemy appeared confused, Lee replied, so he was confident of his objective. But as McHenry left, Lee called out to him that a few British cannon were firing at them and that the British were doing a very unusual thing for a retreating army—they were constantly changing their front.[18]

This seems to have been the first sign that Lee was losing his nerve. Some suggested that Lee was a traitor who purposely sabotaged the American effort that day. What is clear is that he advanced so slowly that he had not engaged in battle by 10:00 a.m. Lafayette, with a smaller command, finally attacked on his own initiative, and Scott and Wayne came to his aid. Lee's men, however, milled about in confusion, for their general had issued no orders—until, that is, he commanded a retreat.[19]

At this point, Washington came upon the scene and asked angrily why there was so much confusion. Hearing Lee's vague reply, Washington took command, charging forward to rally the men and assist Lafayette. With Washington's leadership, the officers imposed order and resisted British attack. After retreating about fifty yards, they suffered another assault, but this time pushed the British back. Clinton called off the fight and retreated in the dead of night.[20] The striking difference in the two American generals' command efforts was not lost on anybody, least of all those who, like McHenry, witnessed it. Washington's bravery brought inspiration to the men who felt humiliated by Lee's conduct.

But the fight between Lee and his superiors was not yet concluded. Washington had upbraided Lee publicly during the battle and the latter demanded satisfaction. When Washington referred him to Congress, Lee at first demanded permission to resign, but then changed his mind and insisted on a court-martial that would, he thought, acquit him. McHenry must have been pleased to write the letter authorizing Lee's arrest. To Lee's surprise, the court determined he had disobeyed orders, misbehaved before the enemy, and affronted his commander-in-chief; he was suspended and later dismissed from the army.[21]

Vindicated, Washington now hoped to hit the British in New York with a joint sea/land attack, only to find that the French fleet's ships ran too deep to enter the harbor. So the general turned his eyes to Newport, Rhode Island, where British Brigadier General Richard Pigot encamped. A sea/land offensive could be mounted by the American General John Sullivan and Admiral Comte d'Estaing, commander of the French fleet. But for some reason Sullivan moved a day early without consulting the Frenchman, and when the British navy appeared, d'Estaing had to meet them rather than assist Sullivan. A gale injured both fleets, which then headed to ports for repairs. With d'Estaing gone, Sullivan was on his own. Seeing the futility of his situation, Sullivan retreated, harassed by the British along the way.[22]

Americans were certainly disappointed and many were even bitter about d'Estaing's withdrawal. But Washington knew that he still needed the French fleet, and through McHenry urged Sullivan to allay any low spirits Newport caused.[23]

McHenry himself was ill. He had returned to camp from a sickbed only two days earlier, having spent the better part of two weeks eight miles away at White Plains because of an "ugly anomalous fever."[24]

The turns of both the war and his health depressed him. Events since Monmouth, he wrote a friend, had left the army in the same geographical position as in 1776. Moreover, the British were currently too strong for the Americans to attack. When McHenry discovered that enlistment periods had increased from months to either three years or the duration of the war, he wrote, incredulous, that the recruiters were trying to establish "a permanent and regular army, as if our prospects not only included Canada, but extended as far as New Orleans."[25] After three years McHenry, like much of the population, had finally become impatient; he simply wanted the war to be won and done.

Worse, the war went badly over the next few months. In separate incidents, the British massacred Colonel George Baylor's Third Continental Light Dragoons and fifty of Count Casimir Pulaski's Legion. New York's

Mohawk and Pennsylvania's Wyoming frontier valleys had been repeatedly attacked by the Iroquois and the British, who also burned the privateering port of Little Egg Harbor in New Jersey, destroying ten ships.[26] Then, despite the fact that Washington had sent reinforcements south, the British landed at Savannah on December 23. Six days later the city fell.

Furthermore, serving George Washington was harder than McHenry had anticipated. He admitted the difficult living conditions to his father. "In sleeping in the open fields—under trees exposed to the night air and all the changes of the weather I only followed the example of our General," James admitted. "Tho' long in the army I was but a hospital soldier." Despite those difficulties, this was harder. "When I joined his Excellency's suite I gave up soft beds—undisturbed repose—and the habits of ease and indulgence which reign in some departments—for a single blanket—the hard floor—or the softer sod of the fields—early rising and almost perpetual duty."[27] Thus, despite the benign facade the younger McHenry generally presented to his father, James found the life hard and unremitting. Although he had only served Washington for a matter of months, his optimism had become ambivalence.

Still, McHenry suppressed his discontent. He had, after all, made a commitment. And he had also begun to develop a sense of pride in their efforts and sacrifice. So he stayed and spent September and October writing letters about supply and insignificant British movements.

By late fall, however, McHenry yearned consciously for a change. As he missed ten days at Headquarters in this period, he was probably sick again. He wrote to a friend that military duty "has not a little impaired my health," and began to think of a "voyage to Europe for its re[covery]." McHenry continued to indulge these thoughts, and shared them with Hamilton, another dissatisfied assistant at Headquarters. These were good, talented, ambitious men working for Washington, who understood their frustration. Unfortunately the nature of the job involved limited rewards. Often an aide's determination to prove himself worthy of honor left him feeling the despair of the second-rate.[28]

Still, they stayed with Washington, but it was frustrating to spend much of 1779 watching and assisting the campaigns of other generals. Since British General Clinton had moved the war to the South and Washington commanded in the Middle Colonies, he could do little more than send aid to the American commander of the Southern Department, General Benjamin Lincoln.[29] It must have been agony to watch from the sidelines.

Moreover, from January through most of June, the southern fighting was indecisive. The Americans won a victory at Kettle Creek, Georgia, but suffered serious casualties at Stono Ferry, South Carolina, while the British kept Savannah. There was also a limit to the assistance Washington and his aides could offer. Occasionally he ordered men and supplies south, but generally he ran his own command.[30] McHenry wrote numerous letters settling issues of rank, the location of shoemaker's tools, the need for military discipline to prevent mutiny, and so on.

Far more important was Major General Sullivan's anticipated summer campaign against the Indians, who had killed fifty citizens of New York's Cherry Valley the previous fall. Their deadly raids on western settlements had to be stopped or they might distract the war effort. Washington believed this could only be accomplished by destroying all of the Iroquois' (Six Nations: Mohawk, Oneida, Onondaga, Cayuga, Seneca, and Tuscarora) settlements and corn in western New York and taking hostage as many of their men, women, and children as possible. Only then might the Indians willingly negotiate a peace. Washington would stay near the British in the New York City area while Sullivan campaigned westward against the Indians.[31] McHenry, accordingly, wrote a number of letters ordering support for Sullivan, both in the form of men and supplies. Local authorities were also notified.

By May McHenry wrote Sullivan that Washington expected the western campaign to begin, but problems in the Commissary and Quarter-Master General Departments caused delays.[32] Sullivan did not march until July 31. Moreover, he failed to appreciate the need for surprise, for when he rendezvoused with Brigadier General James Clinton at Tioga, he stopped and built a fort. They did not, in fact, advance from Fort Tioga until the end of August. After some early resistance at Chemung near Elmira, New York, Sullivan and his men cut a swath up through the Finger Lakes. But because he had lost the element of surprise, Sullivan generally encountered vacated settlements, which he destroyed. Washington had hoped that hostages would create a desire for peace on the Indians' part, but instead they became more determined to resist and remained a problem for the Americans for the rest of the war. Even so, Washington counted the expedition a success, albeit a limited one. Few American lives had been lost, the Iroquois Confederacy had been split and part of it neutralized, and the rest of the Indians now understood that their raids would occur only at personal cost. Rather than attack the Americans directly, they would now attack their Indian allies.[33]

Washington also kept careful watch on British General Clinton, who advanced 6,000 men up the Hudson, taking two incomplete American forts at Stony and Verplanck's Points. The Americans, however, avenged these losses with a feat of daring. General Anthony Wayne led a night attack at bayonet point on the British at Stony Point. He captured the fort, destroying it and its usefulness to the enemy.[34] His audacity earned him the nickname "Mad Anthony Wayne."

Inspired, the Americans now planned another attack. This was the brain-child of Major "Lighthorse" Harry Lee, who had extensively surveilled the area. McHenry sent Major Lee the plans, approved by Washington, for a surprise attack on Paulus Hook. Without firing a shot, Lee took 150 prisoners. McHenry sent Washington's congratulations and urged Lee to report his exploits to Congress. Both American victories were stunning and relatively bloodless.[35]

These victories impressed McHenry deeply. Clinton, he thought, must be made to feel the full impact of the situation. It was the perfect time to discourage the British and Tories while uplifting American morale. To achieve both of these ends, McHenry wrote his first piece of political propaganda.

He took his time to write the piece and, as was the custom, chose anonymity, signing himself with the mysterious letter "Z." McHenry gloated over the American success at Paulus Hook. The post had seemed so secure that Clinton could reasonably have "laughed over the midnight bottle without imputation of folly." The fort was, after all, on a peninsula with miles of hazardous approach. But "[a]ll these obstacles were surmounted, and another ray plucked from that star [England] whose lustre is nearly extinguished." But why, "Z" wondered, had Clinton forsaken the post without a fight? How, he asked, "will you explain to ministry the mystery of your campaign? . . . . [Y]ou have rendered yourself ridiculous to the world. . . . You have suffered yourself to be successively defeated by a people boastingly called cowards, and ridiculously rebels." Worse, McHenry argued, Clinton had embarrassed the king. "[Y]ou have taken away from your prince the chief support of his speeches: He will be no longer able to tell his parliament of his reliance on the bravery of his troops, and the courage and conduct of his commanders." The essay was an effective piece, and later that year, John Laurens attempted to get McHenry's "darling" printed. He clearly wanted to make a mark beyond that of secretary.[36]

McHenry knew the daily dangers others risked, and this now hit harder as he began corresponding with those in the secret intelligence rings Washington created. After the death of Nathan Hale, Washington realized safer means of attaining information about the British had to be found. Hale's task had been to infiltrate and then escape without any means of support. He was, of course, caught and executed. Washington did not want this to happen again, and he sought a more stable system of intelligence.

The general put the matter in the hands of Robert Townsend, a patriotic New York merchant. Townsend set up a small coterie of spies, mostly relatives who could visit each other frequently without exciting British suspicion. Neighbors could communicate in a variety of ways, including leaving clothes on the line. The operation was small, secret, and carefully run in Manhattan and Long Island. Not even Washington knew the identities of all the players, who possessed aliases. Robert Townsend was Samuel Culper Jr., and he generally passed his information to Washington through Major Benjamin Tallmadge, also known as John Bolton.

Thanks to John Jay's brother James, the Americans passed information secretly and easily. James Jay, in London, had run across a clear ink that became visible only when used on a good-quality paper. He immediately recognized the uses for a different ink, one that remained clear on paper until brushed with a special solution. So Jay invented this latter, invisible ink, and sent it to Washington. Ironically, throughout the war Washington continued to receive this important anti-British weapon from London.[37]

The American spies thus wrote light letters concerning weather and family, hiding their intelligence in-between the lines in invisible ink. So, when a letter from Samuel Culper Jr. or John Bolton arrived at Headquarters, the message would be exposed and, for preservation, copied by one of the aides. McHenry had been writing Bolton for some time, but in September McHenry addressed Culper Jr., who considered giving up his business to gather intelligence full-time. Washington shuddered at the thought, arguing that the business was the spy's best cover. Without an obvious livelihood, the British might watch his movements more carefully. Culper Jr. obliged the general and a few days later reported that the French fleet under d'Estaing had been sighted off the American coast earlier in the month.[38]

In fact, Admiral d'Estaing moved against Savannah, which had been taken by the British. Eight days later General Lincoln joined him with American land forces. D'Estaing pressed an assault on October 9 but the move failed, costing over 800 American casualties. Count Pulaski was killed and d'Estaing himself withdrew wounded.[39]

Upon hearing the news, Washington assessed the damage. McHenry wrote General Wayne, "Altho' we were repulsed in the storm of the works of Savannah, we met with no opposition afterwards in removing our stores and baggage," making it easier to fight another day. More importantly, Washington thought, the Americans "have greatly crumbled the enemys force in this quarter. The allied men and officers harmonised perfectly, and behaved with great bravery on the occasion." It was an excellent sign that the French and Americans could now fight together without the petty squabbles that had erupted earlier in Rhode Island. Since the defeat was not an unmitigated disaster, the general looked to the future.[40]

As 1779 drew to a close, Washington prepared for winter, assigning quarters and what few supplies existed, but by mid-December he came to realize the extraordinary difficulties of the wintering army's situation. Hence McHenry implored help in a circular letter directed to the governors of the various Middle States. "The situation of the enemy with respect to supplies is . . . alarming . . . [soon] we must depend on the precarious gleanings of the neighbouring country," he wrote. "We have never experienced a like extremity at any period of the war." Furthermore, "there is every appearance that the army will infallibly disband in a fortnight. . . . I . . . entreat the vigorous interposition of the State."[41] To make matters worse, on New Year's Eve McHenry had to write to the Board of the Treasury that reenlistments had emptied the military chests. Most of the army had not received pay since September 1.

British General Clinton now thought to revive the southern campaign. On December 26 Clinton left 20,000 men in New York but took Cornwallis and 8,500 men to Charleston.

As the war moved south, the restlessness of Washington's military Family increased. Hamilton wrote John Laurens, who had returned to his home in South Carolina, that he had "strongly solicited leave to go to the Southward. It could not be refused; but arguments have been used to dissuade me from it, which however little weight they may have had in my judgment gave law to my feelings." Washington needed Hamilton. "I am chagrined and unhappy but I submit," he lamented. "In short Laurens I am disgusted with every thing in this world but yourself and very few more honest fellows and I have no other wish than as soon as possible to make a brilliant exit. 'Tis a weakness; but I feel I am not fit for this terrestreal Country."[42]

McHenry had been fighting similar feelings all along. Unlike Hamilton, he had not yet reached the point of requesting a military position in the southern campaign. Instead, he wrote silly little poems to fight off the doldrums. At other times he kept a diary, practicing his writing skills by describing waterfalls and trees. Often he encouraged others to drop their usual reserve and laugh, which no doubt contributed to his popularity in the Family. On more than one occasion McHenry "engaged in writing an heroic Poem of which the family are the subject," Hamilton wrote. "He celebrates our usual matin entertainment, and the music of those fine sounds, with which he and I are accustomed to regale the ears of the fraternity." Fellow aide Harrison provided special material. "His sedentary exploits are sung in strains of laborious dulness. The many breeches he has worn out during the war are enumerated, nor are the depredations which long sitting has made on his _____ unsung. . . . I have borrowed the wit of the present collation from McHenry."[43]

McHenry's official correspondence was filled with the usual severe winter problems. There was not enough food, and as much as Washington disliked the practice, he ordered supplies taken from the populace. While the army paid locals with notes, everyone knew these certificates had little value. Despite this commandeering, supplies remained insufficient, forcing the general to release soldiers whose enlistments were over rather than try to sign them up for another tour; he could not keep men he could not feed. Under these conditions, Major General William Heath suppressed at least one mutiny.[44]

There was also trouble at higher levels. Squabbling among the American commissioners to France threw a pall on the war effort. Of the three commissioners, Silas Deane, a merchant from Connecticut, had arrived in France first back in 1777. Eager to get arms to the Americans, Deane had worked to speed the process. Virginian Arthur Lee, who arrived later, suspected Deane of lining his own pockets in these matters and in 1779 decided to make his concerns public. Franklin defended Deane (historians today generally agree with him) but the damage to Deane's reputation was severe. Indeed, he would become quite disenchanted with the Americans' ability to win the Revolution and very prematurely urged a rapprochement. Many thought Deane a traitor and he eventually became an expatriate. Then in March Quartermaster General Greene reported the "evils" in his department to Washington, who sent Greene's report to Congress.[45] But at last the spring of 1780 arrived, Congress attempted to stabilize the currency, and Washington began recruiting for another fighting season.

By July 11 McHenry, after long deliberation, decided to make another change: after two years with Washington McHenry now wished to serve as a "volunteer" rather than assistant secretary. After all, when he had joined Washington's staff, McHenry had really hoped to do something more than write letters. Volunteer status would leave him free to seize any opportunity that appeared, especially in the southern campaign. He determined to speak up. This arrangement required Washington's cooperation, and McHenry made his request in writing, indicating that he would continue to waive pay as he had in the past. Treading carefully, he asked Hamilton to deliver his letter. Having respectfully and clearly stated his case, McHenry ended by noting, "If I receive your permission, to serve as a volunteer or accept of such a station in the army as may place me in a wholly military light, I shall be happy, because in it, I combine, with what I owe myself, that duty proper to my country."[46]

Washington understood but worried that he might be asked to find McHenry a military station. "You know it is not in my power to produce anything for you in that line," he added.[47] After all, McHenry had no official position or rank. To achieve a command would require an act of Congress. With McHenry's assurances that no such service had been considered, Washington found it "agreeable" that McHenry serve as a volunteer.

But, if Washington lacked the power to guarantee McHenry military rank or station, he could give the young man a position more martial and less secretarial. In fact, Washington could achieve two ends at once. Lafayette, a congressionally commissioned officer, had returned from France and required a unit to command, but as much as Washington genuinely cared for Lafayette, he feared the latter's impetuosity. McHenry was four years older than the Frenchman and, although it was probably more a function of personality than age, he was certainly more cautious. Washington gave the marquis command of a light division in New Jersey and made McHenry Lafayette's aide. While this did not give McHenry rank, the position was more martial, as Lafayette needed more assistance with his command than his correspondence. As aide, McHenry would serve the important function of cautious adviser to the eager marquis.[48]

McHenry had begun his service to Washington hoping to be rewarded by some sort of true military position. His new assignment to Lafayette, available to him only through Washington's interposition, was a step further along that line. It would certainly be better than putting the general's thoughts on paper, a position for which McHenry would never again settle. He could, moreover, be pleased at the friendships he had made, a number of which would prove valuable. Most important was his relationship with Washington himself. Although McHenry wished to leave the Family, he admired the general, having seen his courage firsthand. But, despite a soldier's pride in a difficult job done well, McHenry looked forward to the position with Lafayette. The future held promise.

FIVE "Sorcery and Majic"

James McHenry

MCHENRY TOOK THE JOB as aide to Lafayette, but he also started to agitate for military rank. By the middle of 1780 he enlisted his friend Hamilton, who wrote glowingly of McHenry to James Duane, an influential member of Congress from New York. "You know him to be a man of Sense and merit," Hamilton noted. "A more intimate acquaintance with him makes me hold him as such in an eminent degree. He has now no military existence properly speaking—no rank." But Hamilton had one to suggest. "For my own part were I to decide for him considering his length of services, his merit, the relation in which he has stood, I would give him a Majority." Although most of the aides to Washington served as lieutenant colonels, this rank distinguished them from aides to other generals, who usually ranked as majors. Surely, Hamilton wrote, Duane would "be glad to serve Mr. McHenry from motives of justice, of friendship to him and (shall I not add) of friendship to me." Hamilton also wrote his fiancée's father, General Philip Schuyler, one of New York's wealthiest and most influential men. Schuyler could offer McHenry the rank of lieutenant colonel with the New York state militia but not with the Continental Army.[1] If McHenry were to tie himself to any state militia, however, it would be with Maryland, where his family now lived.

McHenry was, moreover, soon reminded that his family's prospects affected his own. His brother John's unspecified financial troubles made him reconsider traveling to Europe on business. The prospect of an ocean separation displeased James terribly. "You have indeed been greatly unfortunate in trade. I feel for you with the heart of a friend and a brother. But the circumstance in it which gives me most uneasiness, is that I am to lose you for I know not how long." James had missed John. "I always wished that you might be near me, I loved you with all your faults; I thought you would one day get rid of them; I had my own to be forgiven." The thoughts pained him. "We were but two, but we were everybody to each other; for I believe our friendship was perfectly mutual. It is therefore that I find the intended seperation [sic] aggravated to one of the greatest evils. You have made me melancholly." But he had to consider the larger situation. "In what you are doing you may be acting wisely. . . . But, is it necessary that we should both be unhappy in order to acquire a little money[?] You see what a temper I am in." He now tried to collect himself. "Indeed I would not have you absent for all the money you [may po]ssibly make. But I will try [to recon]cile myself to whatever may happen, and trust to your prudence, and the arrangements of providence to bring us together."[2]

Interestingly, James mentioned no personal concern over money. Given his volunteer status with the army, this could not have been an inconsequential matter. Few family business records survive, but his third of the family estate must have been secure or sufficient for a military man. After their earlier disagreement, however, James surely would not write anything that might make him appear to be a sponge.

John's decision did limit James's options, however, as there was not enough money for both to go to Europe. James and John had discussed such a trip. "I have one request to make before you leave America," James wrote. "Make no provision for my going to Europe. I give this up forever, if it infringes on your prospects. Can the money in France be of use; if so, do not scruple to say it, that it may be subjected to your order."[3] Happily, John's finances recovered. But James continued to hold the idea of a European harbor somewhere safe in the back of his mind, retrieving it whenever ill health became an issue.

If McHenry could not travel to Europe, in September he did leave for Albany to attend Hamilton's wedding to Elizabeth, the daughter of General Philip Schuyler. Thus, the guest could personally thank his host for the general's efforts to procure McHenry rank.[4]

The marriage brought out the romantic muse in the Irishman, who tendered Hamilton a long poem for a wedding gift. Hamilton, a fellow poet, liked this verse for it was one of McHenry's best. Although it addressed Hamilton and his marriage, it tells much about McHenry himself.

McHenry had obviously given thought to love, marriage, and happiness in general. The man who would be happy "must build his hopes on love," understanding that with caring acts love's divinity and its intimacy with faith are preserved. In the poem McHenry treated each of these as sacred beings, partly out of convention but also out of reverence. Yes, he had thought of love and marriage, but had rejected the idea, concluding that he "could not be happy with a wife."[5] As no woman appeared to be a good fit, he declared that matrimony was simply not for him. In a few years he would change his mind.

Soon after Hamilton's wedding, the American war effort had its own cause to celebrate. McHenry, Hamilton, and Lafayette attended the Hartford conference between the French and Americans on September 21, 1780. Here, Washington and Count Rochambeau, lieutenant general of the French army, met for the first time, sizing each other up. Pleased with the qualities they found in each other, signs boded well for Franco-American cooperation.[6]

But trouble of another sort fomented. Traveling back to headquarters now, Washington and Lafayette planned to stop at West Point, where the general could quickly inspect the fort, the chain across the Hudson River designed to halt British ships, and socially acknowledge General Benedict Arnold and his wife.

Expecting to reach West Point in time to breakfast with Arnold on the morning of September 25, at the last minute Washington decided to inspect some redoubts on the Hudson's east bank. McHenry and one of Knox's aides rode ahead to inform Arnold of the change. While they ate breakfast and exchanged pleasantries, Arnold received a communication that agitated him. He checked on his wife; then told McHenry, who noted his agitation, that he would return to meet with Washington; and left.[7]

However, when Washington arrived Arnold had not returned. The general breakfasted, then rode to West Point alone and found no Arnold. In the meantime Peggy Arnold hysterically accused others of wishing to harm her baby. No one yet understood what had happened.[8]

It all became clear when Washington returned and opened a packet of letters that had just arrived. American soldiers had caught a British spy with "a plan of the fortifications of West Point; an engineer's report on attack and defenses of the place; a return of garrison, ordnance, and stores; and a copy of the minutes of a council of war held by Washington three weeks before." The most damning item was a pass for the spy, Major John André, written in Arnold's handwriting.[9] Arnold was a traitor.

Arnold had obviously received word of André's arrest while visiting with

McHenry, and he then hurried for the British lines. Immediately, Washington sent McHenry and Hamilton to capture Arnold, but it was too late; the traitor had already boarded a British sloop.[10] Peggy Arnold, who used hysteria to hide her own guilt, soon joined her husband.

Four days later, Lafayette sat at André's trial. As there was no doubt of his guilt, there could be no sentence other than death; only an exchange for Benedict Arnold could save his life. André requested to be shot honorably as a soldier, but spies merited only a hanging, and so André died as had Nathan Hale.[11]

The discovery of Arnold's treason shook the country, casting a shadow of fear and doubt. Arnold had once been a hero to the Americans, who relied heavily upon public virtue to help win the war. If he could succumb, who else was vulnerable? Not Washington. If his steadfastness and resolution had not stood out in sharp relief before this, they did now. After Arnold's treason, Washington and all of his supporters emerged the true heroes. All of the Family, including McHenry, knew it. Looking once more at themselves and each other, they became more observant but also more supportive. Good spirits would be important to overcome this blow. And there was cause for hope. The French had, after all, brought men, a navy, money, and supplies. It was important to remember that the cause was not lost but rather had been saved by the ordinary foot-soldiers who had caught André.

No, the war was not lost, but it would be decided in the South. On October 7 the Americans defeated the British at King's Mountain, South Carolina. Seven days later, an important change of command occurred.

General Horatio Gates had commanded the southern army, but Washington had always preferred Greene. Washington, however, did not have the best relations with Congress, whose approval he needed to fill command posts. Greene had served as quartermaster general, and whenever Congress questioned where money and supplies had gone, it was Greene's thankless task to explain and justify all of his purchasing and distribution decisions. Naturally, Greene and Congress had disagreed and not always politely.

But Congress's choice, Gates, the hero of Saratoga, led his men to serious defeat at Camden in mid-August. Far worse, Gates fled from the battle and traveled the enormous distance of 180 miles in three days![12] Americans gasped in shock and humiliation. After Arnold's treason and Gates's cowardice, however, Washington no longer needed to worry about his political status; in mid-October Congress rewarded him by approving Greene for the southern command.

McHenry was thrilled, as he and Greene had been friends ever since McHenry had joined Washington's family. Greene had, in fact, witnessed the oath McHenry swore to defend the United States. They may have met even earlier, since it had been Greene and Magaw who had decided to try to hold Fort Washington on Manhattan. The fort had, of course, fallen and led to McHenry's term as prisoner of war. So the men had known each other for some time. Greene was also convinced that McHenry had served Lafayette well, tempering the Frenchman when necessary. Needing to establish a loyal staff of his own, Greene soon wrote to Congress, expressing his "earnest desire to have Doctor James McHenry as an aide de camp upon the southern command . . . and that the said Doctor McHenry . . . be intitled [sic] to the rank of major by brevet."[13]

But if Congress allowed Greene the southern command, they had no desire to suffer for him. There were others in line for rank ahead of McHenry; to make him a major, the typical rank of Greene's aides, would bring political repercussions. Thus New England unanimously opposed the notion, as did New Jersey, Virginia, and McHenry's own state of Maryland. Just as McHenry's career had become caught in the web of higher politics when he was in the Medical Department, again his career became entwined in the knotty politics surrounding the southern command. He had lost his greatest chance to see action in the South.

As a result of this political opposition to his promotion, McHenry stayed with the marquis until November 26 when it became clear that Lafayette's Light Corps could accomplish little more and was disbanded. McHenry stayed until December 28 to help in the transition to winter quarters, but by then his work was done. McHenry now had no post.[14]

By late January 1781 McHenry made his way to Baltimore with a brief stop at Philadelphia, renewing his political contacts and composing another political tract.[15] Ironically, McHenry's eyes now turned to politics. He had learned that even in the army power lay with politicians, and he wanted to be a decision maker, not a victim.

Within Washington's Family, McHenry had made friends who would help to shape his future. Regarding Maryland, the most important was Tench Tilghman. Although a Philadelphia merchant before the war, he was closely related to Mathew Tilghman, his future father-in-law and a very important man in Maryland politics. Mathew was part of the "country" or "popular" party which had ousted the Tory "court" party early in the Revolution. He was also wealthy, knowledgeable, and extremely organized, holding a variety of significant executive positions throughout the war. He had led the assembly and all the provincial conventions, served in the Continental Congress, and at present served in the Maryland Senate.[16]

It was probably through this connection that McHenry came to know Charles Carroll of Carrollton, one of the wealthiest men in the state and its Senate, who guided that body without "ruling" it. The Carrolls were wealthy, aristocratic, and influential Catholics with an important history in Maryland. Charles Carroll of Carrollton, with fine features and a direct gaze, was generally conservative and had overcome misgivings to sign the Declaration of Independence. He now led other key Marylanders such as his cousin, Charles Carroll, Barrister, and Samuel Chase, who dominated the Lower House.[17] Through Tilghman, then, McHenry became acquainted with many of the most important men in Maryland.

By 1779 they, too, were aware of McHenry, as illustrated by an incident involving Samuel Chase. Solidly built, with an oval face and brows that knit easily, Chase was also a delegate to the Continental Congress and had used privileged information for personal gain. Unlike those among whom he circulated, Chase was born to an Anglican clergyman and a woman from a good Maryland family, but he did not come from a moneyed background. Given a solid education but little else since his mother died soon after giving birth, he was instead a man on the make, looking for every opportunity to improve his financial position. He had studied law only to find that the wealthy clients had other attorneys. For his fees Chase had turned to the multiplying number of debtors created by the turbulent wartime economy, and in his eagerness to acquire wealth, overextended himself in land speculation. Representing debtors both in court and in the House of Delegates meant that he was simultaneously advancing his own interests. He thus courted the debtors whom other lawyers avoided, and soon he became the champion of those who might be dispossessed. Via this route, Chase hoped to realize his dream of becoming one of the landed gentry.[18]

Chase saw an opportunity to make money in 1778 when, as a member of Congress, he learned that body planned to buy large quantities of wheat to help supply the expected French fleet. He directed his partner to corner the Baltimore wheat market in order to raise the price and make a windfall at Congress's expense. When Hamilton discovered this profiteering even as soldiers everywhere risked their lives, he could not restrain himself. Anonymously, Hamilton exposed Chase in the *New York Journal and General Advertiser*. Naturally, the Maryland Senate (Carroll of Carrollton's bailiwick) formally chastised Chase. Chase proclaimed his innocence against the overwhelming evidence, letting the matter lie until March 1779. Then, in an obvious attempt to deflect the attention from him, Chase declared that Samuel Adams had called Mathew Tilghman and Charles Carroll, Barrister, traitors. The Maryland Senate investigated and found the charges baseless, but in May Daniel of St. Thomas Jenifer, president of the Maryland Senate, traveled to Philadelphia. There Samuel Adams, with McHenry as witness, denied ever accusing Tilghman or Carroll of treason.[19]

This episode revealed several things. A new rift had emerged between Chase and Charles Carroll of Carrollton, who was naturally upset that his cousin had been irresponsibly accused of treason, and who had encouraged the Senate in its earlier censure of Chase's speculation.[20] The tension between the conservative Senate and more liberal House of Delegates would last for years.

It also reveals the origins of McHenry's involvement in Maryland politics. For when Daniel of St. Thomas Jenifer wrote the Senate of his conversation with Samuel Adams, he referred to McHenry as his witness without bothering to explain who McHenry was. Undoubtedly through the Tilghmans, the Senate already knew. Moreover, as witness, McHenry could not help being aligned with the party growing in opposition to Chase, the more conservative Senatorial cadre of Carrolls and Tilghmans. Now known and aligned within Maryland's high political structure, McHenry would not be forgotten.

In fact, two years later on January 25, 1781, the Maryland Council, the highest and wealthiest political body under the governor, almost voted McHenry into their group when a member resigned.[21] Extraordinarily, McHenry, an outsider, nearly became an adviser to the governor.

This was possible due to the structure of Maryland's government. The general populace voted for only two offices, the Lower House and the county sheriff. An electoral college chose the Senate, whose members had to be worth at least £1,000. The legislature chose the council and the governor annually. Advisers to the governor, the council also included wealthy men, and here lies its immediate significance for McHenry: if a member died or resigned midterm, the council itself chose the replacement. On January 17, 1781, Daniel Carroll resigned his seat. Five men were nominated to replace him, and three of them, including McHenry, tied for the position twice. In the end, the council decided the election by lot. Only chance had kept McHenry from this post.[22]

The fact that the council even considered McHenry for the post was surely due to the fact that colonial and revolutionary governments like Maryland were run by a relatively small group of, say, 50 to 100 men who all knew each other fairly well. When one segment of that group became interested in someone, the others could not help but hear of it. The Carrolls and the Tilghmans had certainly exerted their influence on McHenry's behalf.

Doubtless pleased to find a group of men who appreciated his talents, McHenry stayed in Baltimore until March, while he and local Maryland dignitaries each took the other's measure, approving what they saw. McHenry was welcomed practically everywhere, for he was a close associate of General Washington's and could tell locals much about the war effort that they would be hard-pressed to learn elsewhere. For his part, McHenry became more fully acquainted with Maryland politics.

But soon the war effort reclaimed McHenry's attention. He was still Lafayette's voluntary aide-de-camp and that now began to mean something. In fact, this was the beginning of the second significant event McHenry would experience while serving under the Frenchman's command. Early in 1781 George Washington decided that Benedict Arnold, now serving the British in Virginia, must be dealt with, and Lafayette was the man to do it.[23] McHenry, as Lafayette's aide, would at last see action in the South.

It did not, however, escape anyone's notice that fighting in Virginia might well lead to the war spilling northward to Maryland. Since McHenry was in the perfect position to get the best intelligence available, he began an extended correspondence with Maryland's Governor Thomas Sim Lee that would last until the end of the war. This reinforced McHenry's growing acquaintance with the most powerful men in Maryland, helping him prove his worth at the most significant levels.[24]

When McHenry reentered the service, Hamilton left. He and Washington had finally come to an impasse. Although Washington demanded more from himself than from others, he could be difficult to work for, as he was always formal and stiff and consequently impossible to relax around. And, bearing so much responsibility on his shoulders, he occasionally lost his temper.

Hamilton, on the other hand, was Washington's most trusted aide; whenever the general found himself in a bind, he turned to Hamilton. Indeed, perhaps because of the trust he placed in the young man, the Virginian had repeatedly reached out to him personally. Many have suggested their relationship evoked that of father and son. Such a connection would certainly be natural in such an intimate setting where one man is much older than another. And, of course, the military term for the staff was "family." Certainly both McHenry and Lafayette agreed to this close kind of friendship that bordered on a father-son relationship with Washington. Recently, however, Ron Chernow has suggested that Washington hoped for friendship with Hamilton rather than a filial connection. However one defines the connection between the two men, it was intimate yet complicated, for Hamilton rebuffed Washington's overtures, always keeping their relationship professional and not personal. Washington accepted this, continuing to value Hamilton's work. But Hamilton, like McHenry, wanted to see action, and especially desired a command. Twice Hamilton had nearly received one, but in the one case the general said the aide could not be spared, and in the other Hamilton could not be promoted over those in line above him. Angry, Hamilton awaited an excuse for a rupture. So when one day Washington lost his temper with Hamilton, believing the aide had kept him waiting ten minutes, the latter could no longer bear it. Hamilton disagreed over the length of the wait, and chose this time to part ways. Even Washington's apologies, Hamilton wrote McHenry, could not soften him.[25] In light of Hamilton's situation, McHenry must have felt most fortunate, even if he was serving Lafayette rather than Greene.

Lafayette, for his part, quickly saw the wisdom of using McHenry's contacts and popularity in Maryland, for it fell on the Irishman's shoulders to mobilize and coordinate Maryland's activities. The most pressing problem was to get the Frenchman's troops near Virginia immediately, marching them south from the Middle Colonies to the northernmost tip of the Chesapeake Bay, a place called "Head of Elk." Boats would then transport them to Annapolis in southern Maryland, from which they could later move into the most advantageous part of Virginia. McHenry therefore spent February and the early part of March locating all types of vessels, some armed, others for dispatch, more to serve as transports or scows. He contacted not only the governor and council but also the merchants of Baltimore. With their assistance, Lafayette's needs were met. McHenry himself contributed $110.76½. By March 9 McHenry joined the troops on board the ship *Nesbit* and continued to oversee transporting sick soldiers to a hospital.[26]

Throughout the rest of the war McHenry continued to communicate with the governor and local merchants about Maryland's safety. In fact, at McHenry's recommendation, Baltimore merchants created a committee to oversee the city's war efforts. They soon voted McHenry president of the committee, surely a good thing as they had lost their cohesion. The most serious problem was that Samuel Purviance had fallen out badly with the popular party's leaders in Annapolis. Chase and Carroll had invested in companies that fought Virginia for the ownership of western lands, but Purviance had joined Virginia's side. The alienation of Purviance led to the political distancing of Baltimore from power in state politics. The Baltimore community had not recovered, and McHenry slipped into the political power vacuum, facilitated by his expertise in military matters. In April, Baltimore merchants decided they needed a decent harbor defense and determined to construct two "lookout boats," which McHenry believed would be ineffective. Convinced that he alone could not sway the Baltimoreans, McHenry privately urged Governor Lee to advocate a galley and the expedient worked.[27]

In the meantime, General Daniel Morgan had won the Battle of Cowpens and Greene had met General Charles Cornwallis at Guilford Courthouse. Although the Americans withdrew in a technical loss, Greene's troops had seriously punished Cornwallis, who now found himself in need of men, supplies, and respite.[28]

McHenry still hoped that Lafayette might join Greene, but the latter expected orders to move momentarily, he knew not where. In the interim, there was no point in sending for the Frenchman. Instead McHenry spent the rest of March on board the *Nesbit* serving Lafayette and Maryland simultaneously. The work was strenuous and by the end of March he was sick once again.[29]

As if being sick were not bad enough, on April 3 Congress finally agreed to make McHenry a major "from the time at which Genl. Greene applied in his favr. (last octobr.)."[30] One might expect this recognition to have pleased McHenry, but he had long since stopped thinking in terms of rank and now thought in terms of flexibility. He had not completely lost his desire to see important military action, but he knew that being a volunteer without rank had its advantages. He could take whatever opportunities presented themselves without having to ask anyone's permission, and he could serve in the army for as long as he wished—then leave it should something come up, say in politics.

By July, something did indeed come up in politics. His friend, Colonel Uriah Forrest, had returned to Maryland and pushed for McHenry. Forrest was auditor general for the state, had served with the Maryland forces, and had likely met McHenry at Washington's Headquarters. Now based in Annapolis, Forrest had ample opportunities to put in a good word for his friend. For his part, McHenry was still ambivalent. He desired a political position, was tired of the war, yet still found it difficult to leave. Realistically he knew that his health had suffered during his war service: "Too much, perhaps, attached to my country, and too little attached to myself, I forego everything to gain—nothing." His exhaustion showed: "I take no care for myself, and the care I take for others, is either not known or will be forgotten." McHenry envied Forrest, at home in his own bed and in the bosom of his family. Since Forrest proposed a place for him in either the council or the senate, McHenry expressed his preference for the council, which he thought would be less taxing physically, but in truth he would accept either position. "I am not averse to sacrifices. I would do a great deal for mankind were I able, but I cannot see the necessity of killing myself."[31]

By September, however, it became apparent that an interested Maryland hesitated to give him a post because they thought his rank as major tied him to the army. Quickly, he wrote Governor Lee in a hedging letter that he had not asked Congress to give him rank. Greene had made the request, and at the time McHenry had desired it, but after Congress's initial refusal he had considered the matter closed. When Congress finally gave him the rank, he was insulted by their sluggishness and believed he was due a lieutenant-colonelcy, the rank of Washington's aides-de-camp, despite the fact that other aides to Greene and Lafayette possessed majorities. McHenry had therefore simply ignored Congress and continued to serve as a volunteer. But, in the event that Governor Lee required it to satisfy Maryland politicians, McHenry enclosed a resignation of his military office, asking Lee to use it only if necessary. He was still not burning any bridges unnecessarily.[32]

Despite all of these maneuverings, McHenry was not quite ready to give up on the military. He had devoted so much time, energy, and health to the Revolution already that some part of him still did not wish to let go. So he continued to pursue a place of military importance, even if without rank, attempting unsuccessfully in early April to transfer to General Mordecai Gist's command.[33]

In June he was called back to the southern army, not knowing if he would serve Lafayette or Greene, but suspecting the latter. Since Lafayette still wanted McHenry, Greene deferred, writing to McHenry, "I wish you with me exceedingly, but there is no inconvenience to which I would not subject myself to oblige the Marquis. . . . I am persuaded you are useful to him in moderating military ardor, which no doubt is heated by the fire of the modern hero."[34] The desires of Washington and Lafayette won the day.

McHenry continued to pine for another commander late into August. "I almost sigh to think, what distinguished riches in history you have gained under a great general," he wrote to Colonel Otho Holland Williams, who served under Greene, "while we in this quarter, have not yet deserved a corner." McHenry cared deeply for the Frenchman and the affection was mutual. Still, McHenry was convinced that Lafayette was too low in the military hierarchy to lead an important or decisive command. Americans were not eager to give important commands to foreigners. Despite this, McHenry served Lafayette well. His rapport with the Baltimore merchant community had come in handy when Lafayette needed money, because, on July 1, McHenry helped arrange and witness a personal loan of £1500 to Lafayette from Baltimore merchants.[35]

By now it was clear that Lafayette's task was to keep a close eye on Cornwallis and harass him occasionally without provoking him to attack, for the British had 7,000 men in Virginia while Lafayette had half that number. In fact, with this disparity in men, one of Lafayette's first problems was to convince Cornwallis that the American army was actually much larger. Lafayette's pursuit of Cornwallis, however, convinced locals that the American army was on the offensive, and militia from all over appeared to join the effort. Accomplishing this, McHenry wrote, required "sorcery and majic, and I have reason to think that it had its effect." Under the circumstances, it was all the army could do. "We have done nothing, and, I hope will do nothing; although, there is nothing I wish for so much as to do something. This is an enigma, which I must leave to time to explain."[36]

But Cornwallis would not let this state of affairs continue. Although he was on the Virginia peninsula with the York River to the north and the James River to his south, he had not yet settled on a location. Deciding to cross the James and move to Portsmouth, the British general thought he could accomplish two goals at once: he hoped to leave the peninsula and injure Lafayette's command. Thus he planned his own "majic."

Cornwallis sent part of his forces ahead across the James in a way that suggested he was crossing with the entire army and left Lieutenant-Colonel Banastre Tarleton in the rear to act as a decoy. The Americans began pursuit, and Lafayette sent Wayne ahead in reconnaissance. When Wayne saw Tarleton and only a few British units remaining on his side of the river, Mad Anthony decided to attack. Before long, however, he saw his mistake—the bulk of the British army lay before him and he was about to be swallowed. Cornwallis expected the Americans to beat a hasty retreat, but to his astonishment, Wayne deployed his men in a bayonet counterattack. A short fight ensued that allowed Wayne's men to execute an orderly retreat. All in all, the Americans were pleased that the losses were not greater and they had fought well. Cornwallis moved south toward Old Point Comfort without having inflicted a serious blow on the Americans, but the British commander soon decided that this site was less defensible than Yorktown in the north, to which they returned.[37]

The British move northward in early August heightened McHenry's fears for Maryland. "Cornwallis," McHenry wrote Governor Lee, "is a modern Hannibal." He warned the inhabitants of Baltimore that if they could not provide a galley and a boom for the city's protection, they might be wise to transport everything movable, people and things, out of the city.[38]

To the Americans' surprise, Cornwallis remained at Yorktown. Yet McHenry continued unenthused. Not until August 28 did he begin to partially comprehend the possible significance of Yorktown. For he now heard that French Admiral François J. P. de Grasse was sailing his fleet from the West Indies to the Chesapeake.[39] This created an unexpected opportunity for the Americans, because Cornwallis's force rested on the York River next to the Chesapeake Bay. If the French could control the bay, Cornwallis would have to move by land, and by land he could be surrounded. Cornwallis's army was vulnerable. So Washington secretively moved his troops from New York to Virginia, warning Lafayette not to allow Cornwallis to escape south to the Carolinas. To that end, Lafayette sent Wayne north of the York River to guard the few British troops on that side while the Marquis, and McHenry, tried to keep Cornwallis against the York.

McHenry communicated this information to Governor Lee via private letter. At last McHenry had awakened to the possibilities. After all of his military service, he would not give this up. "A propos, should the state make me a civil man, I must beg a week or two's indulgence in this quarter, but this will be a hereafter consideration." Maryland did not ask him to leave. By September first Cornwallis was nearly encircled. "Cornwallis is at York . . .

General Washington . . . at or near the head of Elk; Count de Grasse in the Bay; and some of his frigates in [the] James river," McHenry told Governor Lee.[40] McHenry shared Washington's concern that the French fleet might not be able to stay long enough to force the British to surrender.

Certainly the British were not going to give up without a fight. The arrival of Admiral Thomas Graves and the British fleet attempted to aid Cornwallis by sea. But the French sailed out of the bay to meet them and engaged the British off Cape Henry. The two fleets continued maneuvering and engaging until they were off the coast of North Carolina, when they slowly started to move back north. Finally, on the night of September 9, the British ships left for New York. The French commanded Chesapeake Bay. Thus, when Washington arrived, prospects could hardly have appeared brighter, especially when de Grasse informed Washington that he would try to stay until the end of October if necessary. McHenry remained cautious, for "when we reflect that war is like an April day, it will temper our mind to disappointment."[41]

Washington, however, did not intend to be disappointed. He spent the rest of September perfecting the American and French positions and earthworks. The allied land forces surrounded Cornwallis in a semicircle, leaving only the swamplands unmanned. Occasionally the British fired on the American soldiers, but did little harm.[42] Washington now ordered the digging of parallel trenches, by which he could close in for an assault.

On October 6 McHenry wrote the Maryland governor, "[t]onight we begin to work upon our first parallel. This siege will be a very anxious business." Three days later the first parallel was nearly complete with hardly a problem, but digging the second parallel, still closer to the British, might mean storming some of the British works nearby and result in casualties. American spirits were nonetheless high. "A Major General and his division mounts the trenches twenty-four hours in every three days; and this is a place in which few men wish to sleep."[43] Though McHenry served his turn and had hoped to open the second trench, that honor went to Baron von Steuben's men.

Part of the second parallel required ground occupied by British earthworks. Washington ordered those works taken, one by the French, the other by the Americans. On October 14, Colonel Alexander Hamilton finally got his command, leading the American attack with Laurens and some of Lafayette's men. Hamilton did not, however, lead his own New York men, but instead commanded the First Rhode Island, many of whom were black and former slaves. It was evident to many that this revolution for liberty was hypocritical if slavery was not somehow addressed. Hamilton would later help found an antislavery society in New York, Laurens planned to free his slaves, while Washington freed his at his death. McHenry would continue to own a small number of domestic slaves even while publicly acknowledging an equality of mind among the races. Certainly this intimate group reflected a tendency for those who served in the army to be or become more antislavery than others.[44]

Lafayette and McHenry observed from the second parallel where they were "exposed to a heavy fire from the enemies gun during the attack on the redoubt." McHenry was "much fatigued by three days and two successful nights' duty," but the effort was crucial. Even as a voluntary staff officer, McHenry could now honestly say that he had served in the frontlines of battle. After all his maneuverings to be assigned to another command, there was now no more important place than with Lafayette and Washington. The attack was a resounding victory and the Americans were ecstatic. "As soon as the success of the Am[erican]-arms was ascertained, the Marquis desired Major McHenry to hasten to the redoubt and congratulate Col. Hamilton [and] Laurens in his name." McHenry did. "The first officer he recognized was his friend Col. Laurens—when—embracing him he exclaimed here is Caesar but where is Alexander—He is safe replied Laurens."[45]

Still, the British were not quite ready to surrender. Two days later the British attacked the second parallel and spiked the American guns, but this did no permanent damage to the American attack. Cornwallis could now only retreat across the York. Some British crossed the river that night but high winds and rough water prevented sending the entire army over. They had no choice but to surrender.

On October 17 a British officer under a white flag opened negotiations with Washington, and the next day commissioners agreed on terms. Two days later the papers were signed, and that afternoon the surrender ceremony occurred. Cornwallis, pleading an illness that few believed, sent his second-in-command to surrender his sword. Ever mindful of protocol, Washington referred the British officer to his second-in-command. The British were then directed to lay down their arms. As Americans watched the lobsterbacks mound their guns, no one, including McHenry, knew that it was the end of the war. In fact, more fighting did occur, taking the life of John Laurens. But they must have sensed it was the beginning of the end.[46]

For Britain, Yorktown was a catastrophe in an otherwise terrible year. She had suffered "defeats in India, the loss of West Florida and Tobago, heavy losses of merchant shipping, Minorca invaded, the French and Spanish fleets riding once more in the mouth of the Channel."[47] If England was not willing to stop fighting, she was finally willing to talk about peace. Now McHenry had to know that it had all been worth it. This last year of service to the cause had been awkward while he searched for a place in an important command, a place where he could be useful and receive recognition. It had also been a year of accomplishment, of "sorcery and majic," for Lafayette and Maryland had needed him. In the end, McHenry and the other men in his circle of friends were rewarded for their earlier service to Washington with active roles at Yorktown, the most decisive military engagement of the war. It must have been a sweet victory indeed.

In the euphoria after the victory at Yorktown, McHenry left the military. A serious blow had been dealt England, persuading the king's ministers to negotiate for peace. Now Americans had to face the aftermath of war and the challenges of self-government. This was the world McHenry was about to enter.

In his absence, a Maryland electoral college had selected McHenry state senator, and he was sworn into office November 30, 1781. McHenry had created this opportunity through a combination of hard work and networking. Finding his way into Washington's military Family had been the critical step. Working for Washington, McHenry had met Uriah Forrest, Tench Tilghman, and his cousin Mathew. The last served on the committee that examined the account of the Electoral College's decision and reported McHenry's election to the Senate.[48] Clearly, Maryland politics beckoned, and therein lay McHenry's future.

PART TWO

Politics, State and National

SIX "Transition from the Military to the Civil Line"

George Washington

MARYLAND'S CAPITAL, ANNAPOLIS, was small and charming. Its little harbor edged the city and goods lined the wharves. Brick and cobblestone streets radiated out and up the hill, past decorative clapboard houses. At the top of the rise stood the imposing yet graceful white capitol. From the building one could see the entire town and far away into the distance. It felt important.

Senator McHenry surely felt important, too, as Maryland faced serious political problems. Washington, for one, was "convinced your transition from the Military to the Civil Line will be attended with good consequences." As a new member of the Maryland Senate, McHenry moved with men at the top of the social rank. Unlike in other states, Maryland's "aristocracy" still controlled the government. Elsewhere the Revolution had created power vacuums that had opened politics to the middle class. But in Maryland the division in the aristocracy had simply led to the ousting of the Tory or proprietary faction; the remaining patriot elite then very carefully admitted other men of similar political views with wealth and connections. There was no large influx of the middle class into the power structure. McHenry was an exception.[1]

The most critical issues were economic. Financing the Revolution had been supremely difficult since the Continental Congress lacked taxing power and thus did not have a steady source of income. Somehow Congress had managed on state requisitions, foreign loans, various issues of certificates, and paper currency. States had issued their own paper money as well. But wartime inflation caused depreciation throughout the colonies, and the problem did not disappear with the cessation of hostilities. After a short-lived economic boom, depression would hit hard later in 1784 and all groups would struggle to meet their financial responsibilities. As the economy dragged, national, state, and personal finances worried everyone.

Maryland was certainly one of the more troubled states, working often on a depleted or near-empty treasury, with difficulty procuring credit and its money in England tied up in stocks. By 1781 "the pecuniary resources of Maryland appear to have sunk to their lowest point of depression," and the state was "forced into an open and solemn acknowledgment of her utter inability to pay her debts for some time to come." The state was often forced to impose new taxes and print more money, and sometimes it failed to make requisition payments to the Continental Congress. A year earlier the General Assembly had overruled protesters like McHenry by authorizing the payment of taxes in monetary equivalencies like pork, beef, flour, and similar items.[2]

With all the enthusiasm of a newcomer McHenry tackled a prime source of trouble, paper money. Publishing his views, he argued that the "prudent" people of Maryland were right to question the value of state paper money because too much had been issued based on no external value. Naturally it depreciated drastically. New emissions must be based on a standard—specie in the form of gold or silver coin that could be raised by a property tax. Furthermore, landowners should not be allowed to pay this tax in equivalencies, for that only encouraged people to hoard their specie as insurance against a financial emergency. In other words, McHenry believed the coin was available, just hidden. Make this new property tax payable in specie or something similar and then new paper money could be issued.[3] This would both standardize and increase the value of Maryland's currency while discouraging the popular tendency to save coin.

The essay got the Senate's attention, leading McHenry to pen another clarifying the first and adding a new wrinkle: the amount of specie needed for a new emission equaled that required to start a state bank. A state bank would provide Maryland with a well-regulated medium and would also help the General Bank established by the Continental Congress.[4] A valiant effort, McHenry's "Act to Establish the Credit of a Bank" passed the Senate but not the House.

McHenry had done well for a neophyte. He must have expected that his bill might fail in the House since Maryland had, over the years, divided on currency. In general, conservatives like Charles Carroll of Carrollton, who detested the capriciousness of paper money, sat in the Senate, while others like Samuel Chase, whose personal finances relied on the depreciation of paper money, often controlled the House of Delegates. In sponsoring his bank bill, McHenry clearly aligned himself with the conservative Senate against the fiscally more liberal House. It would be easy to misread this division as one of classes, assuming that the House of Delegates, theoretically more democratic, represented the majority view in Maryland. Debtors, it is true, were often farmers, no matter what class they came from, and tended to favor paper money, while nondebtors of varying wealth usually lived in the cities and disliked the medium. There were, however, many exceptions to the generality, and no one knows how many of each group existed. Sometimes debtors appeared affluent, while nondebtors lived modestly. McHenry, though, was a member of the Senate and a city dweller whose bills did not risk alienating his constituents.[5] Under the circumstances, getting his bill passed would actually have been a minor miracle. Still, its loss surely disappointed McHenry.

He also spent part of January in the midst of an old controversy that only tangentially concerned him. Back in 1778 Alexander Hamilton had written an inflammatory diatribe against Marylander Samuel Chase, a member of the Continental Congress who had used "secret" information for profit. When Congress had decided to buy flour to supply the arriving French troops, Chase and his associates cornered the flour market. Upon hearing that a congressman had done this, Hamilton, incensed, had excoriated Chase in print under the pen name "Publius."[6]

Now, in Annapolis in 1782, Chase's defenders wanted Publius's identity. Chase had been acquitted by the Maryland legislature because Congress's decision to purchase flour had not, as Hamilton thought, been a secret and anyone could have done what Chase did. Somehow Chase's friends realized that McHenry knew Publius, but McHenry said only that he was not a Marylander. Yet McHenry did inform Hamilton of the acquittal so that the New Yorker might decide for himself whether to retract his allegations. Hamilton "respect[ed] . . . the decision of such a body too much not to be induced by it to *doubt* and *examine*." What, he asked, did McHenry think? No response survives, but Hamilton never retracted and McHenry never betrayed Hamilton.[7]

Three months later the next session of the Senate began. This time McHenry abandoned the ambition of his earlier bank bill. Instead, he successfully proposed that naval officers be allowed to grant registers for vessels and that the governor proclaim a day celebrating the birth of France's dauphin.

Otherwise, it was business as usual. The Senate agreed to the repair of a causeway, the building of a college and prison, the selling of confiscated British property, relief for petitioners, and further payment on the accounts of Maryland troops.[8]

More important, the Senate now considered the Impost of 1781, sent from the Continental Congress. At the urging of the Confederation's superintendent of finance, Robert Morris, Congress proposed an amendment to the Articles empowering Congress to levy a 5 percent impost, or tax on imported goods, to provide the Confederation with an independent source of revenue. The problem was that the impost plan, as an amendment to the Articles, required ratification by all thirteen states to go into effect. Most Maryland politicians, like McHenry, favored the impost and defeated the few in the state who feared increased congressional power. The import duty was, however, controversial since it would provide indefinite security for more foreign loans. As a result, the impost was later killed by Rhode Island.[9]

As this second session of the Senate drew to a close, McHenry returned to Baltimore. In January he had been made a justice of the peace, and although he did assist in a few cases, the workload was light. To make matters worse, he was soon ill with what was probably malaria and had no less than five bouts that lasted into the fall and quite nearly killed him.[10] Under the circumstances, it should be no surprise that an August letter he wrote Hamilton revealed a very depressed or "melancholy" man.

Being "on the point of gaining immortality by a fever" had caused him to confront the fact that it was not merely the Maryland Senate that was not making progress. Neither was he. In fact his public service prevented him from making personal financial headway, for his salary "might perhaps defray about two thirds of our expenses while attending the Senate . . . provided one was unmarried and lived frugally."[11] Perhaps McHenry and Hamilton ought to quit public service and concentrate on their own affairs. After all, McHenry complained, the people actually valued the wealthy more than their public servants, often electing a man of fortune rather than reelecting one who was the poorer for having served them.

His lack of personal autonomy upset him most. He had long fought for the country's independence while neglecting his own. "I find that to be dependent on a father is irksome, because I feel that it is in my power to be independent by my own endeavours. I see that the good things of this world are all to be purchased with money and that the man who has money may be whatever he pleases." He urged Hamilton to decline his recent election to Congress, and instead to finish his law studies and care for his family. McHenry admitted, however, that he was probably more in need of this advice than Hamilton. "My dear Hamilton, adieu. Remember a man who lives in this world, without being satisfied with it. Who strives to seem happy among a people who cannot inspire happiness, but who thinks it unbecoming the dignity of man to leave his part, merely because it does not please him." He knew, however, that he was being self-indulgent. "I am melancholly you perceive. This plaguy fever has torn me to pieces and my mind yet shares in the weakness of my body. But I will recover spirits, as I recover strength."[12]

To ease his financial situation, the young senator decided, like other volunteers, to take the pay he had waived for his service in the Revolution. Maryland had set aside some confiscated western lands for soldiers to purchase with their settlement certificates, and McHenry arranged to make such a purchase. However, Maryland's auditor refused McHenry the necessary certificates, since serving as secretary to Washington was not, strictly speaking, a military position. Without the certificates, McHenry would lose his chance to buy the land. He was forced to ask Washington to intercede, and he responded by requesting "congress to recommend his case to the state of Maryland." It worked.[13]

Sometime in between his bouts of illness McHenry visited Philadelphia and lifted his spirits by enjoying its feminine diversions. He flirted with a Betty Miller, writing her a short and humorous sonnet. He had played the gallant before. Back in June 1775, McHenry had to assure a man named Arthur Harper that he was not in love with "Polly" so that Harper's way to her was clear. Also, in 1777 he wrote a quick note of goodbye to Miss Kitty Ashfield, assuring her "that he wishes her every real form of happiness."[14] So we know that he flirted.

But we also know what McHenry *thought* of women, thanks to the survival of a remarkable letter to another woman that did not belong in the category of flirtation. He was lured into correspondence with a Miss Betsy Orrick, whom he believed wrote him a letter "without any date or signature."[15] According to eighteenth-century etiquette, a young lady simply did not initiate correspondence with a man, so that her letter seems to have been filled with trepidation. What would McHenry think of her behavior? How unfair it was that women were so circumscribed. And how necessary for women to retain what privileges they had! Such dissembling, of course, permitted her to retain a modicum of both pride and modesty.

James easily assured her that he was no slave to propriety. "When I sit quietly down, to reckon up the mistakes we so frequently commit in form-ing the details of life, it would seem rather a misfortune to be over wise or delicate. . . . We should comply with customs, but not at the hazard of our own happiness."[16]

Up to this point, James had merely been receptive and courteous. But Orrick had apparently struck a nerve, for he chose to address her concerns about the station of her sex and to explain his attitudes toward women in general. He professed advanced views regarding women's intellectual capac-ity even while couching his regard in the gendered and "protective" roles of his day. "I hope you do not think I desire to see them [your sex] more abridged. Indeed I wish them all kind of protection, and perfectly agree with you, that they stand pretty high in polite literature, nay further, that in almost every science they have done something to be distinguished."[17]

Despite his gallantry, James clearly saw himself as pushing women's ac-complishments into areas not traditionally considered feminine. He even had a retort for those who might dismiss women for not having achieved more. "I would say also, that if the other sex have acquired a predominence in *fame*, it is certainly built on the works of a very *few*; while it may be ar-gued in favor of the ladies, that they have not shared an equal number of chances with the men.—Had as many tryed [sic], it is probable as *many* would have been successful."[18]

Neither was James alarmed by the attempts of those who forecast social and political doom for men when considering the advancement of women. "But I have heard it urged by their enemies why do they not claim more ear-nestly their honors[?] They should gradually slide into government and strip man of the usurpations and usages which he has so insultingly established." They thought to reduce the argument to the absurd, saying that woman "should lead him by a prudent policy to a love of the household duties— teach him the arts of . . . the nursery—and the works of the wheel and the needle—assume by degrees his character—his laborious pursuits . . . his dangers—and all those trophies he gains in the field and the cabinet." Gen-der roles, in other words, would be turned upside down. McHenry, however, merely dismissed their worries and stayed the course regarding women's in-tellectual capacity. "But the irony of such insultors apart, the ladies undoubt-edly hold a very respectable rank in the republic of learning, and were their literary powers more generally exerted and applied I am persuaded man would loose in time much of the empire he so petulantly possesses."[19]

There it was. When pushed into a serious reflection on the place of women in eighteenth-century society, McHenry held that nature had made them man's equal while society had deprived them of opportunity. Such admissions on the part of his contemporaries were rare.

Nonetheless, in the inner recesses of his heart, he hoped women would not become too liberated. For one thing, he feared what he called woman's "inclination to tyranny" (he did not reflect on male autocracy) that he believed coexisted with her tenderness. But additionally, men truly valued the traditional qualities of women and their ease in ways that "increase the cordiality of acquaintanceship, and render the fair the sweeter companions."[20]

Having confessed all of this to Miss Betsy, young James suddenly realized what he had done. "I have trusted to paper that *secret* which gives your sex dominion and mastery over ours." He had exposed what men trusted other men not to reveal: that women were not simply men's equals but the caretakers of a part of life that made them powerful in men's eyes. His was a serious breach. "Masons, we know may talk freely with each other on the mysteries . . . and are only culpable when the art is exposed to one out of the compact." Implicitly, he requested Miss Betsy to honor its secret status.[21]

In fact, the secret power of women was more widely known than McHenry implied. In *A Father's Legacy to his Daughters* published in 1774, Dr. John Gregory had admitted that women were "designed to soften our hearts and polish our manners . . . 'And sweeten all the toils of human life.'" They were also, he said, "our companions and equals" and "not . . . domestic drudges, or the slaves of our pleasures." Does the denial prove the rule? Perhaps not. Having asserted female equality, this dying father went on to advise his daughters not to read too deeply, especially in religion, and to be careful that what they did read elevated rather than degraded them. He also spent the bulk of the essay telling them how they were to act in order to be desirable to men. Dr. Gregory's essay, consequently, was far more traditional than the opinions expressed by the much younger McHenry.[22]

Certainly the exchange between James and Betsy reminds us of the famous communications between Abigail and John Adams, when she urged that he remember the ladies while helping to create the new country. Although John seemed surprised and even bemused by her request, McHenry's letter confirms that the nature of woman's role in this new society was apparently a matter being widely discussed—and sometimes derided. If this generation of men was not ready for the power shift involved in a real equality between the sexes, one can see the stage being set for the postrevolutionary role of women as "republican mothers"—an ideal that was traditional insofar as it emphasized motherhood, but a step forward as it encouraged a more advanced and patriotic female education necessary so that women could in turn transmit it to the next generation.[23]

Now, however, in 1782, McHenry's attention was drawn to Miss Peggy Caldwell. The nine-year-old girl he had met in Captain Allison's household when he first crossed the Atlantic had blossomed into a lovely twenty-year-old woman. Her miniature shows an ivory-complected, oval face surrounded by light brown (powdered?) hair. McHenry took her most seriously. After all, she was a woman of the same social milieu as McHenry, the same religion, and with similar expectations. Furthermore, her father had left her a substantial amount of money.[24] Yet James appears to have been most attracted to her personality, confessing to her that he had modeled this poem's character on Miss Caldwell:

> [T]hink not fantastic, foolish, vain
> what fixes or revives your reign;
> think not that wealth directs the soul
> or love inspires from pole to pole.
> no fair e'er held the fickle heart
> by dress absurd or awkward art,
> no, nor riches ever yet could raise
> in human breast love's sacred blaze.
> These only serve to point your charms
> excite new joys spread fresh alarms,
> for contrast is the soul of bliss
> without it, vain your melting kiss![25]

McHenry continued, extolling her "spotless heart," for he clearly respected and admired Miss Caldwell. She was a young woman of good sense, prudence, innocence, and judgment—but a wealthy woman who worried that men would pursue her money rather than her heart.

At the time he wrote this letter McHenry could not pursue any woman, being dependent on his father. But in less than two weeks his problem would be gone, though at a terrible cost; shortly after he returned to Maryland his father died.[26] James and John were the only two McHenrys left. The property appears to have been divided equally between them, with James opting to become a full but silent business partner with his brother in "John McHenry & Co." James was now financially independent.

Still grieving, McHenry braved mid-December's winter chill and headed for the Senate in Annapolis, ignoring his own advice to Hamilton. Perhaps this time he was grateful, for he could keep busy in matters that would not constantly remind him of his loss. There were the usual petitions for relief. McHenry presented a bill to pave Baltimore's streets and also obliged the legislature by drafting short expressions of gratitude for the long services of Major General Nathanael Greene and the Count Rochambeau.[27]

One issue, however, must have pained the senator. The House of Delegates passed a bill forbidding the naturalization or immigration of British citizens during wartime; if enacted, an immigrant like McHenry could no longer escape Ireland and settle in Maryland during a war between the United States and Britain. Was there a fear of spies or was this a dig at McHenry? The Senate defeated the bill and charged McHenry with a reply that, unfortunately, does not survive.[28]

Far more consequential than any of these measures were the national and state economic concerns. The Continental Congress had been making valiant efforts to pay the war debt and restore greater balance to the nation's finances. One major problem in controlling the economy that had emerged during the war involved the circulation of many different currencies—states, the national government, and merchants all circulated paper in various forms that had competing and fluctuating values. To address this problem, in 1781 Congress had retired its paper money and was successfully paying the interest on the foreign loans. Both to meet its obligations and retire the varying circulating media, Congress often made the requisitions that states owed the central government payable in the medium they at present hoped to terminate. While these actions made sense, it could be difficult for the different states to keep track of the general debt, much less their portion of it. Concerned, McHenry moved that congressional delegates keep the Maryland Senate "well informed, from time to time, of the state of the foederal debt." Nor was the federal debt aided by the fact that someone was counterfeiting continental bank bills, forcing McHenry to present an act punishing such conduct.[29]

States, in turn, had their own finances to manage. In fact, to McHenry's dismay, Maryland began to pay debts through financial maneuvers that he believed were seriously problematic. Some undermined the state constitution. For example, the Senate continued the Intendant of the Revenue on its own authority despite McHenry's protests that Maryland's constitution required monetary bills to originate in the House of Delegates. Others violated the sanctity of contracts, which would surely cause future issues, for who would enter into legal agreements that were not binding? In addition, quite dangerously, Maryland had established what McHenry called "retrospective" laws, or laws that could impact a citizen retroactively. It might be as simple as changing the terms of a contract without the involvement of those involved, or making a legal act illegal and prosecuting someone for an action done while it was legal. The potential for the abuse of power was staggering.[30]

Alarmingly, Maryland proposed to meet Congress's 1783 requisition by allowing debtors to deduct one-sixth of the interest owed their creditors and pay it instead to the state. Aghast, McHenry denounced this as unjust and unconstitutional. Above all, he argued, it violated the sanctity of contracts and was especially dangerous because the assembly planned to make it effective on *already existing* loans and hence make it retrospective. This would, McHenry charged, destroy the general faith in contracts and eventually "the trade and prosperity of the state." Less effectively, he argued that it was also "a violation of the thirteenth article of the declaration of rights," which provided for a proportional tax; this was not proportional since it taxed only the creditor and not the debtor. Perhaps his weakest point was his last, that the proposal was "opposed to the letter and spirit of the eleventh section of the constitution . . . which declares, that 'the house of delegates shall not . . . blend with a money bill . . . any matter . . . not immediately relating to and necessary for the support of government, or the current expences of the state.'"[31] Splitting hairs, he insisted that these were future national, not state, expenses, though he undoubtedly believed that the requisitions were indeed a debt the state owed the national government. Money was needed for the requisitions and was scarce everywhere, especially among debtors; where else could the legislature turn for the funding? The dilemma was real. It may have violated laws and contracts, but the measure passed, despite McHenry's and Charles Carroll of Carrollton's fiscally conservative protests. There both the matter and the legislative session ended.

McHenry returned to Baltimore where restlessness seized him. He served as Judge of the Orphan's Court charged with protecting inheritances and apprenticing to a trade children ranging in age from two-and-a-half to eight years.[32] But he apparently disliked it, since during the ensuing year he attended only the first of five court sessions.

Nor could he have been pleased with Baltimore's impotence in the ongoing war effort. When new Governor William Paca requested armed sloops to fight British ships marauding the Chesapeake, the merchants replied that they could supply the ships but could not sustain any "capture or loss" and would require payment within a month. Four days later the governor and council declared the terms unacceptable.[33]

This only increased McHenry's disquietude, reviving thoughts of serving in Europe. It was not unusual for him to consider traveling to Europe when he was sick and in need of a change of climate or when the country was experiencing problems abroad. This time he was merely restless. He contacted Washington, who in turn wrote congressmen R. R. Livingston and James Madison; they lamented that no free position existed, even for a person of McHenry's talents.[34]

McHenry cast about for another way to alleviate his discontent. Although he was now financially secure, he had no personal life and the Maryland Senate promised little that was exciting and new. Whether to chase away the doldrums or to conduct business, McHenry headed to Philadelphia for a short stay.

There Miss Peggy Caldwell lifted his spirits. Later, when he left Philadelphia for the Maryland Senate, he wrote a friend, Major John Armstrong, cheerfully praising the weather and the beautiful women of Pennsylvania and Maryland. He wished Armstrong to deliver Miss Caldwell a message:

> assume the attitude of persuasion—awake her feelings by some well chosen story—take care at the same time of your own—then pause—and while, as she is wont, she casts her eyes thoughtfully, languishing on the ground—tell her—that although the edges of her little silky present, are much fretted by the attention paid to it—and here and there a thread actually destroyed— yet what is left—which I intend to wear round my neck as an amulet—still retains the power which she gave it entire and undiminished.[35]

It now seems clear that Peggy Caldwell returned at least some of his affection, since she gave him a keepsake. After all, there must have been a great deal about him that appealed to her. Not only were their cultural and religious backgrounds similar, James McHenry was now an eligible bachelor. He was an attractive man who had served his country honorably during the Revolution, for a time as an intimate of George Washington. Since his father's death, he was now independent, well off, and trained to a very respectable profession. Furthermore, they had known each other for over ten years. Indeed, he had taught her penmanship, so there must have been some level of comfort between them. Without a doubt, Miss Caldwell was fast becoming a force in his life.

Now the Senate elected McHenry to the Confederation Congress (formerly the Continental Congress). He was pleased, as he had been nominated twice before but not elected. It was an important post, and he now realized that politics, despite its frustrations, offered what he had been seeking for so long: usefulness and recognition. Furthermore, his newfound financial independence made his continuation in politics possible. McHenry would finish the month of May in Annapolis at the Senate's spring session and in June leave for Philadelphia, Miss Caldwell, and the Confederation Congress.[36]

SEVEN "A Delicate Task"

James McHenry

MCHENRY ARRIVED AT PENNSYLVANIA'S State House (now known as Independence Hall) on June 11, 1783.[1] It must have gratified him to enter the red brick building with its imposing white steeple. He had been here before, known delegates, and as a military physician had even applied to Congress for men and supplies. Here the Declaration of Independence had been approved and signed. Now he joined the ranks of those who belonged to this history.

As he sat at the Maryland delegation's small table, McHenry could survey the other men. He saw James Madison of Virginia, old friend Alexander Hamilton of New York, and the current president of Congress, Elias Boudinot of New Jersey. He soon discovered that, with the war nearing an end, these men possessed opposing visions for the newborn nation's government.

One group of early patriot revolutionaries had urged the war but favored their "local" authorities and a weak central government run largely by committee. Soon, however, the nationalists emerged, whose experience fighting the war led them to support a strong central government run by departments. Indeed, from 1781 to 1783 nationalists like Madison and Hamilton had dominated the body, but now their terms were ending and over the next two years the group's influence in that body would wane. Because the Articles of Confederation fixed term limits to three years in any six, they could not be immediately reelected. And although congressional disagreements involved fundamental views of government, differences manifested themselves most clearly over financial issues.[2]

McHenry fell comfortably into neither category; while he frequently took national positions, he also protected Maryland when a conflict arose.

Rather than quickly choosing to urge the interests of one level of government over and against the other, McHenry attempted to balance the conflicts between the emerging nation and his state.

On Friday, June 20, less than two weeks after McHenry's arrival, trouble erupted. The problem existed because of the federal government's lack of financial resources. This meant that most of the army had been furloughed the previous fall without compensation. (They were supposed to be issued certificates acknowledging their service and pay due. The certificates, however, did not arrive until six days after their dismissal.) With no peace treaty yet ratified, however, a skeleton army had been maintained for emergencies until April, when Congress finally declared hostilities at an end. Unfortunately, Congress delayed authorizing Washington to furlough the remaining men and in the interim the army languished in a general atmosphere of discontent. Now, several hundred Pennsylvania soldiers who belonged to this skeleton army gathered in mutiny outside the State House, angry because they had not been paid. The Pennsylvania soldiers wanted justice. They wanted pay.[3]

The next morning a bewildered and outraged Congress demanded "[t]hat the Superintendant of Finance report to Congress the obstacles which have hitherto impeded the settlement of the accounts of the army; and that he report to Congress the most eligible means to obviate those obstacles." They also soon discovered that the Philadelphia militia would neither guard the Congress nor appear in a show of support; the militia would assist only if violence actually broke out.[4] Washington was sending General Howe with a contingent to suppress the mutiny, but until they arrived Congress was on its own.

Soon the mutineers grew restless. While on Friday they had been orderly, on Saturday their numbers and impatience had amplified. Angrily they fixed their bayonets, surrounded the hall, and sent their demands to Congress. That body, however, considered itself "grossly insulted by the disorderly and menacing appearance of a body of armed soldiers" and the danger made it "necessary that effectual measures be immediately taken for supporting the public authority." Since Pennsylvania would not guarantee Congress's safety, it would adjourn to Princeton, New Jersey, on the following Thursday. For appearances' sake, Congress waited to leave the building until three o'clock, their usual hour of adjournment, when the soldiers allowed them to leave peacefully.[5]

A few days later, in a letter to Thomas Sim Lee, McHenry admitted that he had pressed Congress to reassemble at Annapolis rather than Princeton. Hosting the Congress would be an honor and good for trade. It would not happen, however, because of fellow Marylanders. "[I]t was unlucky for Annapolis that a detachment of our line in passing through Philadelphia exhibited the same mutinous disposition as the Pennsylvania troops. But for this, perhaps, a favorite scheme might have been carried into effect." Unfortunately, it was clear that "a removal to Annapolis would not have secured Congress from the soldiery, and this alone was enough to prevent it."[6]

McHenry was not unique in seeing this as the ideal opportunity to coax Congress to another city. His was, in fact, only an early maneuver in an extended battle over Congress's permanent location. Even before leaving Philadelphia, both New York and Maryland had made Congress attractive offers.[7] But McHenry could accomplish little as he was now Maryland's only representative, and the Articles prevented a single delegate from voting. Only one thing was clear—Princeton was just too tiny for Congress to stay long.

So McHenry kept up the battle. By August 7 Daniel Carroll arrived, giving Maryland a vote in Congress. Two days later McHenry asked Governor Paca for the authority "to inform Congress . . . that the public buildings were at the service of Congress. . . . It may have influence." He also wrote the mayor and citizens of Annapolis, suggesting that they "suit the price of boarding to the economical taste of the Eastern [New England] Gentlemen."[8]

In fact, Congress voted on its future location no less than twelve times. McHenry urged Annapolis as either a temporary or permanent home, depending on which fit the moment's debate. In October, after debating for two days, Congress chose the Delaware River (later the Potomac) for its home. "Had Annapolis succeeded in this vote it would [have] the permanent residence. . . . I have but one other stand left—which failing Congress it is likely to go to Philadelphia."[9]

He tried to win the temporary residence, hoping that it might eventually *become* permanent. Finally, after a series of serpentine votes and debates, Congress agreed to meet next at Annapolis and then alternate with other cities. McHenry had won at least a minor victory, which must have pleased his absent colleague, Annapolis Mayor Jeremiah Townley Chase. "Tell the good people of Annapolis—that I fought hard, and did not escape without some wounds."[10]

Now Congress considered what to do with the mutineers who had caused both the flight to Princeton and the debate over Congress's new location. The ringleaders were, of course, undergoing military trial, but Congress would execute the sentences. McHenry favored mercy. He reminded Congress that, until the mutiny, they were officers who had "behaved with that fortitude and patience which have so distinguished our army." They were "worn down by poverty and grown desperate by necessity," had merely sought justice, and had done no actual violence. Finally, he begged Congress not to let "the first fruits of their long and perilous contest, *our peace*, be watered with the blood of two of their companions. . . . It is said Draco's laws were written in blood—but no one has ever dared to praise them."[11] Congress agreed, letting the matter drop until 1786 when one of the ringleaders, Lieutenant John Sullivan, applied for his old war pay. Congress simply refused.

In the meantime, Congress heatedly attacked Robert Morris, superintendent of finance. Earlier in the spring, it had instructed him to issue the soldiers three months' pay. Why, Congress demanded, had that not happened? Morris answered in late July. He dissembled, called for taxes, and passed the buck, refusing to admit that he had used requisition money to pay army contractors and holders of the loan office debt rather than the soldiers. The committee formed to review this response, on which McHenry sat, was not pleased. Morris's attempts to blame the paymaster clearly rang hollow, for it was Morris who had delayed signing the notes. The committee, now distrusting Morris, resolved that he must inform Congress just how he planned to execute their charge, "that such plans and regulations may be known to Congress, and undergo their revision before they are put into execution."[12]

Congress was also angry because Morris's actions contributed to the growing tendency of states to assume the national debt by paying their Continental Army soldiers directly. Naturally, Congress feared the decentralizing effect of this, which was leading states to act as if independent rather than confederated. When New Jersey paid its Continental soldiers, Congress passed an act denying states requisition credit for these payments. Recently Maryland had found the money to advance five months' pay to its own Continental soldiers by revoking an act paying Congress's requisitions. Alarmed that Maryland had done this, Congress insisted on the requisitions, and asked that Maryland "be called upon to take into their most serious consideration the pernicious tendency of the measure complained of."[13]

Embarrassed, McHenry moved the postponement of this matter until the Maryland delegates could consult with their state. There must, he claimed disingenuously, be a serious reason why Maryland would have done such a thing. Maryland had, he insisted, "the strongest inclination to do everything in their power to support and maintain inviolate the confederation." With this motion he bought time, but not Congress's forgetfulness, for in 1785 he would still be trying to find a way to get some form of credit for the advance. He had indeed become a politician, for he confessed to another Marylander, "I had a delicate task in this question to vindicate in Congress what I condemned in the [Maryland] Senate."[14] No doubt many congressmen found themselves defending their states' interests in the Confederation Congress while at home supporting national interests.

Of fundamental national interest was the Virginia Cession, which would determine how much authority Congress had out west. Strictly speaking, Virginia's early charter claims entitled her to an almost unbounded western territory. This had caused states without claims to western lands, especially Maryland and Pennsylvania, to contest Virginia's claims even before the Revolution. Private speculators from those states, hoping to profit in this confusion, had purchased land and then appealed to Great Britain for support. During the Revolution, the speculators appealed to the Confederation, but when Virginia determined to help cement the union by giving up her western lands, she insisted that western land companies' claims be ignored.

Maryland, for her part, wanted Virginia to give up the lands, but strong private interests also demanded that Virginia's proviso be dropped. Interestingly, McHenry did not argue against the proviso (which clearly would have lined him up with the land companies), but against the cession itself. Because McHenry was not connected to private western land speculation, his opposition may be taken at face value: namely, that Virginia would still be too large and that a fair settlement could not be made until extensive surveys were run. He therefore moved to postpone consideration of the cession, calling the plan "too comprehensive & indefinite."[15] Nationalists and Virginia, of course, thought the matter much too important to await such a survey and the next year the Virginia Cession passed Congress. If the nationalists were right, so was McHenry, since western land disputes in unsurveyed areas plagued Congress and the nation for years.

McHenry's personal life centered increasingly on Miss Caldwell. Indeed, by mid-July they were deeply in love and a train of letters to "My dear Peggy" began. They had already discussed marriage and McHenry was quite tempted to "overcome my fears and speak to her parents tomorrow; she shall be mine."[16] But he had a job to do and neither one of them thought it proper he should neglect it.

When Congress moved from Princeton to Annapolis in early November, however, McHenry stole some weeks to go to the Caldwells in Philadelphia. At this visit he asked successfully for Peggy's hand, and thereafter pestered her to set a date. James was quite anxious; he was more than ready to give up his long bachelorhood for this sweet maiden. But he had to attend Congress and find a decent house in Baltimore since his bachelor quarters would not do. Even so, he tried to convince Peggy to marry as soon as he could leave Congress—possibly in early January. Peggy, on the other hand, wanted to wait until the spring, giving him time to find her a house, finish Congress, and allow her to stay with her family through the winter. Peggy's mother solved their problem: they would marry in January and McHenry would return to Congress, leaving Peggy in Philadelphia until the spring when a house was available and the weather was better. This seemed to satisfy everyone.[17]

So he returned to Annapolis and politics an engaged man, only to be frustrated when he found that the Confederation Congress lacked the quorum necessary to conduct official business. Instead McHenry attended the Maryland Senate, which had moved so that Congress could meet in its hall, making Congress's "residence in this state as agreeable as in [Maryland's] power."[18] All of this, the Maryland Senate hoped, would encourage the Confederation Congress to stick by its decision to locate the capital on the Potomac, Maryland's southern border.

Finding so little happening in Annapolis despite being an elected member of two political bodies in session at that very moment, McHenry traveled to Baltimore for a few days in December. "Half my business thither," he wrote Peggy, "was to communicate to my brother my plan of being with you in January. He will be prepared to accompany me the moment I can withdraw myself from Congress."[19] This done, he returned to Annapolis.

Although word had arrived from Europe back in January (1783) that a peace treaty had finally been negotiated, it took some time to implement the new peace. The British at last evacuated New York and now General Washington would resign his commission as commander-in-chief to the Confederation Congress while it stayed in Annapolis.

They all understood the significance of the event about to unfold before them. Few men in history possessing Washington's military power and popularity had voluntarily given it all up. But, during the previous year, Washington had suppressed a potential coup, the Newburgh Conspiracy, which would have tried to make him king or Caesar, and had instead slowly disbanded the army. Now he was resigning. It was an act of true republican greatness, and everyone knew it. It reminded them of the ancient Roman hero Cincinnatus, who had left the plow to command Rome's armies, only to return to his farm after winning the war. Excitedly, the general assembly of Maryland put McHenry on the committee that chose the new and elegant Mann's Tavern for Washington's residence, and the Senate prepared an address thanking the general for his long and dedicated service.[20]

McHenry had kept in communication with Washington ever since leaving the service, and they counted each other as friends. In fact, because of the Family intimacy, McHenry was a man with whom Washington could relax. The senator could even bring out the softer side of the general. The previous year, when Washington hoped for word about the peace negotiations from McHenry and had not heard because of the latter's ill health, he wrote, "Do not my dear Doctor, tease your Mistress in this manner—much less your Wife when you get one.—The first will pout—& the other may scold—a friend will bear with it, especially one who assures you, with as much truth as I do, that he is sincere."[21] No one could have looked forward to the general's visit more than McHenry.

By Saturday, December 20, 1783, Washington arrived in Annapolis. As his resignation was unprecedented, the general had asked Congress what protocol it would like observed. The members of Congress decided first that the seven states attending possessed the power to formally accept the general's resignation and also that the event should be public. Then they assigned McHenry, Thomas Jefferson, and Elbridge Gerry of Massachusetts to determine the particulars.[22]

The room in which Washington resigned overflowed that day. The spectators entered a large, square room with enormous windows on the far wall facing the audience. They crowded into the space until a balustrade stopped their progress, leaving them to stand and await the general. In front of the windows stood the podium used by the president of the Confederation Congress. Above the audience the balcony bulged with more onlookers whose bodies pressed against the creamy, pale green wainscoting.

At noon a door in the far left corner opened. After the government officials sat, the general appeared, dressed in full regalia. He advanced part way into the room, standing so that he could at once face the audience and officials. He stood, tall and commanding. McHenry described the scene to Peggy.

> To day my love the General at a public audience made a deposit of his commission and in a very pathetic manner took leave of Congress. It was a solemn and affecting spectacle; such an one as history does not present. The spectators all wept, and there was hardly a member of Congress who did not drop tears. The General's hand which held the address shook as he read it. When he spoke of the officers who had composed his family, and recommended those who had continued in it to the present moment to the favorable notice of Congress he was obliged to support the paper with both hands. But when he commended the interests of his dearest country to almighty God, and those who had the superintendence of them to his holy keeping, his voice faultered and sunk, and the whole house felt his agitations. After the pause which was necessary for him to recover himself, he proceeded to say in the most penetrating manner, "Having now finished the work assigned me I retire from the great theatre of action, and bidding an affectionate farewell to this august body under whose orders I have so long acted I here offer my commission and take my leave of all the employments of public life." So saying he drew out from his bosom his commission and delivered it up to the president of Congress. He then returned to his station, when the president read the reply that had been prepared—but I thought without any shew of feeling, tho' with much dignity.[23]

Thus Washington's war ended, as did the session of the Maryland Senate. Congress, however, remained sitting in hopes of attaining a quorum to ratify the peace treaty with England. McHenry lingered, hoping more delegates would appear so that he might sign the document that formally ended the war, but in early January he could stand it no longer and left for Philadelphia.

James and Peggy married on January 8, 1784, in the small, private ceremony McHenry had desired. She was twenty-two and he thirty. He remained with Peggy as long as he could, but in March life intruded upon the newlyweds. Governor Paca wrote that McHenry's presence was needed in the Confederation Congress. The new husband moaned, reminding Paca that *his* leave had been planned and complaining that he had only recently left that body.[24] Further, he knew that he *should* go to Baltimore to make arrangements for his new family, as Peggy was already pregnant. But since Maryland had no representation in Congress, he agreed to head for Annapolis, via Baltimore, instead.

McHenry arrived at the Confederation Congress on March 27. Certainly his pet project during this session was his plan for the light-duty employment in an "invalid corp" of veterans who were handicapped and otherwise unemployable due to their service in the Revolution. He also supported navigation acts to bolster American shipping, and unsuccessfully attempted small alterations of commercial treaties in ways he thought would benefit trade. In these cases he could promote all of his constituencies without conflict of interest.[25]

Thinking more nationally, he agreed when Congress offered credit *plus interest* to any state paying requisitions *in advance*. But McHenry's suggestion that interest apply only to payments made in specie failed, despite the government's need of that medium.[26] In any event, Maryland was unable to pay advance requisitions, specie or not.

McHenry also sat on the committee considering what to do with the northwest posts. The Old Northwest was now American land populated by Native Americans and scattered settlers, with posts held by the English. Without an American military presence, the land would be beyond U.S. control. Yet those delegates who disapproved of a peacetime military questioned whether Congress even had the authority to create such an army. Nationalists, however, favored this defense force and it was fairly clear that the posts required maintenance. The committee called for 700 men provided by state militias, including interested officers of the late Continental Army.[27]

Throughout, leaving Congress for Peggy was uppermost in McHenry's mind. Their correspondence was generally filled with sweet nothings, but the need to keep in touch was strong. Although he had taught her penmanship when she was a girl, Peggy was not given to letter-writing; she simply did not trust the "post." Letters were often mislaid or opened by others. Yet she promised to write, and after her first few successful attempts she was really quite pleased. "How delightful it is," she wrote, "that at such a distance, we can communicate our thoughts to each other, & by this means be able almost to imagine ourselves present with each other." James was so eager to set Peggy up in Baltimore that he left Congress as soon as enough other Maryland delegates appeared to do business, returning in June only for the last few days of the session. In the interim, he moved Peggy and their child-to-be to Baltimore.[28]

While in his new home McHenry attempted cautiously to expand the business. In October his father-in-law wrote from Philadelphia that he had, as requested, written a commendatory letter of introduction to his London contacts. But Londoners were doing badly in the American trade so he did not know how helpful it would be. Also, now that the Virginia Cession had transpired, McHenry and his father-in-law vaguely considered purchasing lands in western Virginia, but no record survives to indicate if that materialized (many years later McHenry attempted this but the records are unclear about his success).[29]

McHenry would not return to Congress until after the birth of their first child, Grace, on November 2, 1784. Instead he stayed home and played the roles of merchant, husband, and father. Only in December did the new father resume his political chores, first in Annapolis at the Maryland Senate. But he was not at the session long, so he accomplished little during his stay. Instead, McHenry packed up his family and five days before Christmas transported them to Philadelphia. He traveled on to New York, where Congress would meet on January 11 of the new year, 1785.[30]

Now serving his second term in Congress with a stable personal life and good health, he remained in New York through November for the bulk of this very busy session. Of course there was the usual supply of petitions from individual soldiers for promotion or recompense. But the end of the war also brought more western problems before Congress. As McHenry had anticipated, the question of boundaries continued, for although the Virginia Cession had been settled, North Carolina had also surrendered western land (present-day Tennessee) to the United States. Then, the previous November, North Carolina had tried to revoke that submission. McHenry's committee decided two things: that North Carolina could not revoke the cession *and* that Congress could not refuse the offer of the land.[31]

Western issues were complex. As Peter S. Onuf has written, "Once the states began to relinquish their western claims, Congress had to organize, distribute, and defend the new national domain." It was essential to do this, as the sale of these lands would provide much-needed income for the national government. This in turn meant sorting out relations with Indians, settlers, and squatters.[32]

Now, in 1785, McHenry rejoined the Committee for Indian Affairs, which concluded that a treaty was essential to establish boundaries between the Indians and white settlers (and squatters) in what would later become Indiana. McHenry worked diligently, drawing up the committee's report. In an attempt to establish peace with the Indians, control white settlement, and maximize land-sale profits for the government, a treaty conference would be held at Post Vincent on the Wabash on June 20 of that year, to which commissioners, money, and food would be sent. Squatters on the land were to be dispossessed, by arms if necessary. The issue of squatters emerged in another of McHenry's committees, which unsuccessfully urged Congress to forbid American settlers on Indian lands outside current state territory. All of this was required because there had not been the time to properly survey the western boundaries and land as McHenry had earlier urged.[33]

Reports of more land disputes resulting from conflicting surveys poured into Congress. Settlers in Kaskaskia (in present-day Illinois) bickered so bitterly that another of McHenry's committees suggested a commissioner survey the land and arbitrate the conflicts in favor of the longer-established settlers. There was even some question as to whom the land and buildings at Fort Pitt belonged: the United States or Craig, Bayard & Co. (in what is now Pittsburgh). The company got nowhere.[34]

These committee decisions were soon moot, however, for Congress took up what became the Land Ordinance of 1785. With the passage of this ordinance western land would be surveyed and sold, with the money going to the national government to help pay off the national debt and, presumably, provide a fund for national expenses. Despite the fact that there was basic agreement over the general plan, Congress still wrangled over the size and price of the lots. McHenry suggested larger amounts of land be sold with a lower price per acre; this would speed up the process of selling the land, and bring money into the national coffers more quickly than if smaller lots were surveyed. Of course, it would also make it easier for those with more money to purchase large amounts of land to later sell in smaller lots at a profit. Congress compromised, agreeing to the alternate sale of fractions of townships with smaller individual lots. While McHenry privately continued to consider becoming involved in this sort of land speculation, there is no evidence he did so until decades later, about 1812 or 1813, when he did attempt (it is not clear if he was successful) to buy some Kanawha River land in Wood County around what is now Parkersburg, West Virginia.[35]

Congress, of course, also sought other sources of funds, including foreign loans, regulating interstate and international trade, and levying imposts and export duties. These last caused McHenry to deliberate in a letter to Washington about whether or not Congress ought to have the power to lay imposts and exposts, and in so doing regulate trade. Robert Morris' 5 percent impost of 1781 had been defeated and the financial problems under which the country labored had not improved. So, in 1783, a congressional committee comprised of Madison, Hamilton, Nathaniel Gorham of Massachusetts, Pennsylvanian Thomas Fitzsimmons, and John Rutledge of South Carolina revived the idea of an impost to provide the national government with a stable source of money. Getting this power, however, again meant amending the Articles of Confederation, and thus the amendment again would require ratification by all thirteen states. By 1785 eight of the states had indeed ratified the amendment. Such an amendment would strengthen the central government, McHenry admitted, but he believed the South would dislike giving this greater power to the central government. After all, the sponsors of the duties partly hoped to foster shipping in American vessels, McHenry believed, while discouraging trade via British ships. This meant that New England's shipping industry, with its emphasis on international commerce, would benefit. The South, however, relied on imports that would increase in cost with higher imposts, and it had only a small shipping business to benefit from the possible changes. Moreover, increased (Northern) American shipping might well lead to demands for a navy (which had been disbanded at the end of the war) to protect the merchantmen. "But is it true that a navy is at present necessary?" McHenry questioned Washington rhetorically. "And if necessary, is it true that our people could go to the expence of supporting it? . . . [C]an we pay our present debts?"[36]

McHenry, typically, fell completely into neither camp and spoke for compromise. "Perhaps the point of true policy lays between forcing the growth of our shipping and doing nothing that may forward their increase. Perhaps the Southern States should give up something and the other States should not ask everything."[37] McHenry thought an American navigation act that encouraged the growth of shipping but did no harm to southern states might be wise and just might pass Congress. But Congress could not agree.

In the case of import duties, McHenry's concern for Maryland tempered his nationalist tendencies. He was, after all, very aware that Maryland was seriously behind in her requisition payments. This made her a debtor state to the creditor states and that, he feared, made a navy dangerous. After all, in 1781 (during the war), when states were not always meeting their requisitions, Congress created no less than three committees to consider just how Congress could find the money to govern. One committee, comprised of

Madison, James Duane of New York, and Rhode Islander General James Varnum (Continental Army) brought forth an amendment that historian Merrill Jensen says "would allow Congress to use the army and navy to enforce its decisions upon the states, seize their vessels, and prohibit their trade."[38] The idea that the national government might use armed force to compel obedience from a state was not anything Congress wanted to entertain, but the mere suggestion worried some. Although the notion was stillborn, McHenry had not forgotten it and feared for his small, debtor state. "I would only add," McHenry wrote to John Hall, "that the States to whom we are in debt are numerous enough to compel us to pay them, which I dare say they will attempt as soon as a favorable opportunity offers. If Congress were in possession of a *marine* it is not difficult to divine in what manner it would be directed."[39] In the end, New York refused to ratify the new impost, so McHenry need not have feared the navy or the impost's tendency to harm the South while benefiting New England.

McHenry's belief in the prospect of the coercive use of a navy by Congress against debtor states, however, helped keep the matter of Maryland's requisitions before him, since the state's problem would not disappear. In July, McHenry had thought it possible Maryland might be reimbursed in certificates for requisition money the state had collected but not sent to Congress, choosing instead to pay the Maryland line. McHenry believed this reimbursement might be possible even though in using this money for her own troops Maryland had acted against Congress's wishes. After all, he thought, an individual acting as Maryland had would have received certificates. Congress, however, had no intention of rewarding Maryland for using requisition money to make the advance.

Ironically, part of Maryland's requisitions difficulty lay in the fact that Congress now required specie payments, a practice that McHenry had advocated but with which Maryland and other states had difficulty complying: they simply lacked the specie. Further, Congress charged interest on unpaid requisitions, hurting delinquent states.[40]

Then, in 1784, Congress began to allow states to pay one-fourth of their requisitions in a form of paper known as "indents" (certificates of interest due). Continental loan officers had begun issuing indents in 1782 when Congress stopped paying the interest on the loan office debt. Of course the holders of the debt had protested vociferously, leading the loan officers to issue the indents, which acknowledged the interest due in a sort of promissory note.

In 1785 Congress increased the fraction of requisitions payable in indents from one-fourth to two-thirds. In general this was thought to benefit those states that had little specie on hand. However, different states possessed varying amounts of indents; the southern states, for example, possessed very few. As a consequence they were left having to pay their requisitions in hard currency—specie—which was becoming increasingly rare. McHenry described this clearly to a correspondent in Maryland. "Its [the requisition's] principles as you will perceive are only calculated for one part of the union; I mean for those States which are in possession of the great bulk of continental securities where they may be purchased at *eight* for *one.* To these States it will prove a blessing, to Maryland it cannot," he moaned. He also knew who benefited. "The States which it favors are Pennsylvania New Jersey and so on Eastward to New Hampshire inclusive . . . [t]hese States have it in their power to discharge their *two thirds* of their quotas at a very easy rate." Maryland was not so lucky. "[A]ll the . . . continental securities belonging to the State of Maryland or its citizens will hardly exceed *one fourth* of our quota. Of course Maryland must pay *three fourths* of her quota *in specie* or run in debt." The best solution to Maryland's problem, McHenry thought, was for the state to buy certificates (securities), enough that the interest on their indents would equal two-thirds of Maryland's requisition. They should be purchased quickly while they were cheap. His colleague from Maryland, William Hindman, agreed.[41]

In an unusual move, James encouraged John McHenry & Co. to assist Maryland in the purchase of continental certificates. This appears to have been a completely altruistic matter, for nowhere in any of the correspondence is there any mention of profit for the McHenry brothers. In essence, since the state was temporarily low in funds, the brothers agreed to purchase the certificates on the state's behalf, fully expecting to be quickly reimbursed the amount the company spent by Maryland. The national government would then issue Maryland the appropriate indents to cover the certificates' interest, which Maryland could use to pay the 1785 requisition. It was definitely an arrangement in Maryland's favor.

Purchasing the certificates was also the beginning of a financial setback for the McHenry brothers that would be troublesome for the next decade. Somewhere the arrangement broke down. By the middle of 1786 John McHenry & Co. did indeed purchase £4,000 sterling of certificates for Maryland. They soon discovered, however, that the state lacked the money to reimburse them; she had expected incorrectly that she could sell large quantities of pig iron in London to finance the purchasing of the certificates. But even that money only amounted to £1,500 sterling. By mid-July it was clear to McHenry that his company was in financial trouble.

As the brothers' original arrangement with the state was oral, the terms are unclear. James and John both thought they were to buy whatever they could find at a good price, and did so. Daniel of St. Thomas Jenifer, Maryland's intendant of the revenue, maintained that he had never thought in terms over £950 sterling. This surprised McHenry since he thought he had orally told Jenifer how much they were going for. Wherever the misunderstanding occurred, Jenifer tried to mitigate the problem, suggesting that Maryland might be able to find £1,500 for the McHenrys. Since the treasury was empty, the Council authorized that amount in credit.

It was little assistance to the two brothers and they found themselves financially "embarrassed." They tried to sell the certificates in Maryland but there was no market, and then through Peggy's stepfather in Philadelphia, where a good price might be managed. But the stepfather, William Allison, found that he could not sell them for the McHenrys since they were not Pennsylvania residents.[42] They were forced to take a large loss.

Since the company had not received satisfaction from the state, "[i]t now therefore became an object with them to fall into the agents [Jenifer's] debt a sum that might serve as an offset to their loss and thereby compel him to an equitable settlement. They accordingly in January 1787 agreed with the agent for a parcel of iron . . . shipped . . . for Liverpool by his order." But the ruse would not work. "[B]efore the agent would give the company any power over the same he obliged them to give the [promissory] note in question . . . the better to obviate what he saw was intended."[43]

Indeed, the November session of the 1790 assembly would call McHenry to account for the company's promissory note to the state for over £2,000. Why, it would want to know, had this not been paid? He would recount his story to the assembly, which would agree that the state owed the McHenrys, but only £183, and that the McHenrys owed Maryland £2,030.[44]

The assembly's reasoning may be surmised, for the documents do not bear out McHenry's argument that a contract existed between the state and the McHenrys, as there was no meeting of minds. The only clear contract that existed was the note the brothers signed saying they owed the state £2,030 in exchange for pig-iron, and to this note the assembly held McHenry. It had been a bad bargain for the company all around. McHenry would protest the matter again in 1796, and that spring William Marbury, agent for the state of Maryland, would suggest appointing mediators to "ascertain the amount of Damages"; nothing would come of it, although by this time the McHenrys' finances had recovered.[45] One might have expected this incident to have left such a sour taste that McHenry would want nothing more to do with public service. This was not the case, but he learned to never again mix his own finances with that of the public.

But now, in 1785, the year was drawing to a close, his term in the Confederation Congress was ending, and McHenry decided to return home. He had been parted from his wife and daughter much of the year and they wanted to go home to Baltimore. Most of Congress apparently felt the same way, as very few states attended that December.

Feeling this way, McHenry reacted poorly when, on January 6, 1786, he received notice that he was required in the Maryland Senate. Although politics provided him much of what he needed to feel useful, public service had left him little time for a family life. "As it is not in my power to attend the Senate without doing the greatest injury to my family and private affairs," he found it necessary to resign. McHenry could not help adding that during the previous decade, "the whole of which has been devoted to the service of my country, no part thereof has given me more pleasure than the time I have served in the senate, and that I shall always recollect that honorable period with peculiar satisfaction."[46] Hence, as his elected term in the Confederation Congress ended, so did his time in the Maryland Senate. His "delicate task" of balancing Maryland's and the nation's interests in the two political bodies was done. McHenry now gladly submitted to the demands of family life.

EIGHT

"For the General Good"

James McHenry

ALTHOUGH MCHENRY HAD RETIRED from government, its lure remained. Politics was work, it separated him from his family (and his brother, for one, complained), it lacked real financial reward—but he kept coming back for more. He enjoyed the fray too much, and he was fortunate that he had money enough to pursue his calling.

In September 1786 a recently organized Baltimore group known as the "Association of Tradesmen and Manufacturers" sponsored McHenry for the assembly as their candidate. He appealed to the group on a number of issues, among them state-sponsored religion. Mechanics had come to fear that the creation of the Episcopalian Baltimore College constituted the first step toward "establishing" that denomination in the state. Not only was McHenry unconnected with that institution, he was also a member of a small Baltimore congregation that would suffer should episcopalianism be established, and his upbringing in northern Ireland had taught him the pitfalls of state-sponsored religion. But McHenry also appealed to the workmen because of his Revolutionary War service, which they respected. They further identified him as a physician, though it is unclear whether they appreciated that his income came primarily from investment in a mercantile house. Then, too, McHenry still lived in Fell's Point, a working-class area of town, leading the mechanics to believe McHenry might have real sympathy with their ideas.[1] Perhaps part of his popularity among this group was a matter of personality—McHenry, as an immigrant, had not been raised as a member of the colonial elite and, although well off and a gentleman, would not have possessed the airs of the local "aristocracy."

Although he lost that race to the incumbent, McHenry could not stay out of politics when paper money was at issue, and during these troubled financial times the paper currency forces would not rest. Naturally, those heavily in debt hoped to pay their creditors in depreciated currency. While a number of farmers were debtors, the group also included many who had purchased more confiscated British property than they could handle or had taken on other risky speculative debt. Samuel Chase, leader of the paper money forces, gave debtors a political voice.

During the Revolution Chase had purchased confiscated British property for next to nothing, planning to pay the state for it in depreciated paper currency. To effect this, he sponsored a paper money bill that the Senate rejected. This precipitated a personal financial crisis for Chase, who, with his allies, appealed to the voters. Since he appeared to be fighting for the interests of the poor, his position was popular and so was he.[2] "Instruct" your delegates, he urged Maryland voters, that you want a new emission of paper money. After all, he insisted with some eloquence, power comes from those governed and "the right of the people to participate in the legislature is the foundation of all free government."[3] Instruction had also been traditional throughout the colonial period.

Chase's argument irked McHenry on two counts. First, he only approved of paper money if backed by specie, which the state did not have. Second, he held that voters did *not* have the right to instruct, or by petition to oblige their delegates to vote a particular way, and he wrote an essay to counter Chase's position. McHenry considered instruction to have many marks against it. For one thing, the Constitution gave the assembly the power of deliberation and authority, while the people retained other rights to themselves. "Instruction" would be an unconstitutional infringement on the assembly's power. Even worse, he argued, it would lead to chaos. There would be too many conflicting instructions. And who was to do it—any eligible voter or only those with enough property to hold office? What should be done if new instructions appeared on an old and apparently settled topic? He saw nothing but trouble with this policy.[4]

On the other hand, if Chase advocated his own interests, McHenry did the same. Merchants like McHenry generally favored a conservative money policy; they, after all, dealt with coin and paper daily and felt every change in its value. While James did not wish ruin on Samuel Chase, he did want his own vision of prosperity for Maryland and the Confederation realized, and he disagreed with Chase about the path to that end.

Chase's efforts, however, met with defeat. "The failure of the paper money movement meant financial collapse for Samuel Chase. His lifelong dream of accumulating the landed estate of the true gentleman ended in a nightmare of unpayable bills and unreachable hopes."[5]

Although McHenry's side won that battle, he did not reenter into full political participation until called back in 1787. In 1785, nationalists had recognized that their decreasing numbers and influence in the Continental Congress required them to find other means to achieve their ends. In March of that year some of them had met at Mount Vernon to discuss problems on the Potomac and the Chesapeake. These commissioners determined that Virginia ought to call for another commercial convention of all states to be held at Annapolis in 1786. This was poorly attended, but their discussions revealed that commercial issues intertwined with the political, and so they called for a general conference to consider strengthening the central government.[6]

Their call was aided by Shays' Rebellion, an uprising of farmers in western Massachusetts. These farmers, many of whom were veterans of the Revolution, found themselves barely subsisting on the land. As poor as they were, the state also struggled financially, and it chose to impose heavy new taxes on these farmers. Then, when the farmers could not pay, the state took their farms for taxes. As a result, the farmers agitated for either a new issue of paper money to provide more (depreciated) currency or laws staying farm and home foreclosures. When legal channels did not work, the rebellion began. The state now had to impose law and order but could not afford an army to suppress the rebellion. As a result, well-off Bostonians paid for a private army to do the job, certainly a disturbing precedent. Leaders around the country took heed, and many saw this as further proof of the need for a strong central government.[7]

Indeed, the notion that Congress's powers should be augmented—a perennial nationalist position—gained increasing acceptance throughout the states. People had talked about it for years. As early as February 1785 McHenry received a letter from Maryland's financial officer, the Intendant of the Revenue, Daniel of St. Thomas Jenifer. "But, my friend, requisitions will never do; Congress must have permanent funds," he complained. "If . . . [Rhode Island] should continue to be inflexible [on the 5 percent plan to raise revenue], I fear there must be a new convention especially appointed by all the states to increase the powers of congress, or it will be obliged from necessity to assume them, as political bodies have heretofore generally done."[8]

The time for this new convention had come at last, and it was to meet in Philadelphia on the second Monday in May 1787. When McHenry received word that Maryland had chosen him to represent the state in this conven-tion, his desire to reenter public life combined with his concern about the country's financial state, thus sending him to Philadelphia.

According to his notes, McHenry arrived in that city by the middle of May to find himself the only delegate from Maryland, for his state was so con-sumed by its paper money war that few would agree to leave (although three claimed illness).[9] In the early winter of 1786 the legislature knew it needed to jointly appoint delegates, but the lower house had insisted on adjourn-ing to address the public on the currency issue. When it reconvened in late March 1787, the lower house quickly compiled a list of important Maryland-ers, including McHenry, as candidates for the convention.

It did not, however, escape the Senate's notice that the men on the list op-posed paper currency. The Senate suspected paper money forces of trying to send conservatives out of the state and in their absence passing a currency bill. So it responded in kind by adding the strongest advocates of paper money to the list of nominees, namely Samuel Chase and his friends. All of them declined. Hence the first five men elected delegates to the convention were mostly fiscal conservatives, who, with the exception of McHenry, also declined. In the end only two of the five delegates were friends of Chase— Luther Martin and John Mercer.[10]

So it was that on May 14, the opening day of the convention, McHenry attended only to find that no other Marylander had yet arrived. Unfortu-nately, the state had solely authorized the actions of at least three delegates.[11] McHenry alone did not constitute a delegation and hence had no authority. All he could do was wait.

His waiting lasted over two weeks, but for much of that time the con-vention lacked a quorum and could not begin business anyway. Not until Friday, May 25, were nine states properly represented. McHenry began at-tending the following Monday, to keep informed even if he could not vote. His colleagues included such old friends and luminaries as George Wash-ington, Benjamin Franklin, Alexander Hamilton, and James Madison. They were all sworn to secrecy, and then the general elected the body's president. Even so, McHenry kept an important diary. According to Max Farrand, edi-tor of the convention's records, McHenry's diary especially illuminates the latter part of the convention, ranking only behind Madison's diary and the convention's official *Journal*. Richard Beeman is certainly right when he de-scribes McHenry's notes as fragmentary. They could hardly be otherwise, as McHenry was called away for a good part of the convention. Others also took notes, of course, such as Luther Martin, another Marylander not yet in attendance, who later compiled his notes in a pamphlet he called *The Genuine Information*. Robert Yates of New York and Rufus King of Massachusetts also kept sketchy accounts.[12]

One other source of material for the convention came from William Pierce, a delegate from Georgia. Pierce wrote character sketches for those who attended, and although he recounted the positive, he generally incorporated criticism as well. McHenry proved typical. On the one hand, he was "a very respectable young Gentleman, and deserves the honor which his Country has bestowed on him." Moreover, McHenry's talents were "specious," a word that did not possess today's meaning but, according to Samuel Johnson's 1755 dictionary, had as its first definition "showy, pleasing to the view." He was, however, no "genious," but an unremarkable politician, "nor has he any of the graces of the Orator." Indeed, Pierce criticized many delegates for their oratory, a trait the Georgian apparently prized. McHenry himself would probably have agreed with the assessment: he was respectable, talented, but no genius or orator.[13]

Many of the fifty-five delegates had already spent a great deal of time in this assembly room of the Pennsylvania State House, now known as Independence Hall. The Declaration of Independence had been approved there and the hall had hosted the Second Continental Congress. The building itself was made of warm, red brick; the Liberty Bell hung in its steeple; and the hall was handsome. As the men entered, light poured in from windows on the side walls, and in the middle of the far wall stood a raised dais with a pediment design flanked by columns, in front of which Washington sat. On either side of those columns rose two large fireplaces fronted by a gray-streaked marble. Each state delegation sat in Windsor chairs at a small table covered in green cloth with a candle, ink, and quill pen. Immediately, the convention decided on secrecy, a rule that grates against modern notions of open government, but it proved extremely important that the men felt themselves able to speak freely, without the fear of political repercussions. In this way they could honestly push for ideas they believed in. Indeed, none of the delegates expressed serious concern over the requirement for secrecy at the convention. They understood that, even if republican governments should be generally open to the citizens, there were times when the extreme sensitivity of issues or situations would not permit it. They determined that matters would be discussed only among the delegates, and nothing could be written for the consumption of others. They also ordered the shutters closed and doors locked and guarded by sentries despite the heat that would grip Philadelphia later that summer, so that a passerby could not eavesdrop.[14]

On May 29 Governor Edmund Randolph presented the Virginia Plan, named for his state, suggesting an aggressive new outline of government to consist of three branches and enumerated powers. His long and involved speech led Hamilton to ask the more fundamental question: Should the United States unify under a strong central government or remain a loose league? This question consumed members the next day, some fearing they lacked authority to create a radically new system, others thinking a bicameral body like Parliament or most state governments safer than a unicameral body like the Continental Congress. But even the latter were not sure the situation required a new national government. After a day of wrangling they realized that a decision had to be made to move forward, and when a milder motion failed suggesting the creation of a "more effective" government with three branches, even those who preferred the lesser version chose to vote for a new and stronger "national" and "supreme" government in order to start the discussion.[15]

Now concentrating on the framework found in the Virginia Plan, the convention agreed easily on a government with three branches, yet debated how many representatives each state would have. Randolph urged representation by population, but McHenry feared that "this gave the large States the most absolute controul over the lesser ones [and] it met with opposition which produced an adjournment without any determination."[16] McHenry, from the small state of Maryland, assumed that it could never support the population of those geographically larger, and was relieved at the opposition proportional representation met.

Delegates also naturally debated the legislature's powers, even whether the national legislature might "call forth the force of the union against any member of the union failing to fulfill its duty."[17] Years before, while in the Continental Congress, McHenry had feared that a navy might be sent against Maryland for not paying enough of her requisitions. The old specter rose again. But McHenry could not speak, could not vote, and did not betray this fear in his notes. He had been in politics long enough to know that the proposition meant nothing unless it was enacted. Indeed, it was not.

The next day, June 1, a far more immediate danger faced McHenry. He "[received] an express from home that my brother lay dangerously sick in consequence of which I set out immediately for Baltimore."[18] He raced home to the only member of the McHenry family left, a brother whom he dearly loved. John's "debauchery" had produced two results: an illegitimate son named for and taken in by him; and the dire consequence James had predicted—the onset of venereal disease, probably syphilis. Before the discovery of penicillin the disease often lingered painfully for many years— but it almost always proved fatal. John paid for his earlier actions, and James agonized at the thought of losing him.

It must indeed have been a serious attack, for it took two months of his brother's constant medical attention to bring John to sufficient health that James felt he could return to Philadelphia. He arrived in that city and to his in-laws on August 4.

When he returned, the convention's work to date was just rolling off the printer's press.[19] The plan he now saw took him aback, for he had failed to appreciate the appeal of the Virginia Plan. McHenry saw before him a brand new government, not an alteration or amendment of the Confederation. He needed to know what his fellow Marylanders thought. So he suggested they meet.

During McHenry's absence the other four delegates had arrived with new credentials indicating that any one delegate could now represent the state. They did so only too well, as Maryland's divisions at home also split the delegation. Two of the men, Daniel Carroll and Daniel of St. Thomas Jenifer, were fiscal conservatives and had very little trouble with the new shape the national government was taking. But paper money men John Mercer and especially Luther Martin did not like the new plan at all. The division here, however, did not occur over the issue of paper money. Martin volubly and consistently asserted that the plan favored big states against small states like Maryland.[20]

McHenry and Daniel Carroll had the most extensive experience in elective, deliberative office, each of them having been first elected in 1781 and serving pretty consistently thereafter.[21] McHenry's political background and personal temperament disposed him toward compromise, although only after he was convinced that his point had lost. This made him valuable in a legislative setting.

It was immediately apparent to him that the division in the Maryland delegation was completely counterproductive, for only a unified "yes" to a matter counted as an affirmative vote. So when the delegation divided, as it usually did, their vote counted as a "no." Divided, they were incapable of helping any matter pass.

Because of this, McHenry hoped to prearrange some agreement in caucus outside the convention. Then, perhaps, Maryland might be effective on some issues. McHenry suggested they go through the plan paragraph by paragraph and decide whether they could unite. But Mercer, who opposed the plan, asked the delegation if they thought Maryland would go along with a government drawn on these lines. This question ignited the volatile Luther Martin—who insisted Maryland would never accept the plan—and he personally opposed it. Then he accused Jenifer of weakness, who angrily retorted that he had supported Martin when it had been meaningful but that the convention had simply left them behind. Before tempers got completely out of hand, McHenry called them to order.[22]

For his part, McHenry believed Maryland would accept a "wise system" and suggested a number of steps. First, the convention should reconsider amending the articles. Perhaps it was the doctor in him, recently brought out so forcefully by his brother, that made him wish to save the Confederation. This "body politic" was a system with which he was familiar and to which he was attached. But Carroll, Mercer, and Jenifer all disagreed. McHenry might not like it, but this patient was really dying.

All McHenry could hope for now was to make minor changes in the system wherever he saw a flaw or where he thought Maryland might need protection. Worse, he realized that the delegation was getting nowhere so he asked the other gentlemen to consider sections of the new system he thought troubled. With the exception of Martin, who was going to New York, they agreed to meet the next day. Indeed, the four remaining delegates found it easy to come to agreement on McHenry's three points. Without Martin, tempers were cooler.

McHenry's concerns all came out of his Maryland background. For example, the Senate repeatedly proposed money bills that were supposed to originate in the lower house. Since this feature of the Maryland constitution was chronically violated despite McHenry's protests, he presumed this would occur nationally as well. He therefore proposed both houses be eligible to initiate money bills and the other Maryland delegates agreed to support this. Although the convention defeated it, the convention gave the Senate power to amend such bills.[23]

McHenry also questioned whether a nine-state vote to ratify the Constitution was sufficient. Just where he stood on this the records do not say, but the delegation chose to support a unanimous ratification. Maryland stood alone on this position, however, and a Virginian eventually moved the number nine for ratification, which won the debate.[24]

Next McHenry turned to the issue of navigation acts, which were vital to Maryland's, especially Baltimore's, financial future. He wanted to make it more difficult for Congress to pass them, hence he proposed, and the other Marylanders agreed, that a positive vote by two-thirds of each delegation be required for passage rather than simply two-thirds of the present members. This was lost in a now infamous deal that Paul Finkelman calls "the dirty compromise" between New England and the South, notably South Carolina. New England agreed to forbid export taxes and to allow the international slave trade for another twenty years while South Carolina assented to the passage of navigation acts important to the North by simple rather than super majorities. Still, McHenry and General Pinckney of South Carolina successfully urged the equal treatment of ports in all states. "That clause, together with certain restrictions on the powers of the states, ensured that no matter what system of political economy was adopted, internally the United States would be the largest area of free trade in the world."[25]

McHenry's other significant contribution to the Constitution was to second a motion made by Elbridge Gerry of Massachusetts, who actually spoke on the matter, prohibiting ex post facto laws and bills of attainder. The latter were old English laws that permitted sentencing an individual or group to death without trial. Their crime was considered so great that the prisoner was "tainted" and so lost other civil rights, including that of owning property, which then reverted to the state. The potential for abuse by monarchs was striking. During the American Revolution, every state had passed such laws for use against the Tories, allowing the states to confiscate their estates to sell and so help the ailing finances of the revolutionary governments. Clearly, Gerry and McHenry thought this should not persist, and the convention readily agreed.[26]

McHenry, of course, already had a record of fighting retrospective laws in Maryland and felt strongly about this matter. Back in 1782 (see chapter 6), he had opposed a bill that allowed debtors to deduct one-sixth of what they owed their creditors and pay that amount to the state instead. McHenry had opposed this bill on many grounds (including its opposition to Maryland's constitution), one of which was that it was a "retrospective" law and thus "ruinous . . . inasmuch as it tends to destroy all faith in agreements, which is the basis of public and private credit." It is surely no coincidence that McHenry used the word "retrospective," for that is the word used in Article XV of Maryland's 1776 Declaration of Rights (a part of the state's constitution), which prohibited criminal ex post facto laws. Although Maryland thus categorized ex post facto laws as criminal, it is clear that McHenry disliked retrospective laws of any sort. In any event, we do not know if Gerry brought these matters up coincidentally or if the two men had spoken. But the last is very likely, as Gerry and McHenry were both members of a group Richard Beeman calls "potentially dissident delegates" who met in the evenings to discuss the work at hand.[27]

There was, however, some debate over ex post facto laws. James Wilson of Pennsylvania thought the prohibition unnecessary and worried that the provision might cause general concern about just how much power the national government was aggrandizing, but Daniel Carroll—McHenry's colleague from Maryland—countered that state governments had indeed passed such laws. McHenry knew this only too well. The prohibition passed. In 1798, the Supreme Court (including Samuel Chase) in *Calder v. Bull* would limit this ban on ex post facto laws to criminal cases, without complaint from McHenry.[28]

During the rest of the convention McHenry generally watched out for Maryland's interest, frequently monetary, and that usually meant trying to *reduce* powers the plan gave to the national government. On the other hand, when he asked that states be allowed to raise duties to clear harbors and build lighthouses, the convention agreed only if it first received congressional approval. Ironically, protecting Maryland's harbors increased the national government's power. McHenry also successfully moved that the president have the authority to convene one or both houses of Congress in a crisis.[29]

Such were McHenry's contributions to the Constitution—minor to be sure, but based on experience and interest, with some contributions, such as helping to bar ex post facto laws and bills of attainder, that have been important. No doubt this applied to most of the members of the convention. Having missed that half of the convention wherein the larger framework was structured, he could at the last minute only add insight earned by experience.

Still, the plan had been more than McHenry had expected, and although he had gotten over the initial shock he experienced on his return from Maryland, he was not the type to pledge himself easily. Instead, he needed to take

the time to consider all sides before committing himself; this was a personality trait exhibited even when deciding to join the Revolution as a young
man. Only after real contemplation would McHenry commit, and then he
would remain steadfast.

At this moment, he still had questions about the proposed government.
For one thing, he was uncertain that Maryland's constitution allowed ratification of this new document by state convention. James Madison had acknowledged the problem, but he favored state conventions for several reasons. The state ratifying convention's power emanated from the people,
making the Constitution a fundamental law and difficult for the state governments to challenge. Or, to put it another way, the constituent power—
the power to constitute a government—would be best exercised by popu-
larly elected ratifying conventions constituting expressions of the popular
will. In addition, Madison was concerned that state legislatures would not
vote to reduce their power by ratifying the Constitution. The conventions,
on the other hand, would actually speak for the people of the several states
rather than the desires of the state governments. Although Madison's point
won, McHenry remained uncomfortable, for he had sworn to uphold Maryland's constitution before attending this convention.[30]

So McHenry hesitated. This was a far more elaborate government than
existed under the Articles of Confederation—and hence a far more expensive government. He thought it would worry "the people on account of its
expence." Armies, navies, law courts and a "princely president" would be
costly. In addition, "it was plain that the revenue for these purposes was to
be chiefly drawn from commerce. That Maryland . . . would have this re-
source taken from her, without the expences of her own government being
lessened." This new government would clearly cost far more than that under
the Confederation.[31]

Undecided, McHenry rehearsed the pros and cons of the new system. The
new government would be stronger and more expensive than he thought
necessary—but the old Confederation was clearly too weak. In the end the
new frame of government won the argument for three reasons. First, his experience and humility led him to "distrust [his] own judgement, especially
as it is opposite to the opinion of a majority of gentlemen whose abilities
and patriotism are of the first cast." Second, if any of his fears proved correct, the document was not written in stone—it could be amended. Finally,
the potential evils he foresaw under the new Constitution did not equal the
political evils under the "present confederation." Shedding his reluctance,

he confided to his diary: "I am clear that I ought to give it [the new Constitution] all the support in my power."[32] On September 17, 1787 he joined most of the other delegates and signed the document.

Somewhere around this time, supporters of the Constitution began calling themselves "Federalists." This name had been taken by New Yorkers and other eastern men before the convention to distinguish themselves from those emphasizing states' rights, and the term quickly came to refer to those who now supported this new "federal" document. Their opponents saw them instead as nationalists, consolidationists, even monarchists. McHenry, a new advocate of the Constitution, was now a Federalist.[33]

When he returned to Baltimore he knew that he would have to campaign for office in the October elections for the General Assembly, since this legislature would decide if Maryland would hold a state ratifying convention. If the legislature called for a ratifying convention, then elections for delegates to that convention would also have to be held. Proponents of the Constitution were sorely needed in this next session of the assembly.[34]

McHenry, then, "a friend of the Constitution," ran for Baltimore's seat in the assembly. His opposition in the election, however, was Samuel Chase, who had recently moved from Annapolis to Baltimore. Both were generally popular with the laborers who were becoming more active politically, but Chase had made a name for himself by defending debtors both in court and the legislature. Now each side made conscious attempts to woo the public's support, beginning a type of campaign new in Maryland. Most of the city's mechanics had been agitating for a protective tariff that the Maryland assembly had refused to pass, so the mechanics looked to the new federal government for protection. Knowing that Baltimoreans favored the new Constitution, Chase hid his opposition, merely stating that he thought amendments might be in order. He did, however, proclaim himself in favor of a convention, a stance that most took to be proratification. Thus, by leading people to believe he favored the Constitution even while he secretly opposed it, Chase beat McHenry.[35]

McHenry also, through no fault of his own, influenced another election in Maryland. Daniel Carroll, a Federalist as well, appears to have run for the Continental Congress and lost. (Carroll merely referred to an election to Congress, leaving it vague as to which assembly he meant. But he elsewhere referred to the Continental Congress as "Congress" so this seems likely.) He soon discovered that Luther Martin had circulated a rumor through the taverns that McHenry considered Carroll a monarchist. "[T]he weight of Mr. McHenry's name" cost Carroll the election. Carroll, of course, became alarmed for his reputation and appealed to McHenry, who traced the issue to a list of names he had copied from Mercer while at the Constitutional Convention. These names had "for" and "against" written next to them, which Mercer said indicated those who favored a king. Luther Martin then copied the same list. Carroll denied being a monarchist and when McHenry confronted Mercer he said he had *meant* that the list indicated those who favored a national government, and not those who desired a king. By creating confusion, Chase and Martin had successfully defeated two Federalists.[36]

Although not an elected member, McHenry attended the legislature on November 29 to report what had transpired at the Constitutional Convention in Philadelphia. Two months had elapsed since he had signed the Constitution and his earlier reluctance had vanished, the Constitution's virtues crystallizing in his mind during the election campaign. So when he appeared before the Maryland legislature, he "descanted with Energy," perhaps giving the best speech of his life.[37]

McHenry let the events of the convention speak for themselves. He forcefully presented the weaknesses of the Confederation: it could not provide for the common defense, security, or general welfare. Indeed, the widespread social and political turmoil indicated "that all were on the brink of Ruin and disolution . . . perhaps this was the last, the only opportunity we should ever have to avoid or remedy those impending evils."[38]

Having now sounded the alarm, he proceeded through various sections of the Constitution, explaining the opposing interests and the resulting decision. Most important, he calmed the legislature's mind. Martin insisted that large states hoped to overpower the small through proportional representation in the House of Representatives. But, McHenry reminded the assembly, there was equal representation in the Senate; and, because it could amend or reject money bills, the larger states' representation in the House should be effectively countered. Admitting that he disliked aspects of the document, he thought it the best that could be achieved. Generally he described the individual decisions as compromises or the result of concern for the general welfare. Unlike Martin, he emphasized unity over discord: "the whole . . . is the result of that spirit of Amity which directed the wishes of all for the general good, and where those Sentiments govern it will meet I trust, with a Kind and Cordial reception." McHenry had judged right, for most Marylanders understood the nation's problems and wanted a positive solution.[39]

McHenry's approach effectively left Luther Martin in the role of suspicious accuser. Yet since Martin honestly believed the larger states would gain inordinately under the Constitution while Maryland would suffer, he said so. This was, in fact, the crux of his argument, which he elaborated in detail and later published as *The Genuine Information*. The legislature disagreed.[40] In fact, the new Constitution so pleased them that it decided in favor of a ratifying convention.

Now the question was who would be elected to the ratifying convention—Federalists, who favored the Constitution, or those opposed? Both sides saw clearly the need to garner as many seats as possible.

Not surprisingly, the same division of men occurred over the Constitution as had existed during the paper money controversy. Luther Martin and John Mercer joined with Samuel Chase, who spearheaded the opposition in Maryland. Of course, everyone realized that the new Constitution denied states the right to print paper money or emit bills of credit, and some attributed Chase's contrary stance to this fact. It was certainly ironic that men on both sides of the paper money controversy had refused to attend the convention for fear that very issue would erupt locally, only to find that the new document would wrest that issue from their hands and settle the question for good.[41]

But Chase faced an exceedingly difficult task, for most of Maryland seemed to want the new Constitution. Baltimore, where Chase now resided, was especially anxious for the Constitution's ratification since it wanted tariffs. Chase now found himself in a strange dilemma. He had publicly, and loudly, insisted that the electorate could "instruct" their representatives. Were he elected in Baltimore, he would have to support the Constitution or deny the right of instruction. He found a way out. Despite the fact that he no longer resided in Annapolis (Anne Arundel County), he decided to run there. His side made a last-minute campaign, circulating handbills that "emphasized the Constitution's lack of a bill of rights, its failure to prohibit a standing army in peacetime, the president's emergency power to control state militia without consent of the legislature, and the federal government's broad powers of direct taxation." Apparently these arguments hit their mark. "Carroll noted that 'a wildness appeared in many which showed they were really frightened by what they had just heard.'" Having left no time for a Federalist response, Chase and his friends were elected by a slim margin—about fifty votes. Still, only three counties brought forth Anti-Federalist victories in Maryland.[42]

Back in Baltimore, confusion also led to exciting last-minute campaigning. As of the first day of the elections two men, David McMechen and Samuel Sterett, ran unopposed for the seats available. By the end of the first day of voting, however, people became suspicious that these two men just might not favor unconditional ratification. Their fears were correct, for McMechen and Sterett were indeed Anti-Federalists who would have "demanded amendments as a precondition to ratifying the Constitution, which was widely perceived as a delaying strategy for subverting ratification altogether."[43]

So, on the second of three voting days, the Federalists put up their own candidates, Doctors McHenry and Coulter. Again, McHenry was not identified as a merchant. Was this done in order to better appeal to the laborers or to seem more gentlemanly? Perhaps it did both, depending upon their intended audience. In any event, the two doctors insisted that ratification should occur first, before any amendments were added, and this was what most of Baltimore wanted to hear. But the results of the first day's election worried many, for hundreds of votes had obviously gone to opposition candidates that might have gone to Federalists had the contenders' true positions been known. To counter the effects of the first day's results, gangs roamed the polls and kept "peaceable German citizens from voting." Ironically, Chase, supposedly a supporter of the unfortunate, would later complain that officials had not enforced the property qualifications and so the poorer sort had flooded the polls. It was indeed the previously disenfranchised of Baltimore who wanted the Constitution—and McHenry and Coulter won by a landslide.[44] Their votes of 962 and 958 were *so* much greater than Sterett's 385 and McMechen's 380 that the legislature upheld their election. No doubt such irregularities should have been grounds for a new election, but it was already mid-April and the convention was scheduled to meet on April 21. There was no time to clear up the controversy properly. Probably McHenry thought the opposition got what it deserved. For its part, Federalist Baltimore celebrated with a parade emphasizing the unity of the thirteen states.

McHenry did not arrive until the second day of the ratifying convention, April 22.[45] In his absence the other Federalists strategized, determining first to thwart the opposition's efforts at debate and second to ratify the Constitution unconditionally.

The Constitution's opponents had their tactics planned as well. Their real goal was to defeat the Constitution although they knew it would be difficult. Yet there were two alternatives: they might convince the convention to adjourn until the results from more states were known, but that too was unlikely; or they could aim for conditional ratification—that is, amending the Constitution prior to ratification.

Both sides understood that the success of this last strategy would be the death knell of the Constitution as they knew it. For adding amendments prior to ratification would require a new convention—at which anything at all might happen, from violent arguments to a return to the Articles of Confederation.

Given this strategy, it was a cardinal mistake that the Constitution's opponents did not arrive until the fourth day of the convention. This allowed the Federalists ample time to solidify their position, becoming an almost unbreakable, unstoppable phalanx against which those who opposed the Constitution would be powerless. For when the Federalists arrived they quickly decided, even before the convention began its official business, not to debate the individual sections of the Constitution. Disputes could bog down the convention, defeating the new government through sheer dissipation of energy. So they justified their refusal to argue by saying they had been elected to ratify the Constitution and do nothing else. Here they used Chase's instruction argument against him, for they were indeed a temporary body formed for only one purpose.[46]

But why were the Federalists so concerned when they vastly outnumbered their opposition? Because Maryland alone was not at issue. Six states (Delaware, Pennsylvania, New Jersey, Georgia, Connecticut, and Massachusetts) had already ratified the Constitution, but problems remained. Governor Edmund Randolph, the man who had presented the Virginia Plan to the Constitutional Convention, now favored conditional ratification. Moreover, New Hampshire had proven problematic, leading Federalists there to follow Madison's advice and adjourn its convention so that Federalists could fall back and regroup to foster a positive outcome. Federalists did not want this to happen again. The momentum had slowed, so that now important Federalists such as George Washington considered Maryland key to future ratification in other states, especially Virginia. If Maryland and South Carolina failed to ratify, Virginia, whose convention would meet after these, might hesitate as well. The Constitution might be lost. In fact, Washington wrote McHenry that the opposition in Virginia hoped to defeat the Constitution by arguing that states should not ratify, but that all should adjourn (like New Hampshire) in deference to Virginia. "Should Maryland fulfil this p[r]ognostic South Carolina may indeed be staggered and the prediction of the foes to the Constitution will thereby be realized." Indeed, Washington said that "the postponement of the question would be tantamount to the final rejection of it—that the adversaries of the new Constitution [in] Virginia and Maryland view it in this light."[47] On the other hand, if Maryland and South Carolina ratified the document, then eight of the requisite nine states would have agreed to the Constitution and Virginia would almost surely follow.

This led Maryland Federalists to "steamroll" the Constitution through the state's convention. When Chase arrived they allowed him to talk, at length, but offered no response whatever. They simply refused to engage in debate. Then William Paca, another opponent of the Constitution, arrived and asked for permission to submit possible amendments the following day. But when the next day's session began another delegate suggested they vote on ratification. When Paca tried to introduce his amendments, yet another new delegate called him out of order and the speaker upheld that call. The vote was taken, then, without debate and without considering any amendments.[48]

Only after ratification did the convention consider Paca's amendments. In fact, they created a committee to consider them, on which McHenry served. The committee agreed to thirteen of the proposed amendments but disputed three others. These three would have kept the militia within the state, guaranteed the sanctity of election dates, and "suspended" direct federal taxes if the state paid them first. This dispute over these three proposed amendments finally prevented the committee from recommending *any* of the amendments, so the convention adjourned having merely ratified the Constitution. This must have pleased McHenry, for he considered the amendments a ploy to harm ratification in Virginia.[49] The Federalists had stood shoulder-to-shoulder and won, outmaneuvering Samuel Chase at his own game.

South Carolina ratified on May 23 and then, ironically, New Hampshire became the ninth state to ratify on June 21. Within days Virginia did the same. A new government was to begin. Baltimore, thrilled, celebrated with another parade. The number thirteen became mystical, representing the union of all the states. Despite their disagreements, McHenry doubtless concurred with a prayer favored by the Constitution's opponents: "May the all-wise and omnipotent Being, who made us masters of a fair and fruitful empire, inspire us with wisdom and fortitude to perpetuate to posterity that freedom which we received from our fathers!"[50]

NINE "A Friendship Independent of Brotherhood"

James McHenry

FEDERALISTS HAD TO CONTROL the new form of government to launch it on as strong a foundation as possible. Yes, the Constitution had been ratified by the requisite nine states, but Federalists now needed to incorporate everyone who might assist in starting the new national government, and some former opponents now joined. Of course, both the current Federalists and their opponents understood the importance of Maryland's fall 1788 elections. According to the Constitution, the populace chose representatives, but the legislature chose senators, and Federalists knew that the outcome would greatly determine the partisan cast of the new federal government.[1] Federalists would naturally do what they could to elect their own to both houses of Congress. Federalists and their opponents now centered their attention on this campaign.

By all accounts Baltimore had the most exciting election, doubtless because McHenry and Chase opposed each other for the House of Delegates. In a number of ways this election mirrored the last with heated rhetoric, street brawls, and commandeered polls.

But the election was also fierce because of the part played by mechanics and laborers. Well-organized now after years of struggle, the Association of Mechanics and Tradesmen continued to push for protective tariffs, and since Maryland had ignored their petitions, the association saw the new federal government as the means of attaining their ends.

Given these circumstances, Chase had a real dilemma on his hands. It did not escape anyone's notice that, after having won one election in Baltimore, Chase had retreated to Annapolis for the next election because of his opposition to the Constitution. How could he now hope to win Baltimore's seat in the House of Delegates when he clearly did not reflect the city's views? Chase could do so only by dividing the opposition, and that is what he attempted. First, he played on class antagonisms to divide the mechanics by convincing the poor among them that their wealthy brother mechanics were enemies. (Chase, it turned out, overestimated the extent of class conflict in Baltimore.) Second, Chase would attack the alliance between the mechanics and the merchants. "[B]y persuading the mechanics generally that merchants were behind their woes, Chase could draw attention away from his own anti-federalism, where he was most vulnerable."[2]

Using this strategy, Chase and McMechen branded McHenry and John Coulter the "wealthy enemy of the common man," even suggesting that affluent employers and merchants had threatened to fire any workers who voted against the Constitution. They also spread a vague rumor that a Federalist, probably McHenry, had spent enormous sums on the campaign in an effort to "buy" his way into office.[3] If so, such records do not survive, but it would be no surprise to find that both sides spent what they could to get elected.

McHenry and Coulter responded by listing legislative acts supported by Chase but unpopular with the "common man," such as taxes on liquor stores and tools, the last of which made a strong impression on the mechanics. Federalists also reminded voters of Chase's efforts to leave the "common man" behind and acquire wealth, even to the point of cornering the flour market during the Revolution.[4]

Yet the crux of the campaign remained the Constitution, for Chase continued to support amendments and ran on that issue. McHenry maintained that sending a delegate to amend the Constitution was analogous to being bled by a "physician who thirsted to drink their blood."[5] If anyone should amend the Constitution, he argued, it should be a Federalist.

As the campaign progressed, political rhetoric became vitriolic and political rallies turned into fistfights.[6] In each case, the opposition accused the Federalists of initiating the violence, which they naturally denied. But they did take obvious pleasure in publicly warning Chase to stay indoors lest the populace get ahold of him.

To their credit, all of the candidates agreed upon rules for an orderly election, including polling hours and the number of official observers. The polls would also be open for two days to allow those from the farther ends of the district time to reach the voting locations. Further, "All citizens were forbidden to come to the polls or walk in the streets with weapons, sticks, colors, fifes or drums. Masters were requested to keep slaves and servants home until the voting ended at sunset; captains were urged to keep sailors who were not citizens from coming on shore." Despite these precautions there was heavy drinking, gambling, and fighting for possession of the polls by partisans, with each accusing the other of reprehensible conduct. In an era of viva voce, or voice vote, one could not keep one's vote secret and feelings could easily get agitated. Nor did anyone think of requesting secrecy, since voting was an intensely public affair. Both sides did agree that the second day's fight resulted in Federalist control of the polls; McHenry and Coulter won the election.[7]

When McHenry and Coulter arrived at the 1788 session of the House of Delegates, so did Samuel Chase, determined to contest the election. The House agreed to investigate if the principals paid the cost. Witnesses were called (one proudly boasted he had bet two beaver hats that those opposing the Constitution would win), and days were devoted to the question, but the Federalist House finally dropped the matter at the end of the session. All Chase really succeeded in doing was irritating the House, although the exasperation was probably mutual. This campaign marked Chase's last bid for elective office, as his future would lie in the appointive judiciary. Over time, "[h]e would metamorphose into one of the republic's most outspoken conservatives, an almost hysterical enemy of . . . the 'rabble' who had rejected him."[8]

McHenry again sat on numerous committees. One agreed that Adam Fonerden should be given a monopoly on his "card-teeth cutter," while others considered incorporating a Marine Society in Baltimore, a divorce petition from one Grizelda Hannah, a petition for relief for the widow Mary Cox whose husband died at the battle of Germantown (granted), and Nathaniel Smith's claim for service as an artillery officer.

Despite this record, McHenry spent little time at the fall session of the assembly as family matters preoccupied him. Two years before, Peggy had delivered a healthy boy, named "Daniel William" for James's father and Peggy's step-father, respectively. She was now due with their third child. After a week at the legislature McHenry returned to his wife; when convinced that all was well, he went back to Annapolis. Anna, their second girl, was born on November 20, 1788, prompting McHenry to take a leave of absence from which he did not return.

Frankly, the family needed good news. Captain William Allison had died a year and a half before and his widow Grace had considered and rejected settling in Baltimore to be near Peggy. Then, in January, Peggy's half-sister Polly passed away after suffering an illness that lingered for at least three months. Peggy had returned to Philadelphia during this time, and for some days after the death her depression left her unable to do more than help her family cope. Once she even asked her brother Jack to write James for her, as she had neither the time nor emotional reserves to do it herself.[9]

Moreover, James worried about his brother, since the syphilis still ravaged his body. At the very time that Peggy was due to bear Anna and James was in Annapolis, John went to Philadelphia for a consultation with doctors and wound up having an operation. "I am very sorry you cannot be here however as there is very little risk in the opperation [sic] there is no necessity for your presence." Despite this apparent calm, he included in his letter to James a makeshift will, leaving his "natural and adopted son John McHenry [Jr.], got on the body of my former House keeper," to James's care.[10] Happily the operation went well.

If John was holding on, the McHenrys' oldest child, Grace, was not, as she died not even four months after the birth of her younger sister. Years later McHenry wrote of this to Hamilton. "I lost my eldest child, a daughter, after she had discovered whatever can promise to flatter parental expectations. Is there ought [sic] in this world can console for such losses?"[11]

While McHenry had concentrated on family, his colleagues had developed a system of voting for their six new federal congressmen that was "the strangest in the nation."[12] To prevent the Constitution's opponents from carrying the two or three districts where they were popular, the legislature had required each nominee to reside in his district—but voters of all districts could choose any six nominees from any part of the state.

Furthermore, to foster Federalist unity throughout the state, they also devised Maryland's first truly partisan ticket, causing the opposition to respond in kind. By the time Maryland's elections for Congress had been held in January, Federalists had won two-thirds of the positions across the state. They took both federal Senate seats and all of the six seats in the House of Representatives. Federalists had managed the elections so well that when the state's presidential electors met in Annapolis in February, Washington won Maryland's vote unanimously, as he did in the rest of the country.[13] Maryland Federalists had achieved their goals at both the state and federal levels.

The president-elect was to travel north in April from Mount Vernon to the capital in New York and would naturally stop in Baltimore along the way. Baltimore made McHenry chair of the committee to welcome George Washington, and he may have appreciated the diversion. So a mere five days after Grace's death, McHenry wrote Washington congratulating him on his election—"You are now a king, under a different name; and, I am well satisfied, that sovereign prerogatives have in no age or country been more honorably obtained."[14]

This quote is striking for many reasons, not least of which is McHenry's approving use of the term "king" when Daniel Carroll had so recently lost an election over accusations that he favored a monarch. In fact, some political ideas remained in flux, as there were many who embraced both monarchy and republicanism at one and the same time, even in England, and especially before the Revolution. Perhaps McHenry had not quite left this commingling tendency behind.[15] But probably the best way to understand McHenry's quote is the way he would later describe the government himself, that is, as the best mix of the three classic forms of government: monarchy, aristocracy, and democracy—all thrown together in a republican form.

McHenry also invited Washington to stay at his home while en route to New York. McHenry had moved from Fell's Point and built a country home west of the city about a mile from the Patapsco River that he had named "Fayetteville," in honor of the Marquis De Lafayette. But Washington knew just how troublesome such a stay would be. "[H]owever pleasing it might be to me, on any other occasion, to render this proof of my regard for you, I cannot consistently with my ideas of propriety (under the existing circumstances) consent to give so much trouble to a private family." He further explained that "[t]he party that may possibly attend me—the crowd that always gather on novel occasions—and the compliment of visiting (which some may incline to pay a new character) all contribute to render a public house the fittest place for scenes of bustle & trouble."[16] Although Washington was undoubtedly right in his assessment, McHenry was disappointed. Futilely, he protested, "you did not know that my house is very large." But, although Washington had stayed in private homes before this, while traveling as president (including a future trip to New England) he did not stay in private homes; the matter was settled.[17]

After receiving his certificate of office, Washington began the trip and Baltimore was prepared. An assemblage met Washington at the county line on April 7, parted their horses for his passing, and then followed his entourage into the city. Cannons saluted him upon his arrival while he rode on horseback to the city's finest hotel, Grant's Fountain Inn. At six in the evening the city honored Washington with a supper, followed by two addresses from the citizens of Baltimore extolling Washington, his service to his country, and the glorious future of the United States and also expressing their support for "placing public credit on the most solid foundation." McHenry helped write one of the addresses and was the first of ten who signed it.[18]

Mrs. Washington followed her husband to New York a month later and was similarly celebrated. The McHenrys entertained her during the afternoon of her visit and she was later treated to a supper, fireworks, and a band.[19]

The celebrations infused McHenry's spirits as well as those of the general populace. He was truly optimistic about the country's future. Even the Constitution's opponents, he wrote Washington, believed he would be a good president; all they could do was worry whether future presidents would be as worthy. "I beleive [sic] with them that you will have the merit of giving stability to the government, but I am also disposed to think, that the next generation will be as competent to the preservation of their liberties as the present, so that on this point I am perfectly at ease."[20]

Certainly it was important for Washington to acknowledge these communities on his journey as a way of helping to unite the whole. For their part, Maryland Federalists had now "begun to develop a network of correspondence, linking county leaders with the party elders."[21] So, as 1789 initiated a new national government, it also brought in a fledgling national political network upon which Federalists would try to capitalize. McHenry helped to create that network for Maryland.

Washington's visit also served to put McHenry back in closer touch with the Virginian than their letters had allowed.[22] Other Baltimoreans hoped to use McHenry's friendship to advantage, and McHenry could not object, for this was the way of politics and both he and Washington knew it. They accepted their roles.

McHenry became the state's Federalist leader, helping to develop a partisan alliance within his state, and as such he served several functions. For one thing, McHenry and General Otho Holland Williams guided Washington's distribution of patronage in Maryland. McHenry also corresponded and kept in active contact with both national and local Federalists, frequently coordinating partisan activity. He influenced election campaigns behind the scenes, wrote political essays for newspapers, and drafted bills and got them through the legislature. It must be admitted, however, that this was all done even while the thought of party activity—which the founding generation considered devoted to the individual rather than the common good—was anathema. It was, in essence, party activity before parties became acceptable.[23]

Of greatest importance was McHenry's ability to get the ear of the highest Federalists in the nation and seek patronage for fellow Marylanders. From the start others applied to McHenry for recommendations to Washington, and McHenry did not hesitate to write the new president his suggestions for posts. Following McHenry's suggestions, the president appointed Robert Purviance naval officer for the port of Baltimore, Robert Ballard surveyor for the port of Baltimore, retained Mr. Eichelberger as customs weigher and Major Lynch as measurer, and finally made John Caldwell, better known to McHenry as Jack, his brother-in-law, "United States attorney to the Inferior federal court for this State." In 1789, Washington asked for and followed McHenry's advice, appointing William Paca to a district judgeship. The president was, in McHenry's own words, "very attentive to my recommendations." In fact, from 1789 to 1795, McHenry secured no less than thirty jobs for loyal Maryland Federalists, which were especially significant as they reached well into the middle class.[24]

It was natural that Washington should be so conscientious, for he would need information about Maryland in the future and McHenry was a man he could trust—a known quantity. Washington did not hesitate to correspond with trusted confidants throughout the states.

By the end of May, however, McHenry's spirits deflated. Both Washington and McHenry's brother John were ill. McHenry urged Washington to hire a personal physician, and suggested Dr. Craik, an old and favorite doctor of Washington's. The president thanked McHenry but insisted that he was now much better. His physician, Dr. Bard, had spared nothing, but he feared the president might have had anthrax, signified by a fever and large tumor on his thigh. But the fever had abated, the tumor had been removed, and all he required now was rest.[25]

Yet McHenry also admitted to Washington that distress in his own family had added to his alarm. His brother John had become his full-time patient and they planned to travel to some "health" springs out west in hope of relief. His two-year-old son Daniel was also sick so all three set out on July 3.[26]

Their goal was the Appalachian Sweet Springs, one of a number of springs gushing from the mountains that today separate West Virginia from Virginia. Three weeks later they arrived at the Warm Springs with its "blood hot" water. "A large quantity of air is continually rising from the bottom in bubbles and the vapor has a sulphurous smell. . . . We bath[e] in it twice a day," he informed Peggy. "The first time Daniel went into it very reluctantly; and now he leaves it with as much reluctance, and goes to it with pleasure. I think it has been serviceable to his complaint." John, however, was not recovering. "We propose two days longer stay, and then try the Sweet Springs, which is forty three miles from this place."[27] But it was of no avail. John did not improve. In September, to avoid being trapped in the mountains for the winter, the McHenry men journeyed home.

At home again, McHenry returned to the House of Delegates on November 6, 1789. He served on committees considering the usual—petitions for divorce and financial relief, the courts' calendar, and what its officers would be paid. He supported funds for Saint John's College, helped to decide tax rates for the coming year, and delivered a report regulating the assize of bread. McHenry unsuccessfully argued for decreased regulations on tobacco to improve shipping between districts.[28]

More important, Maryland still had to deal with the debts left over from both the Revolution and the paper money era. McHenry served on the committee that attempted to consolidate and settle the debt, and he delivered its fiscally conservative report to the assembly. The committee had studied all of the amounts that the state owed (bonds, certificates, losses for confiscated lands, etc.) as well as what was owed to the states, and found that the state's financial obligations were too straitened to offer most of the debtors any relief. In issuing certificates and bonds, McHenry reported, the state had borrowed from wealthy Marylanders and other creditors and was thus a debtor. But those who purchased the certificates or bonds on credit were in their turn debtors (presumably to the state, as it is hard to imagine McHenry, given his record, even considering impairing contracts between individuals). The question now being considered was whether, since the state hoped to consolidate and settle these debts, the debtors could in any way be relieved of their burden. In general, the committee found that the state's obligations to its creditors took precedence over its wish to relieve debtors. However, for reasons that are unclear, but perhaps because they involved prerevolutionary accounts, debtors who purchased these certificates or bonds only in 1769 and 1773 were reprieved from interest payments. On December 16, the report was read a second time and agreed to paragraph by paragraph. Opponents made four unsuccessful attempts to defeat the House's concurrence, but fiscal conservatism triumphed. The House then ordered the committee to draw up an "act to establish funds to secure the payment of the state debt within five years, and for the punctual payment of the annual interest thereon," which passed the House on December 22.[29]

Toward the end of the session, the assembly learned that other states were bringing claims against the new federal government for war expenses. McHenry argued such a course of action would help reduce Maryland's debt to the federal government. But self-interest may also have been at work, for the United States government still owed him back pay and the federal government might authorize states to settle federal debts toward veterans. It had happened before. In fact, the next day the assembly directed the governor and council to give certificates to veterans with valid claims and charge them to the federal government.[30]

By Christmas 1789 McHenry returned to Baltimore and his family, where he saw that John had grown worse; the disease persisted, racking body and spirit. Still, James wrote that he felt "my attachment to him grow every day stronger and find nothing to blame in him now which I have not always blamed." James admitted that John had a temper that had grown "naturally hasty" during his "long and severe indisposition." But, James insisted, "in every other respect he is the same man, with the same understanding, the same good heart, and the same attachment to and affection for his friends which has ever distinguished him in my eyes."[31]

John was now so ill that he had withdrawn from their mercantile business. As early as May 30, 1788, Hugh McCurdy announced in the *Maryland Journal and Baltimore Advertiser* that he was opening a new dry goods store called the "Golden Fan" at the site of the business "lately occupied by John McHenry." McCurdy was James's new partner, a wealthy merchant in his own right and, James judged, a "deserving" young man. James appears to have enjoyed much the same silent partner relationship with McCurdy that he had with John, helping only occasionally with correspondence during the transition period.[32]

With constant attention from James, however, John seemed to improve, leading James to hope in April that the "warmer weather will still further improve [his health]." But James was deceived, for on May 7, 1790, John died.[33]

John's death devastated James. Despite the fact that they had both been fighting the disease for a number of years, James was not ready for the loss, and perhaps could never have become prepared for it. He tried to describe it to Jack, Peggy's brother—"Ours too was a friend[shi]p independent of brotherhood which every new day rendered more dear and valuable." He had not merely loved his brother, but had liked him. "So much wit, so excellent [an] understanding, so much affection and goodness of heart seldom found to center in one individual. All this it pleased God to take from me and I feel myself yet as one shipwrecked and alone upon a desert[ed] and uninhabited country."[34] James alone survived of the original McHenrys. Now only the family resulting from his marriage could comfort him.

In the midst of this grief, John's estate had to be settled. James hired lawyers and wrote letter after letter to the company's business associates informing them of John's death. He also had to decide what to do with the merchant house. It had really been John's province; James had only supplied capital and occasional help, basically serving as a silent partner. But since Hugh McCurdy was running the business well, James stayed on. Otherwise he paid John's debts and called in sums unpaid; the entire process took years.[35]

James's grief was profound, and it would take some time before he would feel ready to go out in the world again. He described his feelings to Washington. "Every sorrow and consideration whatever has been swallowed up, or diminished, in the depth of affliction I have felt on the loss of my brother." Overwhelmed with sadness, his public success seemed less meaningful. "I have estimated the value of public applause, and well know that neither talents nor merits insure it with posterity. The one I do not want, the other I have not the talents to attain." He was also fortunate. "I am independent in my circumstances. I have retired to the vicinity of the Town a little spot from which I can see its smoke and hear its noise without being offended with either." Finally, McHenry did not think he could be interested in public service again. "I resist all solicitations to venture upon the ocean of politics, and intend to devote the remainder of my time to my own ease, to devotion, the recollections of a dear brother, the happiness of a little family and literary amusements." So for over a year McHenry quit politics. What little business he conducted concerned either John's or his father-in-law's estates.[36]

TEN "Not Wholly Lost to Ambition"

James McHenry

BY JANUARY 1791, however, signs of recovery slowly appeared. McHenry pulled himself out of his grief long enough to write Hamilton an apology for his "long silence, but I can assure you I have never forgot you." McHenry also sent Washington a gift of asparagus. Otherwise he continued to assist the administration by scouting out eligible and qualified Federalists for government positions. But he insisted that at this point (although in reality he was waffling) he wished nothing for himself. "I would remain where I am. My mind in the loss of a brother has received a severe shock."[1]

Perhaps to help relieve the distress, in July the family traveled to Philadelphia. Peggy wanted to see her mother, who had been sick for some time. In fact, on August 2 Grace decided to write a will, dividing everything equally among her four surviving children: Peggy, of course, and her older brother Jack Caldwell, but also the two Allison girls Grace and Jane. As the girls were still young, the elder Grace arranged for them to live with the McHenrys. The trip proved wise, for Grace died soon thereafter.[2] Now James and Peggy cared for their own three children, Peggy's two half-sisters, and John McHenry Jr.

While in Philadelphia, the nation's temporary capital, McHenry saw Federalist friends. In fact, despite the fact that McHenry said he wished no position for himself, he and Hamilton discussed a foreign posting as minister at The Hague. Before John's death, he had written Hamilton that, although he was "easy in [his] circumstances," he was still "not wholly lost to ambition" and was interested in a foreign appointment where he might both serve his country and improve his writing. McHenry was again open to the idea, believing he could acquire loans for the United States, and that a

change of scene might do him good, spiritually and physically. The Marylander, however, requested that Hamilton sound out the president without
giving the source away. McHenry had asked enough of Washington already,
and for characters in need of office, unlike himself. Hamilton complied,
placing McHenry on the list of officers he would recommend for foreign
posts whenever that issue arose.[3]

When he returned home, however, Maryland offered him a Senate seat.
Hamilton assured him that holding a state post would raise no impedi-
ment to one abroad since political positions commonly fluctuated.[4] William Short received the post at The Hague, however, and McHenry served
in the Maryland Senate for the next five years.

During this time McHenry shed his gloom and truly reentered the political world, serving in the 1791 Senate session. In a progressive move, he
successfully sponsored a bill freeing "conscientiously scrupulous" Quakers from having to take an oath to serve in state office. He also fruitlessly
urged a tax-supported public school system. Mainly, however, he represented Baltimore, which was critical because the city had yet to be incorporated as a municipality with its own government. Baltimore simply could
not choose the form of government it wanted, which meant important decisions regarding the city were made by the state legislature. McHenry in-
troduced acts or sat on committees which proposed the following: paving
the city's streets; empowering port wardens to collect duties; incorporating
Baltimore's fire insurance company (in which he owned stock); appointing a health officer to quarantine diseased ships; and proposing a turnpike
between Baltimore and what would eventually become Washington, D.C.,
thus facilitating business between the two locales. Lastly, the city won a
bank, which pleased McHenry: "I look upon it to be one of the most important acts, as it respects Baltimore, which has ever passed our legislature."[5]

Whether in the Senate or at home, McHenry again corresponded regularly with Washington and Hamilton, especially through writing letters of
recommendation for political posts. In fact, the president now relied on
McHenry to discover in advance if candidates would accept a post. Constant public rejections to service in the new government looked bad and
the Virginian knew it.[6]

Sometimes McHenry wrote directly to Hamilton about positions over
which he had influence. For example, Otho H. Williams had become seriously ill. His position as Baltimore's collector of customs was a lucrative one,

netting over £2,000 sterling a year or around $276,000 in 2008 dollars. (The U.S. Mint was created in 1792, so an American currency did not yet exist.) Clearly such a position ought to go to a deserving Federalist. McHenry recommended Robert Purviance, a down-on-his-luck Baltimore merchant who knew the ins and outs of the port's business and had a large family to support. George Salmon, another loyal Federalist, could then replace Purviance as naval officer. Salmon was "popular, a man of *honor* and a respected judge in our criminal and orphans courts. If neither can be appointed I request that I may hear from you before you determine upon a successor."[7]

The political relationship between old friends McHenry and Hamilton grew. They wrote constantly about local and national politics, keeping each other informed of news in their own bailiwick. As each served the other, they also forwarded their own ends, and they expected to be consulted on matters that affected them. Indeed, they planned and plotted with open regularity on matters so delicate that McHenry grew concerned. "Knowing that I was apt to lose letters out of my pocket, and recollecting that you are a little subject to lose them by not putting them into yours, I thought it best that we should burn them." Surviving letters bear repeated references to epistles never found.[8]

As a partisan leader, McHenry decided to work actively in the election of fall 1792 against John Francis Mercer, who had served at the Constitutional Convention but had walked out and not signed it and now ran as an Anti-Administration candidate, opposing Washington's administration. McHenry did this despite being extremely ill, possibly with malaria, for half of September and admitting to Hamilton that he despaired of life. "Adieu. If I should get to heaven before you I shall remember you. I must go to bed." Before his sickness, however, he had written an article against Mercer under the pseudonym "Valerius" for the *Maryland Journal* and he followed up on the piece after he regained his health. Nor did he confine himself to newspaper articles. "I have also employed Major Hopkins of Anne Arundel County [Mercer's district], who is under considerable pecuniary obligations to me to circulate hand bills which contain popular charges against Mercer and fixes upon him some falsehoods."[9]

Despite the fact that McHenry acted independently, Mercer believed that Hamilton had engineered the resistance. Trouble between Mercer and Hamilton had begun while the former served in Congress and the treasury owed him money. When Mercer requested payment, Hamilton unwisely asked if Mercer would vote for one of Hamilton's key plans, the federal government's assumption of state revolutionary war debts. Mercer took umbrage at the implication that his vote was for sale. Although a witness insisted that Hamilton had been joking, Mercer refused to believe it, and this incident helped to set up the election imbroglio that now occurred.[10]

McHenry had learned that Mercer intended to use Hamilton's plans "as an excuse to attack the Federal Government."[11] Hamilton's policies, outlined in a series of public reports, did indeed serve to create an active political opposition to the administration, for they could now attack a target that was not the revered Washington. Distinct partisan alliances emerged around this time (1792), with those who supported the Washington administration denoted "Federalists" and those in opposition variously referred to as "Republicans," "Democrats," "Jeffersonians," or "Democratic-Republicans." The generally favored term, however, is "Republicans."

Hamilton's ideas did, in fact, form a whole that he believed would reestablish the country's economy and credit and include the entire Revolutionary War debt. He wanted to fund the Continental debt and support this with both a federal impost and a tax on liquor. The federal government would also assume the state war debts, and establish a national bank to provide a dependable source of stable currency. It would also, when possible, support manufacturing. Above all, government would "bring about economic changes which in turn would alter society for its own benefit."[12]

Sound as Hamilton's ideas were, there were also good reasons for opposition to parts of the plan, and those who disliked these matters coalesced around James Madison and Thomas Jefferson. States like Virginia and Maryland, which had paid off much of their debt, saw themselves as coming up short since they would now be asked to help pay the debt of other states. They also feared that the assumption of state debts would weaken the credit of individual states.

But at this point two historical schools of thought emerge. One school argues that a far more distressing issue existed—which especially concerned Madison—within assumption itself. Its origins dated back to the point at which soldiers had been furloughed at the end of the war. At that time, the United States had had no money to pay the soldiers, so they were given certificates, sometimes referred to as "promissory notes." Many soldiers (or other first holders of these promissory notes), however, needed money immediately and sold their certificates for whatever they could get (fair market value), usually for far less than the face value. Those who bought the certificates took a chance that the country would someday honor this debt.

Hamilton now proposed paying only those currently in possession of these certificates, and not the soldiers who had risked their lives. Madison, it is argued, found this very disturbing, and suggested "discrimination," that is, paying the secondary holders the face value, while finding the soldiers and giving them the difference between what they had already received and the face value amount. Madison considered the debts to the soldiers to be a matter of honor.

The other school of thought, articulated by Forrest McDonald, argues that Madison really had no concern for veterans or first holders of the certificates. Instead, Madison's goals were to gain a southern location for the capital and extract whatever financial benefit could be found for Virginia. According to McDonald, "The Virginians had been extremely artful. They used the first trade, which would give them the permanent capital, to provide a cloak of respectability for the second, which would be worth a net to their state of more than $13 million in the final settlement."[13] In addition, there were also others, like Thomas Jefferson, who unalterably opposed a National Bank, proposed in the third report. As a result, in June 1790, the House had approved funding the national debt without the assumption of state debts, sending Hamilton into a tailspin. Only after Hamilton met with Jefferson and Madison at dinner did Madison, a member of the House, agree not to oppose assumption if the New Yorker would agree to support a southern location for the capital.[14]

McHenry, however, was long an advocate of banks and funding and his reticence toward assumption had now disappeared. This placed him squarely behind Hamilton's plans for he was convinced that they would place the nation and the states on solid financial ground. When he heard of Mercer's designs to assail Hamilton's plans, McHenry decided to attack.

Mercer, however, immediately presumed that Hamilton lay behind the assault and asserted so publicly. This was a serious charge that Hamilton had to address. But he and McHenry had spoken and corresponded on so many matters that he could not honestly recall if he had suggested attacking Mercer or not. McHenry admitted they had briefly discussed Mercer and agreed on their "disapprobation against his political principles." Nonetheless, McHenry insisted "the little I did against Mercer was not the consequence of any thing you said about him. . . . I can safely acquit you of having either led my mind to give him opposition, or to have excited in it any ideas which were not in it before." The controversy between Mercer and Hamilton ultimately vanished, but not before focusing the current campaign. As a result, the opposition gained ground in the assembly and Mercer won office despite McHenry's activities.[15]

In fact, Federalists began to lose ground around the state, and the mechanics turned away from McHenry toward the opposition. This change on the part of the workers was less a shift away from McHenry than it was a renunciation of Maryland's Federalist proto-party itself. While McHenry had been consumed by the loss of his brother and had temporarily withdrawn from politics, the Federalists within Maryland had split. Because Maryland's congressmen failed to secure Baltimore rather than the Potomac River for the new nation's capital, angry Baltimoreans and the entire Chesapeake now gave their votes to the opposition. Since many also disliked Hamilton's new program, the voting pattern persisted. The national Federalist partisan alliance's loss of the Chesapeake Bay emerged clearly in the election of 1792, and their power would continue to degenerate for the next decade.[16]

Having gained in the Maryland House of Delegates, Republicans continued their fight to weaken the Constitution despite the fact that the Bill of Rights had gone into effect the year before. In fact, the House proposed further amendments, but Federalists "scattered in air the long string of amendments . . . so we remain a free . . . and a tolerably virtuous people."[17]

McHenry now wondered about the political fate of fellow state senator William Perry, who had warned McHenry of Mercer's election tactics. Not only was Perry a colleague, he was an old friend—Perry had taken his sick wife to the Sweet Springs the same summer McHenry had taken John. Mrs. Perry had died there. So the ties between the two men were old and close.

Perry had worked tirelessly for the Federalists—and therefore for Hamilton—and McHenry very much wished to reward him with a federal post. In fact, he had practically promised Perry a post in return for help in the election. McHenry was certain he was safe in this matter since as early as July 15 he "had a letter . . . from my friend in Philadelphia. He says 'Should an opportunity occur I shall not forget nor neglect your recommendation of Mr. Perry.'" To McHenry's humiliation, the position in view went instead to a Marylander named Richardson. How, McHenry wanted to know, had this happened?[18]

It seems that Perry was in line for the position until Hamilton's assistant, Tench Coxe, convinced him that Perry's appointment would not be "advantageous." What Hamilton did not realize, however, was that this information came from political opponents. Hamilton talked to the president, made his own investigations, and found a new prejudice against Perry. The treasurer admitted his own views were "in doubt" but submitted the information to the president. Since Richardson had been recommended by all concerned, Washington chose him.[19]

McHenry was "exceedingly mortified and hurt at Mr. Perry's being refused that inspectorship," but insisted that he "did not once think of blaming you [Hamilton]. I ascribed it to . . . those who were near you." McHenry was right; Coxe had intentionally led Hamilton into appointing a man favored by those who were transforming into Jeffersonian Republicans—and denying a loyal, hardworking Federalist the spoils of victory.[20]

This episode drove a wedge between McHenry and Hamilton. Despite the fact that most office-seekers whom McHenry had recommended *did* receive posts, McHenry was mortified. It truly hurt his credibility. "I know not what to say to Perry when I may see him." He decided he had to make a change. From now on McHenry determined to take a lower profile with regard to federal recommendations. That way he would not promise what he could not deliver. Although he still professed friendship for Hamilton and urged his friend to visit, McHenry ended their political correspondence for the duration of Hamilton's secretaryship. McHenry's communication with Washington also dwindled to a trickle. Perhaps Hamilton and Washington were also embarrassed, for Hamilton admitted that it had "lain heavy on my mind."[21]

This was, after all, an age of "gentlemen." When gentlemen made an agreement, they were honor-bound to abide by it. Since Hamilton, behaving in an ungentlemanly fashion, had backed out of their agreement without even a consultation, McHenry felt that he could no longer trust his friend to treat him with the degree of honor that he, McHenry, deserved. Hamilton admitted feeling concerned because he had to know that he had harmed his friend's reputation within Maryland, and reputation was critical to a man of honor. They were nearly synonymous. Convinced, however, that Hamilton's insult had been unintentional, there was little McHenry could do but turn his back on the insult and withdraw from the situation. But he also had to realize that he could not count on Hamilton to support him; McHenry's reputation was not safe in Hamilton's hands. McHenry chose to withdraw, to the point of noncorrespondence, but the public embarrassment could only persist.[22]

McHenry did, however, return to the Maryland Senate, where he worked toward retrieving his reputation. Probably the most important political issue in the session of 1793 concerned a resolve from Virginia that has since become the Eleventh Amendment to the Constitution. The amendment was generated by national controversy over a 1793 decision by the U.S. Supreme Court. During the Revolution, Robert Farquhar, a South Carolina merchant, had sold supplies to the State of Georgia but never had been paid for them. He sued the state, but died before he could bring his suit to a conclusion. Georgia refused even to appear in the case, because of the old doctrine of sovereign immunity (one cannot sue the sovereign without its consent—in this case, the state government). Farquhar's executor, Alexander Chisholm, brought his suit in federal court, and ultimately the U.S. Supreme Court decided that he could sue the state in federal court without its consent. This decision sent shockwaves through the nation, for if Chisholm could sue Georgia in federal court, then other states faced the danger of being sued in federal courts by former citizens who, as Loyalists, had had their lands confiscated or debts owed them cancelled by state governments. The furor led to the Eleventh Amendment, which declared that the Constitution could not be interpreted to permit any federal court to hear a lawsuit against a state brought by a citizen of another state or a subject of a foreign country. Although McHenry opposed the amendment, the Maryland legislature agreed to it in November 1794 and it was finally ratified in 1798.[23]

In McHenry's private life, however, a serious issue arose. Mr. Bleakley, executor of the Allison estate, had heard some disreputable things about McHenry's business partner, Hugh McCurdy. By January 26, 1794, McCurdy became alarmed, writing to Bleakley in self-defense and requesting a chance to clear matters up; he also asked the accuser's name.[24]

The allegations certainly struck at the two most delicate and important areas of the young man's life, as he was accused of both inappropriate business dealings and a libertine lifestyle. Rumor had it that McCurdy had purchased a part ownership in a western merchant house, to which he was devoting a great deal of time; this upset McHenry as their business arrangement explicitly demanded McCurdy's full-time attention.[25]

The other accusation, that McCurdy was a libertine, offended *and* frightened the young man, for he was in love with Peggy's half-sister Grace Allison. Bleakley feared McCurdy loved Grace's money, which he emphatically denied. "[W]hen I addressed Miss Allison, I did not know whether she had sixpence of a fortune to depend on." Instead, he insisted, "had she not one penny of a fortune, it would be equally the same to me," and he reminded

Bleakley that his own affluence meant "that we need not want for any of the necessarys of this life, either as to Convenience or appearance."[26]

McHenry must have been quite uneasy about this last accusation for he was probably reminded of his brother. Certainly he wanted the best life for Grace, but he was understandably willing to forgive indiscretions (if true) in a single, healthy young man who wished now to settle down with one woman. McCurdy must have proved his worth, for he remained McHenry's business partner and married Miss Allison within the year.[27]

Foreign affairs had also been engaging the nation. Americans followed the French Revolution with great interest, generally supporting it until the execution of Louis XVI and the Terror. When France declared war on Great Britain on February 1, 1793, domestic rivalries within the United States intensified. Americans again divided, Federalists favoring Great Britain and the Republicans favoring France.[28]

With the European war causing such powerful divisions in American politics, McHenry saw that there would be a need for envoys or ministers abroad. So he finally wrote Washington, knowing his request would be one of many. It was important to the "gentleman" in McHenry that Washington not think him either in financial need or vain enough to consider himself indispensable. Instead, McHenry thought that the nation's need for diplomats corresponded with his own need for a change in climate, as his health had been impaired by illnesses in the autumns of 1792 and 1793. This reason fit the gentleman's code more appropriately than trying to convince the president that he was the best man for a diplomatic post.[29]

But shortly after writing this letter, McHenry's anxiety for his old friend Lafayette, who had been imprisoned earlier by the first coalition, overcame his normal good sense. McHenry wrote Washington a letter that betrayed his near-despair. Fearful that Lafayette might meet the guillotine, McHenry now beseeched Washington—again he did not correspond with Hamilton—to send him to France as a commissioner to obtain the marquis' release. Their friendship demanded the attempt, he argued—and the force of his emotions, in fact, had almost the consuming and surreal quality of a dream.[30]

Washington, who loved Lafayette, shared the depth of the Marylander's feelings. He reassured McHenry that "every thing which friendship requires and which I could do without committing my public character, or involving this Country in embarrassment, is, and has been for some time in train, though the result is as yet unknown." In fact, Washington wished above all to keep the fledgling United States out of Europe's wars, and believed he could do little to help Lafayette. In a private capacity, he had sent the marquis' wife over 2,000 guilders, ostensibly in partial payment for services the Frenchman had rendered. But he kept McHenry in mind, and if the Marylander would not write Hamilton, the latter nonetheless placed McHenry on the list of candidates being considered for American minister to France. McHenry, however, lost to James Monroe, and Lafayette was not released by the Austrians until 1797.[31]

In the meantime, McHenry received word from Maryland Congressman William Hindman of Congress's fury that England, despite Washington's Neutrality Proclamation, now officially encouraged the seizure of American ships. England was angry that French Foreign Minister Edmund Genet sought to use American ports to outfit privateers ordered to prey on British ships. Genet's actions undermined American neutrality, leaving England and the United States on the brink of war. Fortunately, New England insisted on negotiations.[32]

Baltimore, which traded heavily with the West Indies, was badly hurt by the English capture of American ships. Anger intensified, and "[f]rom the Baltimore newspapers it appears that the townspeople generally favored preparations for military defense against England. Some people wanted war." So when an article crying for war appeared in the *Baltimore Daily Intelligencer* on April 22, 1794, McHenry immediately replied. The ensuing newspaper debate illustrated clearly the growing division between Federalists and Republicans. George Dent, the prowar essayist, had announced "that scarce a shadow of hope remains of continuing on terms of peace with Great Britain, consistent with national honour or national interest." McHenry responded powerfully. "I am also for war provided we cannot be permitted to enjoy peace upon reasonable terms; but I am not for rushing into it without due forecast and preparation, such as may promise to it a *favorable issue*; nor till the nation which has most injured us *refuses* to do us *justice*." He further asked, "Is peace so light and frivolous a good, as not to deserve even an endeavour to prevent war; or war so slight a calamity, as to make the avoiding it a matter of indifference?"[33] Signing as a "Friend to Peace" he urged support of Washington's attempts to preserve peace and to wait and see what John Jay, special envoy to Britain, might accomplish.

But the question of war persisted. "What real friend to the honour and dignity, and future welfare of this country, would now propose lenient measures with a nation black with the crimes she has been guilty of! . . . AMERICANS AROUSE! . . . your mutilated commerce calls loudly for VENGEANCE!" "A Native American" joined this anonymous writer a few days later, insisting that the British must be "whipped into it [justice] by the brave Sans Culottes." He also insulted McHenry, since everyone wanted revenge "excepting those only who are considerable holders of certificates or western lands, and those who cannot divest themselves of their affections for monarchy."[34]

McHenry ignored the gibe. He did own certificates from the new federal government, and in congratulating Washington's election to the presidency McHenry had written, "you are now a king, under a different name," but he was no advocate of monarchy. The other essayist would have been closer to the mark had he denounced importers, for the Golden Fan's dry goods business relied on undisturbed shipping. McHenry again defended the administration and negotiation, since the British might not risk conflict if they truly believed war might result. Above all, the United States should display its courage only after establishing an "effective military arrangement."[35]

After a response on May 7 by "A Friend to Mankind," McHenry reacted again, this time calling himself "The Remembrancer." Now he complained of Madison and his fellow Republicans in Congress, claiming they were all threat and no strength, holding out the "*olive branch + the sword*" in the one hand and a "*nettle + an empty scabbard*" in the other.[36]

McHenry wrote all of this despite being ill. Knowing now that he would not be sent to Europe he returned to the Sweet Springs, this time for his own health. He experimented on the waters, and even wrote Peggy in great detail about the qualities he discovered. His days were spent drinking and bathing in the waters; eating meals of mush or bread and milk; and chatting, walking, or riding. And, of course, writing Peggy. By late September, however, he received word that she had been unable to find adequate help at home and was now herself indisposed from overwork. He decided to go home.[37]

Back in Baltimore, he heard from fellow Maryland Federalist William Vans Murray, who wrote the news from Philadelphia and the House of Representatives. Above all he lamented the early "leaks" giving the public the substance of the Jay Treaty. The Jay Treaty established peace with England, but at a price many Americans did not wish to pay. Yes, the British agreed to leave the Northwest posts, opened the British West Indies to some American ships, and established commissions to arbitrate prewar debts. However, the treaty implicitly denied Americans the right of neutral trade and freedom of the seas. It would impact American trade with France. Many wondered why the Revolution had been fought if the United States would permit England to dictate the terms of trade. Worse, Murray lamented, the leaks "show'd the feebler part, the mere introduction of the business. . . . The effect was not happy. . . . The roots of the cause however are perhaps to be looked for if any where existing in the remnant of the Democratic clubs."[38] These Democratic clubs were generally spawned by the Republican Party and were conspicuous in their support of the French Revolution. Federalists disliked their politics, their opposition to the Jay Treaty, and their potential to cause their party further trouble.

Federalists like Murray and McHenry now began to fear not just France but French immigrants as well. They worried that the European wars might send as many as one million French immigrants to the United States in as little as three years. In light of their Revolution, it was clear to these Federalists that the French did not know how to live in a republic. (It is certainly ironic that McHenry, an Irish immigrant, subscribed to this view, but he no doubt felt justified by the Terror.) Murray, however, wrote that republicanism was simply second nature to Americans: "So naturally & essentially do the Theories belong to the opinions habits & immemorial practice of the citizens of the U.S. that their General and particular modes of Government can hardly be said to have been *Willed*." McHenry thought that anything legal should be done, but he wondered if federal attempts to lengthen the period of naturalization would work, or if state laws would remain in effect. Congress did indeed pass a law in that year, 1795, lengthening the naturalization period for national citizenship from two years' residence in the country and one year in a given state to five years' residence in the nation and three in a particular state. In Maryland, however, an immigrant could take a state citizenship oath upon arriving, and if worth at least thirty pounds, vote in state elections after one year's residence.[39] Indeed, in the United States, one is both a citizen of a state and of the nation. Although the Supreme Court in 1832 in *Gassies v. Ballon* would insist that a citizen of the United States was also a citizen of a state, the issue of citizenship (including federal, state, and territorial) has continued to inspire controversy (Dred Scott, the Slaughterhouse cases, etc.).

More immediately interesting to McHenry, however, was Murray's confirmation of the prevailing rumor that Hamilton intended to retire. When this event actually transpired McHenry reopened their correspondence. "What shall I say to you? Convince you that though I have been a long time silent I have not therefore ceased to love you nor for a moment felt any abatement of my friendship." He decided to clear the air. "You remember my last letter was an answer to yours respecting Perry [the unsuccessful candidate for an inspectorship]. I concluded on the whole that by discontinuing my correspondence I should free you (and myself) from like embarrassments and leave you in a situation to consult me only in cases . . . where you might suppose my local knowledge might conduce to a more perfect estimate of persons or things." There, it was said. "You see how well I have persevered in this determination, and that it is only now when I can have nothing to expect and you nothing to give that I recall you to the remembrance of our early union and friendship."[40] If the friendship had not died during this dormant period, it had certainly been strained. McHenry, however, was now willing to reopen their relationship and he advised Hamilton to enjoy his retirement.

For his part, McHenry intended to enjoy his own country home as much as possible, tending to business only occasionally. He had, for example, repeatedly urged the establishment of a bank in his city. A bill for a bank had even passed the legislature, and now he and Samuel Chase united to create one. This time an anonymous forty-five-page pamphlet written by McHenry advocating for what became the Bank of Baltimore worked. McHenry and Chase could now work together because the latter's antipathy to the new Constitution had disappeared when he saw it at work, and he was becoming a Federalist. As a matter of fact, he and Chase had come to some rapprochement the year before when Chase, as judge at the Court of Oyer and Terminer, attempted to punish those who had rioted when a ship flew the American flag upside down; McHenry and Chase both favored order. It seems that a drunken ship captain named Ramsdell had refused to right the flag, and the working-class citizenry of Fell's Point, who depended on commerce for their livelihoods, decided that Ramsdell was paid by the British and summarily tarred and feathered him. When the rioters were brought to Chase's court, he ordered them to give bond, which they at first refused. Then, when the sheriff claimed the crowd would not allow him to jail the rioters, Chase offered to constitute a one-man posse. Instead, the rioters changed their minds and gave bond, but when the grand jury refused to indict the ringleaders Chase and the grand jury

exchanged heated words.[41] As far as Chase was concerned, this was insufficient support for law and order.

By the middle of 1795, McHenry now judged Chase a complete convert
to Federalism, and he wrote to Washington "recommending Chase for the
next vacancy on the Supreme Court." He emphasized Chase's conduct *since*
the adoption of the Constitution as well as his service during the Revolution. He was well-educated, informed, and experienced. Despite this recommendation, McHenry admitted that he and Chase were "'on neither
good nor bad terms, neither friends nor enemies.'"[42] Washington hesitated
but eventually followed McHenry's advice.

Late in the fall of 1795, after McHenry again visited the western springs
and then returned to the Senate, Murray reported a scandal that rocked
Washington's administration and eventually affected McHenry. It appeared
that Edmund Randolph, secretary of state, had colluded with the French—
actually worse, that he had been in their pay. When Washington and Pickering confronted Randolph with their suspicions, he resigned in protest. Randolph had not, in fact, taken bribes, but the situation certainly did appear
dubious.[43] Washington now had to fill vacancies.

Who would replace Randolph as secretary of state? By October 29 Washington had asked four candidates who all refused the office.[44] In fact, all
Washington seemed to hear were refusals to fill the offices, so he wrote
Hamilton for suggestions, who also had difficulty supplying names. Hamilton was not thrilled with any of the men who came first to mind—either
they had thorny personalities, the wrong politics, dubious talents, or were
not very well known.

Finally, Hamilton thought of McHenry for secretary of state, comment-
ing that "his views are good." He was, in fact, a Federalist stalwart, and
Washington wanted no more of the bickering that had occurred in the cabinet between Hamilton and Jefferson. Equally significant in light of Randolph's ignominious departure was Hamilton's certainty that McHenry
"would not disgrace the Office."[45]

On the other hand, McHenry was not well known beyond Maryland and
he had had those autumnal fevers, probably malaria, so there was the question of his health. As his reputation was local he "would give no strength
to the administration" but none of the men under consideration were "first
rate" or of national prominence, as the more famous Federalists were already in office, had refused a post, or had left the positions they held.[46]

Washington finally decided to shuffle cabinet positions. Oliver Wolcott,

Hamilton's old assistant, became secretary of the treasury; Charles Lee took attorney general; and Timothy Pickering, who had succeeded Knox as secretary of war and preferred to stay in this position, deferred to Washington's decision and moved over to be secretary of state. But who would be secretary of war?

Since Wolcott and Pickering were both New Englanders, Washington wanted another southerner on board. To that end he had, by January 20, 1796, asked a South Carolinian, a Virginian, and a Marylander to accept office but each declined. None of these men had been on Hamilton's original list.

Now Washington turned to that list and fixed on McHenry. There was a great deal to be said for him: he was a southerner with military experience, a seasoned politician at the state and national levels, a Federalist partisan leader, and a successful businessman. In Maryland, he had channeled federal patronage, campaigned for himself and other Federalists, worked to defeat the opposition, written newspaper essays supporting the Federalist administration, and served in office himself. He was also committed, loyal, and honorable. After the Randolph scandal, Washington valued even more highly a reasonable temper, orthodox views, and an unstained character.

So Washington briefly summarized the situation for McHenry, including the earlier refusals, and wrote that "it would now give me sincere pleasure if you would fill it."[47] Further, as if to make amends for the Perry incident, Washington also asked McHenry to see if his recommendation, Samuel Chase, would sit on the Supreme Court.

McHenry received the request on a Friday and wrote asking for the weekend to decide. As always, he needed time to think, but by Monday he had reached a decision. He had been truly torn between his "ease" and his desire to serve Washington. No one was more aware than McHenry that he had refused elective federal office twice. In 1794 his Federalist colleague Uriah Forrest had begged him to fill a vacated federal Senate seat, for Maryland would give Federalists the majority in the Senate, and "[t]hen on Maryland does every thing Hang." McHenry, however, was not convinced that he was essential; he had refused to run for this position before and was certain another candidate could be found this time as well. On each of these occasions McHenry believed he was dispensable, and he had preferred to remain in Maryland, close to home. But this time he saw that Washington truly needed him, as so many others had declined the position. It would mean financial loss to him, for his sense of honor required that he avoid a conflict of interest by selling both the business his father and brother had established as well as his interest in another mercantile house before assuming his cabinet office. One of the businesses was valued at £3,000 while the other brought in £1,000 per year. He could, however, retain other sources of income, for he had rental properties around Baltimore, and he did own shares of stocks in at least one local insurance company.[48] McHenry was also a loyal man, and he respected and admired Washington more than anyone else he knew. Their years together during the Revolution had created a very tight bond, and he doubtless thought of that experience assisting the general in his Military Family as he made his decision. Hence he wrote the president that "the soothing idea of serving under you, more particularly at this crisis, has effectually and irresistibly silenced all opposition. Such then as I am and with a heart truly devoted to you and the public good, dispose of as you please."[49]

McHenry would be secretary of war.

ELEVEN

"I Am Scarce Mistress of My Conduct"

Peggy McHenry

MCHENRY COULD NOT HESITATE; the secretary of war position had been vacant for some time and he was needed in Philadelphia, the nation's capital, immediately. So he mounted the fastest horse available and braved February's chills despite an already serious cold, promising to return and manage the family's move.[1] But McHenry soon realized the work was far too demanding to return to Baltimore for his family.

Peggy was thus left to manage all the details of the family's move to the north, and she was not pleased. This scenario did not fit her—or the early republic's—general understanding of proper household hierarchical authority. Traditionally, McHenry as husband stood at the pinnacle, representative to the outside world, obeyed by the family. Earlier in the century he could have been described as a patriarch. But by the revolutionary era, a near equality between husband and wife as companions within marriage became an ideal never really met. After all, a wife still owed deference to her spouse should they disagree (much as a junior partner might); she possessed only a restricted legal existence despite revolutionary rhetoric; and her province remained the domestic sphere, although sometimes a wife's duties required that she reach beyond the home and play the role of deputy husband. The children occupied third place and naturally had to honor and obey their parents. But they were not obligated to respect the last category: servants or slaves, who had no authority whatever their age, having to submit even to the master's children.[2]

Certainly Peggy McHenry played her roles in a solid and loving marriage of nearly equal companions. Peggy was always the housewife, but in James's absence also became deputy husband, and her role as mistress of their slaves became more acute. Exactly when the McHenry family first owned slaves is not known, but it is possible that they did so as soon as they could afford them, decades before this. As a city-dwelling, mercantile family, slaves probably were used both as domestics and as help in business. It is at this point, however, that references to slaves are first found in their papers.

For their part, the slaves acted within' an urban context, unlike the majority of slaves who lived in rural, agricultural settings. Baltimore was a highly entrepreneurial city with a labor force more like the North. Slavery had not been essential to the city's early development. Although the institution had been adopted, many slaves were skilled, or hired out; became term slaves; and even bought their freedom. Substantial free black communities were developing in cities all along the seaboard, leading slaves in those areas to an awareness that they could in some ways ameliorate their conditions— even become free while maintaining their families.[3]

The first relationship within this hierarchy to be tested was that between husband and wife and clearly illustrates that the earlier "automatic deference" from wife to husband that had existed earlier, in the colonial period, is too stark a description to fit the McHenrys. Their relationship was born in the republicanism of the revolutionary era and involved a greater equality than that allowed for by automatic deference. In addition, the fortune Peggy brought to the marriage (possibly protected through a trust) appears to have been somewhat larger than James's, perhaps helping to undercut a more traditional patriarchy. In a society where wealth was more important than birth, her contribution to the family's finances mattered.[4] Thus, while James remained the primary decision-maker, in matters that involved her, Peggy came in a close second.

At times, Peggy even took the upper hand. In a poem he wrote her for an anniversary, James professed his complete contentment with her and their marriage—with only one unimportant exception. Whenever other ladies came to call, Peggy persisted in tidying up his books and work notes despite his efforts to stop her. Clearly, her reputation as a housekeeper was at stake, and she would not allow that to be compromised. This was her sphere, her "job," and she asserted her primacy.[5]

Now, in 1796, Peggy apparently did not want to return to Philadelphia, the city in which she had been born and raised. After all, the move would be a great deal of trouble for her to arrange in her role as deputy husband and would be costly as well. Indeed, she seems to have feared the whole endeavor. Her support system of friends and remaining family now lived in the Baltimore area, a very significant matter to women whose lives revolved around family and home. Perhaps she also worried that the move would be fruitless, as rumor had it that James's duties were so onerous he thought of resigning.⁶ Still, the marriage was close and loving, and if she wanted to be with her husband the family would have to move.

But she did not have to act as if she liked it. Peggy's forms of resistance to James's decision in this matter varied. On the one hand she used her supposed female weakness to advantage: although she never specifically denied ability based on her sex, she claimed instead that moving a household was simply too big a job for her to handle by herself. Managing the children and disposition of clothing, glassware, livestock, and especially furniture were too much for her. How could she get proper boxes made for the transportation of the furniture? How could she manage so many loose ends? How, the subtext surely reads, could she be expected to make arrangements within the male world of carpenters and ship captains in which she did not belong? No, she argued somewhat disingenuously, if James wanted the family to move, he should return to Baltimore and supervise it himself. "[F]orgive me I pray for adding to your uneasiness," she wrote. "[M]y mind is so perplexed with anxiety for ourselves & public affairs, wishing to be with you yet fearing to take any steps towards it—dreading the future whether I stay or go, that I am scarce mistress of my conduct." No, she claimed, "I think I cannot leave this, till you can come down."⁷ Now surely she did not really expect James to return for the move. She knew he could not spare the time. Peggy would have to manage this onerous and unpleasant task herself. Very likely stressing real anxiety over these unfamiliar responsibilities, she could, without refusing to follow his directions, stall and try to shift the duty, somehow changing the situation in which she found herself. Interestingly, it never seems to have occurred to either one of them that the family would not try to stay together.

If Peggy "hid behind her skirts," so to speak, she also utilized her position as head of the domestic arrangements to make demands upon James that were difficult for him to ignore. She became *very* particular regarding the family's accommodations, negotiating now for the best familial situation that could be created. The rental house in Philadelphia should be large, but not ruinously expensive and ostentatious. It needed to be in the city, near enough to walk comfortably to everything important: school, the office, shops, and so forth. If they could not do without a carriage, she wished to keep the horses at a livery stable.

By listing such demands, Peggy hoped to avoid falling into a social trap. If their rental were too near the center of the city it would also likely be elegant, leading others to expect a lavish lifestyle and entertaining. This would embroil her in a flurry of expensive sociability that she, as mistress of the household, would have to plan and manage. Peggy must have seen that life while she was growing into womanhood in Philadelphia, as ostentation reigned there before and during the Revolution. The lifestyle was perpetuated after the war, especially among southerners who had come north. Better, she thought, to find a large but "plain" house that would "suit [their] inclination or purse." Since her demands certainly appeared reasonable, McHenry tried to meet her conditions, but such lodgings were not easy to find. Because it was the nation's capital, Philadelphia's rental properties had risen in value from both increasing population demands and competition for prime locations.[8] This scarcity consequently delayed the family's move, probably one of Peggy's goals.

Finally, Peggy had to attend to the disposition of the family's handful of slaves. First she would need to decide whether they should be sold in Maryland or taken to Philadelphia. Making such decisions with respect to the slaves was definitely an incursion into the male world, and proved far more difficult and disturbing than Peggy or James had imagined. At first her complaints about this merely seemed to fit neatly into her overall strategy of trying to bring James home, but as the slaves grew more disruptive over time, Peggy's tactics changed.

For his part, James remained unmoved by Peggy's protests. He certainly appears to have wanted her to acquiesce like a good wife and believed her capable of the task before her. James, it will be remembered, had actually taught her penmanship during her youth, and had repeatedly encouraged her to write, both letters and his own beloved poetry. This ability enriched not only her own life but his and the children's lives with her as well. The republic required women educated enough to teach their children to be upright citizens.[9] So when Peggy claimed incapacity, James simply persisted. In time, however, he realized that his slaves were not mere annoyances but were exerting a challenge to his authority.

It is somewhat ironic that James even owned slaves, since he had placed himself on record as to the biological equality of whites and blacks. He was, in fact, part of a postrevolutionary trend among Maryland leaders to liberalize manumission laws. It was crucial to McHenry, however, that this be done both reasonably and humanely. When serving in the Maryland Assembly in 1789, McHenry had favored a radical bill for the gradual emancipation and nonexportation of slaves (based on Pennsylvania's version); a much milder bill passed that only urged compassion toward slaves, servants, and apprentices.[10] The following year manumission via will was allowed. Ironically, McHenry had qualms about this, for he opposed freeing disabled or infirm elderly slaves as he considered it proper that masters should care for the people who had given so much service. Their widows or children should be freed, however. Such a bill was finally passed in 1796.

But James did take one further step—he met the famous African American mathematician Benjamin Banneker and wrote a laudatory introduction to his 1792 almanac. Then a well-known southern state senator, James had been chosen to bring more public attention to the almanac and help to further antislavery sentiment. "I consider this negro as a fresh proof that the powers of the mind are disconnected with the color of the skin, or, in other words, a striking contradiction to Mr. Hume's doctrine, that 'the negroes are naturally inferior to the whites, and unsusceptible of attainments in arts and sciences.'" He went further. "In every civilized country, we shall find thousands of whites liberally educated and who have enjoyed greater opportunities for instruction than this negro, his inferiors in those intellectual acquirements and capacities that form the most characteristic features in the human race."[11]

Moreover, McHenry did not agree with those who "would assign to these degraded blacks an origin different from the whites," but thought instead that the races were equal and that the progress of mankind would prove this. Slavery too, would become extinct as more whites came to understand the truth of his position. "Let, however, the issue be what it will, I cannot but wish on this occasion to see the public patronage keep pace with my black friend's merit."[12] It was unusual for a slaveholding white of some status to make reference to "my black friend."

McHenry, then, owned household slaves as a convenience. Like so many others of the time, James somehow reconciled himself to the enslavement of "equals." With regard to both women and African Americans, James's egalitarian ideals far outpaced his life choices. In both cases, he acknowledged that innate abilities had been stifled by society, but nowhere admitted his own culpability. He believed—hoped—that time and the new society being created would solve the problems.

It was, perhaps, not too difficult for McHenry to hold relatively enlightened views regarding African Americans. He was, after all, born and raised in Ireland, where black slavery did not exist, but where the English abuse of native Irish did. He knew how easy it was for people to lose rights and much of their freedom. Moreover, 1790s Baltimore and Maryland were not as race conscious as many other places.[13] Slavery had not been critical to Baltimore's economy and various degrees of quasi-freedom had developed, such as term slavery, wherein a slave worked only for a specified period of years. Laws against self-hire were not enforced in that city. The result was a semipermeable racial barrier and relatively liberal attitudes that assured McHenry little social or political cost to his essay on Banneker's behalf.

But the state of Pennsylvania had taken a different course, and this explains why slaves were an issue during the McHenrys' move at all. For in 1780 Pennsylvania had passed a law for the gradual emancipation of slaves in that commonwealth. Many factors had prepared the commonwealth for this event. For one thing, Pennsylvania had fewer slaves than most other states, but it also had antislavery leaders like Anthony Benezet, active since the 1750s.[14] Despite resistance to antislavery ideas, the work of Benezet and others prepared the city for the Revolution's egalitarianism. In a sensitized population, antislavery sentiment grew along with the commitment to American liberty.

Passage of the law was something of a surprise to antislavery Quakers, however. Although the Quaker Party had retired from politics in the 1750s, they remained in political control of the colony until the Revolution, when they regrouped to deal with forced military service, confiscations, and deportation. In their place came the Whigs, a coalition of Philadelphia radicals and backcountry Scots-Irish. In 1778 their acting president, George Bryan, determined to champion the abolition of slavery in Pennsylvania. Bryan would not allow his party to be attacked as interested in liberty only for themselves. After several versions and much politicking, the bill passed by a vote of 34–21. The Revolution was clearly changing Pennsylvania society.

The proponents of the gradual emancipation law of 1780 were indebted to an English court's decision of 1772, *Somersett v. Stewart*. In this decision the judge proclaimed that slavery was so "odious" a matter that its existence and protection required positive law, that is, laws specifically passed by the government and in the law books. In this case, the slave James Somersett sued for his freedom and received it, as his master had brought him from Virginia to England, where the laws of the realm did not uphold slavery. Many thought this decision had put an end to forced servitude in England.[15]

If slavery did not exist in England, and the colonies in 1780 were fighting for "liberty," it seemed important to many Pennsylvanians that their state be no less free than the country they sought freedom from. They were also, as they stated in the preamble, grateful to God for their own good fortune and ready "to extend a portion of that freedom to others." According to *An Act for the Gradual Abolition of Slavery*, slaves born after the act's passage would serve their mother's master under conditions similar to indentured servitude until they were twenty-eight, at which point they would be freed. And those with slaves already born would have to register them by November 1, 1780 or their slaves would be freed. To the masters' dismay, this clause was enforced, and loopholes were plugged with a law that followed in 1788.[16]

There were, however, some exceptions. In the interest of comity, or good will, toward other states, the slave property of "sojourners" residing in Pennsylvania less than six months would be allowed. And, since Philadelphia served as the national capital at the time, the same allowance was made for senators or congressmen from other states. But other federal officials were not given the same consideration. As a consequence, slaveholding members of the administration had to determine what to do about their slaves. They could free their slaves, sell them at home before coming to Philadelphia, or negotiate a contract of indenture with the slaves, hence allowing the master more years of service while guaranteeing the slaves' future freedom. Although some found the law confusing, activist abolitionists ensured its enforcement.[17]

Washington himself had been forced to contend with this issue. By 1791 the president realized that he had stayed in the state long enough to be considered a resident of Pennsylvania with unregistered slaves who could be freed automatically. They could have easily assimilated into the black population of Philadelphia, 87 percent of whom lived in a state of freedom or indenture. While he had considered freeing his slaves, Washington was not prepared to do so at the moment, and any of the slaves lost to his wife's Custis estate would either have to be replaced or paid for. So he returned most of those slaves to Mount Vernon before they understood the possibilities before them. While the cook Hercules ran away in 1797 rather than return to Virginia with Washington, the president freed the rest of those who served him in Philadelphia by simply allowing them to remain behind.[18]

Jefferson, too, had been affected by Pennsylvania's law. He kept at least three "servants" while in Philadelphia whom he paid wages, although that is certainly not proof that they were not slaves. In fact, while in that city, Jefferson agreed in writing to free his slave James Hemings, brother of Sally, who may have mothered some of Jefferson's children. James Hemings had accompanied Jefferson to Paris, where he had learned to cook and become free under French law. Hemings returned to the United States, however, and he now wanted his freedom; Jefferson granted it rather than face possible public embarrassment in a state that would have freed Hemings in any case.[19]

Like Washington and Jefferson, the McHenrys now had to determine whether to bring their slaves north as indentured servants or sell them and hire free labor in Philadelphia. Peggy had an extremely difficult time deciding what to do. It was not because she agonized over the sale of slaves. In fact, at first she thought it best just to sell them, but some were new, and since slaves were only economical over the long term she feared a large and immediate financial loss. No, instead, she fretted over one of the social changes wrought by the Revolution: that is, the development of "whimsical servants," whose pride and sense of personal freedom made them unreliable from an employer's perspective. If they sold the slaves that meant running a household "with an entire set of strange servants not knowing what reliance may be placed on any one of them, hirelings are so whimsical too, & easily offended that one does not know themselves certain of them a day." If, however, they took the slaves north, the McHenrys stood to lose should the slaves escape to an early freedom.[20] Not yet having fully made up her mind, Peggy soon leaned toward indentured servitude.

The slaves themselves further complicated the situation, troubling Peggy in ways she had not anticipated. It became apparent that they understood the matter and determined to influence and manipulate the decision at which their masters would arrive, leaving it only superficially in the McHenrys' control. The McHenrys' female slaves, in ways both direct and indirect, attempted to negotiate their way either to freedom in Baltimore or at least to a future freedom. They would have been familiar with the possibilities, as Baltimore slaves often "negotiated" by arranging their own sales, purchasing their freedom (sometimes on credit), and securing either immediate freedom or a term limit to their service.[21]

What makes the story of the McHenry slaves unusual was not that they negotiated but that they were women interacting with a mistress over freedom at a very early point in the republic. We also know more than is common about the motivations of each side, thanks to the insightfulness and clarity of Peggy McHenry.

In her letters, Peggy generally began her children's names with capitals, but not the names of her slaves. In an era when the use of capitals was abundant, this use of the lowercase is striking. While it is true that Peggy often allowed the rules of grammar and capitalization to lapse, this treatment of the slaves formed a consistent pattern.

Moreover, as Peggy wrote James about what they undoubtedly considered scandalous behavior by the slaves (becoming drunk, disrespectful, or uncooperative), the insensitivity and arrogance of this woman who was probably a relatively kind mistress is striking. There is no evidence that Peggy easily lost her temper with the slaves or was cruel beyond what a degrading system demanded. After all, although Peggy as mistress necessarily saw the slaves as inferiors, she knew their family situations; credited them with cunning, normal emotions; and, above all, appeared to understand their motives. At least her explanations seem plausible—and her explanations are all that remain.

The fates of five slaves hung in the balance, those of four women and one man, each of whom apparently saw the situation clearly and understood its importance for their lives. Both their words and actions, as Peggy describes them, illustrate their general desire for freedom and family, aspirations strong among antebellum slaves.[22] The question in the slaves' minds was how to possess both at the same time. Even as an indentured servant, their freedom lay seven years and hundreds of miles away in Philadelphia. But their families lived in Maryland and could not simply pick up and go to Pennsylvania. Was it possible to acquire freedom and remain in Maryland with their families? Perhaps, but only if they could convince Peggy McHenry to agree to their terms—which was unlikely, as the terms would probably mean financial loss to the whites.

Such, however, was clearly the goal of three of the women, two of whom attempted the same maneuver to achieve their ends. The eldest was a woman named Rachel. Her age, in fact, became her argument, but not until after she had initiated a campaign of disobedience and unruliness to convince her mistress to get rid of her. Peggy's domestic authority was now under fire. She wrote to James, "Your servants want a Master—being all slaves they keep one another in countenance in their impertinence, + vex me sometimes extreemly [sic]." Peggy gave an example: "I called her [Rachel] to take the child in she would not come, I scolded her & she gave me such a serenade . . . I believe she was drunk—she kept cursing the whole evening." Eleven days later Rachel told her mistress that she, Rachel, "was too old to do our business & hoped we would not take her there [Philadelphia]." Peggy now understood that Rachel was playing for her freedom and admitted to James that she hated to "offend" Rachel by telling her to search out a new master. Although Rachel's behavior and strategy were now apparent to Peggy, it had not yet dawned on the mistress that the slave might have either a legitimate position or some power.[23] The situation had, however, led Peggy to an alteration in her correspondence with James. Peggy still complained, but more about the slaves than the move. Instead, Peggy solicited her husband's support. He gave what emotional support he could from a distance, but both recognized that the situation would have to be managed by Peggy. Husband and wife were now, however, united in their determination to control the slaves.

The second woman, Henney, also made Peggy agonize. The slave had been "sullen and impertinent" from the start, but Peggy hoped to bribe Henney into penitence and good behavior: she must either apologize and behave or be sold. But the slave was stubborn and Peggy's authority defied. This Peggy could not allow. Because Henney "did not condescent [sic] to make any apologies," Peggy wrote to James, "the advertisement to sell her, & rachel [sic] will be in tomorrow's paper."[24]

This, naturally, did not improve Henney's disposition. Only two days later little Ann McHenry leaned on Henney, "who pushed her away very roughly & said [Ann] should not lean on her I insisted she should," wrote Peggy. At this, "henney rose from her chair & said faith she would not sit to be leaned on, I was highly provoked & threatened her with the constable she wished to god I would & added if he came once he would never come again to her." As Henney must have feared, the advertisements worked, and when she realized that she would indeed be sold to another master, possibly less kind than the McHenrys, and would lose all hope of freedom, she relented. In mid-April Peggy wrote James that "she seems now to wish to stay with us—and I have told those who wanted her that I believed we would keep her."[25] Henney's ploy to both gain her freedom and stay in Maryland failed because she was young (twenty-four) with many good work years ahead of her. Since there was no financial incentive for the McHenrys to free rather than sell her, Henney went to Philadelphia as an indentured servant.

Rachel, although there is no record of her age, was old, at least by contemporary standards, and there was little work left in her. Peggy had also had some time to reflect and avoid acting in anger. The newspaper advertisement that had led to an offer for Henney had not resulted in one for Rachel. Now Peggy made the best of things and wrote to James, "there has been no offer for rachel she is too old—suppose we let her try to earn twenty pounds & pay for herself."[26] Despite Rachel's age, Peggy, like so many Baltimoreans, still thought herself entitled to some reparation for the loss of a slave, her prior service deemed insufficient somehow. Although the McHenrys received a sum, it was nominal. Her unpleasantness had drained Peggy of any desire to keep her, and because of Rachel's age she was unmarketable. Perhaps Peggy had also since learned that Pennsylvania's 1780 gradual emancipation law had limited indentures, especially of those over the age of twenty-eight. In any case, Rachel had won. She had cleverly finessed the situation so that it actually behooved the McHenrys to let her earn her freedom, and in such a way that she could remain in Maryland with her family.

The behavior of Rachel and Henney was contagious: another slave-woman named Priss joined in. Priss, Peggy wrote, "imitated the example [of Rachel] & said it would be a shame to take such a cripple as her—the poor creature conceits if she was free she could support herself & children when those who can sew twice as fast cannot subsist by their needle." Peggy did not record Priss's fate. But Peggy was right to worry that Priss might not be able to support her family. Many of the city's blacks were living in abject poverty, and as late as the 1830s more than 60 percent of the almshouse supplicants were women.[27]

A fourth woman named Patience did not scheme as did the first three. Pleased when Mrs. McHenry suggested eventual freedom through indentured servitude, Patience was obviously unhappy about leaving her husband and children, a family to which Peggy referred when she wrote to James, "her husband & her I suppose will have a great consultation about it today." One can only imagine the mixture of hope and grief expressed in that family meeting, but they apparently agreed she must go and earn her freedom. In the depths of her sorrow Patience alarmed Peggy by becoming "so much intoxicated that she could not stand."[28] After promising Peggy that it would not happen again, Patience accompanied the McHenrys to Philadelphia.

Indeed, Peggy's reference to the husband opens a world of interpretation and speculation. Interpretively, this slave family was acting as just that, a family, regardless of their legal status. Significant decisions were to be made jointly between the husband and wife, who were to have a "great consultation." And, as a great expression of familial love, the best interest of the individual was placed above physical proximity, offering a freedom that might, in the end, benefit all should Patience manage to purchase their liberty.

Mentor, the only male slave Peggy mentioned, played no games. In fact, he was so clear about his desire for freedom that Peggy made certain his servant's papers were correct, lest he take his freedom upon arrival up north, not waiting to serve out an indenture.

Three, then, of the five slaves used the changes wrought by Pennsylvania's gradual emancipation law to indenture themselves to future freedom in Philadelphia despite the fact that two at least were torn from their families. Rachel, the fourth slave, was the only one to win both her freedom and her family—but she won both only because of her age. Priss's fate is unknown. Despite their "slave" status, they had made quite active choices among admittedly limited alternatives. No more is known about these women, as the McHenry family now moved to Philadelphia and the correspondence between Peggy and James ended. Presumably, however, the arrangement worked to Peggy's satisfaction, as more than thirty years later she provided in her will for the gradual emancipation of two young slaves in her family's care.[29]

FIGURE 1. *James McHenry by James Sharples Senior, from life. c. 1796–1800.*
Independence National Historical Park.

FIGURE 2. *George Washington by Rembrandt Peale, after Rembrandt Peale, 1848.* Independence National Historical Park.

FIGURE 3. *John Adams by Charles Willson Peale, from life, c. 1791–1794.* Independence National Historical Park.

FIGURE 4. *Marie Joseph Paul Yves Roch Gilbert Motier, Marquis De Lafayette by Charles Willson Peale, after Charles Willson Peale, 1779– 1780.* Independence National Historical Park.

FIGURE 5. *Alexander Hamilton by Charles Willson Peale, from life, c. 1790–1795.* Independence National Historical Park.

FIGURE 6. *Timothy Pickering by Charles Willson Peale, from life, c. 1792–1793.* Independence National Historical Park.

FIGURE 7. *Oliver Wolcott by James Read Lambdin, after Ralph Earl, 1873.* Independence National Historical Park.

FIGURE 8. *James McHenry, head-and-shoulders portrait, right profile, by Charles Balthazar Julien Fevret de Saint-Mémin, 1803, Baltimore.* Library of Congress Prints andPhotographs Division.

FIGURE 9. *Margaret Caldwell McHenry (Mrs. James McHenry). Reproduced from the original owned by the heirs of Dr. James McHenry.* In Bernard C. Steiner, *The Life and Correspondence of James McHenry, Secretary of War under Washington and Adams* (Cleveland: Burrows Brothers, 1907), facing page 76.

FIGURE 10. *James McHenry. "From the miniature in the possession of the family."* Rosenthal Collection of Historical Portraits, c. 1880–1900. Accession #99, Special Collections, University of Virginia Library, University of Virginia, Charlottesville, Va.

PART THREE

Secretary of War

TWELVE "A Prudent, Firm, Frugal Officer"

Hugh Williamson

WHILE PEGGY DEALT WITH her predicament, James was sworn in immediately and discovered that political tensions in the capital were more extreme than he could have anticipated. Anxiety over foreign affairs infected both the administration and Congress. The war between England and France helped to sunder the new country's early unity, widening the fissure dividing the Federalists and Jeffersonian Republicans. Washington had hoped to negotiate separate peace treaties with each country, keeping the United States out of war with either, but the terms of Jay's treaty with England were now disseminated, and the fury over it had only increased. Many Americans despised the fact that, as had been leaked, the Jay Treaty accepted the British Rule of 1756, which denied freedom of the seas to American trade with France as long as England was at war with them. The concessions Britain gave—promising to leave America's northwest posts within two years, and granting Americans limited trading rights in the West Indies—felt relatively insignificant. Americans split bitterly over the Jay Treaty, and France, indignant that the country whose revolution she had assisted had made a separate peace with her enemy, now angrily attacked American shipping just as Britain had done for years. Earlier divisions over Hamilton's economic plans now combined with this hostility over foreign affairs, leading McHenry to observe as early as February 9 that "[t]he spirit of party has presided too much. There [is] . . . enmity to some at least of the executive, enmity to the funding system, enmity to our government, and a wild immoderate enthusiasm for French politicks."[1] Ironically the Jay Treaty *might* keep the republic out of war with England only to push it into war with France.

McHenry's job as secretary of war was to prepare for conflict with either country, and the possibility of hostilities was too strong to take matters lightly. There was no time for a slow and easy transition while Timothy Pickering, who had temporarily held the office, showed McHenry the ropes. And there were a lot of ropes to learn, for McHenry entered one of the two largest departments then in existence. Gordon S. Wood has recently stated that the Treasury Department was the largest, with thirty-one clerks and "over two thousand customs officials, revenue agents and postmasters scattered around the country." However, while the War Department had only five clerks, it had to oversee the construction of ships at three different locations, manage an army that included 3,000 officers and enlisted men around the country and in the far-flung frontier posts in 1796, and try to manage relations with the Native Americans. In addition, the budget for the War Department outstripped that of the State Department by about six and a half times. In 1795 it had comprised 38 percent of the federal budget. Perhaps for that reason it was, as Secretary of the Treasury Oliver Wolcott described it, a "difficult and unpopular department," requiring an excess of work. In fact, Pickering's brother-in-law, Judge Paine Wingate, could not decide in which office he thought his relative should serve. He liked Pickering's economy as secretary of war, but understood that the State Department would be "least laborious."[2]

In fact, this general desire for a frugal secretary of war had been made known to McHenry. Among the first to make this clear was Hugh Williamson, who had served at the Constitutional Convention and urged McHenry to accept the position. "Terror has seized the public mind from the apprehension that we should be reduced to a State of insolvency" by men who could not be budget-conscious. "Nothing is so fervently desired," he penned, "as that in our War Department, the Channel through [which] the great Part of our Treasure goes, we may have a prudent, firm, frugal Officer who in private Life having shown that he knows the Value of money may be expected to be equally attentive to the national Property."[3] Immediately, then, McHenry discovered the fundamental tension between a generally desired frugality and a strong defense. But even as he was coming to this realization, Congress made it clear that it hoped to reduce the military.

McHenry had barely entered office when Congress asked, "Ought the military force of the United States to be diminished?" But McHenry's job was defense, not frugality, so he presented four principles that argued against a possible reduction. The military had to be capable of preventing a possible invasion; was essential because the militia was inadequate;

counterbalanced the British and Spanish in the Northwest Territories; and desperately needed Congress to establish an officer's school.[4] In the end, McHenry emphasized the situation on the frontier. Even at this late date, the British had a much larger number of men in the Northwest than did the United States. That country's presence and influence over the Indians could not be ignored.

Congress would have been shocked to hear his other thoughts, which survive as notes jotted down on March 14. Here he argued that if the United States was strong, it could not be "drawn into war" by either England or France. The latter worried him most, for "France will make peace when she is no longer able to make war." He truly believed that "we must create a navy and always maintain a formidable army." Convinced, however, that it would take too long to establish an effective navy, he believed it essential that the country build up strong land forces. He favored an army of 12,000 and twelve ships of the line. Little wonder he did not include this, and its expense, in his formal presentation.[5]

Congress, on the other hand, did not see the situation in the same light. International affairs vexed it but it was not seriously considering war. So, although it gravely considered McHenry's report, it was not convinced. Indeed, another report by Pickering probably undermined McHenry's, for the New Englander believed that the United States had merely to occupy frontier posts: "The sole function of the army, according to Pickering's report, was to preserve a peace already made." Pickering thought it would be "inexpedient" to reduce the army before the country was clear about the "neighboring powers" and the Creeks, but that in a month or two it might be possible to reduce the army and hence save money. Washington, however, did not agree. Late in the previous October, Washington had written Hamilton that it would be "impolitic" to reduce the military establishment. Perhaps this helps to explain why Washington moved Pickering from the position of secretary of war to secretary of state.[6] In any event, if Pickering were to be believed, the situation did not sound serious. Instead of maintaining the army, Congress cut it by 40 percent, from over 5,000 to 3,000 men.

The fact is that the army had only been established at the larger size for war with the Indians in the Old Northwest. Knox, the first secretary of war, had organized this army into a Legion with four sublegions, each with its own cavalry, artillery, and infantry, enabling them to function as miniature armies in their own geographical areas. This idea had originated with Baron von Steuben and worked successfully against the Indians during war in the early 1790s. Mad Anthony Wayne had beaten over 1,000 Native Americans in Ohio at the Battle of Fallen Timbers with the Legion in 1794, and the ensuing Treaty of Greenville opened up parts of the Midwest that had been previously unavailable for settlement. But since that war had been won, Congress no longer saw the need for such an extensive military during peacetime. The Republicans, in fact, opposed such an army on principle, fearing the danger that a peacetime or standing army would be used to oppress the American people. Republicans believed the way to prevent this was to keep the army too small to effectively oppress the populace.[7]

But cutting the army so drastically meant Knox's old legionary organization no longer worked. So Congress decided to return to the regimental framework. McHenry's job consequently became even more difficult. Now he had to patrol an extensive frontier and seacoast fortifications with a seriously reduced army. Nonetheless, by the end of the summer McHenry had complied with the latest law and restructured the new army into regiments and reassigned officers. This restructuring, in fact, would last throughout the nineteenth century.[8]

If the state of foreign affairs could not make Congress continue to support a large army, tensions remained strong enough to cause both McHenry and Washington to watch even the smallest of their activities. Lafayette's son, whom Washington called "Young Fayette" but who was actually named for the president, had done all he could to get his father released and had now made his way to the United States. Naturally Georges Washington Lafayette wanted to see the president and, frankly, the feelings were mutual. Both men, however, were political creatures. Washington grew concerned that even meeting with the young man might have drastic political ramifications in this anxiously divided country. Washington asked McHenry's advice.

McHenry reluctantly acknowledged that Washington's political enemies might oppose a public reception of Lafayette's son. The French party in power had declared Lafayette an enemy of their revolution so that a public reception of young Lafayette *could* be seen as a repudiation of the current regime. Neither France nor the Republicans at home could be expected to approve, and McHenry acknowledged the difficulty of this situation.

Indeed, the situation was potentially even more complicated. One could certainly make the case for publicly receiving the young man on the grounds that he was a U.S. citizen and that France had not declared him a criminal. On the other hand, McHenry wondered just how Lafayette's son had acquired his passport out of France. Did the authorities let him leave with no questions asked, or did the young man conceal his identity? Might it be possible for France to consider him a fugitive?

Because they did not know the answers to these questions, McHenry thought it safer for everyone if Washington received Young Fayette privately, lodging him elsewhere.[9] And, of course, Washington must be prepared for the youth's entreaties in his father's favor.

But the bitterness of political reality overcame McHenry. "Is it possible that I can have written with such seeming coldness where the suffering and exiled son of Fayette is the subject," he asked, and "that I who would share with his father my fortune should be obliged by the imperious situation of things to advise that your goodness to his son should flow for a while in secret and unseen[?]"[10] It hardly seemed just.

Yet justice did win out, for it soon became apparent that the Republicans were not so enamored of the French Revolution that they were ready to forget the services of the Marquis de Lafayette. In fact, they favored receiving and helping the marquis' son in all ways diplomatically acceptable. Washington was now free to take the young man under his wing.

There was also an important ceremonial affair to attend, for on February 22 the president became sixty-four years old and Philadelphia insisted on massive celebrations. Bells chimed, cannons roared, and an elegant supper and ball were held.

The best birthday present Washington received, however, was undoubtedly the treaty Thomas Pinckney had negotiated with Spain. It was a generous treaty in which Americans got just about everything they wanted. Spain agreed to the Mississippi as America's western boundary and the thirty-first parallel as the southern boundary. Most important of all, Spain gave Americans free navigation of the Mississippi and free deposit of American goods at New Orleans for three years with the possibility for renewal. Doubtless Washington hoped this treaty's terms would make the stringent arrangements of the Jay Treaty more palatable. That was not the case. The effect, actually, was quite the opposite as Americans now thought better terms could have been achieved by a more determined and less Anglophile negotiator than Jay.[11]

In fact, the House of Representatives had not yet voted appropriations to implement the Jay Treaty. House Republicans, in fact, were angry at terms they believed benefited England and insulted France. In hopes of blocking the execution of the agreement, on March 24, 1796, they demanded all the papers relating to the Jay Treaty.[12]

Washington's discomfort at this request placed him in a quandary. He asked the members of his cabinet, and Hamilton who was outside the government, their opinions. This, actually, was Washington's style of administration and it served him well. Whenever an important issue arose he presented it to his cabinet and requested their opinions on paper and orally in meeting. He then considered the options and arguments himself and came to his own decision. Through Washington "the Cabinet as an institution for consultation and advice was firmly established."[13]

Recognizing that this was a legal issue and quite busy with War Department matters, McHenry in his turn consulted with Attorney General Lee, asking the latter if the House of Representatives actually had the right to refuse to vote the money necessary to implement a treaty.[14] By March 26 he had considered Lee's response and, mingling his own thoughts with Lee's, had his answer ready for the president.

In substance, McHenry and Lee agreed. On the one hand, McHenry argued that the president was under no Constitutional obligation to share the papers with the House. Only the agreement of the president and Senate were required to make treaties. The Senate had been included in these powers because each state had an equal vote and so each interest would be equally represented. Such was not the case in the House. Indeed, the president "knows such to have been the sense of the convention which framed it." Furthermore, a treaty "is a promise made for the whole nation and becomes obligatory upon the nation, consequently whatever is necessary to be done by the people or by any department of government to fulfil [sic] the promise cannot be refused without a violation of the national faith." On the other hand, if the president thought it expedient to hand over the papers he certainly could, especially if it might "avoid a great evil or obtain a great good." In fact, greater good would probably come from handing the papers over than withholding them, which might create more ill will. He also saw no need to acknowledge that the House had any real "right" to those papers. Nowhere did either he or Lee consider the precedence-setting effect such an action might have. This does not appear to have bothered them.[15]

Washington decided against sending the papers to the House. As he explained it to the congressmen, the treaty had been ratified by the Senate, signed by the president, and it was now law. The House had no part to play in the treaty-making process and of this he had no doubt because—and here he clearly drew from McHenry—he knew the Constitutional Convention had never intended to give it that power.[16]

Madison, who had done so much to help create the Constitution and was now leader of the Republicans in the House, must have been astonished at the response. He countered that treaties required the passage of laws by Congress and the passage of those laws gave the House the right, even duty, of deliberation. Outraged, the House had to respond to the president. Even some Federalists opposed the president on this one, and the House now engaged in a "week of pyrotechnics that brought men to their feet in every corner of the House."[17] It was clearly understood that the House had the power to block implementation of the treaty. Somehow the Republican assault on the treaty had to be broken.

Those Federalists who supported Washington began to act. McHenry wrote Maryland to ascertain public opinion and within five days he decided that serious measures needed to be taken. McHenry called upon the Maryland party machine to "instruct" their representative, Samuel Smith, to vote *for* appropriations. Although McHenry opposed instruction, he was not above using it. Only *with* the treaty, he argued, was the country strong. He wrote confidentially to Robert Oliver, one of the wealthiest and most important of Baltimore's merchants: "Can you do anything in this crisis? Can the Town be induced to do what may save the nation from being considered as violations of public faith . . . ? The address contemplated to the President is a good thing, but . . . may be laid aside for an instruction to Mr. Smith." The instruction, or petition, could be managed, McHenry insisted. "[Y]ou must only communicate with those you can trust in the first instance, and fix upon persons to carry it round the different wards at one and the same hour. By this means a certain party will not have time to take any measures to defeat it." This was critical, he insisted. "Fare well my dear Oliver. It is for Baltimore to save the republic."[18] McHenry, then, appealed to his party organization in Maryland to influence Smith and hence the House. His status as state party leader was critical.

The ploy worked. Samuel Smith, Republican representative from Maryland, informed the House that he would now vote *for* the appropriations, even though he detested it, because he had received such instructions from his state. "Here it was, the ebbing of opposition, the crack in the dike for which Federalists everywhere had worked so assiduously, and for which their spokesmen in congress had waited with taut nerves."[19] While leading Republicans continued to oppose the treaty, Federalists now attempted to persuade other more vulnerable Republicans.

Finally, on April 28, Fisher Ames of Massachusetts rose to speak, his brilliance and passion contrasting poignantly with his ill health. He denounced the notion that the House had any constitutional stake at hand. "On every hypothesis, therefore, the conclusion is not to be resisted: We are either to execute this treaty or break our faith. . . . No, let me not even imagine that a Republican government . . . a government whose origin is right and whose daily discipline is duty, can upon solemn debate make its option to be faithless, can dare to act what despots dare not avow!" Ames feared for the safety of western settlers, for rejection of the treaty would expose them to vicious Indian assault. "In the day time, your path through the woods is ambushed; the darkness of midnight will glitter with the blaze of your dwellings. You are a father: the blood of your sons shall fatten your corn-field! You are a mother: the war-whoop shall wake the sleep of the cradle! . . . I can fancy that I listen to the yells of savage vengeance, and the shrieks of torture."[20] In dramatic climax, the frail Ames spoke the words that cut to the hearts of all present—he feared that, despite his poor health, he might outlive the Constitution.

This was more than the Republican opposition could bear. Others such as Jonathan Dayton of New Jersey and Gabriel Christie of Maryland now changed their vote, and the House divided in a tied 49–49 vote. Then Republican Speaker Frederick A. Muhlenberg broke the tie in favor of an open session vote the next day; the appropriation passed 51–48. "The grand debate was over, the crisis surmounted, the British treaty safe."[21] McHenry, among others, had been instrumental in preserving the Jay Treaty.

Another treaty, this one with the Dey of Algiers, revealed an ongoing element of McHenry's relationship with Washington. Years before, the Algerian despot had attacked American ships entering the Mediterranean and kidnapped American sailors for ransom. In reaction, Congress had set aside money for a small navy and ordered the building of frigates to begin. Ever frugal and suspicious of the potentially oppressive and dictatorial powers of a standing army—or navy—Congress had included a provision that construction would stop upon the successful attainment of a treaty. After three years of negotiating, the United States agreed to pay "protection money" against any future kidnapping by the Algerians. The ransom would cost

$800,000 with a yearly "tribute" of $24,000. Although the deal stuck in everyone's throat, they generally agreed that the money would be well spent.[22]

In the meantime, however, the materials for the frigates had been procured, the keels laid, and the frameworks were now being built. It was an obvious waste of money already spent to simply quit building the frigates. Yet that was the letter of the law. After consultation with Attorney General Lee, McHenry suggested that Washington request a new act to complete the frigates. Congress agreed.

But, in an agreement tangential to the treaty, an armed frigate had also been promised the Dey. The War Department began work on this project in June but only one member of the department, a clerk named Fox, knew anything about naval matters. He could not draw up the plans until Pickering's State Department saw fit to forward the requirements diplomats had agreed upon. Then, as soon as he could be spared, Fox left to inspect and choose which naval yard would build the frigate.

Although McHenry had initiated these measures, he remained uncertain if this was a war or state department matter. Not wishing to step on territorial toes he consulted Washington, who mistakenly concluded that no work had been done regarding the frigate at all. Washington was, in fact, part of the problem. In June he had returned to Mount Vernon and remained there until mid-August. This left the administration of the government effectively in the cabinet's hands. In general the departments ran themselves, but McHenry had so many new matters of concern that he had to correspond repeatedly with the president for final decisions. If even a small matter was forgotten, it could lead to misunderstandings. Furthermore, this extra need for correspondence only added to McHenry's workload and surely helped bring on an illness around the first of July. So, Washington erroneously surmised that frigate matters had stood still. Displeased, Washington chided McHenry "not to put things off until the Morrow which can be done, and require to be done, to day."[23]

McHenry immediately understood the source of this admonition. It harked back to their relationship during the Revolution and the general's Military Family. Washington's quotation is, of course, a paternal adage, and McHenry could understand this in no other fashion. A part of their relationship was stuck in time. McHenry, however, responded without any apparent umbrage. Reassuring his elder, McHenry wrote, "as a child of your own, you must feel an interest in the course of my conduct, that I have endeavoured to follow the maxim you have laid down." McHenry explained that Pickering had, in the interim, agreed to place the frigate under McHenry's direction and that he was in search of the least expensive materials.[24] Washington, who had been unaware of this, now expressed his satisfaction. It was, however, only the first time that Washington would, on partial or erroneous information, be too quick to criticize McHenry.

Foreign affairs, the reason for all these treaties and frigates, remained ever at the forefront and decided internal domestic policy. Certainly most of McHenry's job was determined by foreign affairs. The American West was no exception. Not only did the U.S. military have to take over British forts in the Old Northwest without incident, but any foreign incursions by other powers had to be resisted in proper measure. After the implementation of the Jay Treaty, France now became the force to be reckoned with.

Indeed, Gallic anger seethed over the Jay Treaty, as goods in American ships bound for her were not protected but goods bound for England were. France saw this as both collaboration with the British to starve her into submission and a rejection of republican solidarity.[25]

The sharpness of this impression was not dulled by the American minister to France. James Monroe was such a Francophile that the administration began to question the quality of his diplomatic service. Because he fervently hoped to tie the United States to France he inappropriately overstepped his authority, accusing Jay of accepting an English bribe to support his own treaty. Monroe also took in the exiled Thomas Paine, who had fallen on hard times. Cast out from England, he had been granted French citizenship only to have it withdrawn under Robespierre; Paine was then thrown into prison due to a new law opposing foreigners. His appeals to the then American minister in France, Gouverneur Morris, had been denied since Morris judged Paine's internment less dangerous than the trial that would be necessary to get him out. When Robespierre fell and the Terror ended, Monroe replaced Morris and gave Paine a home. Infuriated at his treatment by the American government, Paine wrote blistering public attacks on Washington while under Monroe's roof. For these reasons, the administration simply no longer trusted Monroe.[26]

Washington wanted to be rid of him. But how? What was legal and proper? Concluding that another minister could not be sent without first recalling Monroe, the administration did so. When Monroe called for a public explanation, Pickering insisted that the president could not be called to answer for his decision to withdraw a subordinate officer. Monroe was simply out.

Who would replace Monroe? Through Wolcott, Hamilton urged Washington to send McHenry. "After turning the thing over and over in my mind I know of nothing better that you have in your power than to send McHenry. He is not yet obnoxious to the French and has been understood formerly to have had some kindness towards their Revolution," Hamilton wrote. "His present Office would give a sort of importance to the mission. . . . He is at Hand & might depart immediately & I believe he would explain very well & do no foolish thing."[27] Once again Hamilton acknowledged McHenry's strengths. He was honest, a committed Federalist, and temperate. But the suggestion went no further, and there is not even any evidence to indicate McHenry knew of Hamilton's recommendation. Washington chose Charles Cotesworth Pinckney instead.

In the meantime, however, France sent three "emissaries" out to the Old Northwest to gather information and spread talk of secession. Alarmed, McHenry ordered his western commander, General Anthony Wayne, to find a legal way to seize the men—Thomas Powers, Victor Collot (McHenry misspelled this "DeCallot"), and Warin—and their papers. For months Wayne and his men observed the "emissaries," waiting for the right time to strike. By the end of August a packet of letters had been intercepted that suggested that Collot answered to Pierre-Auguste Adet, French ambassador to the United States. Handling the matter delicately, Wayne arrested the emissaries without diplomatic scandal.[28]

Despite this success, Wayne struggled for power with another officer, James Wilkinson. At the heart of the problem lay Wilkinson's megalomania. Washington had known of his ambition for years, and had encouraged Wilkinson's attachment to the army precisely because he had, years earlier, plotted to annex Kentucky to Spanish Louisiana with himself in charge. Keeping Wilkinson in the army helped keep Kentucky in the Union.[29]

But retaining Wilkinson had a price, for he was as ambitious as ever. This time, however, Wilkinson aimed for advancement within the army— he wanted to be commander-in-chief out west. In fact, he had been pulling strings in Congress toward this end for some time and had almost received the command. The House had obliged him, but the Senate insisted on Anthony Wayne, hero of the Revolution. Wilkinson, however, had not played all of his cards. For some time he had sown discontent among the officers out west, fostering their complaints about Wayne and helping divide the military. At every opportunity, he informed the secretary of war, establishing a paper trail.[30]

Having lost the vote in Congress, Wilkinson now decided he had no choice but to force a court-martial. In essence, Wilkinson accused Wayne of gross mismanagement. Taking notes on the grievances Wilkinson laid before him, McHenry counted no less than twenty-one points charging Wayne with not dispensing enough power. Wayne had left him "without any general controul and responsibility," he had "no power lodged with him to punish delinquents or enforce obedience. . . . 'The health and comfort of the troops' . . . had been placed beyond any controul . . . implying a distrust in his [Wilkinson's] judgment."[31] The document reads as what it was—the grievances of a power-hungry man.

McHenry and Washington stalled, for they were not even certain that the Articles of War allowed for the commanding general to be court-martialed. Courts-martial had to be called by a superior and, amazingly, McHenry and Washington could not think of anyone in a position to begin the process. After Wilkinson traveled to Philadelphia and threatened to take the matter before Congress and thus make it public, Attorney General Lee concluded that a court-martial was indeed possible if called by the president in his role as commander-in-chief. While others had focused on the Articles of War, Lee let the Constitution sort it out.[32] It simply had not occurred to Washington and McHenry that the president as commander-in-chief could do this. This episode helped to establish that the president, a civil officer, was also the supreme commander of the military. Before any legal action could be taken, however, Wayne died. Since his position was almost ready to expire, the administration simply let it lapse. Wilkinson triumphed—he was now commanding general out west.

Wilkinson was not, however, the only subordinate discontented with his superior officer. Lieutenant Colonel Rochefontaine, commander at West Point, had lost the respect of his subordinates, who claimed he lacked the expertise to properly instruct and command them; a Court of Inquiry exonerated him and returned his command. The real problem was his military inferiors. "The officers of the newly-formed regiment of artillerists and engineers were a difficult lot to control. Most of them were too old for their grade, had little formal education, and were highly critical of Rochefontaine's methods." One Lieutenant Wilson even yelled out a window that

Rochefontaine was a "damned rascal." The two dueled, and, since neither was hurt, continued to brawl. This petty incident, the Wilkinson matter, and the reorganization of the army caused McHenry to draw up new and extensive rules and regulations for recruitment, post commands, and even the distribution of straw and fuel.[33]

As McHenry attempted to subdue and organize this unruly army, Congress explicitly redefined its nature. It was now the army's job to keep peace on the frontier, and that was to be done by restricting the Indians and whites to their own respective side of territorial boundaries. The army would deal with the tribes and detain and take legal action against whites who did not respect the borders. This, of course, "irrevocably committed the nation to a peacetime military establishment."[34]

It was, consequently, McHenry's responsibility to formulate the administration's Indian policy. Knox's Indian War and Pickering's Iroquois Treaty had settled matters in the Old Northwest, but the Southwest remained troubled. Unrest had persisted in the Georgia and Tennessee areas since white settlers, supported by their state governments, frequently encroached upon Indian land. The federal government's repeated attempts to keep the settlers out ended in resentment between the federal government and the Indians, on the one hand, and the settlers and state governments on the other.[35]

Everyone, however, agreed on the need for a new treaty, particularly with the Creeks. So McHenry sent three congressionally approved commissioners to treat at Coleraine on the St. Mary's River. Benjamin Hawkins, one of the commissioners and a man with long experience dealing with the Indians, found the Creeks especially recalcitrant on one point the federal government considered a sine qua non: they did not wish to sell any more land to the Georgia government. They felt there had been too many past "misunderstandings" between them and the government to place any trust in it.

The negotiations nonetheless produced the Treaty of Coleraine, which recognized the earlier boundaries that the Indians preferred and left Washington fearing the Georgians might not abide by the treaty's terms. On the president's order, then, McHenry sent more troops to the area and reshuffled those already there for maximum policing effect.[36] These things accomplished, the Creeks were taken care of at a basic level, at least for the time being.

Of course, McHenry and Washington both realized that there would continue to be trouble between the Indians and whites over land. From the administration's perspective, the hunting-and-gathering lifestyle that supplemented the southeastern Indians' agricultural diet simply required too much land. Since government efforts had not and probably would not stop the press of white settlement, only convincing the Indians to use less land would ease tensions. This, of course, meant asking the Indians to give up a part of their way of life. But both McHenry and Washington believed this was in the Indians' long-term best interest. McHenry hoped to "civilize" the Indians by converting the men to an exclusively agricultural life, with the women spinning and weaving. At least one of the Indian Agents, Silas Dinsmoor, thought the plan might work.[37]

So McHenry sent Dinsmoor and Hawkins, the two new Indian Agents, to draw the treaty's boundary lines and "civilize" the Indians. This complemented Washington's ideas, for he had earlier established public stores hoping that Indians might develop a taste for the white man's goods and try to produce them themselves. McHenry also hoped to encourage this by awarding medals to those Indians in the vanguard.[38]

Finally, McHenry invited the southern Indians to Philadelphia to meet with the president and receive personal assurances of both the government's strength and its goodwill. The Creeks, Chickasaws, Choctaws, and Cherokees all sent delegates. At one point, Washington hoped to make a presentation outlining the government's policies and attitudes. To that end McHenry drew up a speech, had it printed, and gave a copy to the secretary of state. Pickering approached the president in an all-too-typical, behind-the-back approach and strongly objected to its informality. True, Pickering had been successful in his dealings with the Seneca five years earlier, while McHenry's experience in Indian affairs had occurred at the level of committee work in the Continental Congress. But this episode reveals Pickering's unattractive side, a self-righteousness that sometimes led him to sabotage others. At Washington's urging, Pickering then drew up a similar speech of his own, the same as McHenry's in substance that at times even paraphrased his text. Indeed, it is only slightly more formal than McHenry's version. Washington liked neither and gave no speech. Even so, "[t]hese talks were successful in airing whatever grievances the Indians had and in strengthening their ties to the United States . . . they apparently returned home satisfied."[39] No doubt McHenry returned home satisfied as well, for if his speech was not read, the talks he had arranged helped the country to remain at peace with the Indians.

Washington fully recognized the now generally stable state of domestic affairs. Only the war between the French and British caused concern, and that could go on indefinitely. The president decided it was time to retire; he was tired and missed Mount Vernon. The country could elect a new president.

To Federalists, Vice President John Adams of Massachusetts was the clear and obvious choice. He had a long and distinguished national and international career and was Washington's choice as successor.[40]

But the Federalists also had to choose a vice-presidential candidate. Above all Hamilton and other Federalists thought it clear this position should go to a Southerner, for Adams was a dyed-in-the-wool New Englander and votes supporting him would come largely from the Northeast. A strong Southern candidate *should* ensure Federalist unity and victory at the polls. It did, however, occur to Hamilton and others that either northern or southern Federalists might not vote for the other section's candidate and that in this case the Republican candidate, Jefferson, might win. This last possibility was to be avoided at all costs.

For that reason Hamilton considered carefully who should run for the vice-presidency. When Patrick Henry declined, Hamilton embraced Thomas Pinckney, whom Gordon Wood describes as "most talked about" among Federalists for the vice-presidency. Pinckney was a good South Carolina Federalist who had returned from Spain with a very favorable treaty. Southern Federalists would support him. With this decision made, Hamilton now had simply to convince both sections of the party to vote the same way; if party members voted equally for both candidates, one of the Federalists would win. Nor did Hamilton especially care if Adams lost the presidency to Pinckney, for his trust in the man was limited and would decrease in the coming years. Adams was more independent than Hamilton might wish. Pinckney, on the other hand, pleased Hamilton. In fact, near the end of the election, Hamilton may have slightly favored Pinckney over Adams, but if so the southerner had only a small lead in Hamilton's mind. Assuming southern Federalists would naturally vote for Pinckney, Hamilton's call for party unity north of the Potomac might have elected Pinckney. In any event, the main object was to prevent the election of Jefferson.[41]

McHenry seems to have agreed that the Federalist Party should support both candidates. He corresponded with Federalists in Maryland, gathering their ideas concerning the state elections. In support of Adams, McHenry sent close friend and fellow Marylander William Vans Murray newspaper editorials by an essayist named "Phocion" who refuted the Republican attacks on Adams. Murray had written essays under the name "Union," but his approach had been to explain and defend Adams rather than merely respond to attacks. Also, when asked, McHenry supplied Murray information about the vice-presidential candidate.[42] While McHenry agreed with Hamilton that a Federalist should win, he himself did little more than support the party and gather information from his home state. There is no evidence that he pushed any policy that would work to Adams's detriment. Instead, McHenry played a straight partisan line.

As the campaign progressed and Washington reflected on his legacy, the president decided he wished to bid the country farewell. With Hamilton's help—he generally consulted the New Yorker—and assistance from earlier speeches drafted by Madison, Washington composed his Farewell Address. In the address, he explained his reasons for not serving a third term and cautioned against the divisiveness of parties—which is especially ironic since Hamilton and Madison were instrumental in creating intense partisanship. Finally Washington warned of the potential for permanent foreign alliances to drag others into war. He published the address that September in the *Independent Chronicle* and distributed it throughout the country he had worked so hard to build.

It was now, however, time to choose a new president. Ultimately, the electors in the Electoral College could vote for any two candidates they wished, and there was little actual partisan loyalty—although everyone knew who was running for which office and with which group. South Carolina voted sectionally and only for southerners Jefferson and Pinckney (as did an elector in Pennsylvania), despite the fact that they were from different factions. New England, for its part, apparently heard of Hamilton's plans and threw away enough votes for Pinckney to assure Adams's election to the presidency. But the vote was close: Adams received 71 electoral votes, Thomas Jefferson 68, Pinckney 59, and Aaron Burr 30.[43] Adams now became a Federalist president with Jefferson as his Republican vice-president.

At last March 4, 1797, arrived. Wearing a plain black coat, Washington attended Adams's inauguration. Adams was anxious about taking on the presidency, although he believed that he had earned it for his many years of high-level service. It would have been easier for him, however, had people expressed their enthusiasm for him rather than their sorrow in seeing Washington leave. Indeed, Adams felt somewhat chagrined by the affection for the general evident in the teary eyes facing him all around. The only person who seemed happy was the ex-president himself, who clearly thought that he, Washington, had the far better bargain of the two men. It was a strange and momentous event, this first transition of power from one president to another. Everyone—Adams, Washington, McHenry, Hamilton—must have wondered how smooth the transition to a new administration would be.

THIRTEEN

"Are We Forever to Be Overawed and Directed by Party Passions?"

John Adams

THE TRANSITION FROM Washington to John Adams was difficult even in Adams's earliest days. Certainly, Adams himself was part of the problem. Of average height and given the nickname "his rotundity" due to his middle-aged girth, he was brilliant and capable of great and honest introspection. But he could also be suspicious, jealous, stubborn, irascible, and often kept important thoughts to himself. This last quality proved questionable with regard to his cabinet, for Adams had chosen to keep Washington's men rather than imply any criticism of the former president's choices: McHenry as secretary of war, Pickering as secretary of state, and Wolcott as secretary of the treasury.

At present, foreign affairs worried Adams. Gallic anger over Monroe's recall worried Americans. Washington had already sent Charles Cotesworth Pinckney to replace Monroe, and many now considered it wise to send two more men to France to comprise an extraordinary commission. Such a mission had gone to England to negotiate the Jay Treaty, and corresponding treatment might appease France. Hamilton had suggested such a mission to Washington before the latter left office, and now Adams gave the matter serious thought.[1]

But who else should join Pinckney? Adams first consulted with Vice-President Jefferson, who demurred, and then turned to Oliver Wolcott. Adams's idea was to dispatch someone high in the Republican ranks to assuage both the other party and the other country. But when Adams asked Wolcott's thoughts regarding Madison as commissioner, the response astonished him.[2] Shocked, Wolcott blurted out his fears. Madison had opposed the Jay Treaty, fought assumption, and consistently resisted Washington's—and Hamilton's—programs. Madison and Jefferson together had created the Republican party alliance, seemingly destroying unity and transforming everything into a struggle. "Sending Mr. Madison will make dire work among the passions of our parties in Congress, and out of doors, through the states!" But Adams, who had hoped to calm rather than agitate the waters, inquired, "Are we forever to be overawed and directed by party passions?" In "profound gloom and solemn countenance" Wolcott spoke for the cabinet. They did not trust Madison and if Adams chose to send the Republican leader, "we are willing to resign."[3]

This was a bold statement; had Adams consulted the more temperate McHenry, the conversation would almost certainly not have ended in this threat, and if it had, the delivery would have been much gentler. Although McHenry felt strongly about the composition of the mission, he also hoped to have a cordial and cooperative relationship with this new president. In fact, McHenry and his clerks had spent many hours copying all their significant documents for the new president, involving hundreds of pages of materials regarding Indian treaties, agents, talks, the army and navy, forts, and military stores. It was both a professional and considerate act, since McHenry knew that Adams would be only vaguely aware of his office's policies and history.[4]

Hence, Wolcott's astonishing move was indeed telling, for the cabinet's threat to resign reflected both their deep feelings on this issue and their assessment of Adams. Statesman though he was, Adams did not carry Washington's authority. Despite his illustrious political career, he failed to inspire men to follow him, and the cabinet was no different.[5] Indeed, they undoubtedly still thought of Adams as vice president, as the second man rather than the first. Wolcott's outburst showed clearly that the cabinet was, as Adams already knew and accepted, mentally and politically independent of the new president. But they were all good Federalists, and Adams had won the presidency by only three votes; in retaining the cabinet he aimed to keep the support of the greatest number of Federalists. Adams also did not wish to appear to be critical of Washington's choices; ousting them would have thus cost him politically.[6] So Adams faced a group of people with set habits and ideas regarding government policy. Establishing new patterns and authority would be an uphill struggle, and this act of the cabinet's was not a good sign.

Adams made it clear that he did not want anyone's resignation, and there the matter lay, except that it left incorrect impressions. It gave Wolcott the impression that he had single-handedly averted a Madison mission to

France and hence that Adams was relatively malleable.[7] And it gave Adams the mistaken notion that the secretaries were in greater agreement than they were, even that they were in league together.

Adams's error was partly due to the fact that Wolcott and Pickering tended to use the "royal we" somewhat freely. In this case, there is evidence to corroborate Wolcott's use of the term; but such a striking event so early in Adams's administration led the president to assume incorrectly that these three members of the cabinet acted in unison in all things.[8] While it is true that they sometimes acted jointly, they more often differed, and these differences received less attention than they deserved.

In fact, their rejection of Madison was about as far as cabinet agreement went, but Adams simply could not or would not see significant divisions. Pickering was a stubborn man, opinionated and self-righteous. Always convinced that he was correct, he easily rationalized his backstabbing behavior, which could be aimed at anyone—including the president and McHenry. Wolcott hailed from Connecticut, had cut his political teeth in the Department of the Treasury under Hamilton, and consistently fed the New Yorker sensitive administrative information while retaining both his position and Adams's goodwill. McHenry was a Washingtonian, pure and simple. But his temperament was fair enough to wish to serve Adams honorably. He refused, however, to be a "cipher" or rubber-stamp, and would defend his position if he believed the president was wrong.

To complicate matters, late in March, news arrived that France had refused to receive Pinckney as minister-in-residence to replace Monroe and had expelled him from the country. The situation with France was serious, since that country had earlier suspended the Treaty of Amity and Commerce of 1778 in order to free its hands to oppose Washington's reelection. In fact, Pierre Adet, French minister to the United States, had been ordered to proclaim publicly that reelecting Washington might cause war. Although Americans resented such high-handed interference, Washington's decision to retire took the power out of the French threats.[9]

In early 1797, then, Adams faced possible trouble with a France still angry over the Jay Treaty and generally disdainful of the upstart republic across the Atlantic. Taking the lead, the new president called for a special session of Congress to meet on May 15 and asked cabinet members for their written opinions on fourteen points concerning relations with France. Could the United States honorably send another diplomatic mission, and if so, what should the nature of a new treaty with France be, and what ought Congress be told?[10]

McHenry must have groaned to see the questions before him, as he had successfully run this difficult department only through unremitting work; this was especially true since his duties as secretary of war included managing the interior, where the Spanish were causing real problems by their sluggishness in leaving the Southwest posts. McHenry was stretched beyond his limit, taking care of a fledgling navy, seacoast fortifications, the army, and trouble in the West. McHenry immediately realized he did not have time and that he would have to delegate.[11] But the western trouble was international in scope and too delicate to hand to his clerks, who were also overstretched.

McHenry decided to consult Hamilton. In some sense this was business as usual, for under Washington he had sought legal advice from Hamilton and Attorney General Lee a number of times. Washington, Pickering, and Wolcott had themselves repeatedly consulted Hamilton; the New Yorker was good at this sort of thing. Pickering, for example, had requested a point-by-point response from Hamilton regarding the Jay Treaty. McHenry also knew that Hamilton would oblige, since three weeks earlier the secretary of war had received an unsolicited letter from the New Yorker—as had Pickering—giving notice that his services were available. Indeed, this is how Hamilton maintained his status as Federalist Party leader even while he held no government position. In the letter, Hamilton had also urged a three-man commission to France; since the president, McHenry, and Hamilton all favored a mission to France, Hamilton's help would be useful.[12]

Although McHenry clearly intended to rely on Hamilton's work, he would alter whatever did not comport with his own views. "I must intreat you to consider yourself on the ground you once occupied, and to give me your answer at length that I may avail myself of your experience knowledge and judgement." He explained, "I have not time to go into all the detail and research which is necessary. You have all at your fingers ends. I shall rely upon your friendship & patriotism for a sound opinion as soon as your avocations permit."[13] Appreciating the political delicacy of the matter at issue, McHenry also enjoined Hamilton to secrecy.

This episode should have been a warning signal that McHenry needed more assistance within his own office and not outside it. He did not see the problem clearly enough to act upon it until the end of the year. In the meantime, McHenry drew up an incomplete response of his own that illustrated his preeminent focus on the military. He suggested reminding the country of France's transgressions and urged augmentation of the military, arguing "it is visionary for the U.S. to expect that they may continue in a state of naval and military imbecility during these frequently recurring wars between European nations."[14] McHenry never even mentioned whether another mission should be sent.

Fortunately, a more detailed response arrived from Hamilton with which McHenry generally agreed. As he had done in the past when he received advice from Attorney General Lee, McHenry copied what he agreed with, changed what he did not, and handed it to Adams. The most important alteration McHenry made reminded the president that countries do, after all, have the right to accept or reject ministers from other countries. Therefore, "France cannot be considered as a violator of the laws of nations, nor the *simple act of refusal*, as a *just cause of war*."[15] McHenry's reply to Adams, then, favored an extraordinary mission, negotiation, and an increase in defense measures. The position was moderate.

With some difficulty, the rest of the cabinet came to agree that an "extraordinary mission" should be sent. Charles Lee, attorney general, most readily favored such a mission, as well as a more general equalization of relations among the United States, France, and England. Wolcott agreed to a three-man commission (sans Madison) only after Hamilton wrote him urging one. The secretary of the treasury did not want war but was convinced that the French were completely unjustified in refusing to receive Pinckney and wanted France to accept him. Pickering supported the mission even more grudgingly. Of the three cabinet officers he had been angriest with France, writing Hamilton that "we more than doubt the propriety" of sending an extraordinary commission. "This new mission is what the enemies of our government wish for." But he had since changed his mind, possibly because of Hamilton's influence, favoring a mission as long as none of the "fraternizing words" that had characterized the Monroe mission were used. France might be an ally but not a friend.[16] The implacable sternness to Pickering's temperament could not bend far.

Meanwhile, McHenry had to provide Adams with some specific estimate of necessary defense measures. After all, the peace mission might not succeed. In March he had drawn up a preliminary plan and sent it to Hamilton for comments. The two agreed in principle on the steps to be taken, differing mainly on the size of the army (Hamilton, whose military tastes tended to a grand scale, wanted 25,000 men while McHenry suggested only 10,000). In his "Proposals of Defense" handed to Adams on April 8, McHenry divided necessary defense measures into "actual" and "contingent" categories. "Actual" referred to forces needed against France alone; but if Spain allied with France, "contingent" forces would be needed. McHenry's proposal to Adams included the 10,000-man provisional army noted above, which the president and the cabinet increased to 13,000. McHenry also suggested three new frigates, six sloops, improved harbor forts, regiments of artillerists and engineers, and companies of dragoons. He also warned that his plans presumed that France's crippled navy would not attack the coast, that Spain would "remain neutral and friendly along the Mississippi," and that peace would reign between settlers and Indians on the frontier so that western soldiers could be transferred to the East—none of which he honestly believed could be counted on.[17]

Adams's speech to Congress pleased Federalists with its aggressiveness. It also drew upon both McHenry and Pickering. After describing America's complaint against France, he on the one hand assured Congress that "I shall institute a fresh attempt at negotiation, and shall not fail to promote and accelerate an accommodation on terms compatible with the rights, duties, interests, and honor of the nation."[18] But he also emphasized the need for a provisional army; a reorganized militia; and a navy, especially important to Adams, who came from the seafaring state of Massachusetts.

To choose the mission's members Adams called another cabinet meeting. He still liked the idea of three ministers and favored Pinckney, John Marshall of Virginia, and Elbridge Gerry of Massachusetts. Fifteen years later McHenry wrote, "I well remember the meeting, for I have often thought of it since. It was composed of Mr. Wolcott, yourself [Pickering], Mr. Lee and myself. Mr. Adams, in a familiar way, said 'Gentlemen, what think you of Mr. Gerry for the mission?'" It turned out to be a loaded question. "None of the gentlemen offering to speak, I observed: 'I have served in the old Congress with Mr. Gerry. If, sir, it was a desirable thing to distract the mission, a fitter person could not perhaps, be found. It is ten to one against his agreeing with his colleagues.'" The silence was palpable. "Mr. Wolcott made some remark. Mr. Lee and you were silent. Mr. Adams replied: 'Mr. Gerry was an honest and firm man on whom French acts could have no effect. He had known him long and knew him well.' I well remember the meeting, for I was next to incurring his enmity." In fact, according to Gerry's biographer George Athan Billias, Gerry was just as honest as Adams described, and equally independent, which McHenry found so "distracting." Like minds on the mission would certainly be desirable. Adams agreed to substitute his old diplomatic connection Francis Dana of Massachusetts who, however, pled poor health; the president revived Gerry's candidacy.[19]

Behind the scenes, McHenry reconsidered the wisdom of sending three men. No Republicans had been chosen even though this was to have been a bipartisan mission. Although the opposition acknowledged Pinckney's integrity, McHenry worried that he might be insulted by the addition of two more men. "For my own part, I have not been able to discover any advantage attending a trio. It will please nobody, not even those that may be nominated and will not ensure the United States against a single possible evil, nor create to government one additional friend."[20] But he soon realized it was too late, the decision had been made, and it was certainly not worth offending Adams again by urging changes.

The secretary of war's job now was to get Congress to act on the contents of Adams's speech, so he sent his recommendations for the new frigates and the provisional army to Federalist William Loughton Smith, McHenry's main contact in the House of Representatives. Although Smith presented pertinent resolutions in June, the Republican opposition would not increase the army. On the other hand, Congress did approve $115,000 to fortify ports and harbors, agreed to the manning of the three existing frigates, and ordered 80,000 militiamen to stand ready. Since Congress now adjourned, any further measures would have to wait until the next session.[21]

The South and West now consumed McHenry's attention, leading him to adopt a policy that sought dual ends: internal union and external respect. This developed as a reaction to the continuing rumors of conspiracies, some with a basis in reality. Certainly his earlier experiences caused McHenry to distrust the French. "You will see by the inclosed reports to the President the further disclosure of French projects," he wrote to Washington. "It would seem as if nothing short of a dismemberment of the union, and having a part of it under French protection would satisfy the Directory. After gaining this point, at which I am sure they aim France will then play for the whole."[22] So McHenry hired spies to follow each move of every suspicious Frenchman in the West. One of these spies, Felix de Saint Hilaire, came to Philadelphia for money in the late spring and summer of 1797. He gave McHenry trunks full of information, passed discreetly and sometimes piecemeal, before he returned to the West. Some of the letters still bear the fold marks that condensed them into tiny pieces in order to be passed secretly from hand to hand.

But the French knew McHenry was aware of their activities. One letter by Cominges to a "General" (Wilkinson?) said, "If I did not have definite orders to separate this province away from the others, I would not bother to do so because I despise the people so much. McHenry, the new Minister of war is a shrewd man, I know his ploys; keep a close eye on him. The old Knox acted carelessly."[23] The French menace, however, amounted to little more than this. Still, McHenry remained attentive.

France's disdainful conduct continued. France was a major power, had long appreciated her position, and the Revolution had not altered this. Indeed, amateurs who frequently indulged in bullying tactics often handled her international diplomacy. Furthermore, while France was interested in the entire world, there was an important sense in which America was inconsequential to Gallic plans.[24] So, while France plotted to split the West from the United States, it is also true that the French did not consider this to be of great moment.

The West was, however, of importance to McHenry, who sent out military and Indian agents to be his eyes and ears, the most informative being John McKee. Andrew Ellicott, commissioner to draw the survey between Indian and white settlers' lands, had been sent out the previous year and proved another reliable source. Plots relayed by the two distressed the government and mortified most Republicans, since one of their number was involved in the first and most prominent.

This was the Blount Conspiracy, a scheme among western Americans with the potential to cause a serious international incident.[25] The goal, of course, was profit, and obtaining land that did not belong to the United States. Republican Tennessee Senator William Blount had purchased a great deal of land on a bend of the Tennessee River known as Muscle Shoals. Muscle Shoals was not far from another large river, the Tombigbee, which flowed down to Mobile. Speculators like Blount who purchased land at Muscle Shoals planned to build a canal from the Tennessee to the Tombigbee, creating a major north-south water route independent of the Mississippi. The problem was that Mobile was then in the Spanish Floridas. If Mobile could be taken, this new water route would free the United States from dependence on Spain for use of the Mississippi—and also enrich Blount. Knowing that the United States could have nothing to do with such a plan, the speculators plotted independently.

The schemers first spread the rumor that Spain was going to give Louisiana and the Floridas to France. This, they expected, would alarm most westerners, for France would be a more imposing western presence than the weak Spanish. Volunteer soldiers could then be raised to strike at Spanish territory with British help. England would get Louisiana and the Floridas, while the adventurers would receive half the private property and public funds as well as grants of land in thousand-acre parcels. The administration clearly had to act or face a slew of adventurers bent on illegal land grabs—but the government also feared a groundswell of popular hatred against England. To cushion the blow, Pickering gave British minister Robert Liston a chance to disavow the plan before the Senate received the evidence. The administration also continued to support the British. Shocked that Blount had placed personal profit ahead of the country's needs, the Senate expelled him in a 25–1 vote, and considered impeaching him. By 1799, however, the Senate realized it lacked jurisdiction over an ex-member; the next year Blount died.[26] So ended the Blount Conspiracy.

But Blount's was not the only plot. Throughout the spring of 1797, it became clear that the Spanish would not honor Pinckney's treaty and abandon their posts in American territory.[27] For the Spanish, the international situation had changed tremendously. Spain had been allied against revolutionary France in 1792, but three years later the French had made separate peace arrangements with them. Hence, Spain was no longer England's ally, but rather that of France. To secure her pre–Pinckney Treaty holdings, Spain fomented trouble in the American West. Spanish emissaries encouraged new settlement in the area, to be followed by secession from the United States. McKee wrote from Natchez that the Spanish had been giving presents to the Creeks, Cherokees, and Choctaws, and urging the tribes to oppose the United States' boundary survey. McKee also sent word of Wilkinson's collusion with the Spanish to lure Kentucky out of the Union. Rumors like this pervaded the West, but the administration lacked sufficient proof to act.

The Spanish presence in the American West could not simply be ignored, however, so McHenry developed a carrot-and-stick policy to separate the Spanish from the land. As an enticement, the Spanish could destroy their forts and their settlers could petition Congress to keep their homes and count on an equitable adjustment of their claims. McHenry also ordered more gifts for the Indians, with the injunction that they not be seduced by the other countries. Then he ingratiated the most important trading firm in the area, Panton, Leslie & Co., ordering McKee to allow the company un-identified "indulgences" when collecting their debts from the area Indians.[28] This would strengthen American influence in the area without physically threatening the Spanish and risking an unnecessary incident.

But these acts would take time to have effect, and in the interim McHenry received word that the Spanish were actually strengthening their posts at Natchez and Walnut Hills. It seems that they "had heard rumors of a British plan to descend the Mississippi and seize Lower Louisiana" from the Span-ish, who were no longer England's allies.[29]

Clearly, more needed to be done. Adams, for his part, recommended to Congress that a government similar to that in the Northwest Territory be established. Still, the United States did not wish to risk an incident by set-ting up a territorial government until the Spanish were out. Unbeknown to the administration, western settlers in Natchez decided to help solve that problem. The settlers staged a revolt, imprisoning the Spanish governor in his own fort. They demanded that the district's neutrality be respected, that the militia be reserved for Indian attack or riot, that Spanish law be admin-istered mildly, and that trials take place within the district. Although the Spanish retained nominal control, this incident signaled "virtually the end of the Spanish regime in the district."[30]

Now the "stick" portion of McHenry's policy commenced, involving a "hardening of the American position" against the Spanish. McHenry com-manded Wilkinson to remind the Spanish governor of Pinckney's Treaty and of the need to abandon their forts. Further, McHenry ordered the arrest of any anti-American agitators found among the Indians, and the Indians were to be rewarded for informing. More soldiers were being sent to in-crease American strength on the Mississippi. This would place the United States in an optimal position both to keep present territory and, if neces-sary, to create a "new frontier"—that is, to obtain the Spanish Floridas and control of the Mississippi "should hostile acts on the part of France + Spain render a new frontier a just + necessary measure."[31] McHenry's policy now required time to work. No more could be done, short of war. By the follow-ing April, the policy worked—the Spanish left their forts.

In the meantime, Adams retreated to Quincy on July 19, 1797, leaving the government in the cabinet's hands until at least mid-November. Adams simply saw no necessity to stay in Philadelphia, and an ailing Abigail needed him back home. True, most of the government abandoned the capital at some point during the summer because the city invariably experienced an epidemic.[32] But they lodged in nearby country towns where they could communicate with each other easily and swiftly. By retiring all the way to Massachusetts, Adams virtually left the government in the cabinet's hands. Of course, they were expected to correspond with the president, informing him of important matters and leaving any major decision up to him. This year his absence did not matter a great deal.

But it would be an unfortunate precedent. It certainly made the secretaries' jobs more difficult. They could no longer simply speak with the president but now had to write to keep him informed, and correspondence more than doubled. In addition, the cabinet could not resist the rather human conclusion that they were the real government, or the "'actual' administration," as Hamilton called them. Washington, for his part, had been absent only 181 days in seven years, and while he was gone the cabinet had his written permission to execute whatever they might legally and properly need to do. Adams, on the other hand, would be away for 385 days in four years. He was, in fact, absent for four out of his first nine months in office.[33] The long-term consequences would be serious.

More serious to McHenry in the latter part of the summer, however, was the intensity of this year's epidemic. Unlike most other Federalists, McHenry consulted his old mentor, Benjamin Rush, regarding the "prevailing fever." Rush had become a Jeffersonian Republican and still bled with relative freedom, while another physician, Edward Stevens, prescribed quinine bark and cold baths. Stevens and Hamilton had been friends since their childhoods in the Caribbean and the doctor had brought Hamilton through his 1793 bout with yellow fever. As a consequence, most Federalists now preferred Dr. Stevens. But McHenry had a history with Rush, and the secretary of war was not one to forget old friends or treat them unkindly. It is also possible that McHenry still adhered to his friend's teachings. On Rush's advice, McHenry moved both the War Office and his family to a place near Downingtown until the pestilence subsided.[34]

Despite his evacuation from Philadelphia, McHenry once more suffered a severe attack from a "bilious fever," which may have been the disease ravaging the city. This illness hit him hard, all the more so because he did not allow himself sufficient time to recuperate, but kept working on War Office business. Indeed, on September 24 he wrote Pickering, "I am however very far from recovered in strength or appetite, am frequently feverish and on the edge of a relapse."[35]

Try as he might, the illness prevented him from staying on top of his business. He soon had to set priorities, deciding to give special attention to the West. This meant occasionally handing business over to his colleagues. For example, when one of the frigates neared its date of completion and launch, McHenry sent the relevant papers to Pickering, who was closer to the harbor. And in mid-October he wrote Wolcott of his "entire concurrence with the line of march which you have suggested for the troops." Once he was well, it still took time to catch up with the press of business. A week later he apologized to Pickering for not acknowledging receipt of Pickering's letters. "If I have not noticed them sooner it was because I knew that you would find an excuse for it in your friendship for me. The fact is I have been so much occupied with the North West + the South that I am tired of life, I mean of public business which leaves me no time to enjoy it." But in reality, McHenry presumed too much of Pickering and Wolcott, who failed to appreciate the amount of work the office demanded and that the department needed more clerks. They would instead become uncharitable.[36]

Adams, however, was pleased with McHenry's work, especially that connected with the West where McHenry concentrated his attention. "I thank you Sir for your indefatigable attention to all these subjects. The Letters and Instructions to the Officers especially to General Wilkinson appear to me to be well weighed, and judiciously decided."[37]

In October Adams had to consider the content of his upcoming speech to Congress. Again the president consulted the cabinet, this time through correspondence since he was still in Massachusetts. McHenry and Wolcott independently concluded that nothing had changed since the president's earlier speech and that he ought to strike much the same note.[38] Adams agreed and, with Pickering's help, wrote a speech urging both peace and defensive preparations.

McHenry had by now come to realize that his office had to run more efficiently; it had to be able to handle occasional difficulties. Of course, others had experienced similar troubles. When Pickering was postmaster he "allowed himself too few clerks to keep his work always in hand—and he had no subordinate in either of his Cabinet posts other than clerks. Files sometimes were lost or misplaced, and on one occasion Washington was much irritated: 'The business . . . has been shamefully neglected.'"[39]

Under McHenry's War Department, however, one persistent difficulty involved finances—or to be more specific, the departmental accountant.

Back in 1791, Congress determined that poor supplies had contributed to St. Clair's Defeat and gave Secretary of the Treasury Hamilton control of the War Department's finances. As a result, in order to procure money from the treasury, McHenry had to send over a requisition, which also had to be countersigned by the departmental accountant. Although the department had a budget it should have had easy access to, in practice either the secretary of the treasury or the departmental accountant could stymie the process.

William Simmons, accountant for the War Department, occasionally declined to countersign the requisitions. In this case, Simmons stood in the way of the implementation of McHenry's western policy. The accountant had clearly overstepped his authority, and McHenry decided it was time to let him know it. So McHenry called in the president, who in turn asked Lee's and Pickering's opinions. As all sided wholeheartedly with McHenry, the president wrote that "[t]he Secretary of War is the sole judge of the time and manner of making disbursements." This put Simmons in his place—temporarily. It was important, for it "made the Secretary's position supreme under the President in military matters."[40]

But the accountant was only one of McHenry's problems in the War Department, for McHenry's chief clerk, John Stagg, decided to retire. This led two lesser staff members to apply for the position. One had worked in the department for twelve years and naturally believed his seniority gave him preference. Indeed, not getting the position would mean that his "mortification will be extreme." The other, Samuel Lewis, had worked there four years but had a large and growing family to support. McHenry chose neither of them, instead looking outside the department for a chief clerk with legal experience.[41] In fact, he hired Peggy's brother, attorney John Caldwell.

This process, however, finally forced him to assess the needs of his office for more assistants, not just a new chief clerk. The original appropriation had initially supported seven civil servants but now only sustained five. After outlining clearly the duties of each of the five, McHenry pointed out that they were fully occupied with their work—and that the "business not comprized in this assignment to the Clerks, remains either to be neglected or [executed] by the Secretary alone." As a result, so much business came before McHenry in a massive and crude form that he had to wade through it all himself before putting it through proper channels. No doubt things had improved somewhat in 1797 with the death of William Knox, Henry

Knox's mad brother who had served in the War Department, but even sane clerks could not keep up with the press of business. McHenry's complaints did not even include the Marine Department, which required its own group of clerks. The press of business now taxed McHenry so that his tired mind could not summon its usual clarity. "What can more comport with a due regard to national economy," he complained to Adams, "than to put it in the power of the head of an important department to devote a proportionate share of his time . . . to the higher functions of his Office?" This could only be possible "by affording him adequate assistants."[42] McHenry simply had little time to consider the larger problems and policies of his office because he was mired in a mass of details that *should* have been sorted out by a subordinate. So on December 30, 1797, McHenry requested Adams's support in hiring new personnel.

Since Adams agreed, on January 5, 1798, McHenry sent his request for more clerks to the House of Representatives. The House referred it to the Committee of Revisal and Unfinished Business where it languished, while the House concentrated on the more interesting issues of Blount's expulsion and foreign relations.[43]

Adams remained especially concerned about relations with France. What should be done "[i]f our Envoys Extraordinary should be refused an audience, or after an audience, be ordered to depart without accomplishing the objects of their missions."[44] Most significantly, Adams wondered if a declaration of war should follow a rejection of the envoys.

McHenry immediately sent Adams's questions to Hamilton, whom he now treated as something of a free consultant, this time not even pleading the press of business but instead the importance of the subject. A wrong step could be "extremely injurious, or beget disagreeable consequences." Besides, he flattered, "I am sure I cannot do such justice to the subject as you can."[45] This flattery aside, McHenry definitely had his own opinions. He did not think the country was ready for war. Most people, he had written only the previous November, supported the administration but also favored peace and exhibited a strong "apathy" to French insults.

Hamilton agreed that there was "a strong aversion to War in the minds of the people of this Country." Instead Hamilton recommended a "mitigated hostility [as it] leaves still a door open to negotiation and takes some chances, to avoid some of the extremities of a formal war."[46] Hamilton had, of course, provided a detailed response to Adams's questions—and again the two men generally agreed on positions. So McHenry, as he had done before with both Lee and Hamilton, changed what he disagreed with and handed his modified version to Adams.

McHenry suggested a number of things, the first four of which involved naval service. Merchant vessels should be armed, twenty sloops of war found, the three frigates finished quickly, and, in the event of conflict, the president should be given authority to fit out ten ships of the line. Certainly the treaties with France ought to be suspended, troops raised, and a provisional army authorized. But McHenry again thought Hamilton's troop numbers too high, and reduced the number for the regular army from 20,000 to 16,000 and for the provisional army from 30,000 to 20,000.[47]

In addition, McHenry argued, like Blount, that the United States ought to cooperate with England's navy against the Floridas, Louisiana, and Spain's Latin American possessions. If successful, the United States would receive as spoils all the land east of the Mississippi River; to leave no doubt, McHenry added New Orleans to this plan.[48] Since McHenry alone among the cabinet officers answered Adams's questions (Were they also too pressed for time? Did they find out and acquiesce to Hamilton's consultation?), Hamilton's influence on the president was probably great.

While Adams considered these suggestions, the House of Representatives unhappily pondered McHenry's request for more money to complete the frigates. He had been warned when he took the job that they wanted a frugal secretary of war, and the House now protested the frigates' escalating costs. Edward Livingston, a Republican who opposed the navy and defense measures in general, chaired the committee to investigate the frigate situation.[49] It was he who called upon McHenry to explain delays and added expenses. They wanted a full accounting.

McHenry gave them what they wanted, and candidly listed the problems. These had begun with former Secretary of War Knox's decision to create six different navy yards at varying locations along the seaboard. While this divided the spoils, it also decentralized control. Attempts to reduce the corruption had also dragged the process out. To make matters worse, the ships had been enlarged, increasing the amount of high-quality live white oak needed; the cost of labor had risen; and some items had simply been lost. The accounting McHenry gave was clear and aboveboard. If the investigative committee had been hoping for scandal, it did not find one. Others might not be happy with the military expenses, and they might wish to blame McHenry, but they could find no cause.

It had been a complicated first year serving Adams. At the very time that he and his clerks worked heroically to copy documents for the new president, he had agreed with Wolcott and Pickering to resign if Adams chose Madison as a minister to France. He created a carrot-and-stick approach out west that showed promise. Throughout it all he worked, ceaselessly, until he could work no more. At that point he continued consulting with others, especially Hamilton, as he had under Washington. When he finally fell ill, he relied on Pickering and Wolcott. Still, Congress would approve no clerks. The question was, how long could this last?

FOURTEEN "Mitigated Hostilities"

James McHenry

ON MARCH 4, 1798, even as McHenry learned about the success of his western policy, news of the XYZ Affair arrived from the Envoys Extraordinary to France.[1] A coup d'état the previous fall had led to the appointment of a new foreign minister, Talleyrand, who thought he could retaliate against Federalists for the Jay Treaty without serious repercussions. He planned to humiliate and discredit the Adams administration without doing anything serious enough to result in war. The Frenchman remained easy in these expectations partially because he overestimated the Republican ability to thwart the Federalists. So Talleyrand met unofficially with the American envoys and then sent three unofficial agents, later labeled "X," "Y," and "Z," who desired three things before negotiations could begin. The Americans were to account for the harshness of Adams's speech in May of the preceding year; offer a "gratuity" of $250,000; and promise a sizable loan from the United States, presumably for the prosecution of France's war against England.

The envoys were stunned. They had not anticipated being asked for a bribe. Shocked but not wishing to close any doors, the Americans regrouped, telling the French they might consider a monetary exchange *after* signing a treaty, and that they would consult with Adams about a loan. The Directory, however, remained unmoved and the Americans found themselves in a political limbo. With few alternatives, they explained America's position and offered terms equal to those enjoyed by England. Talleyrand only deigned to reply a month later, and then he astonished the negotiators by offering to deal solely with Elbridge Gerry, considered sympathetic to France. Now certain they could accomplish nothing, Marshall and Pinckney left the country while Gerry stayed, believing that his presence prevented war.[2]

Furious when he learned of this treatment, Adams now thought war inevitable and turned to the cabinet. Attorney General Charles Lee agreed, while Pickering argued for war and an alliance with Great Britain.[3]

Taken aback, McHenry nonetheless continued to advocate "mitigated hostilities." He *did* think it "advisable and proper" to inform Congress, but reminded Adams that France held out "terms of accommodation, tho' humiliating and inadmissable in their present nature and form." In fact, France had not treated the United States any differently than other neutral nations. Continuing to reflect Washington's reluctance to get embroiled in "entangling alliances," he opposed Pickering's notion that the country should tie itself to England, whose fate was uncertain.[4] But it was not too late for the defense measures McHenry had been proposing: suspending treaties with France, arming, and increasing the military. Wolcott generally agreed.

Initially unswayed by McHenry and Wolcott, the president composed a declaration of war, but "[e]ven as he wrote, Adams' anger subsided." Congress, he realized, knew only that the envoys had not been received and it was not yet convinced of the need for war. He knew the legislature would be outraged if it saw the contents of the envoys' dispatches, but Lee warned that their publication might anger the Directory and endanger the envoys' lives. So instead, Adams opted for McHenry's "mitigated hostilities," or what amounted to undeclared war. Slowly the advantages of their position became clear to the president. If war had to be, both the country and the Congress needed to be psychologically prepared. After reviewing the dispatches more thoroughly, Adams informed Congress that the envoys could not achieve their goals honorably, and he requested greater defense measures for the coast and American shipping.[5]

Congress was astounded. Federalists were surprised, but Republicans were terrified. War appeared to be literally around the corner, and Congress was not at all clear why. In disbelief, the Republicans convinced themselves that the French had been amenable while Adams fostered hostilities with France, a country the Federalists vilified. Both parties demanded to know the contents of the dispatches.[6]

Adams, surprised by the Republican response and their resistance to defense measures, now sent Congress the papers with relief. But first he blacked out the French names and replaced them with "X," "Y," and "Z." The Republican opposition to defense measures evaporated upon learning of the French demand for a bribe. Affronted, Congress and the country rallied in righteous anger against the French.

It was now clear that American interests on the seas required protection. French picaroons out of the West Indies seized scores of American merchant ships within three miles of American shores, with Philadelphia alone losing half a million dollars within two months.[7] At last Congress set aside the money McHenry had requested to complete the frigates already being built, to purchase or construct forty more ships, and to fortify the harbors.

But soon this portion of defense measures would be out of McHenry's hands. The House Committee on Defense had concluded that oceanic security required a commissioner of marine to serve under McHenry in the War Department. The Senate, however, took the idea a step further, and established an entirely new department. Hence, to McHenry's relief, the Department of the Navy was born.[8]

Moreover, in light of the xyz Affair, McHenry again recommended increased defense measures, and this time Congress acted. By mid-July, Congress approved another regiment of artillerists and engineers; money for ports, harbors, cannon, and arms; and the establishment of armories and foundries. Congress approved twelve more regiments of infantry and six troops of light dragoons for the regular army, which it renamed the "New Army," and added a Provisional Army of 10,000 men. Congress also suspended the 1778 Franco-American Treaty of Amity and Commerce.[9]

While McHenry had repeatedly requested the essentials that Congress now gave him, it did not approve more clerks. If Congress thought about the matter at all, it probably concluded that establishing a Navy Department had solved McHenry's problems. But McHenry's earlier complaint had not included naval matters. Now he was completely overwhelmed; he could only hope that an adequate substructure to the army itself would buoy him.

In the meantime, until the new Secretary of the Navy Benjamin Stoddert arrived from Baltimore, McHenry still oversaw the marine, and in mid-May he was nearly ready to put "one or two" more frigates to sea. The captains of these ships, however, needed carefully worded legal instructions. McHenry had received these the previous year from Attorney General Lee, but as he now favored war with France the more moderate McHenry this time chose to consult Hamilton.[10]

The New Yorker advised that American ships certainly had the "authority to repel force by force (but not to capture) and to repress hostilities within our waters." McHenry added that vessels on the high seas could not be searched by French privateers and that any American prisoners discovered on French boats were to be recovered, by force if necessary. He posted the orders immediately, as trouble had already reached American ports. New York City's harbor forts, begun in 1794 when the country had feared war with England, had failed to stop the French. "[A] French Privateer has made captures at the mouth of our harbor," Hamilton protested. "This is too much humiliation after all that has passed. Our Merchants are very indignant. Our Government [is] very prostrate."[11]

New York's situation involved four different bureaucracies: the federal, state, and city governments as well as the Military Committee of New York City. The two men with greatest impact at these various levels were Hamilton, naturally, and subordinate to him a Revolutionary War veteran, Lt. Col. Ebenezer Stevens. In 1794 Knox had appointed Stevens War Department Agent for New York City fortifications, and McHenry had just reappointed him.[12]

Responding to Hamilton's anxiety for federal assistance with New York's harbor defenses, McHenry arranged an assessment visit. He visited the various parts of the city and surrounding islands, consulted with the Military Committee, and returned to Philadelphia by June 18 to hand in his written report and papers to Adams. Hamilton's letters had indicated an urgency of popular feeling that McHenry did not see. "I find every thing too languid for the conjuncture. I have spoken freely to those that I thought could render service and to some of the young city militia. The latter had no disposition to offer as volunteers under the late law. I hope however to remove their objections."[13]

Back at the War Department, McHenry found to his delight that naval affairs had passed to Stoddert.[14] While McHenry still had to deal with ports and harbors, he could now concentrate on the army.

On the same day, American envoy to France John Marshall arrived in Philadelphia to the greatest fanfare the city had ever seen. Americans cared that the envoys had not groveled to the French and had stood firm for American international independence. This tall, good-looking man with piercing black eyes was now a hero. That evening members of Congress, the cabinet, and the Supreme Court entertained Marshall at a lavish banquet, where politicians toasted their champion to cries of "Millions for Defense, not one cent for Tribute!"[15]

More important, Marshall's report to Adams served to soften the president's attitude toward the French. For although the envoy still smarted from the insulting treatment he had received, and in a public speech remained aggressively pro-American, he nonetheless did not believe the French wanted war; her mistake was thinking "she could bully America into a compliance with her wishes." The envoys' prolonged silence had alarmed Adams, causing him to again think in terms of war. Only Gerry's presence in France had restrained the president; now Marshall encouraged that restraint. "Adams, who had been prepared to ask for a declaration of war before it [Congress] adjourned, now decided to hold off."[16] Marshall convinced Adams that peace might be possible. There was no point in rushing into a war.

This was, in fact, a turning point in the relationship between Adams and McHenry. Since the president now suspected that all he really needed to do was prove to France that America would not be bullied, little more than the defense measures Congress had already enacted were required. There might be further incidents on the sea, but Adams now was coming to believe what the months to come would corroborate—that France really had no plans to invade. Logically, then, the United States needed a navy but not an army. This fit in perfectly with Adams's decades-long preference for a navy anyway.[17]

From now on, it appears, the president supported the navy in every way possible and frustrated the army at every turn. But he did not simply refuse all measures connected with the army, probably because he could not be truly certain what France would do, and also because he had initially supported the measures. Surely he did not fail to appreciate that allowing a slow buildup of the army would make a core available if Adams was wrong and an army really was needed. If Adams was right and the army proved unnecessary, then he prevented a great waste of taxpayer money.

But the army, which no longer interested Adams, was now McHenry's primary concern. Congress had just passed laws increasing the army, and it was McHenry's job to raise that force. McHenry had, in fact, suggested these increases with presidential support; would Adams now tell his secretary of war that he was changing his mind? No, Adams excluded McHenry from his thought processes, as well as from information that Adams continued to receive from Europe. McHenry had no way of knowing that the army was to be a paper tiger.

It was most unfair of Adams not to confide in McHenry, explaining his reasons and intentions. This situation provides an excellent illustration of why Adams was unable to lead the men around him. After all, McHenry did not wish war with France either. The two men could have become allies. Instead, from now on McHenry would find his moves frustrated at every turn, waste an enormous amount of human energy, and receive nothing but criticism for supposed incompetence from every side. If Adams believed his behavior to be politic, it was also cruel.

But the wartime atmosphere led to larger cruelties. In their hawkish enthusiasm, leading Federalists wanted to shut down the voices of their opposition, and they looked to both English and colonial legal precedent for their method. Indeed, because the Federalists feared that "no government . . . could withstand assaults from the press," they considered shutting down the opposition press a matter of national security. Pickering, with significant support from public opinion, successfully proposed to Congress the Alien and Sedition Acts. It would now take aliens longer to become citizens, and until that time the president could easily expel them. The Sedition Act became most famous for imprisoning editors who published anything "false, scandalous and malicious" against the government. While this was designed primarily for use against political opposition in peacetime, and might be useful for Federalists in the election of 1800, it could also be useful (along with the Alien Enemies Law) in the event of war.[18]

It now became an issue that Congress would adjourn in July. If Adams was to have even the bare beginnings of an army to help convince France to back down, the president could procrastinate no longer in appointing a lieutenant general to command the army. But whom should Adams appoint?

At least a dozen names occurred to all, but two stood out above the rest— Washington and Hamilton. McHenry, for his part, favored Washington. In a country so divided between Federalists and Republicans, McHenry believed a name that could unify both parties was critical. He urged Washington to accept the position if offered, because "you alone can unite all hearts and all hands, if it is possible that they can be united."[19]

But there were others, like Pickering, who endorsed Hamilton, and even admitted this later to Washington. The secretary of state argued for the New Yorker on the combined grounds of intelligence and comparative youth. Adams was surprised and not at all swayed. He did not admit his dislike of Hamilton to Pickering, but pointed to too many other officers who had greatly outranked the New Yorker during the Revolution.[20] In this one conversation lay the seeds of a conflict that would rage among leading Federalists for months.

Unwittingly, Adams's choice of a commanding general would set up that conflict. If the choice really was between Washington and Hamilton, then Adams's decision was an easy one. Unbeknown to the cabinet, the president really despised Hamilton, both because he thought the New Yorker had a "Caesar complex" and because Hamilton had actively worked against Adams's election in 1796. "Hamilton I know to be a proud spirited conceited aspiring Mortal always pretending to Morality, with as debauched Morals as old Franklin who is more his Model than anyone I know. As great an Hypocrite as any in the U.S.," Adams fumed. "His Intrigues in the Election I despise. That he has Talents I admit but I dread none of them. I shall take no notice of his Puppyhood but retain the same opinion of him I always had and maintain the same conduct towards him I always did. That is keep him at a distance."[21] All, on the other hand, revered Washington, and the Hamiltonians could not oppose him.

But Washington and Hamilton were not the only available candidates. There were other Revolutionary War generals around who also outranked Hamilton. Some of them were old or in serious debt like Knox, but Charles Cotesworth Pinckney was a possibility. As an envoy extraordinary to France, Republicans could not accuse him of warmongering, and he was a Federalist of good record who was also well connected in the Republican South. Both parties might grumble but would find it hard to object.

Adams, however, valued rank and experience and so he chose Washington. Unfortunately, the president had dallied so long that he did not have time first to sound Washington out on the subject. Although Adams had asked the general for his "name" in a letter on June 22, Adams had not requested an immediate reply and did not get one. Rather than ask the Senate to remain in session longer, Adams took a chance and nominated the ex-president without prior approval.

This decision proved a mistake for several reasons, the first concerning the issue of rank and the psychological and emotional implications it carried. An acknowledgment of accomplishment and rectitude, rank was a delicate matter, and if Washington outranked Hamilton, considering all the psychological factors, he also outranked Adams. True, Adams was the titular and constitutional head of the country—but Washington was the general who had steered the country through the Revolution and the unanimous choice as its first president. And, for all Washington's many virtues, he was also human. His accomplishments had given him an exquisite sense of his own worth. Washington might know intellectually that he owed his obedience to the president, but in reality he would expect to be treated as at least Adams's equal and occasionally Adams's superior. Adams appreciated the delicacy of the situation, but not fully.

Certainly if Washington could not consider Adams his "better," McHenry would also have difficulty. Washington and McHenry had a very close friendship that was nonetheless one of a superior to an inferior. The Constitution, however, placed the men in clear order: president, secretary of war, and general of the armies. Yet none of these men was capable of fully observing this order. Consequently, when Adams appointed Washington, the already overworked secretary of war found himself with two chiefs instead of one.

Another problem was the public nature of Washington's nomination. If Adams was lucky, Washington would accept unconditionally. If Adams was unlucky, Washington would have conditions that Adams, due to the nature of politics, would have little choice but to accept.

Yet Adams took the gamble when he nominated Washington on July 3.[22] Three days later, Adams directed McHenry to travel to Mount Vernon and "wait on General Washington with the commission of Lieutenant-General and Commander-in-Chief of the armies of the United States, which, by the advice and consent of the Senate, has been signed by me." He acknowledged to McHenry that "it is a movement of great delicacy, [and] it will require all your address to communicate the subject in a manner that shall be inoffensive to his feelings, and consistent with all the respect that is due from me to him."[23] Adams also desired Washington's "advice" in forming a list of officers, especially a general staff. He would get more "advice" than he wanted. So Adams played a politician's game, allowing the military buildup to proceed, but only at a snail's pace. This way an alarmed France ought to stop her insults. Then an expensive and, Adams now suspected, unnecessary army could be quickly disbanded at minimal cost once peace terms were established. It was a clever ploy and an important change on Adams's part—unfortunately, McHenry was unaware of it.

FIFTEEN

"I Must Be Allowed to Chuse"

George Washington

MCHENRY'S JULY TRIP to see George Washington at his home in Virginia should have been a pleasure. But travel was never really comfortable for him, and he could not stay long enough to enjoy the distractions of Mount Vernon and its owner. Boarding the mail stage on the morning of the eighth of July, he would not arrive at Washington's plantation until the evening of the eleventh. The trip was long, hot, and dusty, but the matter was too important to trust to the unreliable mail system. McHenry was to ask Washington to command the armies being raised.

It was the beginning of the Relative Rank Controversy, a dispute over how to rank the top three major generals that would consume the next four months and seriously impact McHenry's reputation. The problem began with Pickering, who was once again dissatisfied. He had never thought much of Washington as a general—Pickering often "overestimated his own talent and underestimated those around him." Knowing, however, that the general would rely heavily on his subordinates, Pickering decided to get Hamilton appointed second in command. Since he knew that Adams despised the New Yorker, Washington must demand him. So as soon as Pickering learned of McHenry's mission, he surreptitiously wrote the general a letter supporting Hamilton. Admitting Adams's "disinclination" to appoint the New Yorker, Pickering argued that Hamilton's appointment was "of such vast importance to the welfare of the country, that I am willing to risk any consequences of my frank and honest endeavors to secure it." He was serious—Pickering would do what needed to be done in order to get Hamilton. When certain he was right, Pickering would manipulate to get his way. He had, in fact, attacked and even destroyed at least one person before. In 1795, trusting to his own abilities with French, he had mistranslated a letter that ruined then Secretary of State Edmund Randolph. Since Pickering rarely doubted himself, it failed to occur to him that he might have made a mistake—and he had a marked inability to see that men of differing qualities can contribute their talents to a situation and achieve the desired end. Currently, however, the weight of Washington's opinion was necessary to sway Adams. Washington must be convinced that Hamilton was the "one man who will gladly be *your second*, but who will not, I presume, because I think he ought not, be the second to any other military commander in the United States."[1]

On the morning of July 11 and before McHenry's arrival, Washington replied, agreeing that Hamilton's services ought to be obtained "at *almost* any price." But he argued that Hamilton's brilliance did not outweigh all other tactical matters. Washington believed that *if* France attacked, she would probably assault the South, which was near the French West Indies. It was also strategically weakest and full of Francophile Republicans and slaves that might easily rebel. For these reasons Washington thought an illustrious southerner was in order.[2]

In fact, he had a southerner in mind, Charles Cotesworth Pinckney. The accomplished South Carolinian was on his way back from France now, and might not serve beneath Hamilton, whom he had outranked during the Revolution. Further, Washington knew Pickering to be mistaken; Hamilton would serve below others. He had weeks earlier written Washington "the place in which I should hope to be most useful is that of Inspector General with a command in the line."[3] So, as of the morning of July 11, Washington planned to place Pinckney as second in command, ranking over Hamilton.

In the meantime, however, Hamilton had visited Philadelphia and changed his mind, probably influenced by Pickering. So he wrote Washington a necessarily delicate letter. After expressing surprise that the Virginian had not been consulted prior to his nomination, Hamilton urged the general to accept. High stations require good men, he said, especially since Adams's military ideas were "of the wrong sort." Then Hamilton focused on Washington's prime weakness—his concern for his name. "If you accept it will be conceived that the arrangement [of officers] is yours & you will be responsible for it in reputation."[4] Washington, he hinted, needed to deal with proven and reliable men or his name might be ruined. No one, Hamilton knew, fit that category better than he. After decades of serving together, Hamilton understood Washington. The general's circumspection had often prevented him from unconsidered action, but those who knew of this trait could use it.

McHenry, then, arrived at Mount Vernon on the evening of the eleventh armed with Washington's commission and letters from both Adams and Hamilton. The president's note explained McHenry's mission and requested the general's "advice and assistance." He further informed Washington that McHenry would "consult you upon the organization of the army, and upon every thing relating to it."[5]

It turned out that Washington had conditions to his acceptance of command. He had laid these out in letters that had not reached Philadelphia prior to McHenry's departure, but which he now explained. On the one hand, he told the president disingenuously that "you may command me without reserve." But he was worried about the appointment of generals. He thought that few of the old generals could keep up, that men ought to be asked to serve "without respect to [prior] grade," and he advised "that the greatest circumspection be used in appointing the General Staff." To McHenry Washington was more forthright, worrying about his age and wondering what the country would think of his reemergence after he had been so public about his wish to retire. Only in the third letter did Washington openly assert "that if I am looked to as the Commander in Chief, I must be allowed to chuse such as will be agreeable to me."[6] In other words, he, Washington, must be allowed to pick the general staff, or those generals under his command. This demand struck Adams since the president was commander-in-chief and he believed he ought to pick the general staff, not Washington. But this was new political territory, and Washington and McHenry failed to see the issue.

They spoke at length about the "steps that have been taken," although for some reason Washington never shared Pickering's letter. In the end, McHenry reported to Adams that Washington had "maturely considered" the consequences, and accepted command with two provisos: he did not wish to be called to active command until hostilities began; and there were "officers without whom . . . he would not serve."[7] This, upon Washington's insistence, McHenry reported in writing to Adams. Further, McHenry directed his office to send Adams Washington's letters so that the president would be *fully* apprised of Washington's conditions.

So who was to serve on Washington's general staff? Having mulled the matter over further, with both Pickering's and Hamilton's letters in his head, the commission in his hands, and the entire matter becoming a reality, Washington changed his mind. He chose Hamilton for second in command, serving as both inspector general and first major general, followed by Pinckney and then Knox. After all, although Pinckney had many merits, Hamilton had the preeminent advantage of being a known quantity to Washington. Pinckney was a good man, but who knew what the war would bring? Hamilton had never failed him. Washington had known Hamilton intimately for decades and could always rely on him—his reputation would be safe.

McHenry reminded Washington that Adams would have to agree to the general's list, although the secretary of war did not foresee a problem. After all, Adams had requested Washington's advice. And why should the president object? Every person Washington named was on Adams's list of possible candidates. Washington, however, knew of Adams's aversion to Hamilton through Pickering. For this and other reasons, Washington even suggested McHenry take the commission back to Philadelphia with him until the president agreed to Washington's conditions. McHenry, however, believed this was not only unnecessary, but that it could be construed as either disrespectful or distrustful. If Adams did not agree, he would have to make his position known.[8]

Time was of the essence, for Congress was even now considering the bill that would augment the army, creating what would be called the "New Army," so the two men quickly answered the list of questions McHenry had carried with him. Recruiting for the New Army should begin as soon as the bill passed, while general and field officers for the extra Provisional Army should be decided upon but not appointed. But none of this be could be done without the concurrence of Congress. Since it would adjourn soon, Washington sent McHenry on his way.

That left the general to write both Hamilton and Knox explaining his choices. These letters together illustrate the shifting sand on which Washington stood. For to Hamilton Washington admitted his concern that Pinckney, who was essential, might not serve under Hamilton due to prior rank. Washington clearly understood that rank might be a real issue. So, Washington added, "it rests with the President to use his pleasure," clearly leaving room for jockeying between Pinckney and Hamilton. On the other hand, to Knox Washington maintained that this was a NEW Army and "former rank will be forgot."[9] So, even as Washington tried to insist on forgetting prior rank, he knew this would cause trouble and behaved inconsistently. In the case he cared most about, Pinckney, he allowed room to maneuver. Nor would Washington have dreamt of allowing his own prior rank to be forgotten. Whether Washington's thinking was clouded or he was being disingenuous, McHenry did not question it.

On July 17, the secretary of war arrived back in Philadelphia and went straight to the president, finding the Adamses at breakfast. When the president questioned Hamilton's ranking first, McHenry explained Washington's reasons and produced Washington's letter to Hamilton, indicating that Adams's pleasure was required. Satisfied, Adams wrote a message naming the generals in the order Washington provided. At that point, Pickering entered and informed them that the Senate had adjourned for the day.[10]

But the next day, Adams changed his mind, disagreeing with Washington's decision to forget former rank. Adams himself had a tendency to feel unappreciated, and without the recognition of former accomplishments he would have been lost. His sense of regionalism was also strong. For those reasons he wanted the order to be Knox, then Pinckney, and finally Hamilton.[11]

From Adams's perspective, Knox's mere inclusion was insufficient. Knox was New England's premier general and Revolutionary War hero, the region's military pride. Ignoring his military accomplishments insulted New England. No one felt this more than Adams, old friend of Knox's, proud New Englander, and respecter of rank. To gall Adams even further, the plum position was being awarded to Hamilton, a man the president found highly distasteful.

However, changing the order meant potentially losing Washington. Since the Senate remained in Philadelphia solely for the purpose of agreeing to the nominations of the generals, there was no time for another trip to Mount Vernon. It was either nominate the generals now or wait until the next session of Congress in November.[12]

Fearing the possible loss of Washington, McHenry advised preserving the general's order, letting those nominated appeal any grievances thereafter.[13] The secretary of war now allied with Washington against Adams. If McHenry were lucky, Adams would accept Washington's preferences. But, if Washington was wrong to insist on ignoring prior rank, McHenry was equally mistaken in thinking that these proud men would easily accept a lesser rank with the notion of appealing it later. Later attempts to claim a superior rank would be both immensely difficult and humiliating—far better to settle rank in advance, preventing further discord. Furthermore, unlike Pickering and Washington, McHenry appears to have had no firsthand knowledge of Adams's deep dislike for Hamilton. Hamilton had, after all, very possibly cost Adams votes in the last election, or so Adams believed.[14] Nonetheless, Adams was not admitting these feelings freely, since Hamilton was such a power among Federalists. Only when it was too late did McHenry finally realize the depth of these personal antagonisms.

In the meantime, Pickering created a new and unnecessary problem that insulted the president. Without giving cause, Pickering objected to the appointment of Adams's son-in-law, William S. Smith, as adjutant general. Offended, Adams insisted on Smith's place. Pickering then pushed his luck even further, suggesting the governor of Tennessee, John Sevier, for brigadier general. McHenry knew Sevier to be an "unprincipled man" but "waived objections" as the appointment was to the Provisional Army, which might never be raised.[15]

Adams now sent the nominations for the general staff to the Senate in Washington's order, expressing his hope that any grievances among the officers could be amicably settled among themselves. So the president grudgingly bowed to Washington's wishes, but mentally preserved the idea that the order of rank was not really settled. McHenry, on the other hand, thought that this *did* settle the matter, if only until an officer later filed a grievance. The two men had taken joint action from subtly different vantage points.

Pickering, however, was incapable of letting his objections lie, and now proved his willingness to believe the worst of others without a full investigation. Rumor suggested that the president's son-in-law had been involved in shady, even illegal, business dealings, so Pickering unilaterally urged senators to refuse Smith. The Senate complied, and Adams heard about Pickering's actions. The president felt deeply and publicly humiliated while Smith was later cleared of financial misdeeds. In a few short hours, Pickering had alienated the president, humiliated an innocent man in Smith, and supported an unprincipled man in Sevier.[16]

For his part, McHenry disapproved of Pickering's actions—he should not have tried to influence the Senate. McHenry reported to Washington that "[t]he President felt the disappointment severely. I think it was a hasty measure in the Senate."[17]

The Senate, however, confirmed the other nominations made by the president and adjourned on July 19. Six days later Adams left for home. If McHenry and Pickering had not yet realized the president was angry with them, they could not ignore it now, for Adams left without even telling them.[18] After all, the longer he stayed, the more he would be pressed, especially by McHenry, to take measures to organize the army that he liked less every day. Leaving for Massachusetts was a marvelous stalling technique.

McHenry had to start pulling the army together, and although Adams had not yet called the generals into active service, the secretary of war could now properly ask them for *some* assistance. So McHenry asked Hamilton to consider new rules for the formation and movement of the army, sending a copy of England's guidelines. Hamilton agreed, adding that he would like to talk to McHenry on "a variety of subjects" and would, "without delay, repair to Philadelphia."[19]

Hamilton's visit, however, was not that of an innocent subordinate coming to offer his help. Hamilton had a tendency to overreach. Extremely capable and efficient, Hamilton too often failed to appreciate proper boundaries and took over parts of others' jobs. For example, years before, while secretary of the treasury, he had told agent for the British government Major George Beckwith to communicate with him rather than Secretary of State Thomas Jefferson. Now, with McHenry, Hamilton was about to attempt to blur more lines; it was the beginning of what Howard Mattsson-Bozé has called "Hamilton's campaign to take over." It was not that Hamilton wanted to *be* secretary of war. No, Hamilton's dreams of military glory led him to prefer the position to which he had been appointed. Nor did Hamilton want to destroy McHenry. But it would also be too generous to say he merely wanted to help—he wanted to control. Hamilton was convinced of his own mastery over administrative areas, and believed that his methods were the only proper way to accomplish the goals. So he would run roughshod over others to achieve control if this was necessary. Hamilton apparently expected to go into the War Department, make all of the early decisions, start matters on his chosen trajectory, and then let McHenry oversee the result. This would give Hamilton what he wanted—he would be in charge actually if not nominally. In fact, Hamilton had accomplished this years before: "[S]o completely did he dominate Henry Knox, the Secretary of War [before McHenry], that he became hardly more than a minion of the Treasury."[20]

McHenry, however, did not share Hamilton's ideas on this score and had no desire to repeat Knox's experience. When McHenry officially notified Hamilton and Knox of their positions on July 25, the secretary of war did not expect to see Hamilton walk into the War Department five days later.[21]

Yet that is precisely what happened. Hamilton soon discovered, though, that McHenry was not about to let Hamilton take over. McHenry knew that his work suffered, and he needed and wanted help, it is true—but he would not become Hamilton's minion.

Neither man was pleased. A stiff formality crept into their correspondence, with affectionate greetings and farewells replaced by very proper substitutes. "My Dear Ham" was now "Sir" and signoffs like "Yours affectionately" became the common "Your Obedient Servant." This continued only for about two weeks on McHenry's part, a little longer on Hamilton's.

But Hamilton had more reason for his formality; he was rightly convinced that McHenry was overwhelmed. When it became apparent to him that McHenry would not give him free rein, Hamilton decided to take more drastic measures. Sadly, Hamilton did not attempt to find more clerks for McHenry. Instead, even before he left Philadelphia, Hamilton began a letter-writing campaign designed to discredit McHenry, a technique he had successfully used against others. In this way he apparently hoped to convince McHenry to allow him, Hamilton, to take charge. Hamilton simply assumed that McHenry was the problem, and would discover his error only after he had intentionally damaged McHenry's reputation among the Federalists.[22]

To McHenry Hamilton described the situation he saw at the War Department only too accurately. Despite "scruples of delicacy," both friendship and patriotism demanded candor. "I observe you plunged in a vast mass of details. I know from experience that it is impossible for any man whatever be his talents or diligence to wade through such a mass without neglecting the most material things and attaching to his operations a feebleness and sloth of execution." McHenry must have seethed. He was aware of the problem, for this was precisely what McHenry had long before complained of, but a parsimonious Congress had denied him more aides. "It is essential to the success of the Minister of a great Department that he subdivide the objects of his care, distribute them among competent assistants and content himself with a general but vigilant superintendence," Hamilton went on. "This course is particularly necessary when an unforeseen emergency has suddenly accumulated a number of new objects to be provided for and executed."[23] This letter must have really stung McHenry, especially as he knew how correct the observations were. Hamilton's mistake, however, was to assume that the problem was a lack of organization within the War Department that he could fix if McHenry would let him. The true immediate problem was a lack of sufficient clerks, which Congress had denied

McHenry. But the generals could provide some help, so Hamilton urged McHenry to call the generals to active duty since the New Yorker could not afford to work for free. That step, however, required presidential action and proved the greatest problem of all, one that neither McHenry nor Hamilton yet fully appreciated but that would become apparent in the future—that Adams did not support the New Army and would stall and stymie forward movement whenever possible. Adams would, in fact, make McHenry's job impossible. McHenry's competence could not overcome an unfeasible situation. But it would take time for this to become clear.

In the meantime Hamilton wrote Washington as well, first focusing on the general's fear that Pinckney might not serve under the former secretary of the treasury. Hamilton reminded Washington that Pinckney had held only a slightly higher rank during the Revolution, which Hamilton probably would have outstripped had he not served Washington as aide-de-camp. Thus, he implied, the blame for Hamilton's lesser grade really lay at Washington's feet. Further, Hamilton's service since the war surpassed Pinckney's. Hamilton nonetheless wrote, "I stand ready to submit our relative pretensions to an impartial decision and to waive the preference."[24]

Now Hamilton turned to the matter of McHenry. Convinced that he would have to pummel McHenry into compliance, Hamilton sought the influence of powerful friends. With their help Hamilton might get what he wanted, but to do so he had to destroy McHenry's reputation. Thus he wrote Washington not that he and the Virginian should jointly push Congress to give McHenry the clerks he sorely needed to do his job properly, but instead that McHenry was incompetent and oblivious. "[M]y friend, McHenry, is wholly insufficient for his place, with the additional misfortune of not having himself the least suspicion of the fact! This generally will not surprise you, when you take into view the large scale upon which he is now to act. But you perhaps may not be aware of the whole extent of the insufficiency," Hamilton jabbed. "It is so great as to leave no probability that the business of the War Department can make any tolerable progress in his hands. This has been long observed; and has been more than once mentioned to the President by members of Congress."[25] In fact, the only written complaint by a congressman to Adams was by Robert Goodloe Harper, who had duly reported this to Hamilton the previous spring. As a reward, Hamilton recommended Harper to Washington's new military family but added, "the shade to his useful qualities is *Vanity*."[26]

Continuing, Hamilton wrote that he had traveled to Philadelphia to aid

McHenry "[b]ut the idea has been thus far very partially embraced." Then he warned Washington, "It is to be regretted that the supposition of cooperation between the Secretary at War and the principal military officers will unavoidably throw upon the latter a part of the blame which the ill success of the operations of the war department may be expected to produce. Thus, you perceive, Sir, your perplexities are begun."[27] Again Hamilton targeted Washington's concern for his reputation, this time to use against McHenry. Washington, Hamilton insinuated, would be held responsible for McHenry's mistakes.

Unfortunately for the secretary of war, Washington accepted much of Hamilton's analysis. Although McHenry had written the general approximately once a week since he had left Mount Vernon, he had only reported what had been accomplished, and not what remained in process. Washington was especially concerned about the position of quartermaster general as, unbeknown to McHenry, Washington had prematurely offered the position to Edward Carrington, who had accepted it. Washington now found himself embarrassed since he did not know what had become of the opening. He was right to be concerned; since Congress had not made the quartermaster a general but rather a lieutenant colonel, McHenry had postponed appointing that office until Congress reconvened and a more appropriate rank could be attained.[28]

But Washington felt ill-informed and he was frustrated. He was also overworked, for applications to serve in the army arrived by the dozen. In this frame of mind he received Hamilton's complaint, and returned the feeling. "I am held in the most profound ignorance of every step that has been taken since he left this place. . . . I am not, at this moment, made acquainted with a single step that is taken to appoint an Officer or Recruit a man, or where the rendezvouses are."[29] Washington did not know that Adams had, intentionally, not activated the general staff. Further, McHenry's letters were curt in his effort to at once keep Washington informed but also accomplish his other duties. To make matters worse, McHenry had again fallen ill with his bilious complaint.

Still, Washington complained to Hamilton. "Your opinion respecting the unfitness of a certain Gentleman for the Office he holds, accords with mine, and it is to be regretted, *sorely*, at this time, that these opinions are so well founded." Hamilton's efforts to discredit McHenry had worked. "I early discovered after he entered upon the Duties of his Office that his talents were unequal to great exertions, or deep resources. In truth they were not expected; for the fact is, it was a Hobson's choice [between McHenry, Pickering, and Wolcott]. But such is the case, and what is to be done."[30] Never expressing any true comprehension of the amount of work he was piling on an already overtaxed secretary of war, Washington agreed that he would try to make McHenry see the "propriety" of calling on Hamilton's aid. Washington did not yet appreciate that McHenry had done as much as he could properly do without Adams calling the generals to duty. Hamilton's letter to Washington had hit its mark.

If Hamilton had written only McHenry and Washington, one could excuse it as a matter of personal pique. But Hamilton enlisted Wolcott and Pickering as well. "It is impossible for McHenry to get through all that is now upon his hands in a manner honorable to himself—satisfactory to the public—or proportioned to the energy of the conjuncture." The general officers must be activated or "the Government and all concerned [read: Wolcott and Pickering] will be discredited."[31] He included copies of the note he had written McHenry so that they could not fail to understand him. Pickering, in his turn, urged Adams—the true source of the inertia—to activate the generals. Later in the month, Hamilton wrote the Federalist senator from Massachusetts, Theodore Sedgwick, to the same effect.

The saddest aspect in this whole affair was how pointless Hamilton's campaign was. True, McHenry did not intend to hand his office over to Hamilton, but the secretary did want help, agreed that the generals could provide some of this, and had already asked Adams for permission to call Knox and Hamilton into active service. In other words, undermining McHenry was unnecessary because he was not the problem. The person whom Hamilton needed to influence was beyond his reach—it was Adams himself.

When Washington *did* complain to McHenry about his silence and suggested calling the generals, the general felt somewhat chastened by McHenry's replies. McHenry *had* been hard at work, and the former president now learned about Smith, Adams's departure, and, most important, McHenry's plan to organize the twelve regiments of the New Army, filling one regiment at a time so that complete regiments might be called upon if necessary. He had also asked the president to call Knox and Hamilton into active duty and for permission to hire a secretary for Washington. McHenry planned to divide the country into thirds, appointing Knox in the Northeast, Hamilton in the middle, and Washington in the South. Each general would process and evaluate the many applications from their sections. McHenry further admitted to Washington that he had been in bed for a week too sick to write or move his office and family to the country when the Yellow Fever had reappeared—hence one of his letters to Washington bore another's penmanship. (This year the departments had agreed to remove to Trenton so that they might conduct business more readily in the same location.)[32] This inability to write was especially a problem since McHenry was stuck in the middle not merely of Washington's and Adams's personalities but also geographically. With Adams in Massachusetts, Washington in Virginia, and McHenry in Philadelphia (and sometimes Trenton), the secretary's job now required more extensive communication than ever.

Washington was at once pleased by this new correspondence, chagrined about his hasty and Hamilton-inspired letter to McHenry, and yet defensive of his reasons. Mostly, however, he was glad that McHenry "had suggested to the President, prompt and decisive measures," and that McHenry's and Washington's ideas "accorded so well." Defensively, Washington reminded McHenry that his silence had left the general disagreeably ignorant on certain matters—a situation he hoped would not continue. Washington had "almost" apologized. Indeed, McHenry scribbled on the letter's cover "Approves of my plan—I perhaps too long in informing him what plan I had adopted and he was too quick in censoring me."[33]

But the damage had been done with Wolcott and Pickering. Wolcott surreptitiously agreed with Adams's pro-navy and anti-army position, and would sabotage the army at every opportunity. Despite this predilection, he urged McHenry to call Hamilton into service, and incorrectly concluded— McHenry had written Adams to that effect two days earlier—that he had influenced McHenry to do so. Despite his new anti-army position, Wolcott further hypocritically exhorted Hamilton that "[y]ou must my friend come on with the expectation of being *Secy of War in fact*. Mr. McH's good sense, industry & virtues, are of no avail, without a certain address & skill in business which he has not & cannot acquire."[34] It is hard to know whether to read this as an attempt to make trouble among those who supported the army—assuming that there would be ongoing, intensifying trouble between Hamilton and McHenry—or to take it at face value. If the latter, then Hamilton's letters had accomplished their aim, by discrediting McHenry, who people quickly forgot had performed well under Washington. Moreover, it does seem a bit easy for the man with thirty-one clerks (Wolcott) to criticize the man with only a few (McHenry) for lacking "skill in business." At least Wolcott appreciated McHenry's virtues. In addition, Wolcott was also concerned about the army's finances, for he despised waste. He himself was meticulous in his work, and executed (with a great deal of assistance) a system in the Treasury that Hamilton had created. Wolcott seems to have wanted Hamilton to do the same for McHenry, especially in the area of supplies, where Wolcott believed there was no system. He was wrong. Hamilton had years before created a supply method in the War Department—but events had overtaxed the division and the system was failing.

At this point, Knox protested his rank. He was insulted, considering the arrangement a public degradation. By what rule or military code, Knox wanted to know, was the government justified in ignoring his previous rank? The question clearly implied that he would not serve under Hamilton.[35] Furthermore, Adams now made it clear that the matter was not settled, even as he received Pickering's recommendation that Hamilton be called to active duty. It all began to ferment in Adams's mind, leaving him suspicious of the preference for Hamilton over Knox.

For his part, McHenry's unrealistic hopes of acquiescence left him in a quandary. Indeed, he was still not thinking clearly as he recuperated, was not writing all of his letters, and admitted to Hamilton that he was not sure he had signed them all. But at this point McHenry apparently hoped that the gentlemen involved might come to some amicable agreement. To encourage this, McHenry sent Hamilton Knox's letter and requested the New Yorker's opinion. With a little luck, Hamilton might reconsider and serve below Knox.[36]

Hamilton had another suggestion. Officially he held on to second place. Privately, however, Hamilton proved a bit more malleable. "I am willing to confer—to adjust amicably with the advice of mutual friends, but how can I abandon my pretension."[37] He was not foolish enough to risk losing all military glory over whether he should serve in the second or third position, but he really did not wish to serve below Knox. So he sent McHenry a sample letter asking Knox to accept the appointment and appeal his rank later—the option McHenry had always favored.

Not long after getting Hamilton's answer, McHenry also received one from an overworked Adams. Clearly irritated, the president insisted that the order be Knox, Pinckney, and then Hamilton, but added the odd qualifier that Washington should agree. Only when that order was acknowledged could the generals be called to active service, and Adams, happy to drag his feet about the expensive army, admitted he was perfectly willing to wait as long as necessary to get what he wanted. But he knew McHenry and the other Federalists were not. In fact, he counted upon their eagerness. "Any other plan will occasion long delay and much confusion. You may depend upon it, the five New England States will not patiently submit to the humiliation that has been meditated for them."[38] He believed in rank, he believed the president should be supreme, and he believed that the military representative of New England should be honored. Each of these beliefs was now assaulted, and Adams fumed.

But McHenry did not see the situation the same way. Duty and loyalty conflicted, as McHenry felt ever more painfully the tensions created by his feelings for Washington and his responsibilities to Adams. To his mind, the president had publicly agreed to Washington's order and the Senate had concurred. Now Adams declined to cooperate, Knox made waves, and Hamilton would yield only if forced. Had these three been the only men involved, McHenry's course would have been clear—he would have honored Adams's wishes, as he should have. There was, however, still Washington to consider. McHenry was convinced Washington would withdraw if the order were changed. And McHenry was, above all, a Washington supporter.

Indeed, the secretary of war began to wonder if perhaps Adams had forgotten that *Washington* had drawn up the list and ranked the men. Adams appeared confused when he wrote that McHenry could call up the generals in Adams's order if *Washington* agreed. So McHenry reminded the president of Washington's role. To emphasize his point, McHenry explained that he "had no agency, direct or indirect, before or while at Mt. Vernon, in deciding his mind, either as to the choice or the arrangement of the rank of those he had selected . . . [and when he] showed me his choice . . . I concurred, but [added] that the nominations and relative rank of those nominated must finally rest with the President."[39]

But the president remained adamant. Fearful of losing the general and clearly looking for cover should Adams's bluster turn wild, McHenry consulted Wolcott and Pickering in the kind of meeting they had routinely held during Washington's absences from the capital in the previous administration.[40] McHenry needed another ear and the business of his department often overlapped theirs. Indeed, Wolcott and Pickering had intruded themselves in his business in their support of Hamilton. To some extent they were obligated to listen.

Wolcott and especially Pickering were actually eager to be involved. Pickering, it turns out, had been secretly corresponding with Washington and

Hamilton for a month, sharing the letters with Wolcott—but not McHenry, as Hamilton's letters had developed a conspiratorial tone in opposition to him. Finally, Pickering had suggested solving all their problems by substituting Knox for McHenry as secretary of war.[41] This would quiet Adams without giving in to his ideas regarding rank. Hypocritically, Pickering still pretended friendship for McHenry. But Hamilton did not agree. Knox's ostentation and his wife's large gambling debts had made him a laughingstock at the capital. No, Hamilton did not want McHenry out, just controlled. Not wishing blatantly to contradict Pickering, his best supporter, Hamilton let the matter drop.

Unaware of this, McHenry now included Pickering and Wolcott in his dilemma. Should he acquiesce to the president and risk losing Washington? Should he, with Adams's permission, ask Knox to accept on the grounds of a later appeal, assuring him his acceptance would not bind him if he was later dissatisfied? Or, as Pickering believed, was it time to call in Washington, who would certainly threaten to resign if Hamilton was not his second?[42]

McHenry ruled out the last choice, for it would bring the two presidents to a clear power struggle and an open clash would be tremendously unpleasant. On the other hand, it would be undeniably insubordinate to bypass Adams and suggest directly to Knox that he accept conditionally. Instead, McHenry proposed this to Adams, sending along a slightly altered—and more respectful—copy of the letter Hamilton had composed. If the president agreed, he could just send the letter on to Knox.

Adams exploded, insisting that the law supported Knox and that no rank had ever been established. He was now "willing to settle all decisively at present (and have no fear of the consequences), by dating the commissions, Knox on the first day, Pinckney on the second, and Hamilton on the third." Adams remembered selectively only Washington's respect for the presidency. The secretary of war's attempts to jog his memory concerning Washington's position had not worked. The president reminded McHenry that the authority to decide this matter rested with him. Adams would not change his mind, and he ended his letter with a furious blast: "There has been too much intrigue in this business with General Washington and me; if I shall ultimately be the dupe of it, I am much mistaken in myself."[43]

McHenry could not misread this letter. Even if he thought Adams's memory and reasoning wrong, Adams *was* the president and it was McHenry's job to obey. So McHenry responded that he *would* send out the commissions with Knox's dated first to indicate superior rank, Pinckney's second, and

Hamilton's third. But McHenry was also shocked by Adams's implication that he, McHenry, had intrigued for Hamilton. McHenry certainly had consulted Hamilton repeatedly as he had Lee and Pickering and Wolcott and even Stoddert. Indeed, he had used the former secretary of the treasury as free labor. But he had not conspired on Hamilton's behalf, and indeed he had to prevent Hamilton from taking over his own office. The imputation, now apparent, that he had unjustly favored Hamilton needed to be addressed. "Will you excuse the liberty I take in expressing how much I feel affected at this observation, lest you should attach in your mind any portion of the intrigues, if any have been employed, to me." Having been attacked, McHenry now needed reassurance. "It will, Sir, be a relief to me to be ascertained of your opinion in this particular; because I flatter myself I can convince you, that, abhorring indirect practices, I never even contemplated any; or, should you not be convinced, I can immediately retire from a situation, which demands a perfect and mutual confidence between the President and the person filling it."[44] The telling word here is "abhor." Hamilton and Pickering did not include McHenry in their machinations because they knew he would disapprove. That is not to say McHenry never acted confidentially or secretly. But Adams had implied that McHenry knowingly persuaded Washington to choose a man Adams did not want. This was further than McHenry would go, and if Adams could not bring himself to believe it, McHenry would resign.

The president responded that he believed "pains were taken" to convince McHenry the public wanted Hamilton. McHenry, Adams thought, then reported this to Washington "more forcibly than I should have done" and this decided Washington's mind. On the other hand, Adams allowed that McHenry had acted with integrity even if he had been influenced. The president ended by saying, "I have no hard thoughts concerning your conduct in this business."[45] But this last was not the truth—for Adams remained suspicious of disloyalty in his cabinet. Adams's suspicion was well placed, for he did not inspire loyalty in his cabinet—even McHenry's loyalties ultimately belonged to Washington.

McHenry again wrote Hamilton, asking him a second time to accept a position below that of second-in-command. "I hope you will acquiesce in the necessity which seems to govern," he said to Hamilton, to serve last among the major generals, fourth in the chain of command under Washington.[46] But this time Hamilton refused. He had come too close to commanding the army, and his expectations had risen too high.

The unthinkable now loomed before McHenry: the army faced losing both Washington and Hamilton. Stunned, McHenry hesitated sending the papers he had promised to relay; while he held these documents, there was still some room to maneuver. Without Washington, the army would lose political support and founder. Without the army, the country could not prepare for war with France. The ultimate cost of obeying Adams, McHenry feared, might well be the country's very existence. So once again the secretaries met. Pickering, of course, would not abandon Hamilton, so Stoddert, Wolcott, and McHenry agreed to make one final effort on Hamilton's behalf by drafting "a respectful representation on the subject to the President."[47] They knew it would have to be diplomatic, as the president was already angry and suspicious.

Pickering thus drafted a long letter to Adams that, by joint decision, Wolcott signed and sent as his own since Adams did not connect him with a "Hamiltonian conspiracy." The letter detailed the series of events, argued that no law or regulation supported Knox, and insisted that New England preferred Hamilton. Furthermore, Washington had chosen Hamilton, and since both Knox and Hamilton could not be had, "ought not General Washington's deliberate advice, seeing it has been asked, to influence the final decision?"[48]

McHenry now wrote Washington, first informing him of all that had been done: tents and field equipment would be ready for the spring campaign, a detail of supplies was being compiled, applicants for the most essential positions had been ranked and prioritized, and, with Adams's approval, recruitment could proceed upon the completion of the uniforms.[49] Everything had been begun, but everything also crawled since Adams refused to agree to Washington's order of major generals. Nothing would really move until that had taken place.

At last, McHenry determined that he had no choice but to inform Washington more fully about Adams's position in the last stage of this sorry affair. Now that the president appeared so decisive, McHenry sent the relevant letters to Washington. Since Washington had insisted on naming and ranking the general staff, it was a minimal courtesy to inform the general that this condition would not be honored. What role if any, McHenry wanted to know, would Washington feel comfortable playing in all of this?[50]

Washington, so impatient for both action and news of all that transpired, was stunned when he received McHenry's full account of Adams's intransigence. Since nothing could happen without the major generals, he now understood the delay in the recruiting service. But because McHenry's letter was confidential, Washington's hands were tied. It was, however, finally clear to Washington that he must either submit to Adams or return his commission. At first the general thought he'd wait until Adams responded to Wolcott's letter but soon changed his mind. Instead he requested an official letter from McHenry, and upon receiving it, Washington wrote Adams in strong terms. "[I]f you had been pleased, previously to the nomination, to have enquired into the train of my thoughts upon the occasion, I would have told you . . . on what terms I would have consented to the nomination. . . . They were, that the General Officers, and the General Staff of the Army should not be appointed without my concurrence." Washington had no intention of taking power from the executive, he claimed, but only desired to frame the most effective army. This was his due, for he "had staked every thing which was dear and valuable upon the issue, to trust more to chance than could be avoided." He would not have required this authority if an army had already existed. But since this was generally considered to be a New Army, he believed himself free to do so and to insist that prior rank not be an issue. Too much time and popular enthusiasm had been lost already. Now Washington wished to know if Adams's "determination to reverse the order of the three Major Generals is final, and whether you mean to appoint another Adjutant General without my concurrence." There the letter ended. But a separate letter to McHenry asked for the cabinet's thoughts regarding whether he should withdraw from the army.[51]

Adams was stunned. This letter must have contributed to his belief that he had been conspired against. No one in the government had supported him and he was stubbornly certain he was right. But Wolcott's letter convinced him to return to his previous position. Adams sent McHenry the commissions for the three major generals, all with the same date.[52]

But the president sent no accompanying explanation and McHenry hesitated to interpret this as surrender. Having been accused of intrigue by Adams, McHenry believed he needed some protection. If he gave Hamilton the second place only to find out that was not Adams's intent, McHenry would be open to much censure. So, after a week of consideration, he asked the other members of the cabinet for their opinions, in writing. Pickering, Wolcott, and Stoddert replied. "The only inference which we can draw from the facts before stated, is, that the President consents to the arrangement of rank as proposed by General Washington." Furthermore, "it is our opinion that the Secretary of War ought to transmit the commissions, and inform the generals that in his opinion the rank is definitively settled according to the original arrangement." Only with this written support behind him was McHenry willing to send the commissions, ordering them Hamilton, Pinckney, and then Knox. And so he did, on October 15, three months after the bill to augment the army had been passed.[53]

Knox declined to serve, but Pinckney, about whom Washington had been most concerned, proved eminently gracious. He would serve under Hamilton "with pleasure," and "even offered to serve under General Knox if it would soothe that gentleman's ruffled feelings." Indeed, Pinckney proved a breath of fresh air. "Pinckney coveted public honors, particularly military ones, but his ambition was usually governed by a high sense of patriotism, almost romantic in nature, which prompted him to place the welfare of the nation above his personal feelings."[54] Of all the principals involved in the Relative Rank Controversy, Pinckney behaved with the most grace.

In the meantime, Adams assured Washington that, should any differences arise over rank, he would support Washington's decision. But Adams also did what McHenry should have done more forcefully months before, reminding Washington "that, by the present Constitution of the United States, the President has authority to determine the rank of officers." McHenry had reminded Washington that Adams would have to agree to the list, but could not bring himself to tell Washington his place. With his loyalties so divided, perhaps McHenry did not see this issue clearly himself. Adams, however, could fight Hamilton but not Washington. Instead, the president acquiesced; Washington could choose the generals. Hamilton would hold the second rank even though Adams had opposed him. McHenry, trying to serve the president, had asked Hamilton to step down. An exhausted McHenry confessed the toll it had taken, as he still felt "perfectly tired of the uncertainty in which so many important measures are kept fettered and involved."[55]

Adams too was drained by the business. He, like Washington, had received countless applications to the New Army in addition to mail on every other conceivable subject and had worked hard to keep up, although he now "was even less eager to push the mustering of the army." But he was especially worried about Abigail, who had been deathly ill, causing a distraught Adams to neglect official business. Between Abigail's sickness and the Relative Rank Controversy, Adams complained it had been "the most gloomy summer of my life."[56]

SIXTEEN

"Referred to the General Officers"

James McHenry

MCHENRY HAD TO DO something. The relative ranks of the generals may have been solved, but damage had been done to his reputation, more than he even knew. Frustrated, he desperately wanted the work to pick up speed. Everything moved too slowly, he knew that he was blamed, and he was surrounded by a group of men who wanted to direct him. Moreover, McHenry's subordinates did not always perform. Although McHenry had ordered his superintendent of military stores, Samuel Hodgdon, to send Washington a detail on August 25, he still did not have such a list in November. McHenry excused Hodgdon, not only because the secretary was sensitive to the amount of business before the department but also because of possible political repercussions. Hodgdon had been quartermaster general and held partly to blame for St. Clair's Defeat, but Washington had not lost faith in him and in 1794 gave him this new position. Hodgdon was also "a close friend and erstwhile business partner of Timothy Pickering."[1] To dismiss Hodgdon would have offended both Washington and Pickering. While McHenry might have taken the chance with Pickering, he would not do so with Washington, provided Hodgdon was not completely hopeless. Still, in a department short of clerks, McHenry could not afford any inefficiency.

Indeed, McHenry needed more help if only to free up time to maintain a correspondence substantial enough to please Washington, who wished to be *fully* apprised on every point and whether progress had been made or not. He constantly peppered McHenry with questions, many of which required complicated answers. McHenry could not deny Washington information, since the latter *was* head of the army and was even being incorrectly but commonly referred to as "Commander-in-Chief."[2] But time spent writing Washington was borrowed from his other very pressing duties.

To make matters worse, Washington did not confine his requests to military matters. Even though he acknowledged how busy the secretary of war must be, the general asked McHenry to have a set of "colours" made that his granddaughter might present to a local Alexandria company called the "Silver Grays"; McHenry complied. Surely Washington did not help by asking the secretary to see to his private matters in Philadelphia—they could not avoid being a distraction.[3]

Finally McHenry hit upon a brilliant solution—he would bring all of the major generals together in Philadelphia by calling a "general" conference. If Adams could be prevailed upon to attend as well, everyone's interests could be addressed at once, hopefully bringing an end to the eternal questions and impatient suggestions from both Washington and Hamilton. It would not be easy to manage, however. Washington was recuperating from an illness and uncertain he could come. Hamilton could not make it before November. Of all involved, Pinckney was most agreeable. McHenry set the conference for November 10.

The secretary of war urged the president to attend, but Adams refused to leave Abigail although he knew he *must* come to the capital for Congress's session. He had, however, decided to permit McHenry to fill blank commissions with the names of battalion officers. Slowly, the president began to reveal his thoughts, but not in any organized way that would alert McHenry to a fundamental problem. Petulantly, Adams complained that no one would join the army for $5 a month when common labor on land or sea paid $15, certainly a valid criticism of Congress's pay scale. But, more seriously, he objected that maintaining the army once raised would cost a great deal. And why? "At present there is no more prospect of seeing a French army here, than there is in heaven." Finally Adams admitted to McHenry his reasons for not supporting the army: the cost would be unpopular, and Adams believed it unnecessary. Furthermore, although he did not say so, Adams knew that he would pay the price at election time. But these complaints lay buried in letters about other subjects, and McHenry ignored them. So Adams maintained a minimal support for the army, doing only what was absolutely required of him. McHenry, who had hoped to prevent any future disagreements through the medium of this conference, admitted disappointment that Adams would not attend. "I regret extremely this circumstance, as well on account of the cause, as being deprived of his opinions."[4]

But Adams's absence would give Hamilton even greater freedom to influence the proceedings. Again Hamilton jabbed at McHenry when he wrote Washington that "every day brings fresh room to apprehend that whatever may be the props the administration of the war department cannot prosper in the present *very well disposed* but *very unqualified* hands."[5] Hamilton would not be satisfied until he was completely in charge.

McHenry prepared for the conference and coordinated matters for Washington's arrival. The secretary of war left Trenton, where most of the government had retired to escape the pestilence, and arrived in Philadelphia on November 8. He arranged for the general to lodge at Mrs. White's, where no one had been ill and there was a nearby stable for the horses. A military escort would meet Washington at the middle ferry, giving him an official welcome to the city. Interestingly, Hamilton stayed with the Wolcotts, even though Mrs. Wolcott was extremely, possibly deathly, ill.[6] Adams was still in Massachusetts, but Pinckney was due soon.

Generals Washington and Hamilton began the conference on November 10, centering their work on an agenda of thirteen questions McHenry had prepared. Although their main object was to sort through and determine the officers for the New Army, McHenry requested their opinions on all relevant subjects to circumvent later sources of possible dissatisfaction. Washington had his own set of questions, some of them strategic, four of them concerning uniforms. The substantive questions sought to discover French methods of warfare in order to counteract them.[7]

McHenry had hoped the generals might consider the questions and call for meetings with the appropriate cabinet members when the need arose. Washington and Hamilton, however, wanted all of the basic information in writing, including the present situation of troops on the frontier and the seaboard, the state of military stores, and a copy of expense estimates McHenry had given Wolcott some months before. Although McHenry had anticipated this, his clerks had not been able to make copies in time. With trepidation, McHenry handed over the originals, and the process now fully commenced. As the generals fussed over details, McHenry gave "almost constant attention . . . to the objects, referred to the general officers, since their arrival here."[8] He finally had the help he needed.

To their astonishment, and undoubtedly to McHenry's gratification, Washington and Hamilton discovered the work was far more complicated and time-consuming than they had anticipated. In fact, the work took McHenry (when the office could spare him) and these three eminent generals—Pinckney had arrived—over a month to complete.[9] Working daily, even Sundays as had become McHenry's habit, their task still dragged.

What made the work more difficult was Washington's insistence that only loyal Federalists be considered for the officer corps, lest Francophiles mislead troops at a critical moment. McHenry agreed, but Hamilton thought that Washington carried the rule too far, alienating those who sat on the political fence and making true enemies of the opposition. The rule also excluded some of the best men. Still, Washington was adamant. But this meant that the army became purely political, dividing an already emotionally riven country.[10]

Republicans were, of course, acutely aware of the political nature of this army. They remembered the Federalist use of military force to suppress the Whiskey Rebellion only too well, and they now feared that the Federalists intended the New Army to crush the opposition. McHenry, for one, had no such designs. However, Republican worries naturally intensified with the passage of the Alien and Sedition Acts.[11] As Federalists jailed Republican editors, their fears became reality. Desperate for a way to counteract the growing power of the federal government, Republicans worked at the state level to pass the Virginia and Kentucky Resolutions. Drafted by Jefferson and Madison, they claimed that states had the right to determine a federal law's constitutionality, and proclaimed the Alien and Sedition Acts null and void.

So both sides believed the worst of their "enemy." Even McHenry, in the tense atmosphere of the capital, had grown less moderate and in some areas had fallen into this pattern. Reasoning this way, Republicans branded Federalists monarchists, while Federalists denounced Republicans as Jacobins. "Who is a jacobin?" McHenry asked. "Whoever would disturb an established government or the social order of society to make experiment of an hypothesis is a jacobin. Whoever would take from one man the wealth or property which he possesses to divide it among the idle profligate and pennyless is a jacobin." His faith was also affronted. "Whoever would substitute atheism for religion is a jacobin. Whoever to get rid of a small real or supposed grievance proceeding from the laws of their country pursues measures calculated to spread general discontent in [the] laws and distrust in the governing party is a jacobin. Whoever will endeavor to persuade the people, every man is competent to govern himself is a jacobin." The list went on. "Whoever in short uses a language calculated to make the people believe, that men can be happy without religion, or regular governmen[t] or that religion is the contrivance of priests and government of crafty knaves is a jacobin."[12] No clearer proof of internal political division could exist short of civil war—and civil war is what many Federalists anxiously feared.

Finally, Adams returned to Philadelphia to a government strung taut by both national and international tension. Apprehensive, Congress would convene in early December and Adams would be expected to speak about the state of the union. The president consequently requested cabinet members' ideas regarding this speech. There must have been some awkwardness in this first in-person meeting since the Relative Rank controversy, but they all understood the need to move on.

McHenry answered quickly, but confessed that he had been too busy to consider the matter fully. He begged the president "to consider, what I shall say, as the result, of a too hurried reflexion." His haste actually gives this piece added interest, for he wrote in general terms and explained presumptions he might not otherwise have related. His entire approach to the question concerned American relations with France. McHenry took as unassailable "[t]hat France aims, at universal dominion; that the vices of her government, and nature of her system, render war indispensable to her; that it is a maxim in her policy to prepare the country she designs to subdue by previous divisions, among its citizens, before she strikes it." This is why he saw such danger in the emerging party system. He further believed "that she really intends . . . to bring the United States, or a part of them, by her arms added to her intrigues, into the same state of vassalage . . . to her will, that she has many of the governments of Europe." French history since their revolution "give[s] at least to these positions, an appearance of the greatest probability."[13]

McHenry's thinking had clearly changed over the previous year and a half. In early 1797 he had not thought it likely that France would invade the United States, and this partially explains his repeatedly reducing the large numbers Hamilton suggested for the army. French spies caught in the West and the XYZ Affair, however, had begun to make him nervous. Early in 1798 he thought Americans apathetic about French insults, but by December of that year all of these matters combined with information received from his old friend William Vans Murray—now minister to the Batavian Republic—to convince McHenry that immediate war with France was "indispensable."[14] Perhaps, too, he was more open to the possibility of war because the engine for recruiting an army was now in place.

The situation, however, was a real dilemma to McHenry, leading him to draw a very fine line. Although he thought an "immediate" war necessary to prevent further political division within the country, a declaration of war from Adams might actually encourage that very division, as might a presidential request that *Congress* declare war. Instead McHenry recommended that Adams inform Congress there had been no hopeful signs from France and that defense measures should continue to be vigorously pursued. Indeed, recruiting for the New Army would now begin in earnest. In addition, although the Spanish had left their western garrisons, France had "designs" on the Floridas and Louisiana, especially New Orleans. Because of this Adams should ask for the power, in the event of war, to take "an early possession of New Orleans only" and hold it for Spain. Doing so would help keep Kentucky and Tennessee, always concerned about transporting their goods down the Mississippi, in the Union. McHenry hoped that a presidential speech along these lines would lead Congress to declare war on its own, resulting in a minimal amount of division at home. But if Congress did not, Adams could still defend American interests in New Orleans.

Stoddert and Pickering *personally* wanted to declare war, but did not believe the country was ready. Actually, twice Pickering wrote Hamilton trying both to convince the latter to take a more militaristic stance toward France and to seek advice regarding a possible alliance with Britain. Hamilton, however, would not support these views, and so Pickering put them aside. As a result, Stoddert and Pickering agreed that a recommendation for war from Adams to Congress would fail, and Stoddert argued it would divide that body even further, weakening administration authority.[15]

Ironically, it was Wolcott's response that Adams used, and because Hamilton had been staying with the secretary of the treasury, the paper bore the New Yorker's stamp. Hamilton favored maintaining the status quo. The advantages of this Quasi-War were that public opinion increasingly favored the administration and that "odium is accumulated upon France." The primary disadvantage was that the United States lost rights accorded a country at war. But the advantages outweighed the disadvantages. France would not pursue war unless it was profitable, so that "a declaration of war . . . is inexpedient," Hamilton argued, but prudent defense measures should be continued.[16] Neither should Adams send another minister to France—it was humiliating in light of the xyz Affair—but he should give assurances that a French minister to the United States would be honorably received.

Adams addressed Congress on December 8 following the logic and general order of the Wolcott/Hamilton draft, adding a paragraph about the Spanish leaving the western posts—McHenry's contribution. Although Adams despised Hamilton, the two men actually agreed on many things. But far and away the most significant difference was that, unlike Hamilton, Adams said the United States would not negotiate without receiving "more determinate assurances" that a minister would be received.[17] Adams's position was so much more conciliatory that France just might accommodate the president. It certainly indicated a far greater willingness to send a minister than any of the other Federalist leaders possessed.

Five days later the generals concluded their conference. They had filled reams of pages with the names and suggested ranks of officers throughout the country—except Georgia and the Carolinas, where their information was incomplete. Washington asked Hamilton to place things in writing for McHenry, in what became three letters.

The first letter responded to McHenry's original list of questions. Above all, the New Army ought to be raised immediately, as even those recruits could not be "disciplined in less than a year."[18] To do this, pay needed to begin. So did purchasing. Unfortunately, contractors usually provided inferior quality, but agents frequently defrauded or embezzled. The generals suggested combining both methods, stocking magazines by contract and the rest by military agent. Further, although Hamilton's previous system—the purchase of military supplies by a Purveyor in the treasury—had failed miserably, they now unaccountably sought to create a Purveyor to handle purchasing and accounts within the War Department.[19] It was no solution, and Hamilton would later complain the loudest.

In the second letter, Washington and Hamilton admitted they would like to give Adams's son-in-law proper rank and position, but they had heard the rumors of financial misconduct that could not be ignored. So they asked McHenry to investigate and if Smith were cleared to offer him the position of lieutenant colonel commandant.[20]

The third letter emphasized uniforms, which were discussed at length. An attractive uniform was, of course, desirable for promoting pride and esprit de corps among both officers and enlisted men. Indeed, they decided on the colors of coats, vests, and breeches, while epaulets, plumes, and stars of silver and tin made the list. All of these items were normal parts of the eighteenth-century European uniform that the generals desired to emulate.[21]

Washington, however, should have known better given his own experiences concerning uniforms during the Revolution. Then the main problem had been lack of money, but even after the French became allies and solved that problem, material often lay rotting on the docks. Washington, appreciating the practicality of the American hunting shirt in browns easily made by American vegetable dyes, had asked Congress to adopt that as a uniform, but they had failed to act. He had also urged the creation of a Clothier General, which was done, but the appointee showed little interest.[22]

McHenry, in fact, had just ended a struggle with Oliver Wolcott over uniforms. Although Congress had returned army purchasing power to the secretary of war, the new system was not yet fully implemented, so that Wolcott's signature was still required. Under the system Hamilton had created Wolcott could, and did, stymie acquisitions, and he specifically refused money for uniforms. Since Wolcott thought the army unnecessary, he preferred stockpiling the magazines to ordering military attire. Given Hamilton's earlier covert attacks on McHenry and Adams's disdain for an army, Wolcott simply saw no reason to support the secretary of war. Discussing the matter with Wolcott did not work; he would not budge. McHenry also knew that an appeal to Adams would fail. McHenry had even tried the ridiculously indirect means that he abhorred: he had asked Washington to urge Pickering to influence Wolcott to release the funds! Washington, however, had been preoccupied with his own military duties and then became ill. Instead, the general had done what he had chided McHenry for — Washington had concentrated on his own concerns, namely recruiting men for the New Army and laying out the new Federal City in the District of Columbia, a pet project. The problem persisted, therefore, until the matter was formally out of Wolcott's hands. It is, indeed, interesting that Wolcott behaved this way. As Hamilton's protégé he had spent his early years in the Treasury Department repeatedly consulting Hamilton, asking his advice about numerous things. Hamilton had, in turn, been generous in sharing the benefit of his experience and encouraging Wolcott in the job. Generally, Wolcott adopted whatever view Hamilton had espoused. But by now he had grown more independent, attempting neutrality between Adams and Hamilton. This episode certainly reveals that Hamilton — who complained about the poor uniforms — no longer received whatever he desired from the secretary of the treasury.[23]

Now, even though they knew that material was in short supply, the generals suggested importing fabric. Perhaps, they said, the uniform should even be *sewn* abroad for the sake of economy. They might have taken a lesson from the French, who a century before had decided to uniform their entire army for the first time. France had issued a description of the ideal apparel, but for financial reasons did not press the issue. They emphasized "that all unnecessary luxury should be avoided, and . . . that the uniform of the soldier should be of good French cloth."[24] Even so, it took ten years for the French attire to be generally worn. In choosing European cloth over American homespun, and even looking for the uniforms to be made abroad, Washington and Hamilton had not been practical. Europe was at war, American shipping was being attacked, the United States had only a fledgling navy, and they wanted to import uniforms. Clearly vanity had conquered good sense.

Furthermore, clothing and equipment could not be purchased until Congress passed the yearly army appropriation bill, usually in February or March. Supplies then got on their way by the end of May in order to reach western posts before winter. There was little time for the "purchase and production" of uniforms. There were, after all, a number of items to be generally issued: "a hat, coat, vest, two pairs of woolen and linen overalls, four pairs of shoes, four shirts, two pairs of socks, one stock and clasp, and one pair of buckles as well as one blanket."[25] Trouble with uniforms was bound to occur.

Hamilton, Washington, and Pinckney, however, all left Philadelphia on December 13 satisfied in their minds that the most important matters were now organized and systematized. McHenry's job would be a simple matter of overseeing a mechanism in existence. By "General" agreement, the army had been divided into two commands, with Pinckney heading a southern army and Hamilton commanding the north and west. The worst of the early organizational tasks was now over and recruiting could begin. The generals had, in fact, been kept so busy that Hamilton did not even have time to bid McHenry farewell, or his baggage would have left for New York without him.

SEVENTEEN "A Paltry Insurrection"

Oliver Wolcott

WITH MUCH DECIDED about the army at last, McHenry immediately reported the results of the General Conference to Adams, who in turn referred the account to Congress. Specific bills now had to be drafted for Congress to consider, a task that McHenry readily delegated to General Hamilton, and time was of the essence since the legislature's session would be short. When the New Yorker's bills arrived, however, the most important and intriguing involved the army. Dissatisfied with the size of the New Army of 1798, the Provisional Army of 10,000, and the Volunteer Corps that had been created at the same time, Hamilton now added an Eventual Army of over twenty-eight regiments compared with the New Army's twelve.[1] Had all armies been raised, the United States would have boasted a force of 53,000 regulars, plus dragoons and a Volunteer Corps.

But Hamilton's vision of military grandeur terrified Republicans. Most troubling, Richard Kohn argues, the new law took matters out of the hands of local citizens and allowed the president to substitute federal volunteers for state militias "to suppress disorder or execute the laws." For some "extreme" Federalists, Kohn says, "the military forces authorized during the Quasi-War were designed to intimidate, to create behind the Alien and Sedition Acts a force capable of enforcing the laws, checking or preventing rebellion, and inhibiting partisan attacks on the government." The implications of Hamilton's vision in an era deeply suspicious of standing armies, then, struck a deep and resonant chord—the possibilities for oppression alarmed all Republicans even as the potential pleased some Federalists.[2] The Republicans were worried, however, about possibilities. Even the New Army only partially existed.

Whether or not the army was real, Congress now changed the officer list

Washington and the generals had pored over. Irritated, Washington could not deny Congress's right to do this, but frankly could not fathom why; he could only remind McHenry that the generals had considered each appointment and that Congress should not make changes lightly.[3] The reason, of course, was that congressmen needed to take care of their men at home.

Adams too was concerned about appointments, for he saw these positions as patronage, a way to build political support whether the army became a reality or not. Most of his correspondence with McHenry during these early months of the year revolved around persons he wished to receive field or regimental appointments. Even as he made appointments, however, Adams hampered McHenry's efforts to put the officer corps together. The president resolved not to fix the ranks of these lower officers until the entire service was determined; commissions, of course, could not be sent until ranks were settled. Consequently, as of January 10, 1799, McHenry was only able to send notices without a *determined* rank to congressional nominees. Men naturally hesitated to accept, and the corps remained disorganized. The best McHenry could do was insist that the officers were in active service from the moment of their acceptance, but Adams remained undecided and continued to delay the process.[4]

By mid-February even Hamilton began to appreciate that there were complications; he had expected that once he was involved, all would progress swiftly. That, however, did not occur despite McHenry's full cooperation. Hamilton now suspected a problem within the administration. "I more and more discover cause to apprehend that obstacles of a very peculiar kind stand in the way of an efficient and successful management of our military concerns. These it would be unsafe at present to explain." Hamilton finally began to see that the army lagged *not* because of McHenry but because of presidential policy.[5]

By February the reasons for Adams's obstructionism crystallized. The president had been receiving a stream of important correspondence from Europe that he shared with no one. Both William Vans Murray, American minister to Holland, and the president's son John Quincy Adams, minister to Prussia, reported new French peace initiatives. Talleyrand had sent Murray written assurances that an American minister would be honorably received, which Murray relayed to Adams. While Murray and John Quincy still distrusted France and these indirect methods, they also feared that if the United States ignored these French advances, that country might publish their notes and discredit the Adams administration. If it was a French bluff, as they thought, they recommended calling it.[6]

At home, Adams saw the army and its legislation, which he disliked, growing apace with popular discontent. Although he had initially supported military mobilization, Adams had grown more and more disenchanted with almost every aspect of the New Army. Now he found himself in agreement with Murray and John Quincy: if the French would negotiate, so would Adams.[7]

So, on February 18, 1799, Adams nominated William Vans Murray to serve as Minister Plenipotentiary to France. A better party leader would have consulted with his supporters, building a bulwark from which to fight the inevitable political battle ahead. A great man, Adams was not a great party leader, and he warned no one.

Consequently, this news broke upon the capital as an unexpected blast. Federalists were shocked and Republicans astonished, for although Adams had indicated this possibility in his opening speech of the session, no one had known of Talleyrand's moves, and most Federalists did not care. They believed, like Hamilton, that the only move sufficiently palliative on France's part would be *their* sending a minister to the United States.[8]

The cabinet was as astounded as everyone else, for Adams had kept them in the dark, convinced that they would only try to dissuade him.[9] After all, they all personally favored war—but he conveniently forgot that they had also recommended *against* declaring it. The truth is, Adams had become suspicious and even paranoid about his cabinet, believing they were all supporters of Hamilton and in league against him. If consulted, Adams assumed they would work behind his back to undermine his decision. He remembered Pickering's treatment of his son-in-law and generalized this behavior toward the entire cabinet.

Hoping to minimize the possible dangers of a new mission to France, a group of Federalist senators hurried to meet with Adams and ask him to withdraw the nomination; indignant, the president refused.[10] When they threatened to oppose the nomination, they felt Adams's wrath as he, in turn, threatened to resign the presidency to Jefferson. Lowering the stakes, the men finally compromised on a commission of three including Murray.

As for the cabinet, Stoddert and Lee supported Adams's decision to send another mission, while McHenry, Pickering, and Wolcott opposed it. McHenry, fearing any treaty with France would alienate England and lead to war with that country, had come to believe that this Quasi-War served the United States better than other options. Since he was also certain that France aimed at world conquest, alienating England was the *last* thing the United States should do. The best course, he thought, was to maintain this uneasy peace with France, and strengthen militarily while not estranging England. Then, when France's designs on the United States became manifest, she could fight with England as her ally. Given this frame of mind, a treaty with France would dangerously unbalance the status quo. But when Adams indicated that the commissioners would not leave until the Directory indicated they would be well received, McHenry, Wolcott, and Pickering let the matter rest.[11] It might fade away.

In the meantime, the army had to be raised and paid for. To accomplish this Congress passed a direct property tax designed to raise $2,000,000, and it authorized Wolcott to procure a loan of up to $5,000,000. So the army now resulted in an extremely unpopular tax on regular property owners. To make matters worse, the act provided that taxes would be assessed based on a home's dimensions and the number of windows. This meant that federal tax assessors had to come to individual homes and measure.

This situation could hardly have been more incendiary, for the predominantly German-speaking farmers (*Kirchenleute* or Church People) of Bucks and Northampton counties in Pennsylvania. According to Paul Douglas Newman, these rural counties were already angry about the Alien and Sedition Acts. These children and grandchildren of immigrants had developed a democratic ideology that gave them the "liberty to oppose governmental authority when they found it unfair or threatening." But they also supported authority when they deemed it appropriate. Many of them had served Washington during the Valley Forge winter. They had been permitted to return to their nearby homes for the season, but they had "patrolled the area between the Schuylkill and the Delaware Rivers under General John Armstrong." Their service in the American Revolution, Newman argues, led them to believe that the concept of popular sovereignty applied to them, and that the 1776 Pennsylvania constitution permitted a certain amount of (nonviolent) resistance. Indeed, they had successfully resisted state taxes through peaceful means (i.e., imposing silence at foreclosure auctions). The farmers now incorrectly convinced themselves that this new tax was inconsistent with the United States Constitution, appealing to article 1, section 9, which said that such a levy could only be laid in proportion to a census or enumeration. There had, however, been an enumeration. But they also believed the levy unfair, as it taxed the industrious yeoman farmers and not the wealthy land speculators and merchants who did not build homes that would be measured and taxed. Surely locals also wished to retain control of their region, afraid that the new tax would push landholders who were barely hanging on into tenancy.[12]

When the federal assessors arrived to impose the new tax in this emotionally charged backcountry, the farmers reacted violently. Their most prominent leader was an auctioneer named John Fries, who had served as an officer in the Pennsylvania militia during the Revolutionary War. According to Newman, Fries's ancestry was probably Germanic, harking back to Friesland in the Netherlands, even though his father had immigrated from Wales. John Fries himself had grown up in Pennsylvania and spoke both English and German fluently. During the Whiskey Rebellion, he had commanded a militia company to help subdue those who violently opposed the Whiskey tax. Though Fries was generally supportive of the government, this new law proved too much.[13]

The two counties asked the federal assessors to stay out until the law's status could be determined. When the principal assessor tried to meet with the citizens to explain the law, he was shouted down. Locals captured assessors trying to do their job and warned them away at the end of a gun barrel. Then the local commissioner appealed up the ladder to the U.S. Marshal, who made arrests. Making Fries their captain, the rebels marched to the Bethlehem tavern/jail and freed the prisoners.[14]

At this point the matter came before Adams, who was displeased not only because it illustrated popular dissatisfaction with his administration but also because he was ready to leave for Quincy. He wanted nothing to keep him away from Abigail, so he acted precipitately. He also had a horror of domestic insurrection that made him too quick to fear the worst. It did not help that the matter came to his attention through Pickering, who was rarely moderate. Adams readily agreed that the acts amounted "to treason, being overt acts of levying war against the United States." Under the Constitution, Adams correctly added, he was authorized "to call forth military force to suppress such combinations and to cause the laws aforesaid to be duly executed, and I have accordingly determined so to do." He called upon the insurgents to disperse and then left for Quincy.[15]

McHenry, however, could not execute Adams's orders until he had more information, for no one really knew the insurgents' numbers, their capabilities, or how widespread they were. Upon receiving this intelligence from the

U.S. Marshal, McHenry ordered Brigadier General William MacPherson to prepare his men to march at a moment's notice. The president's plan was to bypass the militia, who were needed at their farms in the early spring, and instead use mainly volunteer companies supported by an impressive number of regulars. This was precisely what Republicans had feared. However, only about sixty volunteers could be mustered, so McHenry again protected himself by meeting with the other secretaries. They agreed that McHenry should call for militias from the governors of Pennsylvania and New Jersey, uniting the state and federal governments against the rebels.[16]

Other Federalists such as Hamilton, Robert Goodloe Harper, and even General MacPherson listened to rumor and feared McHenry had not called enough men. Hamilton warned McHenry "whenever the Government appears in arms it ought to appear like a *Hercules*, and inspire respect by the display of strength." He worried that an inadequate show of strength might turn a riot into a rebellion. Rumor had led Harper to magnify the number of rebels to "at least three thousand effective men." He insisted that all of "the volunteers & regulation cavalry . . . [ought to] be put immediately in motion." MacPherson agreed.[17]

But McHenry's intelligence, in which he was confident, indicated there were only around 100 rebels, perhaps 150 at the most. He ordered Hamilton to direct one company to Newtown and another to Reading where they would rendezvous with other companies. McHenry quickly determined what troops to send, issued the appropriate orders, and within a few weeks all the troops were at their respective rendezvous points. Only General MacPherson's troops lagged behind because Pennsylvania's adjutant general had not sent the proper returns. "Is it not remarkable that however slightly the present Governor of Pennsylvania comes in contact with insurrection that delay becomes unavoidable in quelling it," McHenry observed. Of course, it could not have been easy to get Pennsylvanians to act against their own men. MacPherson was not, in fact, able to leave until April 4. These, along with the militia and volunteers, numbered over 240 men. He ordered other officers, further away, to be ready.[18]

Wolcott, however, would not be satisfied: to younger brother Frederick Wolcott he admitted that the rebellion was not major—"[t]here is a paltry insurrection here, which I am inclined to think will be subdued without difficulty." But to Hamilton he wrote, in complete contradiction, "I am grieved when I think of the situation of the govt. An affair which ought to have been settled at once will cost much time & perhaps be so managed as to encourage other and formidable rebellions. We have no Prest. here, & the appearance of languor & indecision are discouraging to the friends of govt. Mr. McH- does the best in his power—yet his operations are such as to confirm more and more a belief of utter unfitness for the situation."[19] While Wolcott surely hoped to spread calm in his letter to his brother, this observation was certainly accurate. But Wolcott also wanted the Federalists to appear firm, and he remained very concerned about McHenry, as Hamilton's earlier criticisms still resonated.

McHenry, however, had matters well in hand. After MacPherson left, the secretary of war wrote Adams "that the appearance of this force, and a knowledge of that which is held in readiness to march, will be productive of their submission." Adams judged McHenry's decisions "to have been well considered and prudently pursued." In fact, suppression of the rebellion progressed admirably because McHenry was right—it was a small matter. Crucial was the fact that they captured John Fries immediately, surprising him in the midst of calling at an auction.[20] Indeed, they were able to do so because the "rebels" had gone back to their daily business. By April 18 the army had finished the job, having captured a few men here and there, some men even turning themselves in. The Fries Rebellion was over.

By trusting to his intelligence and sending a proportionately reasonable number of men, McHenry made the government appear effective rather than either oppressive or foolish. Hamilton's injunction to send a military might that appeared like a Hercules certainly did not risk having too few men to subdue a rebellion. He was insensitive, however, to the fact that too many men against a small number of rebels could simply make the new government seem oppressive. It would be too easy to alienate the populace. McHenry, however, by believing his intelligence and sending an appropriate number of men, balanced the numbers well. Even so, this area, which before now had supported Washington and his politics, would not vote Federalist again.[21]

EIGHTEEN

"I Have Always . . . Considered You as a Man of Understanding and of the Strictest Integrity"

John Adams

FRESH FROM HIS VICTORY over the Fries Rebellion, McHenry again faced new difficulties. Supplies for the New Army were frequently unavailable or incomplete. Uniforms exposed the problem first. Tench Francis, the purveyor of public supplies, had a predictably difficult time locating sufficient material and manufacturers for the task. Even though Francis had 900 people sewing uniforms, nothing would be available until the end of April. Because the generals had planned so specifically about the uniforms, down to differing regimental buttons, no single generic uniform could be dispersed with discriminative insignia applied later. McHenry should have seen this problem and corrected it, but the desire to build esprit de corps at least partially through these uniforms was strong among the generals. It never occurred to any of the principals involved to make a virtue of that which was simple and American. General Hamilton "lamented that circumstances have prevented the obtaining an early supply of necessary Clothing for the troops" since this delayed recruiting.[1] Nonetheless, by June, eight states were well into their enlistment programs.

The real issue was the basic division of labor between the roles of quartermaster general and purveyor, which Hamilton had borrowed from the Revolution. It was too divided, with no one person responsible for overseeing the operation. A single head of supplies with clear descending lines of purchasing and storage to assure accountability would have achieved much. Instead, there was a quartermaster general and a purveyor, Tench Francis, who made purchases, while the materiel was stored and distributed by Samuel Hodgdon, the superintendent of military stores. As a result, there was also little quality control. Shoes and boots appeared that could not survive a march of twenty miles. "Tis the scene," Hamilton complained, "of the

worst periods of our revolution war [sic] acted over again even with carica-
ture." Not seeing the root of the problem, he tinkered, working out a plan
that gave these two men more assistants and further defined their responsibilities. McHenry liked it, hoping it would work. In fact, he too had erroneously concluded that the trouble lay with the purveyor and superintendent of military stores. Even before Hamilton's complaints, McHenry had
begun looking for a special assistant to the purveyor and had considered
removing Superintendent Hodgdon. But Hodgdon was Washington's appointment and Pickering's good friend and supporter. Tench Francis, the
purveyor, was the son of an extremely important and wealthy Philadelphia
family and could not be easily dismissed. On the other hand, if McHenry
believed their work inadequate, he should have done battle with the political forces. Perhaps he sympathized with them. In fact, firing these men
would not have solved the fundamental problem.[2]

There was, indeed, so much decentralization that Hamilton sometimes
could not even tell when to order through the War Department or the supply
officer. This required knowing federal laws respecting the final organization
of the New Army. Since the original laws remained at the printer's for what
seemed to McHenry like an ice age, McHenry sent the generals copies of
rough drafts. Most of what Hamilton needed, "Ordnance Cloathing and military Stores," was ordered through the War Department, which informed
the supply officer, who managed distribution and kept McHenry informed.
Perhaps anticipating his friend's impatience, McHenry reminded Hamilton of his own duty to facilitate the process by making "estimates of Military Stores . . . to enable order to be taken for their seasonable purchase and
transportation." For now McHenry issued what he could to Hamilton's army.[3]

Hoping to finally fix the various problems, Hamilton traveled to Philadelphia for three or four days to "promote the service" and collaborate with
McHenry about provisions, the paymaster situation, and the growing problem of desertion. McHenry then presented Hamilton's plan to Adams, carefully pointing out that it had been drafted by the New Yorker and approved
by Wolcott. Adams, however, stalled, asking the opinions of the other cabinet members and then insisting it required an act of Congress and would
have to await their next session. There the matter lay.[4] Provision problems,
therefore, plagued the New Army for the rest of its existence, and Hamilton
complained chronically.

Another obstacle to efficient supply stemmed from a fundamental mis-
conception Hamilton had that no one corrected. He believed the United

States more financially and industrially "mature" than it really was. It is ironic that Hamilton, who had attempted unsuccessfully as secretary of the treasury to support industry, failed to appreciate its still-infant state. Perhaps his work in that area had led him to wishful thinking. For example, although no significant fabric industry existed, Hamilton expected uniforms to appear quickly and entire. McHenry himself worked to establish iron foundries in 1798 so that muskets and balls could be produced. The armory at Harpers Ferry, an idea pushed by Washington, was still under construction, and its canal, necessary to harness waterpower for the munitions factory, would not open until 1801.[5] It is no wonder that newly enlisted men had no arms for some time. The country was clearly preindustrial and the machinery to create the goods for an army would take time to develop. Hamilton wanted a speed of mobilization the country could not manage.

Still, complaints within the service became so widespread that McHenry reminded Hamilton of his duty to minimize them. The secretary did not expect to eradicate complaints, for they were part of the nature of the bureaucratic military beast. Officers, however, were *not* to complain about any military matters in the presence of their men and causes ought to be explained to improve morale.[6] Chastened, Hamilton issued a circular to that effect.

But the organization of the New Army was only one of McHenry's concerns. Cordial relations with the various Indian tribes required that survey lines be run; applications for army appointments from Adams, Washington, Hamilton, congressmen, and others required responses; and volunteer companies frequently asked for arms, which required a diplomatic letter from McHenry refusing their request until the army was itself armed. Then, too, forts around the country required attention.[7] Wilkinson saw to the western forts, leaving McHenry to fret over the coastal defenses where French ships might find their way. Congress had allotted money for these fortresses, and leading local citizens headed committees to see they were built.

Certainly the fort being built in Baltimore had a special place in the secretary of war's heart. Not only was the city his home, which he wanted to protect, but the fort was to be named for him. Adams, Washington, many Revolutionary War generals, and all of the cabinet had posts designated after them. This would be Fort McHenry, and its fate lay largely in the hands of the Marine Committee of Baltimore headed by Robert Gilmor. Plans had been drawn up and the federal government engaged an engineer, who found the original plan defective and drew up his own. Unfortunately, the new plan ran over the government's budget by $4,000, which McHenry had to refuse, for the amount fixed by Congress, he said, was immutable. Probably McHenry saw it as a conflict of interest to push funds for his own hometown and not for others and so refused to ask Congress for more money for Baltimore. Rather than allow the project to languish, city subscribers made up the difference and Fort McHenry was built.[8]

Adams, of course, heartily disliked all this expense on the army, so in early August when Pickering gave him letters from Murray and Talleyrand reiterating French willingness to receive American ministers, the president directed Pickering to draw up a set of instructions for them. Adams wanted to be ready when the time was right to send the ministers. "I shall pursue the negotiation, and I expect the cooperation of the heads of departments."[9]

The cabinet, however, was alarmed by Adams's order, for events in France were changing fast. Four Directory members had been deposed, including its president, and everyone speculated about France's future. Would the Directory survive? Would France return to a monarchy? Stoddert argued that Adams should come to the government's temporary home in Trenton, where late-breaking news might convince the president to change the instructions, or even that the mission ought to be suspended. In any event, Adams's presence would give "great satisfaction to the best disposed and best informed men."[10]

But Adams refused to leave Massachusetts earlier than planned, reminding Stoddert that he and the cabinet had discussed all possible contingencies before his departure and everyone knew what to do. On the other hand, he had to admit that changes in Europe might alter matters. "If any considerable difference should unexpectedly arise between the heads of department, I will come," he wrote. But Adams saw no reason to hurry matters, and "[i]f any information . . . should arrive, which . . . would render any alteration in . . . [the mission's] instructions necessary or expedient, I am perfectly willing that their departure should be suspended, until I can be informed of it, or until I can join you." He was not worried. "France has always been a pendulum."[11]

Stoddert, however, feared that Adams's absence from the seat of government would be used against him in the future. During the election of 1800 "[a]rtful and designing men" would surely refer to his absence while important international decisions were being made. This gave Adams pause, and he decided to come to Trenton by mid-October when he would review the situation. But, finding it distasteful to think in such blatant party terms, Adams asked Stoddert not to refer to the election again.[12] Upon arriving at Trenton, Adams found a letter from Attorney General Lee indicating no reason to suspend the mission to France; Stoddert agreed. Adams already knew that Pickering, Wolcott, and McHenry favored a suspension, since he had asked for and received their opinions while still at Quincy.

Then Hamilton arrived and called upon the president to urge postponing the mission. Adams would not believe Pickering's protest that Hamilton's presence was coincidence. The New Yorkers' visit cemented two matters in Adams's eyes. First, he determined to send the mission to France. Even if there were a change in the French government, he told Hamilton, there was no reason to think they would not receive our ministers. And if they did not, it was to their shame and not ours.[13] Second, the idea of a Hamiltonian faction in his cabinet, completely subservient to Hamilton's ideas, became fixed. To Adams's mind they were all of a piece.

That was not, however, the truth. Pickering, true to his nature, vehemently opposed the mission *and* maneuvered against it behind Adams's back. McHenry, however, would have nothing to do with such activities. True, he opposed the mission since he thought Talleyrand's assurances too vague, fearing the ministers might be "received" by France yet not get an audience with the Directory. With all the political changes occurring over there, he saw no reason not to wait until a more stable time. Further, he correctly believed that Federalists at large opposed the mission. But McHenry never worked against the mission. Indeed, he argued that if Adams sent the men, Federalists "must go honestly to work, insist upon our own, and take care to do nothing that might intangle [us] in . . . a quarrel with England."[14] In other words, they must make the best of the president's decision and work with it.

But McHenry did not prevail; Adams's mind was made up. Although Adams knew that sending the mission to France might well alienate the majority of the Federalists, including his cabinet, he insisted on dispatching the ministers. Certainly conspiracy thinking played its part, for when Adams looked at the cabinet, he saw a Hamiltonian cabal. He was mistaken. Certainly McHenry was not in thrall to Hamilton. Neither was Pickering. "Indeed, Hamilton soon became so skeptical of his ability to influence Pickering that on those occasions when he thought it absolutely essential to intervene, he preferred to work through Washington or Wolcott rather than confront the secretary of state directly." Moreover, although Wolcott had started as a Hamiltonian apologist, he had become far more independent, agreeing more with Adams about both the army and economy. They had all sought Hamilton's advice now and then, but none answered to him now. On the other hand, if Adams saw scheming within the cabinet, when they looked abroad, they saw the danger of a French attack. To Adams the mission meant both maintaining peace with France and hurting Hamilton. To the cabinet, the mission meant leaving the country more vulnerable to attack and reducing the military. For both sides, the stakes were high and well rooted in notions of conspiracy.[15]

McHenry, in fact, viewed the Federalist fissure over the mission as potentially catastrophic, since he expected the split to cause the Republicans to take the presidency in the next election. If the Republicans won, he feared, French influence would dominate the government. Since France had conquered European countries by first fomenting political divisions within them, the rifts he saw in the United States indicated that it was happening domestically. Even negotiation held dangers, for a hiatus would allow the French time to palliate the popular will to resist the inevitable invasion. France would conquer the United States. The country's very existence was in peril. No one was more aware than these early leaders that the United States was a most fragile republic. The country remained experimental, a federation achieved only through the greatest effort, which possessed neither a significant army nor a navy.[16]

The stakes were enormous. Yet what could be done? The two sides within the party *were* talking, they were simply at an impasse. Since they fundamentally disagreed over French intentions, they were forced to different conclusions about negotiating with that country.

Ironically, someone of McHenry's temperament might have been able to help reconcile the two sides. Unfortunately, McHenry himself did not see how to make the two sides cooperate any more closely than they already had. How do two sides in fundamental disagreement fashion a common policy? In addition, McHenry lacked the necessary credibility within his own party to effect conciliation. Whatever credibility he had was lost when Hamilton had determined deliberately to undermine him. Moreover, the difficulties, even impossibilities, of raising an army had caused general discontent both with the situation and with him. Still, had he found the vision, he might also have found the strength to foster some party solidarity.

Yet this points to another problem independent of McHenry, for he was a member of a partisan alliance in an age that did not believe in parties and that, consequently, could not fully function as such. Adams especially prized his political independence despite the fact that he knew he needed some sort of party network.[17] Pickering was a different brand of maverick. While McHenry might have been able to appeal to Hamilton on the basis of partisan solidarity, it would be difficult to sway all the principals under that banner.

Only after the envoys had left for France did McHenry complain to Washington that Adams had *both* nominated the envoys and dispatched them without consulting the cabinet. Pickering's machinations had deeply impacted Adams, who feared that a prior consultation with the cabinet would only give them—really Pickering—time to counter his actions. If Adams was going to act without consulting his cabinet, however, McHenry wondered what the purpose of a cabinet was.[18]

In fact, the secretary of war began to wonder just how long this particular cabinet would last. According to McHenry, Adams "believes, and with reason, that three of the heads of departments have viewed the mission as impolitic and unwise." Although Stoddert advised the mission's suspension, he did not disapprove of it and so did not incur Adams's wrath. McHenry found "that he is particularly displeased with Mr. Pickering and Mr. Wolcott, thinking they have encouraged opposition to it to the eastward; seemingly, a little less so with me. Whether he will think it expedient to dismiss any, or how many of us, is a problem." Attorney General Lee and Stoddert thought Adams ought to dismiss one of them, probably Pickering. However, "[t]here are . . . powerful personal reasons, especially at this juncture, which forbid it; and it is more than possible, as these chiefly respect the eastern quarter of the Union, they will prevail." Both Pickering and Wolcott came from the eastern quarter, or New England, and Adams did not like to see his region diminished. "But in my view of the subject," McHenry wrote, "the evil does not lie in a change of Secretaries . . . as these may be replaced with good and able men, but in the mission, which . . . is become an apple of discord to the federalists." The mission, he thought, would surely "operate upon the ensuing election of President, as to put in jeopardy the fruits of all their past labours, by consigning to men, devoted to French innovations and demoralizing principles, the reins of government. It is this dreaded consequence which afflicts, and calls for all the wisdom of, the federalists."[19]

Adams was angry, and knew that his decision to send the mission would probably destroy the party. But he saw more clearly than the others—

because he did not share his information—that France was no real threat. For him, the mission was a way of averting war. Then too, he hoped to defeat the army, the "Hamiltonians," and what he saw as their militarism.[20] If Adams was wrong about McHenry's Hamiltonianism, he was right about France, and that was far more important.

It is too ironic that the same man, American minister to Holland William Vans Murray, sent Adams words of peace from France but *also* had helped to convince McHenry of France's thirst for conquest. This was not hypocrisy on Murray's part, but timing. McHenry and Murray were old friends and colleagues in Maryland politics, and although Murray was younger, the two had corresponded with some regularity. In fact, McHenry's nephew, John McHenry Jr., now served as Murray's secretary.[21] Murray had warned that France conquered only after first fostering internal division. This belief had exaggerated Federalist fears of Republicans. Yet when Talleyrand began to communicate with Murray, the ambassador thought it proper to inform only the president. Now Murray would serve as one of the envoys to France, and John McHenry Jr., whom James had helped to raise, would probably attend as secretary to facilitate the proceedings.

While McHenry's nephew worked for peace, the man to whom McHenry was most dedicated, Washington, died on December 14, 1799, and the nation mourned the loss of its greatest citizen. Federalists did so especially, for Washington was their preeminent leader, the one man who could "unite all hearts" in a time of deeply felt division. It was a double blow to McHenry; he had lost a leader, mentor, and friend.

The mission to France led to exactly what many Federalists feared—a relaxation of the military effort. After all, there was little point in building an army if there would be no war. Harrison Gray Otis, chair of a House Committee to investigate the military situation, learned from McHenry that 3,399 men had enlisted in the New Army, less than one-third of the goal. This was a number the Congress could live with, so that body decided to compromise. A small army would not cost much and could form the kernel of a larger army if negotiations failed. So on February 20, 1800, Congress halted recruitment.[22] The New Army, which had existed primarily on paper, was dying.

Hoping to accomplish something, McHenry now recommended the establishment of a military academy. He, Washington, and Hamilton had favored such a school since the Revolution, when it was clear that few applicants to officer status were adequately prepared. Hoping to remedy this problem now, McHenry suggested a Fundamental School and another for Artillery and Engineering. McHenry even recommended a Naval Academy, all to naught. Congress was in an antimilitarist mood.[23]

As a result, even the small army just recruited did not last long. Before Congress adjourned in the spring, they "authorized the discharge of the officers and men already enlisted, with some exceptions, including the staff."[24] The New Army no longer existed. The general officers now presided over the dismantling of the army they had worked so hard to create.

Pleased, Adams by now had convinced himself that the army was none of his doing, but instead that of Hamilton. Adams ignored the fact that he had approved McHenry's first report to Congress urging an army. Although the president later changed his mind, it was too late and he bore some responsibility for the army.

Now Adams could think of being reelected. It was clear, though, that the party that had put him in office was now fragmenting. "The federal members of Congress held a caucus . . . in which . . . it was determined, that each member in his state, would use his best endeavours to have Mr. Adams and Major General Charles Cotesworth Pinckney run for President, without giving one a preference to the other."[25] This smacked, of course, of Hamilton's plan to defeat Adams in the previous presidential election, and the president saw the writing on the wall.

The last straw came with a close Republican victory in New York's legislative election for the fall of 1799. That state's presidential electors would be chosen by the legislature and so the outcome of this election would affect the next presidential election. Since Adams had won the previous election by only three votes and had carried New York, it was important for Adams to win that state in 1800. When the Federalists lost control of the legislature, Adams irrationally blamed Hamilton. Although Hamilton did not wholeheartedly back Adams, the New Yorker still had no wish to lose Federalist dominance of the state legislature. But the president now considered himself free; he no longer needed to appease the "Hamiltonians."

In fact, Adams would have to build support elsewhere and the "Hamiltonians" now became a liability. To recoup some of his popularity the president would have to disassociate himself from the army and the Quasi-War. He could argue it was *that* wing of the party that stood for the conflict with France, the military buildup, and the taxes that had proved so unpopular. That meant getting rid of the members of his cabinet most visibly associated with these things—McHenry and Pickering, an event McHenry had somewhat anticipated.

Still, he did not expect it on the morning of May 5 when Adams asked McHenry to come discuss the appointment of a new purveyor after Tench Francis's death. McHenry described this incident later in a report he deposited in the War Department's papers with Adams's approval. McHenry had been considering one Jonathan Williams for purveyor, but Adams had decided on another candidate and McHenry deferred. The interview should have been over, but Adams had other things on his mind. He was angry about the New York election, blamed Hamilton, and believed that the cabinet officers were against him. As the president continued he grew angrier. Just thinking about Hamilton gave him greater conviction that what he was about to do was right.

McHenry, Adams declared, was subservient to Hamilton and he listed his proofs. "[I]t was you who biassed General Washington's mind (who hesitated) and induced him to place Hamilton on the list of Major Generals, before Generals Knox and Pinckney. I have the General's letter to that effect."[26] Well, of course Adams did *not* have such a letter, because Washington had written no such thing and McHenry knew it—he reminded Adams of this.

So the situation became more difficult, and Adams became more heated. Perhaps he also needed to justify his desire to rid himself of McHenry; it must, after all, have been difficult to ask a man of integrity and diligence to resign. Overcome by anger and a need to feel vindicated in asking for McHenry's resignation, Adams's onslaught continued. McHenry later reported Adams's views to his nephew. "General Washington had saddled him with three Secretaries, Wolcott, Pickering, and myself. I had not appointed a gentleman in North Carolina, the only elector who had given him a vote in that State, a captain in the army, and afterwards had him appointed a lieutenant, which he refused." Moreover, "I HAD EULOGIZED GENERAL WASHINGTON, IN MY REPORT TO CONGRESS, and had attempted in the same report, to praise Hamilton. In short, there was no bounds to his jealousy. I had done nothing right. I had advised a suspension of the mission. Every body blamed me for my official conduct, and I must resign."[27]

Indeed, Adams's "weak passion was jealousy, that is, suspicion, in the form of a gnawing uneasiness over the way that others, especially the public, regarded him."[28] Adams need not have been so jealous of Hamilton, at least with regard to McHenry—he had differences with Hamilton, always altered anything of Hamilton's he disagreed with, and, most importantly, had only resisted Adams when he thought the army might lose Washington. If McHenry had a reputation for inefficiency, that was largely due to Adams's own stalling tactics.

But Adams did have reason to be jealous of the former president, as McHenry's true loyalties lay with Washington. Insofar as Hamilton was the Virginian's choice as second-in-command, McHenry had supported him. But McHenry *had* been willing to sacrifice Hamilton, asking the latter twice to take an inferior position. Still, after Hamilton became second-in-command, McHenry did rely heavily on his subordinate for the assistance he had long needed.

For the sake of his own dignity, McHenry defended himself. Adams had never given McHenry any indication that he was doing poor work. (For a good reason—Adams knew he had caused most of the delays to which the army was subjected.) McHenry did not see why Adams now felt the need to hide behind the opinion of others; Adams himself had seen the quality of McHenry's letters and papers and could judge for himself. Still, the opinion having been expressed and his resignation requested, McHenry would not refuse.

Having achieved his desired goal, Adams now felt some remorse. In fact, McHenry later reported that Adams admitted there had really been nothing wrong with McHenry's abilities. "For myself, I have always, I will acknowledge considered you as a man of understanding and of the strictest Integrity, and I have had no Reasons to be dissatisfied with the proofs you have given me of your Capacity, in your official intercourse with me, nor with your general Behaviour towards me." This was not merely a palliative offered by the president to a man he had wounded, for he repeated much the same substance about McHenry later to Wolcott. McHenry's real crimes— which Adams did not admit—were both his association with Hamilton (weaker than Adams believed) and especially his superintendence of a *very* unpopular army during a presidential election year.[29]

McHenry tendered his resignation the next morning, which was accepted. He would stay long enough to put his office in order for the next secretary of war, and to help his successor understand the office.

If misery loves company, then McHenry must have been gratified by Adams's treatment of Pickering. Apparently regretting his interview with McHenry,

Adams decided to avoid a face-to-face confrontation with Pickering. Instead Adams wrote the secretary of state, asking for his resignation, but Pickering stubbornly refused. Adams then sent him a note of dismissal.[30]

So the two men most closely associated with the Quasi-War were now out of the Adams administration. Adams could try to create a third partisan alliance independent of the Hamiltonian Federalists called the "Constitutionalists."[31] In this way, the political storm would put an end to the Federalists as an effective national force.

At first, McHenry refused to discuss the president publicly. He was a gentleman and would live up to his own ideas of what that code meant. It was, in fact, more than a week after his resignation before he could bring himself to a written account of what had happened, and that was only for close friends and relatives. "For my own part," McHenry confided in his nephew, "I had never taken a single step to depreciate his character, or prevent his election, or expressed any public disapprobation of the mission."[32]

But the truth is, McHenry was deeply hurt and he could not help but feel bitterly wronged. Now the gentleman in him warred with the wounded man. When he first communicated with Hamilton, McHenry said no more than that he had resigned. But a few days later to Bishop John Carroll, a friend and Federalist leader back in Maryland, McHenry wrote with some freedom—the president had been "indecent and at times outrageous"—and McHenry became convinced that he was dismissed for electioneering purposes. He believed the secretary of the navy helped engineer it. "Stoddert you know is pretty dexterous at intrigue." It was he, McHenry knew, who urged Adams to think of the 1800 election, and the election explained why Stoddert had at first opposed the mission to France but had then changed his mind. McHenry thought "Wolcott is retained only because the President is affraid [sic] . . . of derangements in the affairs of the Treasury."[33]

By the end of the month, however, McHenry wanted everything on the record, penned a full account of the meeting, and submitted a copy to Adams for comment or corrections. The president took his lumps and made none. An account really was necessary, for if McHenry in some measure had expected it, the party at large had not. Without an explanation, McHenry would be considered a rat leaving a sinking ship. So he sent another copy confidentially to Hamilton. "Oh mad! mad! mad!" Hamilton howled. McHenry agreed. From his point of view, Adams had vacillated so much, becoming both irrational and irascible, that McHenry even began to doubt the president's sanity. Adams's care in keeping his own counsel and willingness to change his mind under new circumstances caused him to seem far more inconsistent than he actually was. These apparent contradictions frustrated his colleagues and left them thinking Adams a bit bizarre. It was not the first time a colleague had felt this way.[34] Years before when they had served together in France, Franklin had said much the same thing.

Finally, at eleven o'clock the morning of June 2, McHenry installed Benjamin Stoddert as acting secretary of war. "I placed Mr. Stoddert . . . in the chair I have usually occupied; I then formally laid upon his head eight volumes of the 'code militaire' by Briquet with Caesars Commentaries in French; kept them upon it 'till he was nearly stupified, when I pronounced him duly installed and as well qualified to discharge the duties of Secretary of War as the President."[35] McHenry was content that he had left his office with as much honor as he could muster under the circumstances, and then he left for home—for Baltimore.

Now Adams authorized demobilization of the New Army to take place by June 15. Hamilton managed the details.[36] Ironically, the country returned to the western constabulary force McHenry had so successfully set up during his first years as secretary of war. In fact, his early work bore long-lasting fruit, enduring into the late nineteenth century, and helping to protect settlers on the frontier. McHenry could take pride in that.

Finally, although Federalists like McHenry had worked themselves into a mental state bordering on paranoia about France, their carrot-and-stick policy *had* preserved peace between the two countries. For when France saw that the United States was indeed pursuing a military buildup, Talleyrand sent out conciliatory messages. Although McHenry was wrong about France's wish to conquer the United States and the final mission that Adams sent to France, his work in building up the military had indeed helped to frighten France into respecting American sovereignty. If it was not the outcome McHenry expected, it was nonetheless the greatest of endings— Peace!

PART FOUR

Retirement

NINETEEN

"To Retire to the Shades of Tranquility"

James McHenry

THE RETURN HOME must have been bittersweet. How much to tell, what face to put upon the matter of his resignation? Now, especially, the injustice must have assaulted McHenry's feelings. He had tried throughout his adult life to serve his country with honor, but in the end had been sacrificed and disgraced. McHenry understood the politics, but he was wounded. He was strong, it was true, but he would not play a leadership role in party affairs again.

When McHenry resigned he intended also to leave public affairs, so that when Federalists held partisan meetings as early as mid-May, McHenry did not attend. He had "given up the faction, and means to retire to the shades of tranquility and the pursuits of science, on his Estate in Maryland." But such a resignation was far easier said than done, for he was concerned about his reputation among family and friends, as well as the country's future. Thus he drew a *very* fine line, one so delicate that even he occasionally crossed it. "I reserve . . . to myself the entire privilege of feeling a proper concern for those of my friends who may be engaged in public scenes as actors or sufferers, and of . . . communicating . . . my own comments upon public occurrences. Thus far . . . I may indulge in public affairs, without disturbing the tenour of my life, or that tranquillity of mind which I aim at." McHenry's friends, however, were influential Federalist leaders; his letters could not help reverberating politically.[1]

In fact, he was home for less than two months before his behind-the-scenes involvement in election politics began to grow. He did indeed take a back seat in party affairs, leaving the hard work of campaigning to younger men like Robert Goodloe Harper, who had recently moved to Maryland. But according to McHenry, Maryland Federalists were in a quandary.

Before McHenry had left office, Federalist leaders at the capital had decided to implement Hamilton's plan from the last election again in 1800.
Stanley Elkins and Eric L. McKitrick refer to this as "the Federalist cabal to
prevent John Adams from succeeding himself." Gordon Wood agrees that
"Hamilton and some other High Federalists began working to find some
alternative to Adams as president." They would campaign far and wide for
two candidates, Adams and Pinckney, publicly supporting Adams for the
presidency. But secretly they would convince a few key electors in Federalist
states *not* to vote for Adams and hence elect Pinckney president. This was,
of course, possible because the votes for president and vice president were
not yet distinguished on the ballots. It also assumed, incorrectly, that South
Carolina would only vote for southerners Jefferson and Pinckney. Hence
they thought that Federalist electors in all states would vote for Pinckney,
but that Adams would lose southern votes and not be reelected president.
This was also the activity that, in 1796, had led Adams to despise Hamilton.
It did not work then and it would not work in 1800.[2]

Now, in Maryland, the lower-level Federalists knew only that the party
urged votes for both Adams and Pinckney, but the state leaders knew the
larger strategy and disliked relying on other states to throw the election
of 1800 to Pinckney. Harper, for one, wanted Maryland to favor the South
Carolinian over Adams. To complicate matters, the previous year Maryland
had changed its elector system. Before this, the General Assembly had chosen presidential electors, but Maryland had joined many states in switching
to a vote for electors by district. Federalists were now uncertain they could
deliver the requisite number of electors. So Federalists and Republicans in
Maryland squared off, Republicans arguing for district votes, Federalists
pushing for a vote in the General Assembly.[3]

For his part, McHenry was now willing to communicate his true thoughts
about Adams to a larger circle of friends. He made it clear that he believed
Adams's foreign policy to be dangerous, and designed "to answer electioneering purposes." His real problem, McHenry thought, was control: "he
would be everything, and do everything himself." Unfortunately, "he wants
the prudence and discretion indispensable to enable him to conduct with
propriety and safety even the colloquial intercourse permitted between a
President and foreign ministers." This is a remarkable statement given Adams's years of successful foreign service, yet fellow diplomat Franklin had
thought much the same thing. It may well have been important that Adams
did not generally serve alone. His passions tended to get the better of him.

Administratively, this meant that "he is incapable of adhering to any system, consequently must be forever bringing disgrace upon his agents and administration," a trait that clearly had hurt McHenry and the cabinet, who were unaware of the secret information Adams had about French intentions. Finally, "his foibles, passions, and prejudices, are of a stamp which must expose him incessantly to the intrigues of foreigners, and the unprincipled and wickedly ambitious men of either party; and that the high and dearest interests of the United States cannot possibly be safe under his direction."[4] This was strong stuff from a man who claimed he had left politics behind. While still obeying his rule of writing to friends rather than engaging in open campaigning, he had decided to tell his thoughts to others, even at the cost of further dividing his party.

Most ironically, he criticized the party for behaving the very way he now chose to act. In his defense, this was a first for him, and unlike the others, he did not hold office. Previously, McHenry had written essays for newspapers and pamphlets and in public had argued politics, trying, as he might say aristocratically, to "guide" the public mind. Even as secretary of war he had written newspaper essays, unlike many other Federalists who professed disdain for the populace. Now, even as McHenry decried their secretive behavior, he adopted it. In a private letter to Wolcott, he complained, "Have our party shown that they possess the necessary skill and courage to deserve to be continued to govern? What have they done? They did not, ... knowing the disease [Adams], the man and his nature, meet it when it first appeared, like wise and resolute patriots; they tampered with it, and thought of palliations down to the last day of the late session of Congress." He was right, of course. "Nay, their conduct, even now ... is tremulous, timid, feeble, deceptive, and cowardly. They write private letters. To whom? To each other, but they do nothing to give a proper direction to the public mind." The Federalists were too insular. "They observe, in their conversation, a discreet circumspection generally, ill calculated to diffuse information, or prepare the mass of the people for the result. They meditate in private. Can good come out of such a system?" McHenry clearly thought not. "If the party recovers its pristine energy and splendour, shall I ascribe it to such cunning, paltry, indecisive, back-door conduct? Certainly I shall not, but to a kind and watchful Providence alone ... I carry, you see, my religious principles into my politics." It was a stunning indictment and the sharpest statement by any Federalist about the group's failings. They held themselves aloof from the people and did not "deserve" to govern. Nor were they honest and upright within the partisan alliance, but gossiped, plotted, and intrigued among themselves rather than forthrightly leave Adams behind for another candidate.[5]

Instead the party had embraced Hamilton's plan, but by late August Hamilton feared failure. He now wanted to rebuke the president publicly, exposing his behavior; without this, Federalists would have "the air of mere *caballers* and shall be completely run down in the public opinion."[6] Interestingly then, in his own way, Hamilton saw part of the problem. But if he put his name to such an exposition, people would know his information came from the cabinet and they would be linked against Adams.

Hamilton decided the stakes were worth it. Because McHenry had deposited an account of his "retirement" conversation with Adams in War Department files, Hamilton considered the account to be "public domain" and on that premise resolved to use it. So he published an attack on Adams using McHenry's account without asking permission. Angry, McHenry chided Hamilton in no uncertain terms. "I shall expect never to be again treated by a friend in the same manner. The truth is, had you asked it, I should not have consented to their publication." Although he thought the Federalists wrong to have supported Adams for the presidency, the campaign was now well under way and McHenry considered an attack on their candidate both unwise and unseemly. Furthermore, the account, though honest, was humiliating for McHenry. Worse, it had been made public by a "friend." Disappointed, when Hamilton apologized, McHenry nevertheless forgave.[7]

Indeed the letter *was* unwise, as many leading Federalists now lost whatever small amount of enthusiasm they had previously mustered for the campaign. McHenry wrote Wolcott that "there is every symptom of languor and inactivity . . . among the well informed federalists, which every new recurrence to the conduct and character of the Chief, seems rather to increase than diminish." For example, "Mr. Charles Carroll of Carrollton [a leading Maryland Federalist], did not go down to Annapolis from his Country residence, to aid in the election of members for our Legislature. I also know many others who did not vote on the occasion."[8]

In the end, Maryland voted by district and returned a bare majority of six Federalists to four Republicans. When the electoral college turned in a tie vote between Jefferson and Burr, the decision was sent to the House of Representatives. Many Federalists, who for so long had thought of Jefferson as the enemy, now considered handing Burr the presidency. This news alarmed Hamilton, who knew Burr well since they were both New York

City lawyers. As yet civil in public, Hamilton privately thought Burr a base opportunist and urged McHenry to use all of his influence for Jefferson rather than Burr.[9] After some reflection McHenry concurred.

Ultimately it became clear to many Federalists that Burr would not cooperate, while Jefferson would not dismantle the government. Before this realization, however, the election was deadlocked. For a period of six days and thirty-six ballots the House of Representatives struggled. Finally Federalist Congressman Bayard of Delaware announced in caucus that he would cast a blank ballot; this allowed him to save face but amounted to a vote for Jefferson. Bayard's decision in turn influenced Maryland and Vermont, as the three states' Federalists had agreed to act jointly—some refused to vote but the others cast blank ballots. The election had also been personal, invading the familial realm. "Congressman Nicholson [Republican] of Maryland 'left his sick bed—came through a snow storm—brought his bed and prevented the vote of Maryland from being given to Burr.' The wife of [Federalist] Congressman Craik of Maryland threatened to divorce him if he did not vote for Jefferson." Indeed, Federalists had now helped to elect a "Jacobin" president.[10]

Desire as McHenry might to stay out of direct involvement in politics, the Republicans would not let him. They tried to dishonor the party they had beaten, especially attacking Federalist spending, and an investigation into the Treasury branched out into a general investigation of departmental spending. Since the War Department had both the largest and most complicated budget, McHenry himself came under attack.[11]

Indeed, every secretary of war since the department's inception had been derided for excessive spending. It was one of the first things he had learned about the office. McHenry, who had the additional misfortune of having to create an army unpopular to Republicans during a peacetime war fever embraced by Federalists, was especially vulnerable to these attacks. To make matters worse, the War Department office and most of its papers burned to the ground in November 1800, making it impossible fully to answer the charges.

Still, McHenry had his defenders. When the investigating committee reported its findings to the House, Roger Griswold rose to complain. Although a member of the committee, he had barely been given a chance to peruse the findings before they were reported. Moreover, he considered the report so misleading that at points it could be labeled false. For one thing, the committee deceptively reported that the army and navy had not accounted for $3 million and $4 million, respectively! The real problem lay in the bookkeeping system, which considered entire balances unaccounted for until *all* vouchers were in. Small monetary disputes, then, left million-dollar accounts open. With such large sums under discussion, the public naturally believed there had been widespread embezzlement. Griswold, however, argued that "the losses of the government have been less than are generally experienced by merchants in transactions of equal extent." Republicans even criticized the government's paying to move clerks, papers, and secretaries to the new capital in Washington, D.C. In McHenry's case, the government paid rent on a house to which he had committed prior to his requested resignation. Griswold pointed out that all of this was not merely legal but also reasonable.[12]

McHenry naturally had to defend himself against such accusations made by the House. So he drew up his own very pointed and specific rebuttal, included as many documents as he could muster, and sent his ninety-one-page defense to the House.[13] Despite Republican opposition, McHenry's defense was read. It was long, thorough, and left to lie on the table. The Republicans did not attack him publicly again.

Nor did McHenry ever reappear on the national scene; he wanted to maintain only a minimal state involvement. Fortunately, he still had wealth enough to live a life of quiet leisure, reading, gardening, and enjoying his estate, Fayetteville. In this way he spent his last years, watching the country become far too democratic for his tastes. But he was not doctrinaire, for he recognized the positives as well. Although he feared the trampling of laws, he admitted in a letter to Lafayette that this had not happened. Instead, "the general prosperity of the country is on the increase, and the laws, except perhaps where certain political questions are concerned, executed with the usual fidelity and integrity."[14] His fear of the Republicans had been unfounded.

Now the country changed, leaving McHenry and his ideas behind. Even his old friends, both personal and political, departed. William Vans Murray, who had served as one of the three ministers in Adams's final mission to France but who had remained a good friend, died in December 1803. Then Hamilton was killed in 1804, victim of his own special hubris. His constant opposition to Aaron Burr—admittedly an opportunist—finally caused Burr to challenge Hamilton to a duel. They fought in Weehawken, New Jersey, and Hamilton died. Ironically, the former secretary of the treasury died heavily in debt, and McHenry was among those asked to subscribe for the support of Hamilton's family.[15]

TWENTY

"At the Twilight's Last Gleaming"

Francis Scott Key

IN 1805 JAMES and his son Daniel decided to hold a weekly "family" entertainment, at which all of the nuclear family were expected to play their parts. Everyone was to contribute a written piece, in any form— letter, essay, poetry, lecture, or short story. Collectively, these pieces were addressed both to the other family members and to their descendants, with the intention, they said, of helping them create their own happy families.[1] Once these papers were bound, they called this year-long project their "Domestic Bagatelles." These bagatelles provide a rare glimpse into early nineteenth-century family life.

"Bagatelles" possessed a privileged history in early American literature. The word is defined as "an unimportant or insignificant thing; a trifle," and Benjamin Franklin excelled in these kinds of light-hearted and humorous essays. Among his most famous are *The Ephemera* (1778), in which a wise old fly of seven hours lectured to those around him on the vicissitudes of life; and *The Dialogue between Franklin and the Gout* (1780), wherein gout becomes a person who has come to teach Franklin to change his ways and eat less while exercising more. "Attention is given to setting, plot, point of view, characterization and dialogue. Comic detachment is created through rapid transitions. . . . The cast is depicted with gentle humor."[2] Bagatelles often, although not always, contained some moral point.

This was the world of bagatelles into which the McHenrys plunged. James and Daniel could hardly have chosen a better year, for the family was intact, healthy, and reasonably happy. James repeatedly expressed his pride in the children, his nephew, and his sense of good fortune. The boys were young men trying to find their own paths in a society open to them, while the daughters sought to understand their place. James consistently strove to impart his wisdom to the next generation, which often thought it knew better. With one exception, the servants and slaves revert to the background after treatment in the earliest bagatelles. Despite the fact that the whites used the term "family" initially to include everyone, all of the focus, resources, and most of the power revolved around the whites.[3]

James and Peggy, moreover, were not the only family members whose roots extended beyond the Atlantic. Their household servants also hailed from the other side of the ocean, and their roles became apparent as early as the second week's bagatelle. This was written by son Daniel with a sense of humor probably inherited from James. Proclaiming that the McHenrys had adopted a set of rules for a happy family, Daniel proceeded to enumerate them.

> The first, or principal, rule upon which all the rest depend is, that the servants do what they please. The second which is like unto it, is, that they do as they please. The third teaches that all are made of dust, that servants are on a footing with thier [sic] masters, and may contradict, argue and swear with impunity. The fourth requests them to leave thier other work on Sunday, and wait at table, that they may learn to be more expert next Friday [a fast day] when company is expected to dine. The fifth forbids thier paying respect to the younger part of the community, either in word, or deed. The sixth allows them to take the life of thier master, or at least to threaten it if he provokes them, by exercising authority. The seventh permits thier frolicking at thier will, and pleasure. The eight [sic] regulation, suffers them to steal. The ninth exhorts them to lye, and bear false witness against each or any of the community. The tenth provides silent admiration for the honorable act of despoiling our neighbours. You may observe according to the extent of these commandments, that they are well calculated, to make good servants, than which nothing can be more conducive to the peace & tranquility, of a *happy & united family*.[4]

This piece was clearly a bagatelle in the general fashion of Benjamin Franklin. Its moral is that a happy family lets the servants do as they please. It makes fun of the haplessness of the master, positing that the true power lies in the hands of the servants. The social relations are absurdly topsy-turvy; resistant slaves and whimsical, unreliable servants were complained of by many "masters" in the early republic.[5] It is a production with a cast of characters (servants) that is designed to be superficial, light fun. It is revealing nevertheless.

Only a member of the upper or upper-middle class would have written such a composition. Nor is it a surprise that it was written by a youth to both his current and future family. It never seemed to occur to him that the striving of servants might portend a social mobility that can go both ways. Indeed, the definition of "servant" and its status was experiencing flux in the early republic. England's laws recognized a number of "servant" positions, but in the United States only two such "legal" categories now existed: indentured servants and apprentices. Slaves, a different legal group, were referred to as "servants" as a colloquial euphemism, behind which masters hid the reality of the power structure.[6] Although his slaves clearly questioned the social hierarchy, Daniel seems to have simply assumed his future family would have "servants" too.

There were, in fact, ten servants in the McHenry household, three from Europe and seven African Americans. Each, of course, had his or her role, and on February 16 James decided to describe them in case future references to them appeared throughout the oncoming year. He started with twelve-year-old James Holden, an Irish lad described as "a smart boy, slovenly in his dress, perverse occasionally, and [who] will sometimes forget to tell the truth."[7] This child had been caught up in the wars emanating from the French Revolution, as he had accompanied British troops in their unsuccessful invasion of Holland under the Duke of York sometime prior to 1802. He could not have been more than nine at the time. The English had left him in Holland, where he seems to have been thrown in with a group of poverty-stricken Dutch who sold up to seven years of their service for passage to Maryland. They were called "redemptioners," with circumstances very similar to the more familiar indentured servants.

This probably explains the origins of the two Dutch sisters, Margery and Kitty Hyderback. McHenry considered these women "stupid," with an "utter inaptitude to benefit by instruction. . . . They are good natured, but will never learn anything."[8] As they arrived in the McHenry home in the same year as young Holden, it seems likely that they, too, were redemptioners. While they may indeed have been dimwitted, it remains true that they surely had little to no incentive to sweep, a factor the McHenrys never acknowledged.

Interestingly, at this point McHenry began to descant "On national errors." McHenry believed there was a "vulgar error" leading to a popular stereotype that the Dutch and Germans were obtuse. Such anti-German sentiment had found expression during the Fries Rebellion. Federalists

Robert Goodloe Harper and Uriah Tracy respectively had called the Germans "ignorant, bigoted" and had denounced the Germans as "stupid, ignorant and ugly."[9] For his part, however, McHenry did not wish to imply "that the Dutch and Germans are a stupid people." McHenry's chosen version of the Enlightenment emphasized the equality of people. "It does not appear to me, that there is any intrinsic difference, in the intellectual powers of men, inhabiting different countries or born in different latitudes, or that man because born in one country must ever remain dull and stupid, while his fellow man, born in a different country shall become civilized and learned."[10] Indeed, he proceeded to list the various Germanic accomplishments and famous persons with which he was familiar. Perhaps his largesse was not merely magnanimous but also personal. He was surely also dismissing what could be seen as old English aristocratic attitudes toward the Irish and colonials. If so, he still thought Margery and Kitty dimwitted.

The rest of the servants were African American slaves, and McHenry had the same complaint against Saragh the cook that he had against the Dutch women. "She is good tempered, but not very active, nor yet much to be commended as a plain cook. What she is taught one day, she is too apt to forget the next." He did not question her intelligence, however, instead noting that she was "married" with a child named Jenny.[11]

Her husband Edward, or Ned, earned McHenry's respect, not for hard labor, but for his "steady habits." While his single day's output might not be great, Ned accomplished a good deal in a week. Probably for this reason, he was given a fair amount of responsibility. "He has the care of the cows, of the Hot-house, of the garden, of the Pidgeons, of the rabbits, of the guinea pigs, of the fowls, and, lately of a monkey." In addition, Ned "assists to saw wood, waits table on Sundays, and on days of company. . . . He is also employed in miscellaneous business, goes regularly to chapel, keeps lent and observes the fasts and holydays of his church."[12] Ned had evidently found the personal resources to work, but did so at his own pace.

Also a "tolerable" worker was a girl named Emma, who had been hired out as a "seamstress and lady's maid" by a Dr. John Murray. Perhaps Emma also helped with little six-year-old Rachel, used mainly as a messenger from one part of the house to another.[13]

Augustus, on the other hand, was well made and strong and so took care of the carriage and the horses, "but cannot be praised for order attention or regularity in his business." James considered fourteen-year-old George "cunning" for he lied and stole. In fact, George was "suspected of a propensity to consider small articles, which do not appear to be under the immediate protection of their owners, as belonging to himself."[14]

Probably it was George who figured at the center of a series of bagatelles from early February to late April. The story unfolded with James's report that although the hens were suddenly barren, the old cock had taken a shine to the two chickens. There was still hope, then, for eggs. But soon the cock himself disappeared leaving no signs of "fowl" play. Naturally Daniel and James suspected theft, the eighth rule of a happy family. Luckily, the old cock had sired a fine brood of chicks that included a male. Daniel now assumed there was a breeding plot and correctly predicted that the young cock would disappear by Easter—he was sure to a cockfight![15]

Daniel, eighteen, had been right. He was the age his father had been when he crossed the Atlantic in search of a new home. Daniel did not need to travel so far, for unlike northern Ireland during James's youth, Maryland held open countless opportunities for the free white male of some education and property. Like his father, however, Daniel's constitution had not held up well to rigorous study. Now he was learning at home but was becoming more interested in farming than some scholarly pursuit. This attention paid to the farm animals was an early sign. Writing these weekly essays was time-consuming, however, so that by early April Daniel instead began contributing his astronomical studies.

Younger brother John was not having as much trouble with his studies. In fact, at fourteen (or fifteen?) John was attending the local "french institution," St. Mary's College in Baltimore. Although the school was near, John lived there and returned when he could, writing often. Daniel identified letters written in five languages: English, French, Latin, Greek, and gibberish. Indeed, the school's rigor required that the students not speak in their native tongues. James was pleased. A "liberal education," he wrote, was "more important to children than the greatest wealth, which any parent could leave them."[16]

James had given some thought to whether or not he should send his son to a Catholic school, and was asked this very question by an acquaintance. The question itself, of course, reflects the centuries of European conflict between Catholics and Protestants, and Maryland's own historic founding as a refuge for Catholics that was, ironically, settled largely by Protestants. The tension remained, so it was natural that issues might exist. James concluded that the priests knew the trouble their institution would bring down upon them if they took to teaching Catholicism to Protestant students.

For her part, eleven-year-old Margaretta grew tired of hearing about her brothers' educations: "I wish papa would choose girls education, as a subject for his next bagatelle." It took James a month before he decided how to address this. Whereas the boys were encouraged in Latin and Greek, James's immediate concern was to help Margaretta become a desirable marriage partner. "I shall only observe, that a religious education, or a due sense of religion, is best calculated to inspire the fair sex with energy and resolution, to perform the duties of their station, however severe its exactions, with patience, and without murmuring." Perhaps his lack of enthusiasm came from remembering that as a young man he had argued for the equality of women's intellect. Now fifty-two, he apparently felt uncomfortable not preparing his daughter for the potential hardships of marriage. James presented her with two letters from others on the subject. The first, written by Augustus to Maria, was followed by her reply. Augustus wrote, "Your duty, my dear, is comprised in a narrow compass. Obey this mighty master, and hold yourself subject to his orders. What, in everything? Yes, in everything . . . two persons possessing co-ordinate powers, [cannot rule] without its being productive of contests between them . . . and almost perpetual disorder and distraction."[17] It is fortunate that Maria had the last word, reminding Augustus that Eve was created from Adam's rib, so that "God indicated clearly, that the woman was to be ever held and considered, as a *part of himself*, and treated accordingly." She bade him remember "that no tyrant can be happy." The lesson was clear—Margaretta was to be religious and duty-oriented, ready to submit to her husband's will at all times.[18]

Older sister Anna at sixteen was already taking on a certain self-possession indicating her entry into young womanhood. She only contributed two bagatelles, one a speech written to convince Richard III to spare the lives of the young princes, and the other a poem about the peaceful Nile growing stormy and overflowing its banks. This serious young woman was now on occasion given "temporary government of the household" in order to prepare her for her woman's role. But even this young woman craved more, trying to convince her parents to let her travel to a city 100 miles and 18 hours away with only a hand fan to fight the city heat.[19]

Peggy appears to have been too busy to contribute anything, but she did read the bagatelles to the assembled group, which sometimes included James's nephew John, who had just passed the bar and been admitted to the

General Court. Peggy was probably encouraged to make her contribution. Since their youth James had urged Peggy to write, and she had, of course, written letters during their separations, but she also joined in the family love of poetry. Hers tended to be religious and revealed little about her except that this facet of life was truly important to her.

Periodically James returned to character-building themes, warning about bad tempers, and advising how to attain happiness. Christianity, he said, led to happiness through a clear conscience and trust in God. But it was also necessary to have both regular work and times of ease, to indulge in culture, to govern one's passions, and to cultivate habits of thought and recollection. Interestingly, he also warned against expecting too much from one's friends, or trusting them too far. Instead, one should "unite the innocence of the dove with the wisdom of the serpent!"[20] Was he thinking of Hamilton, Pickering, Wolcott, or Adams? Edification was indeed more than one learned in school.

By the end of the year, Daniel admitted that he could not maintain the bagatelles and keep up with his studies. He reminded the family to no avail that all were supposed to contribute. His studies understandably won the battle.

In truth, it was a good year for the McHenry family, and the bagatelles reflected this, with their references to poems, sleighing, parties, theater, classical authors, and recordings of the weather. The servants lived another life, one of privation with little incentive to accomplish anything. Still, they clearly found ways of making life more interesting, cockfights and all. James wrote: "It will occur from this short detail of our domestics, that our little world is like the great one, of different characters, possessing a full share of the imperfections of human nature."[21]

After 1805, McHenry remained active in his church and the community. Proudly watching the city grow, he published a Baltimore directory in 1807. But the familial happiness would not last. McHenry's youngest child, Margaretta, contracted tuberculosis at the age of fifteen. In desperation they traveled west to Bedford Springs to bathe in its warm, sulfuric waters, but the girl was doomed. In November 1809 James and Peggy lost their Margaretta, "who was very dear."[22] Only the middle three of their five children survived.

He also lost his retirement's written labor. McHenry had been writing a novel, supposedly somewhat similar to a popular work called the *Trav-*

els of Anacharsis. But he packed it with other items to be sent west to his son's home, where McHenry intended to continue work on it. Somehow the manuscript vanished.[23]

Also gone was any desire to be active in politics. The role of interested spectator suited him until 1809 when the ghost of his secretarial past proved that it would not die. Adams began publishing his own recollection and interpretation of his presidency, and publicly denouncing his old cabinet members. The former president did this as therapy, a way of releasing years of pent-up anger. He had a deep-seated need to be appreciated by posterity, and he had been upset by Mercy Otis Warren's 1805 publication of the *History of the American Revolution* in three volumes. Warren's work had not merely failed to treat Adams as a central character in the Revolution; she had also described him as much changed by the 1780s, more inclined to monarchy than republicanism. Intensely hurt, he complained to Warren and wrote his own version of his presidency for the newspapers.[24]

This especially angered Timothy Pickering, still active in politics, who contacted McHenry. Their friendship had actually grown since his resignation. McHenry probably knew only a portion of Pickering's earlier duplicitous conduct, although the Marylander surely would have forgiven it anyway, as that trait ran strong in his character. Pickering now urged his old colleagues to rebut the ex-president, but McHenry instead chose to take the high road. He thought a public rebuttal would only grant Adams's charges unwarranted attention when McHenry wanted to leave those years behind. He did not respond to Adams. He did, however, fume. He found Adams's letters "puerile," full of "errors, some important forgetfulness and not a few striking misrepresentations."[25]

Pickering, however, needed help reconstructing events. Although McHenry would publish nothing himself, he nonetheless decided to cooperate. This retrospection led McHenry to expound his view of the cabinet's system of foreign affairs. He believed their foreign policy was "General Washington's. We held with him that we ought never to quit our own to stand upon foreign ground; under no pretext to weave our destiny with that of any European power; that our true policy was to avoid permanent alliances with any portion of the foreign world; to trust to temporary ones for extraordinary emergencies, and to suitable military establishments to enable us to act up to and avail ourselves of our maxims." McHenry mistakenly saw Pickering and Wolcott as having parallel devotions to Washington. "Three of the gentlemen who were heads of departments with Mr. Adams were also heads of departments with General Washington. These gentlemen could never for a moment depart from his maxims, they were the soul of their system; they could not tear them from their hearts and retain their honor and integrity." McHenry clearly believed Washington's policies "to be the only sound ones for their country, the only ones proper for the guidance of our foreign affairs and, in no instance," McHenry insisted, did the three "ever advise or countenance departure from them."[26]

A clearer statement of McHenry's general approach to foreign policy would be hard to find. Furthermore, he believed that he, Pickering, and Wolcott all possessed this overarching loyalty to Washington. While it is quite possible that he never appreciated the extent of Hamilton's influence on Pickering and especially Wolcott, it is also possible that he generally thought Hamilton's views a mere reflection of Washington's. Striking too is the apparent fear that Adams did not place a premium on independence from foreign powers, or at least that Adams's policies would result in an unnecessary dependence. Despite the intervening decade in which that did *not* result from Adams's peace settlement, McHenry continued to believe it would.

Although the United States maintained neutrality, England and France had not ended their war in Europe. Napoleon continued French aggressions while George III's madness led to the Regency and some confused politics even as England warred against France. In the United States, a new party governed. The Republicans, like the Federalists before them, attempted to remain neutral using every method short of war.

Still, newspaper accounts alarmed McHenry. Both countries captured American ships, but England was more offensive: it impressed American sailors, and it published Orders in Council limiting American trade as if there had been no revolution. Then, too, diplomacy was failing. The 1806 Monroe-Pinkney Treaty with England collapsed almost immediately. When Jefferson disastrously implemented the Embargo to avoid either fighting or submitting, the ineffectiveness of that option became clear. Instead this policy caused a partial resurgence of Federalism in the Maryland House of Delegates but Baltimore remained staunchly Republican. Lesser attempts to influence Europe during the Madison administration also failed, such as Macon's Bill No. 2 which reopened American trade with both countries— unless one recognized American rights, whereupon trade with the other country would halt.[27]

As tensions escalated with Great Britain, every election increased in importance. McHenry, supporting a Federalist Party convention for the state senatorial election of 1811, published "The Three Patriots, or the Cause and Cure of Present Evils, Addressed to the Voters of Maryland," which urged the people to choose "suitable electors."[28] It was indeed an important election, for it sent a group of war hawks to Congress.

By the early summer of 1812, the country's frustration over foreign affairs reached new heights, driving President Madison to appear before Congress and cite a long list of grievances against the British, especially their continuing impressment of Americans. Arrogantly, England did not respond. Congress, considering Madison's argument, now concluded it had only two choices: submit to England's will or fight. It declared war—the War of 1812.

No longer active in politics beyond writing the occasional essay, McHenry pushed on with plans to accompany his newly married son Daniel west to Cherry Tree Meadows, farmland near the westernmost edge of Maryland. In the Appalachian Mountains, the area was ruggedly beautiful and the family built a log house at what is now known as Deep Creek Lake near the Lake Pointe Inn. This land would be Daniel's home. Once there James began to experience pain in his lower legs that intensified until they were both completely paralyzed. All his family's nursing was to no avail. He diagnosed himself as having a combination of gout and rheumatism in a letter to Robert Oliver, an old friend in Baltimore. The pain confined him to his room and forced him to remain there through the winter. He could not return to the city. "Do not blame me. The journey would destroy me. Keep this to yourself. To all I seem better than I am."[29]

But not every day was lost. McHenry found the capacity to find delight in the world around him, writing his friend Charles Carroll of Carrollton:

Where Alleghany lifts his head,
as silent as among the dead,
I pass my time.

Except the barking of a dog,
Or grunting of a hungry hog
No sound is heard.

Sometimes, indeed, a wolf will howl,
And, sometimes, there is heard an owl
At midnight screech.

. . . .

For me, I like these solitudes,
These mountains high and stretching woods,
Majestic scene.

I like in lonesome woods to ride,
The notched trees my only guide,
Till tir'd of thought.

. . . .

Should Rattlesnake across my way,
Lay basking in the sunny ray,
I fear it not.

If undisturb'd, it will not bite;
If anger'd, will not spend its spite
Till notice given.

Not so that reasoning creature man,
Who poisons by long and settled plan
Without a rattle

. . . .

I like, in winter, a warm fire,
And here I have my hearts desire
Great store of wood.

. . . .

I like the cabin stor'd with health,
Where pride and circumstance of wealth
Are all unknown.

. . . .

I like to hear by hunter told,
His various feats of emprise bold,
Against the foe.

. . . .

Soft, sir, if eating be in favour,
Here's venison of finest savour,
Wild fowl and trout.

. . . .

Old wine, tis true, is rather rare;
But then here's plenty and to spare
Of water pure.

Now say, would you the friend disown,
Who for these mountains leaves a town,
To Rogues and riot.[30]

Friends back in Baltimore urged him to stay there as long as possible, for anyone previously associated with Washington and the Jay Treaty that favored Britain was now persona non grata in the city. The "Rogues and riots" McHenry referred to in his poem had indeed terrified the city; those who supported the war effort would simply brook no opposition. At its worst, on the night of July 27, a crowd gathered at the site where an antiwar newspaper was printed called the *Federal Republican*. Those inside determined to resist; the crowd outside turned unruly; and those in the house fired into the crowd, killing one Dr. Gale (first name unknown) and injuring others. The civil authority finally appeared as General John Stricker arranged to take those inside the house into protective custody. The crowd, now a mob, at first agreed but then grabbed the men from jail, beat them badly with whatever implements they could find, poured hot candle wax into their eyes, tarred and feathered and generally tortured the men. Revolutionary War General James Lingan died from his wounds.[31] Mobs did not rule the city, but everyone feared another outbreak of violence, as the war did not go well for the Americans.

Much later, McHenry's poem inspired his friend Charles Carroll to respond in kind.

He's gone to the mountain he's lost to the City
McHenry the jovial the gay & the witty
Oh! sigh ye Librarians! Oh weep all ye friends
No longer his converse your science extends
No more shall he aid ye in dressing a dish
No more play his part on your mutton & fish
Ye shall droop o'er your pheasants your sallad & wine
While he shall the myrtle & laurel entwine
In vales and deep glens while he's hunting the deer
Ye shall drop on the board sympathetic the tear
Allegany became to McHenry his Heaven
Lamenting the hour to solitude given
And you, ye fair ladies, presiding the while
To grace at the table your welcome & smile
Shall ye not regret the loss we deplore
While round him the panthers & tigers shall roar
The gun of the hunter at distance is heard
The wolf to your presence mild dames is prefer'd;
And yet you must say with sincerity own
From your sight none so courteous so polish'd has flow'n

The Scholar the Gen[t]leman Washingtons friend
On rattlesnakes even reflection can lend
And force a fine Moral from fruits & from flow'rs
From woods herds & flocks & from cabins & bowers
Who likes all rurality [?] wild fowl & trout,
And to hear what his neighbours & friends are about
Who likes too his fare of beef, ven'son & game,
And the stream of pure water (forgotten to name)
Alass! The old wine is so scarce, I suspect
We soon all his wisdom revers'd, may detect;
Believe me, he'll come from his mountain & quiet
And write verses here, on the rogues & the riot.[32]

While McHenry stayed in the mountains, the war pressed on and, like the Quasi-War, it proved difficult to man; only on paper did the army boast 36,700 men. The attempted invasion of Canada by fewer than 10,000 Americans against more than 40,000 Canadians and British miscarried badly, although Fort York (Toronto) was taken and the legislative assembly buildings in the nearby town were burnt down. The naval war fared better, capturing 50 British ships and 250 merchantmen.[33]

In the mountains, McHenry sometimes experienced pain so severe he could not even hold the pen to write friends. But on better days he relished the activity, requesting copies of government speeches and reports. Politics remained in his blood, perhaps now more than ever, since the events and issues helped to keep his mind off his plight. Yet the war worried him, and the politics that had led to this state of affairs preoccupied him. In his hopeless dreams he visited politicians, even meeting with Madison who vaguely admitted errors leading to the war and then asked McHenry what he should do. But he had no answers, it was too late, the war was on.[34]

Still, McHenry felt better once he had returned to Baltimore and Fayetteville. The travel had been difficult, but he had made it. Ambulatory again, he even dared take on the presidency of his Bible Society. And soon Baltimore's own Oliver Hazard Perry won an important victory on the Great Lakes at Put-in-Bay. For their part, McHenry's friends clearly thought the end was near for him. One after another, Pickering among them, congratulated him on the capacity of his Christian faith to sustain him during his suffering while he awaited a happier afterlife.[35] His faith gave him great comfort.

Sadly, McHenry's improved health did not last. Early in 1814 his paralysis returned, never to go away. If his self-diagnosis of gout was correct, this temporary period of increased well-being was not unusual. As a physician, he could not have been surprised by his relapse. The children, of course, feared their father's days were numbered, so the elder son, Daniel, came to visit while his expectant wife stayed with her own parents. Even after the grandchild's birth, however, Daniel made no move to leave. Recognizing that he was the cause of his son's delay, McHenry urged Daniel's departure. Daniel died that day, having been thrown by a horse. Peggy later wrote: "[H]e left us in health in the morning, & before night was brought home a corpse. I leave you to judge what our situation was, for I cannot describe it, but I recollect all consideration for myself was lost in apprendsion [sic] of the effects of the shock, on the dear affectionate parent then laying *on a bed* in extreme pain from which he was never to rise; for my poor [daughter] Anna who was advanced in pregnancy & my widowed daughter-in-law— surely we should have been overwhelmed had we not been upheld by an Almighty arm. . . . He rode, unknown to us, a vicious horse who had the habit of throwing his rider—he threw our beloved."[36]

McHenry mourned:

My son, my son, so lov'd, so dear,
My son, my son, oh cruel death,
This morning health, now on his bier,
And I not breathe his latest breath.

Bring all that's left of this dear friend,
Close to my bed his body lay;
Now help me o'er his corpse to bend,
To kiss, and kiss, his lips of clay . . .

Where now his worth, who cheer'd my sight
And careless of his time and health,
Watch'd my sick couch, night after night,
As misers watch their hoarded wealth.

Where now his worth? Forever flown?
My joys all center'd in his grave;
And must his worth, no longer, known,
Lie buried in oblivions cave? . . .

Come then, religion, gift of heav'n,
Soother of sorrows the most deep;
Come thou to whom the pow'r is giv'n,
Bid me, no more, to wake and weep.[37]

This dreadful scene was soon compounded when, in the second week of September, the war drew near. American efforts to take Canada had failed and Napoleon had surrendered in Europe. Stronger now, the British turned their attention to the Chesapeake, sending Major General Robert Ross and 4,000 veterans from France to maraud the American coast. Entering the bay, Ross set his sights on Washington, D.C.

The capital was, in fact, poorly defended, as Secretary of War and former Brigadier General John Armstrong concentrated his attention on Canada rather than his own backyard. He refused to believe that the British had any interest in the city. As a result, Congress had voted no money for its defense, and Fort Washington down the Potomac River was simply insufficient for the task, especially since the British chose to attack via the Patuxent River instead. From there they marched north until they met the American force just outside Washington at a place called Bladensburg. Brigadier General William Winder had raised a unit of largely green militia. Despite Winder's best efforts, he could not keep them in disciplined order under fire. The battle turned into a rout. After this, the British marched to Washington unopposed. Finding that the government had left the capital rather than surrender, Ross set fire to the public buildings.[38]

Now the British set their sights on Baltimore, economic capital of the Chesapeake. Here they faced a more prepared city. Older than the capital, Baltimore had been concerned about security since the Revolution when McHenry presided over the committee to improve Baltimore's defenses. Then, at Maryland's request in 1794, President Washington found enough money to build a small redoubt and a twenty-gun battery. Army engineer J. J. Ulrich Rivardi also made recommendations regarding the defense of Whetstone Point. Baltimore's Marine Committee, headed by Robert Gilmor, oversaw the construction of Fort McHenry, which was built largely thanks to city subscribers. It had been repeatedly improved and strengthened over the years, so that in 1814 it stood as an impressive earthwork five-pointed star with brick supporting walls, complete with barracks, armory, and batteries. Most important, it commanded the main water entrance to Baltimore's harbor, the Northwest Branch of the Patapsco River.[39]

But this was not the only way for the British to approach Baltimore. Another was to sail along the Ferry Branch of the Patapsco and land west of the city—but the citizens had scuttled ships there, making it impassable. On the other hand, spreading further out into the bay and hence more safely accessible to the British lay a long, fingerlike stretch of land called "North Point." The British land contingent of about 4,000 disembarked here. After a march of about five miles, they approached the city from the east. The fight for Baltimore was about to begin.

Baltimore prepared under the direction of Major General Samuel Smith of the Maryland militia. Realizing its vulnerability, Baltimore had been digging earthworks and entrenchments along its eastern approach ever since news arrived of the capital's burning. Batteries were built. But hoping to prevent the enemy's reaching the city, on September 11 Smith sent Brigadier General John Stricker (also of the militia) with a force of 3,185 down Long Log Lane to meet the British.[40] McHenry's only remaining son John, named for his dead uncle, marched with the rest.

Peggy remembered that "[o]ur terror was inexpressible. my husband could not be moved, my daughter would not seek safety by leaving us, my only son thought it his duty to leave his Father, tho' his attentions were so needful to him, to go out in our defence . . . we thought we should never see him alive again, when we parted with him."[41] Stricker's men halted by a Methodist church about midway between Baltimore and North Point; here they spent the night under a full moon in a clear sky.

Early the next morning, the British landed and began their march toward the city. The Americans sent ahead a smaller body of 250 skirmishers who opened fire when they encountered a small advance party led by British General Ross. Astonished, Ross pushed to the front to assess the situation but was cut down by three militiamen, one of whom had climbed a tree to pick peaches. As Ross died, the American skirmishers fell back to the main body of men. The British opened fire at about 2:30 in the afternoon. Despite confusion and disorder, the Baltimore line held, returning fire for over an hour. At last Stricker ordered his men to fall back and regroup, while the British remained behind. The British lost 39, with 251 wounded, while the Americans counted 24 killed and 139 injured. It would be difficult for the survivors to rest, however, as a driving rain began around midnight.

In the bay, Vice-Admiral Cochrane decided to provide a diversionary force to support the British land forces. By dawn he positioned five British bomb ships two miles from Fort McHenry and began to fire. Each bomb, about thirteen inches wide and 190 pounds, was powerful enough to bring down even substantial buildings. Unfortunately, Major George Armistead (U.S.

Army), who commanded at the fort and who had been commissioned four-teen years earlier by Secretary of War James McHenry, soon discovered that his American guns lacked sufficient range to damage the British vessels ex-cept when they approached the fortification. Throughout that day the for-tress and its men survived hundreds of bombs hurled in its direction. Not only was it strong but many bombs missed their marks, some burst in the air, and others never exploded—such as the one that landed on the pow-der magazine.

As night approached, the battle had not been won. The British soldiers on land had not made it to Baltimore just as the naval bombardment had failed to destroy Fort McHenry. Nor could the British ships enter the harbor even if they could scurry past the garrison's guns, as Commodore Rodgers had scuttled twenty-four ships, schooners, and brigs across this branch of the Patapsco as well.

The night of September 13 would prove a long one for the inhabitants of Baltimore. Their homes shook under the assault. McHenry, at his estate just beyond Baltimore, could surely see from his window the mortars as they exploded while he lay helpless in his bed, fearful for the fate of his city, his country, and especially his son.

Francis Scott Key, a Baltimore attorney, could certainly see the explo-sions. Before his death General Ross had released Dr. William Beanes into Key's care, and then decided to keep the Americans under guard lest they warn Baltimore of the impending attack. Key, then, watched the battle from a British cartel ship in the harbor. Because of failing eyesight, Beanes re-peatedly asked Key if Fort McHenry's flag still flew. Yes, Key answered. It was an impressive flag, forty-two feet long by thirty feet wide and with fif-teen stars that still flapped loudly in the air over the center flagpole.

Finally, around midnight, 1,250 British rowed toward shore attacking under the withering guns of Fort McHenry and its surrounding emplace-ments. The attack lasted two hours. After the British retreated to their ships, the rain finally stopped, but they continued to bombard the fort. At dawn, Key thrilled to see the battered and torn flag that still flew. It was clear that Baltimore and the United States, through a combination of militias that prevented the British from reaching the city and the regular army soldiers within Fort McHenry, had won. "The city was defended not through the ef-forts of the federal government but by the mobilization of the local commu-nity under the leadership of Samuel Smith." The British left later that day. Fort McHenry had withstood an onslaught of from 1,500 to 1,800 shells;

amazingly, only 4 men had died, 24 were wounded, and 2 buildings were damaged.[42]

To James and Peggy's joy their son John not only "was foremost in battle at North Point" but was also "restored to us alive." He was, however, "much weakened . . . his laying on the ground one night in a heavy rain brought on a billious cholic, from which he suffered much by repeated attacks."[43]

Baltimore exulted, and no one was more moved than Francis Scott Key. "My heart spoke," he wrote. "Even though it had been a hanging matter to make a song, I must have written it." He began composing even before leaving the British ship and initially called it the "Defence of Fort McHenry." It was set to a trendy English drinking song and quickly made the rounds of all the taverns.[44] He had certainly lived the words he wrote: "O! say, can you see by the dawn's early light, / What so proudly we hailed at the twilight's last gleaming?"

When news of the Battle of Baltimore and the surrender of the British fleet at Plattsburgh on Lake Champlain reached the diplomats in Ghent, negotiations began in earnest. By Christmas Eve they concluded a treaty of peace. Even as the commissioners parlayed, however, Americans under Andrew Jackson battled the British in Louisiana, with the largest battle taking place at New Orleans on January 8, 1814; they did not know as they fought that the war was already over. The war effort thus ended with no less than three stunning American victories in which the country took enormous pride. The British never again bothered American ships on the seas or impressed another American sailor.

While the country was now at peace, trouble would not leave the McHenry family alone. Along with John, their only other child Anna became sick with a bilious fever at the end of her pregnancy, causing her to bear a "very delicate infant" that died in two months. Happily, she would bear another child, a healthy baby boy, in less than two years. Anna's husband, however, Baltimore attorney James Pillar Boyd, also fell ill that fall with an intermittent fever. Any of these illnesses could have killed their victims, and Boyd took this very much to heart. After this sickness, his infant's death, and the ravages of war, Boyd seems to have felt ever more keenly the fragility of life. He turned to religion for comfort, which at first pleased his parents-in-law. After all, McHenry's religion had given him much consolation. But it soon became apparent that Boyd's need for religion had grown excessive and that his mind was now "disordered." Boyd never recovered, becoming a burden to the family. By 1816 his madness placed him in the Baltimore Hospital.[45]

In the meantime, McHenry's son and nephew, both named John, took care of family business. The nephew, John McHenry Jr., took his family to James's western property, where Daniel had lived. McHenry's son John, for his part, became guardian of Daniel's son, Ramsey McHenry.[46]

Surely McHenry counted himself lucky that his wealth could support the family members who needed it. Like many other successful merchants of his day, McHenry had diversified, investing in local real estate, which he either rented or sold at a profit, and buying stock in local companies (i.e., fire insurance) and a bank. Thus bolstered financially, his faith sustained him through his chronic, sometimes extreme, pain.

McHenry now prepared for death, and old friends visited when they could. The end finally approached in March 1816 when he caught an "obstinate fever."[47] Weakened as he was, James still held on for over a month. But on May 3, at the age of sixty-two, McHenry died.

His adopted country had taken from him all that he was willing to give it. James McHenry had lived a life of honor and integrity, while his kindness and generosity of spirit had made him widely loved. His loss to his sorely tried family, however, was incomparable, and Peggy sorrowed. "[M]y dearest and best earthly friend was taken from me . . . I sought to rejoice that he was not only relieved from great misery here, but received to that world of inconceivable bliss to which he had long aspired."[48]

Today, Fort McHenry stands as a nation's tribute to a man who served it well.

Notes

ABBREVIATIONS

HL	Henry E. Huntington Library
HSP	Historical Society of Pennsylvania
LC	Library of Congress
MdHS	Maryland Historical Society
MHS	Massachusetts Historical Society
NYHS	New York Historical Society
PHS	Presbyterian Historical Society
WLC	William L. Clements Library
WMQ	William and Mary Quarterly

INTRODUCTION

1. Mattsson-Bozé, "James McHenry," chap. 8.

CHAPTER 1   "Of a Persevering Temper"

1. Heretofore, the only full-length biography of McHenry was Steiner's *Life and Correspondence of James McHenry*. Steiner reported, "The date of James McHenry's birth is uncertain. It is usually given as November 16, 1753, but the family records give the year as 1752, and in a letter to Timothy Pickering in June 1813, McHenry gave it as November 25, 1751. The first is probably the correct date, as his only sister, Anna, who died in 1771, was born in 1751." Steiner, *Life and Correspondence*, 1. Most convincing to this author is that footnote 1 on page 2 of Steiner, *Life and Correspondence*, indicates McHenry spoke of "being twenty when his wife was twelve." So James himself essentially gave two separate years for his birth, but 1753 makes the most sense. Indeed, since family records report 1752, the year the Irish were to switch to the new Gregorian calendar, quite possibly 1752 was recorded as the Julian calendar year, whereas 1753 was otherwise used because it was true to the Gregorian calendar.

Steiner also reported the family tradition that James was sent to the colonies because of ill health from excessive studying. I believe that James McHenry's ill health was not the sole reason but rather a primary contributing factor in his decision to journey to the North American colonies. I have found nothing to indicate what caused Anna's death. I merely suggest typhus as a very likely cause. Steiner, *Life and Correspondence*, 1. Barker and Cheyne, *Account of the Rise*, 8, 9, 367.

2. Hooper, *Travel Writing and Ireland*, 23. McDowell, *Irish Public Opinion*, 41. Dickson, *Ulster Emigration*, 17. Fischer, *Albion's Seed*, 613.

3. Foster, *Modern Ireland*, chap. 3. Glasgow, *Scots-Irish in Northern Ireland*, 44–48. Harvey, "A Few Bloody Noses," 15. Holmes, *Presbyterian Church in Ireland*, 13.

4. McDowell, *Ireland in the Age of Imperialism*, 173. The most accessible chronicle of the oppression of the Scots-Irish Presbyterians is Glasgow's *Scots-Irish*, chaps. 3 and 4. Although her account is unfortunately marred by her emotional commitment to the Presbyterian cause, the acts she cites did exist and her general thrust is upheld by other sources such as Beckett's *Short History of Ireland*, 93–112. Foster's *Modern Ireland*, however, presents a more balanced and thorough account, and the reader can generally find Foster's treatment of the Presbyterians following his discussion of Catholics in any chapter.

5. Glasgow, *Scots-Irish*, 47–55, 73–74. Foster, *Modern Ireland*, 85–86. Beckett, *Short History of Ireland*, 80–82, 86.

6. Glasgow, *Scots-Irish*, 83, 113–14.

7. Powell, *Britain and Ireland in the Eighteenth-Century Crisis*, 13, 104–11. McDowell, *Ireland in the Age*, 173. Dickson, *Ulster Emigration*, 60. Hooper, *Travel Writing and Ireland*, 17. Cronin, *A History of Ireland*, 89–91.

8. Foster, *Modern Ireland*, 157–58. Steirer, "Philadelphia Newspapers," 247.

9. James McHenry to Arthur Harper, June 6, 1775, *Papers of James McHenry* (Washington, D.C.: Library of Congress Photoduplication Service), reel 5, container 14, series D correspondence, Personal, 1775–1822 and undated.

10. Steirer, "Philadelphia Newspapers," 86–93, 138. Bridenbaugh, *Cities in Revolt*, 179. Nash, *Urban Crucible*, 209–10. This volume is an abridged edition of *The Urban Crucible: Social Change, Political Consciousness, and the Origins of the American Revolution*, published in 1979 by Harvard University Press.

11. This description of McHenry is based on a miniature of him published in Steiner, *Life and Correspondence*, and average height is assumed since contemporaries often commented on those who were tall (Washington, Jefferson, Marshall) and on those who were short (Burr).

12. "Taxables in the City of Philadelphia, 1756," *Pennsylvania Genealogical Magazine* 22, no. 1 (1961–1962): 12.

13. "Records, First Presbyterian Church, Philadelphia, Pennsylvania, 1747–72," vol. 1A:98, Presbyterian Historical Society, Philadelphia. Caldwell's and Allison's names recur through August 2, 1762 on 132.

14. Steiner, *Life and Correspondence*, 75.

15. David Caldwell, "Will of David Caldwell," Wills Books, Book M, 1762, #209, Historical Society of Pennsylvania, Philadelphia.

16. "A Register of Marriages, Baptisms and Communicants Kept by and for the Use for the First Presbyterian Church in the City of Philadelphia from the Year 1760 to the Year 1806," Presbyterian Historical Society, Philadelphia. Steiner, *Life and Correspondence*, 78.

17. Doerflinger, *A Vigorous Spirit of Enterprise*, 138, 141–42, 178–79. Nash, *Urban Crucible*, 317–22.

18. Wood, *Radicalism of the American Revolution*, 25–26.

19. Ibid., 32–37. Freeman, *Affairs of Honor*, xix.

20. *Pennsylvania Packet and General Advertiser*, June 15, 1972. Munroe, *University of Delaware*, 22.

21. Ryden, "Newark Academy of Delaware," 207, 211. Sloan, *Scottish Enlightenment*, 77–82. The academy was moved to Delaware by the Reverend Alexander McDowell. Pears Jr., "Colonial Education among Presbyterians (Concluded)," 169. Lewis, "The University of Delaware," 18.

22. Coad, "James McHenry: A Minor American Poet," 35.

23. Steiner, *Life and Correspondence*, 2–4.

CHAPTER 2   "The Commencement of Our Independence"

1. Rush, *Autobiography of Benjamin Rush*, 32,38–39. Reiss, *Medicine in Colonial America*, 14–15. Brodsky, *Benjamin Rush*, 66.

2. Rush, *Autobiography*, Appendix 1, 363–64. Reiss, *Medicine in Colonial America*, chap. 5. Brodsky, *Rush: Patriot*, 91. More detailed information regarding Cullen and fevers can be found in Porter, *The Greatest Benefit to Mankind*, 260–62.

3. Rush, *Autobiography*, Appendix 1, 362.

4. Ibid., 80.

5. A good account of this is in Miller's "A Contracting Community," esp. chap. 1. Also see Gillett's *History of the Presbyterian Church*. Powell, "Presbyterian Loyalists," 139.

6. Barkley, "The Presbyterian Church in Ireland," 17, 29. Nybakken, "New Light on the Old Side," 819–20. This is a significant contribution to our understanding of Philadelphia Presbyterianism at the time of the Revolution, showing why the Scots-Irish Old Side did not see the issue of church "control" in the same fashion as the New Side.

7. Rush, *Autobiography*, 79. Hawke, *Benjamin Rush*, 84. Gibson, "Benjamin Rush's Apprenticed Students," 127–32. Exactly when McHenry joined the group seems impossible to determine. Steiner reports family records as suggesting the year 1772. But Rush's list of apprenticed students (drawn up years later and therefore in retrospect) dates McHenry's apprenticeship to 1771. That would push his year of immigration back to 1770. Immigration records for this period from Ireland to Philadelphia are limited to indentured servants. McHenry's name does not appear. And the Presbyterian church records give no clue because of their very nature as listings of births, deaths, marriages, and pew rentals. At present I see no way of solving the matter. For the sake of continuity, however, I am following Steiner's dates. Also see Brodsky, *Rush: Patriot*, 81–85.

8. Reiss, *Colonial Medicine*, chap. 1. Brodsky, *Rush: Patriot*, 84. Steiner, *Life and Correspondence*, 5.

9. Rush, *Autobiography*, 83–84.

10. Maier, *From Resistance to Revolution*, 51, 73–76. Reid, *Constitutional History*, 12, 13, 17. Bailyn, *Ideological Origins*, 100–102. Greene, *The Ambiguity of the American Revolution*, 4.

11. Maier, *From Resistance to Revolution*, 116–17, 146, 170, 178–80, 199. Bailyn, *Ideological Origins*, 102–3.

12. Rush, *Letters of Benjamin Rush*, 1:83–84.

13. Ryerson, *The Revolution Is Now Begun*, 33–38. Unger, *American Tempest*, 172. Carp, *Defiance of the Patriots*, 79, 131, 165.

14. Ryerson, *The Revolution Is Now Begun*, 33–38. Rush, *Autobiography*, 109–11.

15. Ferling, *Almost a Miracle*, 24, 26.

16. Rush, *Autobiography*, 109–11. Ryerson, *The Revolution Is Now Begun*, 33–38. Bailyn, *Ideological Origins*, 118–19.

17. D'Elia, *Benjamin Rush: Philosopher*, 9–13. Nash, *The Unknown American Revolution*, 100–103.

18. Wingo, "Politics, Society, and Religion," 2, 62, 104–7, 145.

19. Ibid., 23, 224, 226.

20. Ryerson, *Radical Committees*, 79–83.

21. Agnes had been ill for some months, as in May James had written his brother John a letter chiding the latter for lack of information on the illness. James McHenry to his "Dr. Brother," May 8, 1774, The Papers of James McHenry, MS 647, MdHS. The family now composed only three—the father and two brothers.

22. David Hackett Fischer, *Paul Revere's Ride*, 76, 84, 200, 320–21, 262, 270–73. Rush, *Autobiography*, 112.

23. Steiner, *Life and Correspondence*, 2. James McHenry, The Papers of James McHenry, MS 19,006, n.d., reel 1, container 3, LC.

CHAPTER 3   "The Events of War Are Uncontroulable"

1. Washington was elected commander-in-chief on June 15, 1775. Ford, *Journals of the Continental Congress*, June 15, 1775, 2:91. Middlekauff, *The Glorious Cause*, 302.

2. The use of the word "Hospital" is somewhat confusing since smaller hospital buildings and huts were used. To distinguish these actual hospitals from the larger administrative units, I will capitalize "Hospital" when referring to the latter. Ford, *Journals*, 2:209–11. Middlekauff, *The Glorious Cause*, 525. Ferling, *Almost a Miracle*, 332.

3. Note of pay due McHenry from Dr. John Cochran, Director of Military Hospitals, July 25, 1775, McHenry Papers, reel 3, container 11, LC. Carp, *To Starve the Army at Pleasure*, 26.

4. Applegate, "Preventive Medicine," 379–82. Middlekauff, *The Glorious Cause*, 528–29.

5. Brown, *The Medical Department*, 11–12. Applegate, "Remedial Medicine," 450–51. Ferling, *Almost a Miracle*, 332–33. Middlekauff, *The Glorious Cause*, 532–33.

6. Middlekauff, *The Glorious Cause*, 318, 321, 324–26. Ferling, *Almost a Miracle*, 113–14. Foner, *Thomas Paine and Revolutionary America*, 73–75.

7. James McHenry to "My very Dear Brother" John, January 31, 1776, McHenry Papers, reel 1, container 3, LC.

8. Ibid.

9. Dupuy, *The Compact History of the Revolutionary War*, 68–71. Middlekauff, *The Glorious Cause*, 316, 298, 310–13, 346–47. Ferling, *Almost a Miracle*, 117. Paul, *Unlikely Allies*, 179, 197–98. Schaeper, *Edward Bancroft*, 66–67.

10. Brown, *Medical Department*, 8–13. Ford, *Journals*, 2:249–50. Middlekauff, *The Glorious Cause*, 519–26. Ferling, *Almost a Miracle*, 332. For more on organizational problems within the Hospital Department, see Carp, *To Starve the Army at Pleasure*, 26–29.

11. Ford, *Journals*, 4:344.

12. Brown, *Medical Department*, 21. Gibson, *Doctor Bodo Otto*, 104–6.

13. Middlekauff, *The Glorious Cause*, 334–39. Maier, *American Scripture*, 147. Ferling, *Almost a Miracle*, 119.

14. Gibson, *Dr. Otto*, 110. For a good description of the controversy within the Medical Department, see chap. 11.

15. Ford, *Journals*, 5:705. Benjamin Rush to James McHenry, August 27, 1776, McHenry Papers, reel 1, container 3, LC.

16. Note of pay due, July 25, 1781, McHenry Papers, reel 3, container 11, LC.

17. The following military account is gleaned from the relevant portions of the following books: Higginbotham, *The War of American Independence*, chap. 7. Dupuy, *History of the Revolution*, chaps. 12–13. Middlekauff, *The Glorious Cause*, 356–61. Lengel, *General George Washington*, 164–69.

18. Harvey, "A Few Bloody Noses," 206. Burg, *An Eyewitness History*, 139.

19. Meier, *Early Pennsylvania Medicine*, 144–45. Porter, *Cambridge History of Medicine*, 205.

20. James McHenry to Benjamin Rush, November 21, 1776, McHenry Papers, reel 1, container 3, LC.

21. Steiner, *Life and Correspondence*, 10–12.

22. Ibid.

23. James McHenry to George Washington, January 31, 1777, McHenry Papers, reel 1, container 3, LC.

24. Harvey, "A Few Bloody Noses," 214. Fischer, *Washington's Crossing*, 232, 235, 248, 265–66, 269, 307, 328–43.

25. The ensuing quotes and interpretation are based on a letter James wrote John on June 1, 1777, McHenry Papers, MS 647, MdHS.

26. Foster, *Sex and the Eighteenth-Century Man*, 5. Rotundo, *American Manhood*, 12–16.

27. Foster, *Sex and the Eighteenth-Century Man*, 102. Kann, *On the Man Question*, 273. Laver, *Citizens More Than Soldiers*, 113.

28. Steiner, *Life and Correspondence*, 10–12.

29. Chase, *Papers of George Washington: Revolutionary War Series*, 10:197.

30. James McHenry to John McHenry, March 5, 1778, MS 647, MdHS. Norton, *Liberty's Daughters*, 160–63.

31. Applegate, "The Forgotten Men of the Revolution," 27.

32. Alexander Hamilton to James McHenry, McHenry Papers, March 15, 1776, reel 1, container 3, LC.

33. Benjamin Rush addressed James McHenry as "Senior Surgeon" (Steiner, *Life*, 16) and McHenry referred to himself by that title in a letter to his father (May 15, 1778, McHenry Papers, reel 1, container 3, LC) but the pay voucher (July 25, 1781, ibid.) calls him "Junior Surgeon." At any rate, McHenry was with the American Hospital at Valley Forge.

34. Meier, *Pennsylvania Medicine*, 152.

35. For conditions, see Fleming, *Washington's Secret War*, 137.

36. James McHenry to Daniel McHenry, May 15, 1778, McHenry Papers, reel 1, container 3, LC.

CHAPTER 4   "I Gave Up Soft Beds"

1. Ford, *Journals*, 5:418.

2. Royster, *A Revolutionary People at War*, 86. Fitzpatrick, "Aides-de-Camp," 2. James McHenry to Daniel McHenry, May 15, 1778, McHenry Papers, reel 1, container 3, LC.

3. Ibid. Fitzpatrick, "Aides-de-Camp," 2.

4. Royster, *A Revolutionary People at War*, 206–7. Fitzpatrick, "Aides-de-Camp," 4.

5. Royster, *A Revolutionary People at War,* 192–93. Middlekauff, *The Glorious Cause,* 401, 419–20. Carp, *To Starve the Army at Pleasure,* 44–45. Lengel, *General Washington,* 272–74.

6. Royster, *A Revolutionary People at War,* 196, 213. Higginbotham, *War of American Independence,* chap. 9. Middlekauff, *The Glorious Cause,* 424–25. Dull, "Franklin the Diplomat: The French Mission," 72:29. Bemis, *The Diplomacy of the American Revolution,* 60. Paul, *Unlikely Allies* 346. Dull, *A Diplomatic History,* argues that Saratoga was not definitive, but came at a fortuitous time because Vergennes already wanted to help the Americans in order to twist Britain's arm by cooperating with France in eastern Europe, and this helped his cause, 59, 90–94. Ferling, *Almost a Miracle,* is in general agreement, 260–62.

7. Crackel, *Papers of George Washington: Revolutionary War Series,* "General Orders," 15:123, 136. Fitzpatrick, "Aides-de-Camp," 6. These are my own observations based on letters McHenry wrote for Washington in 1778.

8. Fitzpatrick, "Aides-de-Camp," 10.

9. Mitchell, *Alexander Hamilton: Youth to Maturity,* 1. McDonald, *Alexander Hamilton,* chap. 1. Chernow, *Alexander Hamilton,* 7, 12, 24, 29, 37, 48–49, 85.

10. Document dated June 9, 1778, McHenry Papers, reel 1, container 3, LC.

11. Dupuy, *History of the Revolution,* 275.

12. Mackesy, *The War for America,* 190, 214–15. Middlekauff, *The Glorious Cause,* 413. Crackel, *Papers of George Washington: Revolutionary War Series,* Washington to Col. Sheldon, May 29, 1778, and Washington to Col. Moylan, June 1, 1778, 15:264, 15:294.

13. Ibid. Washington to Elias Boudinot, June 2, 1778, and Washington to Hamilton, June 4, 1778, 12:13, 16–17.

14. Dupuy, *History of the Revolution,* 275–76. Middlekauff, *The Glorious Cause,* 425. Lengel, *General Washington,* 286–89.

15. Crackel, *Papers of George Washington: Revolutionary War Series,* Washington to Gates, June 27, 1778, 15:563.

16. Higginbotham, *War of American Independence,* 46–47. Middlekauff, *The Glorious Cause,* 429.

17. Ibid. Lengel, *General Washington,* 294.

18. Steiner, *Life and Correspondence,* 19.

19. Middlekauff, *The Glorious Cause,* 432–33.

20. Higginbotham, *War of American Independence,* 246–47, and Middlekauff, *The Glorious Cause,* 432–33, are kinder to Lee than Dupuy, *History of the Revolution.* Lengel, *General Washington,* 303–4.

21. Crackel, *Papers of George Washington: Revolutionary War Series,* Washington to Lee, June 30, 1778, 15:597. The account of this battle can be found in Dupuy, *History of the Revolution,* chap. 21; Middlekauff, *Glorious Cause,* 429; and Harvey, who, in *A Few Bloody Noses,* argues instead that Lee was Washington's scapegoat to "spin" the problems, 302–5. Lengel, *General Washington,* 305–6.

22. Ibid., 307. Middlekauff, *The Glorious Cause,* 437.

23. Crackel, *Papers of George Washington: Revolutionary War Series,* Washington to Sullivan, September 1, 1778, 16:454–55.

24. James McHenry to Hugh Williamson, September 12, 1778, McHenry Papers, reel 3, container 11, LC. Royster, in *Revolutionary People at War,* 129–31, points out that the general population felt the same mood swing after Monmouth. But, he reminds us, they also felt joy at good news, and speculates that these extremes may be explained by their

dependence on the army, of which they were not a part. If so, McHenry illustrates that officers in the army were similarly disposed to mood swings, perhaps also due to their dependence on the turns of the war being made by others.

25. James McHenry to Hugh Williamson, McHenry Papers, reel 3, container 11, LC.

26. Crackel, *Papers of George Washington: Revolutionary War Series*, Washington to Henry Laurens, November 21, 1778, 18:250–51. Starkey, "Paoli to Stony Point," 7–27.

27. James McHenry to Daniel McHenry, August 15, 1778, McHenry Papers, reel 1, container 3, LC.

28. James McHenry to Barnabus Binney, [date uncertain, early November, 1778?], McHenry Papers, reel 1, container 3, LC; Royster, *Revolutionary People at War*, 211.

29. Dupuy, *History of the Revolution*, 324.

30. Crackel, *Papers of George Washington: Revolutionary War Series*, Washington to Pulaski, February 8, 1779, 19:150–51. Ferling, *Almost a Miracle*, 387–88.

31. Dupuy, *History of the Revolution*, chap. 23, and 298. Ferling, *Almost a Miracle*, 352. Calloway, *The American Revolution in Indian Country*, 47, 51–53.

32. Crackel, *Papers of George Washington: Revolutionary War Series*, Washington to Sullivan, May 13, 1779, 20:476.

33. Ferling, *Almost a Miracle*, 354. Graymont, "The Iroquois," in Weiser, *Indians of North America*, 87–88. Lengel, *General Washington*, 311–12.

34. Lengel, *General Washington*, 318. Ferling, *Almost a Miracle*, 355–77.

35. Ibid., 357.

36. Document sized "Z," McHenry Papers, WLC, reel 1. Higginbotham, *War of American Independence*, 258–64; Syrett, *Papers of Alexander Hamilton*, Laurens to Hamilton, Dec. 12, 1779, 2:226.

37. Pennypacker, *General Washington's Spies*, 11, 15, 51. Pennypacker referred to these spy rings as a Secret Service, 2, 3, 16.

38. Ibid., 255; McHenry Papers, reel 1, WLC.

39. Ferling, *Almost a Miracle*, 389–91.

40. Fitzpatrick, *Writings of Washington*, Washington, to Anthony Wayne, Nov. 17, 1779, 17:120–21.

41. Ibid., 17:273–74.

42. Syrett, *Hamilton Papers*, Hamilton to Laurens, Jan. 8, 1780, 2:255.

43. Ibid., May 22, 1779, 2:253–54.

44. Fitzpatrick, *Writings of Washington*, vol. 17, see the following letters—Washington to Brigadier General William Irvine, January 4, 1780, 347–49; Washington to "Brigadiers and Officers Commanding Brigades," January 6, 1780, 358; Washington to Major General Heath, January 14–15, 1780, 395–98.

45. Dupuy, *History of the Revolution*, 483. Fitzpatrick, *Writings of Washington*, 18:89. Paul, *Unlikely Allies*, 344. Dull, *A Diplomatic History*, 116.

46. McHenry to Washington, July 11, 1780, McHenry Papers, reel 1, container 3, LC.

47. "Genl Answer," July 21, 1780, McHenry Papers, reel 1, container 3, LC.

48. Syrett, *Hamilton Papers*, Alexander Hamilton to James Duane, January 8, 1780, 2:364. Steiner, *Life and Correspondence*, 29.

CHAPTER 5   "Sorcery and Majic"

1. Syrett, *Hamilton Papers*, Alexander Hamilton to James Duane, July 22, 1780, 2:363–64, Philip Schuyler to Alexander Hamilton, September 15, 1780, 2:432–33.

2. James McHenry to John McHenry, August 12, 1780, McHenry Papers, MS 647.

3. Ibid.

4. Mitchell, *Alexander Hamilton: Youth to Maturity*, 206.

5. McHenry to Cochran, Steiner, *Life and Correspondence*, 30, 77.

6. Dupuy, *History of the Revolution*, 354. Middlekauff, *The Glorious Cause*, 582.

7. Flexner, *The Traitor and the Spy*, 366. Martin, *Benedict Arnold, Revolutionary Hero*, 1–2.

8. Flexner, *The Traitor and the Spy*, 369–70.

9. Dupuy, *History of the Revolution*, 212. Martin, *Benedict Arnold*, 2.

10. Flexner, *The Traitor and the Spy*, 371.

11. For a good, solid account of this, see Mitchell, *Alexander Hamilton: Youth to Maturity*, 210–21. Flexner, *The Traitor and the Spy*, 86–87, 390–94.

12. Dupuy, *History of the Revolution*, 366.

13. Showman, *Papers of General Nathanael Greene*, 3:51. Idzerda, *Lafayette in the American Revolution*, 3:xxii. Greene, for one, was convinced that McHenry acted as a calming factor on the Frenchman. See Major General Nathanael Greene to James McHenry, July 24, 1781, McHenry Papers, reel 5, container 14, LC; Ford, *Journals*, 18:992–93.

14. James McHenry to Mr. Von Riper, blacksmith, Wayne MS, MS Division, 11:86, HSP.

15. James McHenry to Governor Howley [sic], January 22, 1781, James McHenry Collection, Miscellaneous MS, NYHS.

16. See "Tench Tilghman," Malone, *Dictionary of American Biography*, 18:543–45; and Hoffman, *A Spirit of Dissension*, 113–14. McHenry's ability to enter Maryland politics fits well within a tradition of accepting respectable immigrant merchants into the upper reaches of the political fold. See Burnard, *Creole Gentlemen: The Maryland Elite*, 11, 16. This story of McHenry's networking with Maryland has been published in Karen Robbins, "Ambition Rewarded: James McHenry's Entry into Post-Revolutionary Maryland Politics," *Maryland Historical Magazine* (Summer 1998): 93:191–214.

17. Risjord, *Chesapeake Politics*, 72, 74. Hoffman, *A Spirit of Dissension*, 113–14.

18. Haw, *Stormy Patriot: The Life of Samuel Chase*, early chapters.

19. Hoffman, *A Spirit of Dissension*, 243–47. Hoffman and Mason, *Princes of Maryland: A Carroll Saga*, 330.

20. Chase and Charles Carroll of Carrollton had argued before, over the confiscation of Loyalist property, and would argue again, but they set aside those matters when larger issues required. See Risjord, *Chesapeake Politics*, 75. It is also worth noting that Risjord is quite clear that the rifts were over issues and not personalities, 77.

21. Steiner, *Archives of Maryland*, Thursday, January 25, 1781, Liber C.B., Nos. 24, 36, or 288 of published copy. Burnard, in *Creole Gentlemen*, discusses the wealth of the councilors on page 170.

22. Hoffman, *A Spirit of Dissension*, 179–80. *Archives of Maryland*, 45:287–88.

23. Dupuy, *History of the Revolution*, 424.

24. Most, although not all, of this correspondence is published in McHenry, *A Sidelight on History*.

25. Syrett, *Hamilton Papers*, 2:569. Chernow, *Alexander Hamilton*, 149–53.

26. James McHenry to Governor Lee, February 4, 1781, 4603–46, Maryland State Papers (hereafter MSP). Scharf, *Chronicles of Baltimore*, 414. James McHenry to Governor Lee, March 9, 1781, Steiner, *Archives of Maryland*, March 9, Red Book, No. 32, Letter 53, 114 of published form.

27. James McHenry to Governor Lee, March 14, 1781, Steiner, *Archives of Maryland*, vol. 47, Red Book, No. 32, Letter 51, 127 in published form. Hoffman, *A Spirit of Dissension*, 242–43. McHenry to Lee, April 7, 1781, 4603–48, MSP. McHenry to Lee, April 7, 1781, McHenry Papers, reel 1, container 3, LC. McHenry to Lee, April 27, 1781, *A Sidelight on History*, 11–14.

28. Dupuy, *History of the Revolution*, 404.

29. General Greene to James McHenry, March 22, 1781, McHenry Papers, reel 1, container 1, LC. J. B. Cutting to James McHenry, March 29, 1781, McHenry Papers, reel 1, container 3, LC.

30. Fitzpatrick, *Writings of Washington*, 20:406.

31. See Steiner, *Archives of Maryland*, December 31, 1779, 43:68; January 25, 1780, 43:70; May 13, 1781, 43:494. McHenry to Colonel Uriah Forrest, July 26, 1781, McHenry Papers, reel 1, container 3, LC.

32. Ibid. James McHenry to Governor Lee, September 1, 1781, *A Sidelight on History*, 58–59.

33. James McHenry to Mordecai Gist, April 9, 1781, McHenry Papers, reel 3, container 11, LC.

34. James McHenry to Governor Lee, June 9, 1781, McHenry Papers, reel 1, container 3, LC. Major General Nathanael Greene to James McHenry, July 24, 1781, McHenry Papers, reel 5, container 14, LC.

35. James McHenry to Colonel Otho Holland Williams, August 27, 1781, Ferdinand J. Dreer Autograph Collection, 10:1, volume: Presidents 1:15, HSP. Lafayette to Smith, Young, Neill and Bowley, July 1, 1781, MS 1814, MdHS.

36. Dupuy, *History of the Revolution*, 431–32. The number of men naturally varied, but this number seems to be correct for the beginning of July. Gaines, *For Liberty and Glory*, 155. James McHenry to Governor Lee, *A Sidelight on History*, 24–25. James McHenry to Colonel Otho Holland Williams, July 4, 1781, Dreer Collection, HSP.

37. James McHenry to Governor Lee, July 7, 1781, *A Sidelight on History*, 19–21. Dupuy, *History of the Revolution*, 430–31.

38. James McHenry to Governor Lee, August 6 and 25, 1781, *A Sidelight on History*, 43–44, 54.

39. Mackesy, *War for America*, 273.

40. James McHenry to Governor Lee, August 28, 1781, September 1, 1781, *A Sidelight on History*, 55–56, 60.

41. Ibid., September 15, 1781, 63. Higginbotham, *War of American Independence*, 381–82. Mackesy, *War for America*, 423–44. Lengel, *General Washington*, 336.

42. McHenry to Lee, *A Sidelight on History*, October 2, 1781, 64–65.

43. Ibid., October 6 and 9, 1781, 66–67, 68.

44. Royster, *A Revolutionary People at War*, 244–45. Lengel, *General Washington*, 336–40. Chernow, *Hamilton*, 214.

45. "Taking of the English Redoubt at Yorktown by the American Troops," McHenry Papers, WLC, reel 1. The rest is illegible.

46. Lengel, *General Washington*, 342–44.

47. Mackesy, *War for America*, 435.

48. Nov. 20, 24, 30, 1781, Journals, Minutes and Proceedings of the Upper House, A.1.a., "Maryland Legislative Records," in Jenkins, *Records of the States*. In chap. 6 of *Creole Gentlemen*, Burnard illustrates that Maryland politics had been open to immigrant

men of wealth and gentlemanly bearing throughout the century, despite the predominance of a cohesive majority.

CHAPTER 6   "Transition from the Military to the Civil Line"

1. Washington to McHenry, December 11, 1781, in Fitzpatrick, *Writings of Washington*, 23:380–81. Ridgway, *Community Leadership in Maryland*, 3–5. Burnard, *Creole Gentlemen*.

2. John Thomas Scharf, *History of Maryland*, 2:475–77.

3. "Thoughts on a Plan for a New Paper Money and for Recovering a Currency to Our Old Emissions," McHenry Papers, LC, reel 6, container 4.

4. "Further Remarks on New Money," McHenry Papers, LC, reel 6, container 14.

5. McDonald, *Novus Ordo Seclorum*, chap. 4, esp. 116–31. For more about the paper money controversy, see chapter 7.

6. Mitchell, *Hamilton: Youth to Maturity*, 177–79.

7. Papers for the month of January 1782, McHenry Papers, WLC; and Alexander Hamilton (Publius) to James McHenry, March 5, 1782, McHenry Papers, MdHS, MS 1814. McHenry's low estimation of Chase apparently rose, for on June 14 he presented "an Act to vest in Samuel Chase and Allen Quynn, Esquires, and their heirs, in trust, and for the uses therein mentioned, the theatre in the city of Annapolis; which was read the first and second time by especial order and will pass." *Maryland Records*, Senate, June 14, 1782.

8. Ibid., Senate, May 25, June 10 and 15, 1782.

9. Ibid., Senate, June 12, 1782. Rakove, *The Beginnings of National Politics*, 282–83. Jensen, *The New Nation*, 58–59. Morris, *The Forging of the Union*, 41. Ferguson, *The Power of the Purse*, 116–17, 152. Rakove, *Original Meanings*, 25.

10. *Maryland Archives*, Working File, LHP 1, vol. 2, under LC Offices. Steiner, *Life and Correspondence*, 43.

11. Ibid., 41, 44.

12. Ibid., 43–46.

13. Ibid., 49. See receipts dated November 25, 1783, and March 16, 1792 (LC, reel 3, container 11, series C, 1776–1816). MSP (19970–4/2/26) December 3, 1783. But these were partial payments, and as of March 9, 1792, the United States still owed him—see "No. 1" of that date (same location) for periods not paid. In any event, McHenry's eldest surviving son would, in McHenry's will, inherit the land James "received as Major in the revolutionary Army that under God assisted in achieving our Independence." Maryland State Archives, 11619–1, BA Wills no. 10, 1815–19, 174–78. And Maryland had, in November 1781, set aside for the soldiers. See Scharf's *History of Maryland*, 2:507.

14. James McHenry to Gov. Lee, October 29, 1782, and sonnet, McHenry Papers, LC, reel 1, container 4. James McHenry to Arthur Harper, June 6, 1775, McHenry Papers, LC, reel 5, container 14, series D correspondence, Personal, 1775–1822 and undated. James McHenry to Miss Ashfield, McHenry Papers, LC, reel 5, container 14.

15. James McHenry to Miss Betsy Orrick, August 15, 1778, McHenry Papers, WLC, reel 1, 1777–1798.

16. Ibid.

17. Ibid.

18. Ibid.

19. Ibid.

20. Ibid.

21. Ibid.

22. Gregory, *A Father's Legacy to His Daughters*, 6–7.

23. Many of these issues are discussed in chaps. 1 and 2 of Kerber's *Women of the Republic*. Carol Berkin, *Revolutionary Mothers*, 157–59. Nash, *The Unknown American Revolution*, 203–6. Abigail to John Adams, 31 March to 5 April, 1776, The Adams Papers, An Electronic Archive, MHS, http://www.masshist.org/digitaladams/aea/cfm/doc.cfm ?id=L17760331aa, accessed February 4, 2013.

24. The records do not say how much. Her father, who had died shortly before Peggy's birth, had divided his estate among family members, with smaller amounts going to his parents and siblings, one-third to his widow, and the rest to his children. John received 500 pounds more than Peggy when he reached twenty-one, while Peggy received her inheritance, quantity unknown, at the age of eighteen. See "Will of David Caldwell", Book M, 1762, #209, Philadelphia County, Pennsylvania, Will Books, HSP.

25. James McHenry to Miss Caldwell, November 13, 1782, LC, McHenry Papers, reel 1, container 4.

26. Steiner, *Life and Correspondence*, 50.

27. *Maryland Records*, Senate, December 27, 1782, January 8, 13, and 15, 1783.

28. Ibid., January 3, 1783.

29. Ibid., December 24, 1782.

30. Ibid., December 31, 1782, January 13, 1783.

31. Ibid., December 31, 1782.

32. Maryland State Archives, BA—Proceedings of the Orphans Court, 1777–1787. Liber W.B. 1, MdHR 11, 814.

33. February 20, 1783, 6636–39–96, and February 24, 1783, MSP, 4604–10. See also the Council Letter Book, 1780–1787, 4008–415/416, February 19, 1783.

34. Steiner, *Life and Correspondence*, 51–52.

35. Steiner says this is the same Armstrong who wrote the Newburgh Address that almost led Washington's officers to mutiny. Certainly the name and rank are the same. But later in the same year McHenry would become business partners with Armstrong in a mercantile house in Philadelphia—and the *Dictionary of American Biography* (1:355–58) makes no mention of Armstrong's (author of the Newburgh Addresses) having become a merchant. Steiner, *Life and Correspondence*, 55. Furthermore, Armstrong's biographer quotes the man as having no interest in business. Instead, he went right into politics. Nor is James McHenry ever mentioned in the biography. Skeen, *John Armstrong, Jr.*, 19–20. So it would seem that McHenry's business partner and the John Armstrong Jr. of the Newburgh Addresses are probably not the same man.

36. Steiner, *Life and Correspondence*, 55.

CHAPTER 7 "A Delicate Task"

1. Ford, *Journals*, 24:389.

2. Jensen, *The New Nation*, 54–55.

3. Burnett, *The Continental Congress*, 576. Rappleye, *Robert Morris*, 358–60. Bowling, *Creation of Washington, D.C.*, 30–33.

4. Ford, *Journals*, 24:406. Rappleye, *Robert Morris*, 361. Bowling, *Creation of Washington, D.C.*, 33–34.

5. Burnett, *The Continental Congress*, 576–78. Ford, *Journals*, 24:410. Rappleye, *Robert Morris*, 362–64. Bowling, *Creation of Washington, D.C.*, 33.

6. McHenry to Thomas Sim Lee, June 28, 1783, McHenry Papers, LC, reel 1, container 4. Bowling, *Creation of Washington, D.C.*, 51–52.

7. Burnett, *The Continental Congress*, 584.

8. McHenry to Daniel of Saint Thomas Jenifer, Intendant of the Revenue, MSP, 6636–46/61. McHenry to Paca, August 9, 1783, MSP, 4562–37.

9. Ford, *Journals*, 24:484, 507, 508, 509; 25:649–54, 656, 657, 659, 665, 666–68, 670–73, 675, 707–9, 714. McHenry to Paca, October 11, 1783, MSP, 4562–38.

10. Morris, *Encyclopedia of American History*, 131. McHenry to Paca, October 11, 1783, MSP, 4562–38. Bowling, *Creation of Washington, D.C.*, 58–59.

11. Steiner, *Life and Correspondence*, 57, 148. *A Century of Lawmaking for a New Nation*, vol. 23, November 7, 1785–November 5, 1786, "Pennsylvania Delegates to Benjamin Franklin. http://memory.loc.gov/ammem/amlaw/lawhome.html, accessed Feb. 21, 2003.

12. Burnett, *The Continental Congress*, 573. Ford, *Journals*, 25:547–51 and 24:521. Jensen, *The New Nation*, 389.

13. Jensen, *The New Nation*, 389. Ford, *Journals*, 24:454–55.

14. McHenry to Dear Sir (?), August 2, 1783, MSP, 4562–39.

15. Jensen, *The New Nation*, 9, 23–27. Onuf, *Origins of the Federal Republic*, chap. 4, "Virginia and the West." Ford, *Journals*, 25:972, 554–59.

16. Steiner, *Life and Correspondence*, 59.

17. Ibid., 60.

18. Ibid., 62. Jenkins, *Records of the States, Maryland*, Senate, December 2, and November 27, 1783.

19. Steiner, *Life and Correspondence*, 64.

20. Jenkins, *Records of the States*, Maryland Senate, December 19, 1783. Wills, *Cincinnatus: George Washington and the Enlightenment*, 8–13.

21. Steiner, *Life and Correspondence*, 47.

22. Ford, *Journals*, December 20, 1783.

23. Steiner, *Life and Correspondence*, 69–70.

24. *Maryland State Papers*, McHenry to Governor Paca, March 15, 1784, 4562–48. Jenkins, *Records of the States*, Maryland Senate, November 26, 1783.

25. Ford, *Journals*, 26:176–77, 253–55 and 27:751. McHenry's plan appears to have been accepted, for in 1785 Congress received a petition from agents to the invalid corp.

26. Ibid., 26:296.

27. Ibid., 27:530–31.

28. Margaret McHenry to James McHenry, April 4, 1784, McHenry Family Papers, MdHS, Ms. 647, box 1 of 5. Steiner, *Life and Correspondence*, 85.

29. William Allison to James McHenry, October 19, 1784 and Sam Caldwell to James McHenry, July 10, 1784, MdHS, Ms. 647.

30. By January 13, 1785, Peggy was writing McHenry breezy letters from Philadelphia. See the McHenry Family Papers, MdHS, Ms. 647, box 1 of 5.

31. See petitions in Burnett's *Journals*, vol. 28, from Benjamin Bankson (February 11, 1785), Barton (September 7, 1785), Timothy Bradly (June 7, 1785), and 28:382–6.

32. These problems had been plaguing Congress for some time. Two years before, in 1783, tensions between settlers in Spanish-controlled Natchez and the Spanish government had forced men literally to run for their lives. They now requested American citizenship and permission to return temporarily to Natchez for their families and possessions, which McHenry's committee granted. Onuf, "Liberty, Development, and Union,"

Congress and the Confederation, The New American Nation, 4:179–80. Ford, *Journals*, 24:436–37, 25:602, 692–93.

33. Ibid., 28:125, 178–81, 415, 469–70, 472; 25:602, 692–93.

34. Ibid., 28:155–57, 462–63.

35. Ford, *Journals*, 28:337. Steiner, *Life and Correspondence*, 608.

36. Rakove, *The Beginnings of National Politics*, 320–22, 337–38. Ford's *Journals*, 28:27–28, 29:658; and McHenry's transcripts of "notes from Mr. Adams letters" in the McHenry Papers, LC, reel 1, container 4. McHenry to George Washington, August 1, 1785, Abbott and Twohig, *The Papers of George Washington: Confederation Series*, 3:167.

37. McHenry to George Washington, August 1, 1785, Abbott and Twohig, *The Papers of George Washington: Confederation Series*, 3:167.

38. Jensen, *The New Nation*, 59. Rakove, *The Beginnings of National Politics*, 290.

39. Rakove, *The Beginnings of National Politics*, 290. James McHenry to John Hall, HSP, Dreer Collection, Federal Convention, 2:67. Archivists have mistakenly guessed the year of this letter to be 1784—but the politics it contains belong to 1785.

40. For a more complete explanation of the indent and certificate situation, see Jensen, *The New Nation*, 388–98.

41. James McHenry to John Hall, HSP, Dreer Collection, Members of the Federal Convention, 2:67. William Hindman and James McHenry to Daniel of Saint Thomas Jenifer, October 5, 1785, MSP, 6636–46–167.

42. Most of the affair is in the McHenry Papers, LC, reel 3, container 11, on letters James labeled "References No. 1–9" dated from July 15 through November 16, 1786. The rest is in the MSP, 6636–60–51/1, 51/2, and 26/2 as well as the Maryland State Archives P 220(2).

43. James McHenry to the Maryland House of Delegates, April 4, 1792, McHenry Papers, WLC, reel 1 (1 pos). There are many copies of relevant letters written during this complicated transaction as well as a disjointed account of what he told the assembly in 1790 (see McHenry Papers, LC, reel 3, container 11, series C, November 10, 1790). However, the clearest and most comprehensive account was written in 1792 when he organized a complete representation of what occurred for the assembly's consideration.

44. Ibid. Also Jenkins, *Records of the States*, Maryland Lower House, November 19–20, 1790.

45. See William Marbury to James McHenry, April 7, 1796, McHenry Papers, WLC, reel 1, and James Winchester to James McHenry, November 16, 1796, McHenry Papers, HL.

46. James McHenry to George Plater, January 6, 1786, HSP, Dreer Collection, Soldiers of the Revolution, 3:87.

CHAPTER 8   "For the General Good"

1. Steffen, *The Mechanics of Baltimore*, 87–88. Steffen says the mechanics supported McHenry for three reasons: he was a veteran, he lived in "Fell's Point, which many believed made him sympathetic with the needs of the heavily laboring-class population. He was a physician." But according to Steiner, *Life and Correspondence*, 1–2, the family's business was located on Calvert, just south of Market (now Baltimore) Street. Presumably they lived there at first. In 1780, however, John began buying property around town, at least one purchase presumably for James and Peggy's first home. This could have been located on Fell's Point, as Steffen says. By 1789, though, we know that James's family had

moved west of the town of Baltimore to a large home about a mile from the Patapsco that he named "Fayetteville" for his friend the marquis.

2. This account is from the early chapters of Haw, *Stormy Patriot*.

3. *The American Museum*, 334–35. Although this publication did not appear until 1788, the essay circulated during the controversy in 1787.

4. Ibid., 333–34.

5. Haw, *Stormy Patriot*, 143.

6. Gregory Stiverson, "Necessity, the Mother of Union: Maryland and the Constitution, 1785–1789," in Conley and Kaminski, *The Constitution and the States*, 138–40.

7. Gross, *In Debt to Shays*, introduction. Morris, *The Forging of the Union*, 263.

8. Daniel of St. Thomas Jenifer to McHenry, February 1785, McHenry Papers, reel 5, container 14, LC.

9. Stiverson, "Necessity," 142.

10. *Maryland Records, Senate*, April 20, 21, and 23, 1787. Farrand, *The Records of the Federal Convention of 1787*, J. B. Cutting to Thomas Jefferson, 3:339. Renzulli, *Maryland: The Federalist Years*, 49. Whitten, "*The State Delegations in the Philadelphia Convention of 1787*," 1101.

11. Diary of the Constitutional Convention, McHenry Papers, LOC, reel 6. Actually it is quite difficult to tell just when McHenry got to Philadelphia. True, his diary places the date May 14 in the top margin, but he also has notes for the twenty-fifth despite the fact that he did not appear until the twenty-eighth, so he was clearly backdating some things. On the other hand, his new credentials were only passed by the legislature on the twenty-sixth. Had he been in Baltimore the credentials would have taken hours to reach him and then he would have faced an arduous ride by horseback on the twenty-seventh in order to get to Philadelphia, which is unlikely. Probably he was in Philadelphia and the legislature sent him his new credentials by express post as soon as they were passed. This must be Steiner's surmise also, since he placed McHenry in Philadelphia as well. Also see Jenkins, *Records of States*, Maryland, Senate, December 28, 1786.

12. Farrand, *Federal Convention*, 1:xx–xxi. Beeman, *Plain, Honest Men*, 84.

13. Ibid., Appendix A, CXIX, 3:93. Lynch, "A Guide to Eighteenth Century English Vocabulary," http://andromeda.rutgers.edu/~jlynch/C18Guide.pdf, accessed February 4, 2013.

14. Berkin, *A Brilliant Solution*, 64–65. Hoffman, *Governmental Secrecy and the Founding Fathers*, 11–24, 20–21.

15. Farrand, *Federal Convention*, 1:34. Beeman, *Plain, Honest Men*, 100–102. Rossiter, *1787: The Grand Convention*, 171–72. Berkin, *A Brilliant Solution*, 66–71.

16. Farrand, *Federal Convention*, 1:40.

17. Ibid., 1:61.

18. Ibid., 1:75.

19. Ibid., 2:175–76.

20. Stiverson, "Necessity," 143. Beeman, *Plain, Honest Men*, 60. Warren, *The Making of the Constitution*, 124.

21. Stiverson, "Necessity," 144.

22. Farrand, *Federal Convention*, 2:190.

23. Ibid., 2:191 and 280.

24. Ibid., 2:471–82.

25. Finkelman, *Slavery and the Founders*, 22–28. Finkelman, "Slavery and the Constitution: Making a Covenant with Death," in Beeman, *Beyond Confederation*, describes in

great detail how this compromise worked as well as how it benefited the slave states of the Deep South. Indeed, he uses McHenry's notes, which he describes as "quite revealing," 218n85. McDonald, *Novus Ordo Seclorum*, 266.

26. Wilson, "The Supreme Court's Bill of Attainder Doctrine," 54:212–16. Farrand, *Federal Convention*, 2:375.

27. Jenkins, *Records of States*, Maryland, Senate, December 31, 1782. http://aomol .net/megafile/msa/speccol/sc4800/sc4872/003145/html/m3145-0225.html, accessed February 4, 2013. Beeman, *Plain, Honest Men*, 291.

28. Farrand, *Federal Convention*, 2:375.

29. Ibid., 2:587, 553.

30. Ibid., 2:211, 476.

31. Ibid., 2:212.

32. Ibid., 2:649–50.

33. McDonald, *Novus Ordo Seclorum*, 284. White, *The Federalists*, 51n.

34. Steiner, "Maryland's Adoption of the Federal Constitution," 27. Crowl, *Maryland during and after the Revolution*, 118–20. Brown, "Party Battles and Beginnings in Maryland: 1786–1812," 37–38. Steffen, *Mechanics of Baltimore*, 88–90.

35. Ibid., 88–91.

36. Farrand, *Federal Convention*, 3:306 and vol. 3.

37. Ibid., Appendix A, 146CXLVIa, 3:146. Elkins and McKitrick, "The Founding Fathers: Young Men of the Revolution," 181–216.

38. Farrand, *Federal Convention*, 3:146.

39. Ibid., 3:150. Onuf, "Maryland: The Small Republic and the New Nation," 171–200, in *Ratifying the Constitution*, ed. Gillespie and Lienesch.

40. Farrand, *Federal Convention*, Appendix A, CXLVIb, 3:151–59.

41. Steiner, "Maryland's Adoption of the Federal Constitution," 5:28.

42. Haw et al., *Stormy Patriot*, 150, chap. 12, esp. 144–48. Steffen, *Mechanics of Baltimore*, 90–91. Risjord, *Chesapeake Politics*, 284–85.

43. Steffen, *Mechanics of Baltimore*, 91.

44. Wood, *Radicalism of the Revolution*, 210–11. Steiner, "Maryland's Adoption of the Federal Constitution," 5:41–42. Steffen, *Mechanics of Baltimore*, 92 and Crowl, *Maryland during and after*, 135–36.

45. Ibid., chap. 6, "The Ratifying Convention: Annapolis, April, 1788." Renzulli, *Maryland: The Federalist Years*. Elliot, *The Debates on the Adoption of the Federal Constitution*, 2:547–56.

46. A great account can be found in Maier, *Ratification: The People Debate the Constitution, 1787–1788*, 241–47.

47. Crowl, *Maryland during and after*, 148. Stiverson, "Necessity," 144–46. Washington to McHenry, April 27, 1788, *The Papers of George Washington Digital Edition, Confederation Series*, in Crackel, 6:234.

48. Stiverson, "Necessity," 144–50. Rakove, *Original Meanings*, 116.

49. Risjord, *Chesapeake Politics*, 292. Steiner, *Life*, 112.

50. Risjord, *Chesapeake Politics*, 297. Elliot, *Debates*, 2:556.

CHAPTER 9   "A Friendship Independent of Brotherhood"

1. Brown, "Politics of Crisis." This article is basically extracted from her doctoral dissertation cited earlier. Renzulli, *Maryland Federalists*. Risjord, *Chesapeake Politics*, 330–37.

2. A Federal Mechanic to Mr. Printer, September 9, 1788, *Maryland Journal and Baltimore Advertiser*. Steffen, *Mechanics of Baltimore*, 95, chap. 4.

3. Brown, "Party Battles," 197. "An Irishman to the Mechanics, Tradesmen, and Poor Citizens of Baltimore-Town," October 4, 1788, *Maryland Journal and Baltimore Advertiser*. Risjord, *Chesapeake Politics*, 331.

4. Steffen, *Mechanics of Baltimore*, 96–97, and "Continuation of the Speech of Robert Smith," October 3, 1788, *Maryland Journal and Baltimore Advertiser*.

5. Den Boer, *Documentary History of the First Federal Elections*, 2:107–22. *Maryland Journal*, August 10, 1788.

6. Amicus to the Examiner, August 12, 1788, *Maryland Journal*.

7. Brown, "Maryland Elections, 1788–9," 201. Renzulli, *Maryland Federalists*, 111n25. Ridgway, *Community Leadership in Maryland*, 7–8. Den Boer, *Documentary History of the First Federal Elections*, 2:107.

8. Jenkins, *Records of States*, Maryland, Lower House, November Session, 1788. Steffen, *Mechanics of Baltimore*, 99.

9. John Caldwell to McHenry, January 20, 1788, and P. McHenry to James McHenry, January 23, 1788, MS 647, MdHS. John McHenry to James McHenry, November 6, 1788, MS 647, MdHS.

10. Ibid., November 5, 1788.

11. McHenry to Hamilton, in Syrett, *Hamilton's Papers*, 25:439. Steiner, *Life and Correspondence*, 506.

12. Risjord, *Chesapeake Politics*, 332.

13. Ibid., 330–37. Den Boer, *First Federal Elections*, 2:230–34.

14. McHenry to Washington, March 29, 1789, in Abbot, *Papers of George Washington, Presidential Series*, 1:461.

15. Wood, *Radicalism of the Revolution*, 99–109.

16. Abbot, *Papers of George Washington: Presidential Series*, 2:3.

17. Ibid., 2:48. Ellis, *Presidential Travel*, 20, points out that Washington said much the same thing to John Hancock when he, Washington, toured New England as a new president.

18. Abbot, *Papers of George Washington: Presidential Series*, 2:63–65. Kaminski and McCaughan, *A Great and Good Man*, 145–47.

19. Abbot, *Papers of Washington: Presidential Series*, 2:205.

20. Ibid., 2:381.

21. Brown, "Party Battles," 83–84.

22. Washington to McHenry, all in Fitzpatrick, *Writings of Washington*, August 22, 1785, 28:227–30; November 11, 1786, 29:59–60; November 29, 1786, 29:93–5; April 27, 1788, 29:471–72; May 8, 1785, 28:227–30.

23. Hofstadter, *The Idea of a Party System*. Bernstein, *Thomas Jefferson*, 95, suggests the term "partisan alliances." Freeman, *Affairs of Honor*, passim. Brown, in "Party Battles," refers to McHenry as "party leader" in 1796, 153. And she acknowledges that his leadership had been exerted as early as 1789 and developed over the years. But as her focus is not on McHenry it is not surprising that she does not accord him this full status earlier. In fact, while she is aware of the "Valerius" essays, she is unaware they were written by McHenry. I, however, will show that he was clearly a partisan leader almost as soon as the new national government began and that the ways in which he functioned went through stages. Risjord in *Chesapeake Politics* attributes the Federalists' "solid organization in Maryland" to McHenry (409). Renzulli has also appreciated McHenry's role as Federalist leader during these early years. Furthermore, Prince, in *The Federal-*

ists and the Origins of the U.S. Civil Service, has recognized McHenry's significance in Maryland as well, and also notes that in most states Federalist "parties" existed around 1789. See 1, 3, 96–97.

24. Abbot, *Papers of George Washington: Presidential Series*, 2:67, 381–82; and "To the United States Senate," August 3, 1789, 3:106–7, 380. Steiner, *Life*, 124. Syrett, *Hamilton Papers*, 5:472. Prince, *Federalists and the Civil Service*, 96–97.

25. Abbot, *Papers of George Washington: Presidential Series*, 3:75–76, 112–13.

26. Ibid., 3:75–76, 106–7. Fenwick, *Springlore in Virginia*.

27. McHenry to M. McHenry, July 23, 1789, in Steiner, *Life*, 119–20.

28. Jenkins, *Records of States*, Maryland, Lower House, November session, 1789.

29. Ibid., December 14 and 22, 1789.

30. Ferguson, *Power of the Purse*, chap. 10, "Settlements of State Accounts," esp. 217, 281. Jenkins, *Records of States*, Maryland, Lower House, December 23 and 24, 1789.

31. James McHenry to unknown, January 1, 1790, MS 647, MdHS.

32. January and February of the Letterbook of John McHenry & Co., 1790–1810, McHenry Papers, reel 6, series D, LC.

33. Ibid., James McHenry to John Jeffers, April 10, 1790. Steiner, *Life*, 125.

34. James McHenry to John [Jack] Caldwell, May 23, 1790, MS 647, MdHS.

35. Letterbook of John McHenry & Co., 1790–1810, McHenry Papers, reel 6, series D, LC.

36. Steiner, *Life and Correspondence*, 125–26. McHenry to Jack Caldwell, August 17, 1790, McHenry Papers, MS 647, MdHS. The one exception seems to be a letter written on behalf of his Federalist running mate Dr. John Coulter, who had decided to protest payments the House of Delegates demanded for investigating the previous year's election. It seems Coulter had never been consulted as to his willingness to pay and now refused. McHenry thought him in the right. McHenry to unknown, Gratz Collection, case 7, box 31, HSP.

CHAPTER 10   "Not Wholly Lost to Ambition"

1. McHenry to Hamilton, January 3, 1791, in Syrett, *Hamilton's Papers*, 7:409–10. Washington to McHenry, January 31, 1791, McHenry Papers, reel 1, container 4, LC. James McHenry to Alexander Hamilton, May 3, 1791, in Syrett, *Hamilton Papers*, 8:321–22.

2. The Letterbook of John McHenry & Co., McHenry Papers, reel 6, container 14, series D, LC. Grace Allison's Will, August 2, 1791, #58, Book W, Philadelphia County, Philadelphia, Pennsylvania, Will Books #W–X, 1790–1797, HSP.

3. James McHenry to Alexander Hamilton, October 27 and 15, 1791, in Syrett, *Hamilton Papers*, 9:386. McHenry to Hamilton, in Syrett, *Hamilton's Papers*, 5:471–72. "List of Names from Whence to Take a Minister for France," May 19, 1794, in Syrett, *Hamilton's Papers*, 16:422–23.

4. Ibid., Hamilton to McHenry, November 2, 1791, 9:454.

5. Jenkins, *Records of States*, Maryland, Senate, November Session, and November 19, 1791. McHenry to David Stewart, December 22, 1795, McHenry Papers, MS, 647, box 2/5, MdHS. Steffen, *Mechanics of Baltimore*, chap. 6, "Mechanic Republicanism and the City Charter," 121–42.

6. Washington to McHenry, August 13, 1792, McHenry to Washington, August 16, 1792, Washington to McHenry, September 21, 1792, in Chase, *Washington Papers: Presidential Series*, 10:655, 11:7, 136.

7. Williams's salary was computed using http://www.measuringworth.com/ukcompare/relativevalue.php, accessed February 4, 2013. Because a direct historic conversion between the pound and dollar is only available since 1830, it was necessary to first compute the increase in just the pound from 1792 to 1830, and then move to the historic conversion program between pounds and dollars. McHenry to Hamilton, September 30, 1792, in Syrett, *Hamilton's Papers*, 12:510. Prince also discusses this in *Federalists and the Civil Service*, 15.

8. McHenry to Hamilton, October 19–23, 1792, in Syrett, *Hamilton Papers*, 12:602. McHenry did not mention the particular incident(s?) when Hamilton failed to pocket a letter, but they had served together under Washington during the war, at the Continental Congress, and at the Constitutional Convention—such an event could have happened at any time. At any rate, McHenry was certainly serious when he suggested burning their letters. See the following notes in these letters in Syrett, *Hamilton Papers*: McHenry to Hamilton, August 16, 1792, n. 17, 12:214; September 20, 1792, n. 2, 12:407; September 30, 1792, n. 1, 12:511; October 19–23, n. 1, n. 4, 12:603; and Hamilton to McHenry, October 20, 1792, 12:185; September 30, 1792, 12:416; etc.

9. Ibid., September 20 and 30, 1792, 12:407 and 510.

10. Ibid., n. 16 in the introductory note to a letter from Hamilton to Mercer, September 26, 1792, 12:487.

11. Ibid., McHenry to Hamilton, August 16, 1792, 12:214, n. 13.

12. Ibid., McHenry to Hamilton, August 16, 1792, 12:214. For a wonderful account of Hamilton's plans, see Elkins and McKitrick, *The Age of Federalism*, 92–123. McDonald, *Alexander Hamilton*, 190, 234. Chernow, *Alexander Hamilton*, 295–308, 355–56, 374–79, 480. Wood, *Empire of Liberty*, 95–103.

13. McDonald, *Alexander Hamilton*, chap. 8, "Funding and Assumption."

14. Elkins and McKitrick, *Age of Federalism*, 155–61.

15. McHenry to Hamilton, October 19–23, 1792, and August 16, 1792, in Syrett, *Hamilton Papers*, 12:602–3, 12:212–14. Brown, "Party Battles," 118.

16. See Risjord's *Chesapeake Politics*, 266–67, 281, 337, 352–53, 393, 401, 409–10. Brown, "Politics of Crisis," 195–209, and her doctoral dissertation, "Party Battles and Beginnings in Maryland," 98–100, 105–11.

17. McHenry to Hamilton, November 18, 1792, in Syrett, *Hamilton's Papers*, 13:157.

18. McHenry to William Perry, July 15, 1792, MS 647, MdHS. Prince mistakenly says that "[t]here is no instance, moreover, where a McHenry-sponsored applicant was not appointed," *Federalists and the Civil Service*, 3.

19. Hamilton to McHenry, April 5, 1793, in Syrett, *Hamilton's Papers*, 14:287–90.

20. Ibid., McHenry to Hamilton, April 14, ibid., 14:316–17. Although this episode is clearly traced through the letters of volumes 13 and 14 of *Hamilton's Papers*, there is a faithful and well-written account in Cooke's *Tench Coxe*, 247–48.

21. Ibid., 247. McHenry to Hamilton, April 14, 1793, and Hamilton to McHenry, April 5, 1793, in Syrett, *Hamilton's Papers*, 14:288, 317.

22. Joanne Freeman discusses the importance of reputation in *Affairs of Honor*, "[h]onor was reputation with a moral dimension and an elite cast," xix–xx, 59.

23. For more information on this case, see Goebel, *Antecedents and Beginnings to 1801*, 726–37. Orth, *The Judicial Power of the United States*, 12, 18, 20. Jacobs, *The Eleventh Amendment and Sovereign Immunity*, 64–67.

24. Hugh McCurdy to John Bleakley, January 26, 1794, MS 647, MdHS.

25. James McHenry to Hugh McCurdy, February 4, 1794, ibid.

26. Hugh McCurdy to John Bleakley, January 26, 1794, ibid.

27. On November 7, 1794, McCurdy received just over 241 pounds from the Allison estate as Grace's husband, ibid.

28. Miller, *Federalist Era*, chap. six, "The Quarrel between Hamilton and Jefferson." Wood, *Empire of Liberty*, 174–85.

29. McHenry to Washington, March 31, 1794, McHenry Papers, reel 1, container 4, LC.

30. McHenry to Washington, April 3, 1794, McHenry Papers, reel 3, container 11, series C, LC.

31. Washington to McHenry, April 8, 1794, Fitzpatrick, *Writings of Washington*, 33:319. Gaines, *For Liberty and Glory*, 364. "List of Names from Whence to Take a Minister for France," in Syrett, *Hamilton's Papers*, 16:422–23.

32. William Hindman to McHenry, April 14, 1794, McHenry Papers, The Huntington Library (HL).

33. Haw et al., *Stormy Patriot*, 170. See George Dent's (a Maryland state assemblyman) essay to his fellow citizens, April 22, 1794, *Baltimore Daily Intelligencer*. "A Friend to Peace" (McHenry), April 24, 1794, *Baltimore Daily Intelligencer*.

34. Anonymous, April 26, 1794, *Baltimore Daily Intelligencer*. "A Native American," April 30, 1794, *Baltimore Daily Intelligencer*.

35. McHenry to Washington, March 29, 1789, Crackel, *Papers of George Washington, Digital Edition, Presidential Series*, 1:461, http://rotunda.upress.virginia.edu/founders/default.xqy?keys=GEWN-print-05-01-02-0357, accessed February 4, 2013. "A Friend to Peace," *Baltimore Daily Intelligencer*, May 6, 1794.

36. "The Remembrancer," May 29, 1794, *Baltimore Daily Intelligencer*. In fact, McHenry wrote many more essays against the Republicans, but I have not been able to find them in published form—see "Conversations" in the McHenry Papers, reel 6, Miscellany, LC.

37. McHenry to Peggy, the months of August and September, 1794, McHenry Papers, reel 1, container 4 and September 28, 1794, reel 2, container 5, LC.

38. Wood, *Empire of Liberty*, 197. Steiner, *Life*, 155.

39. Steiner, *Life and Correspondence*, 157. McHenry to William Vans Murray, January 4, 1795, McHenry Papers, reel 1, WLC.

40. McHenry to Hamilton, February 17, 1795, in Syrett, *Hamilton's Papers*, 18:274–76.

41. Haw et al., *Stormy Patriot*, 170–74.

42. Ibid., 175.

43. Mary K. Bonsteel Tachau, "George Washington and the Reputation of Edmund Randolph," 15–34. She does a very nice job of evaluating the various historians' responses to the Randolph scandal. Above all, she concentrates on explaining the behavior of all the principals involved, including Washington. The result is some real insight into cabinet intrigue during Washington's administration. Wood, *Empire of Liberty*, 204–5.

44. Washington to Hamilton, October 29, 1795, in Syrett, *Hamilton's Papers*, 19:355–63.

45. Hamilton to Washington, November 5, 1795, ibid., 19:395–98.

46. Ibid.

47. Washington to McHenry, January 20, 1796, in Fitzpatrick, *Writings of Washington*, 34:423–24.

48. Uriah Forrest to McHenry, September 10, 1794, McHenry Papers, reel 1, container 4, LC. Steiner, *Life and Correspondence*, 168.

49. McHenry to Washington, January 24, 1796, in Steiner, *Life and Correspondence*, 145, 164.

CHAPTER 11   "I Am Scarce Mistress of My Conduct"

1. This chapter is also to be found, mutatis mutandis, in Karen Robbins, "Power among the Powerless: Domestic Resistance by Free and Slave Women in the McHenry Family of the New Republic," *Journal of the Early Republic* (Spring 2003): 47–68. Margaret McHenry to James McHenry, February 7, 1796, McHenry Papers, MS 647, MdHS.

2. Norton, *Liberty's Daughters*. Kerber, *Women of the Republic*, chap. 4. Wood, *Radicalism of the Revolution*, 182–84. Lewis, "The Republican Wife," 689–721. Ulrich, *Good Wives*, 9. Jabour, *Marriage in the Early Republic*.

3. Phillips, *Freedom's Port*. Whitman, *The Price of Freedom*. White, *Somewhat More Independent*. Hodges, *Root & Branch*. Oliver and Horton, *Black Bostonians*.

4. Zagarri, *A Woman's Dilemma*, chap. 1. Kerber, *Women of the Republic*. Norton, *Liberty's Daughters*.

5. Oral Sumner Coad, "James McHenry: A Minor American Poet," *Journal of the Rutgers University Library* 8 (1945): 61.

6. Margaret McHenry to James McHenry, March 24, 1796, and February 14, 1796, McHenry Family Papers, MS 647, MdHS.

7. Margaret McHenry to James McHenry, April 24, 1796, ibid. Kilbride, "Philadelphia and the Southern Elite," 175. Tinkcom, *The Republicans and Federalists in Pennsylvania*.

8. Kilbride, "Philadelphia and the Southern Elite." Blackmar, *Manhattan for Rent*, 15.

9. Norton, *Liberty's Daughters*, 255–56. Kerber, *Women of the Republic*, 199–200.

10. Phillips, *Freedom's Port*, 35–36. Jenkins, *Records of the States . . . A Microfilm Compilation*, Maryland, Lower House, December 9, 1789.

11. Steiner, *Life and Correspondence*, 127.

12. Ibid. Bedini, *The Life of Benjamin Banneker*, 178–81. Kerber, *Federalists in Dissent*, chapter on science.

13. Phillips, *Freedom's Port*, 32–33.

14. Robinson, *Slavery in the Structure of American Politics*, 22–23, 29. Zilversmit, *The First Emancipation*.

15. Morris, *Free Men All*, 13–14. Fehrenbacher, *Slavery, Law & Politics*, 28. Finkelman, *An Imperfect Union*.

16. "An Act for the Gradual Abolition of Slavery," in Alexander's *Laws of the Commonwealth of Pennsylvania*, 838–43. *Slavery in American Politics*, 29–30. Finkelman, *An Imperfect Union*, 47. Finkelman, *Slavery and the Founders*, 83–85. Wiecek, *Sources of Antislavery Constitutionalism in America*, 50. Higginbotham, *In the Matter of Color*, 308–9.

17. Alexander, "Act for the Gradual Abolition of Slavery," in Finkelman, *An Imperfect Union*, 47–56. Nash and Soderlund, *Freedom by Degrees*, chaps. 3 and 4, esp. 99. Newman, *The Transformation of American Abolitionism*. The issues surrounding "sojourning" continued to disturb the country well into the 1840s as described in Finkelman, "John McLean," *Vanderbilt Law Review* 62, no. 2 (2009): 528.

18. Finkelman, *An Imperfect Union*, 81. Also, Nash, "Forging Freedom," in Berlin and Hoffman, *Slavery and Freedom*, 31. Flexner, *George Washington: Anguish and Farewell*, 122, 432. Flexner, "Washington and Slavery," *Constitution*, 9. Wiencek, *An Imperfect God*, 315–19. Furstenberg, *In the Name of the Father*, 73.

19. Malone, *Jefferson and the Rights of Man*, 323. Finkelman, "Jefferson and Slavery," in Onuf, *Jeffersonian Legacies*, 204–5. Gordon-Reed, *The Hemingses of Monticello*, 163–68, 176–82, 489–95.

20. Margaret McHenry to James McHenry, February 14, 21, 1796, McHenry Family Papers, MS 647, MdHS. Wood, *The Radicalism of the Revolution*, 185.

21. Berlin, *Many Thousands Gone*. Hodges, *Root and Branch*, 175. White, *Somewhat More Independent*, chap. 6. Phillips, *Freedom's Port*, 49–53. Whitman, *The Price of Freedom*, chap. 4. Levesque, *Black Boston*.

22. Horton, *Black Bostonians*, ix. Frey, *Water from the Rock: Black Resistance in a Revolutionary Age*, 31–33, 315, 320, 326

23. Margaret McHenry to James McHenry, March 9, 20, 1796, McHenry Papers, MS 647, MdHS.

24. Margaret McHenry to James McHenry, February 21, March 7, 1796, ibid. Perhaps the advertisement for Henney is that which ran March 4–10 in the *Federal Gazette* and *Baltimore Daily Advertiser*. It describes a "Negro Woman, about 20 years of age, who has been accustomed to all kinds of housework. She can be well recommended for her honesty and industry." For more information regarding such things as the owner, price, reason for sale, etc., the reader was told to "enquire of the printers." As few such ads appeared in the *Federal Gazette* at this time, the young woman would have been quite marketable. "For Sale Advertisement," *Federal Gazette & Baltimore Daily Advertiser* (Baltimore), March 8, 1796.

25. Margaret McHenry to James McHenry, March 9, April 14, 1796, McHenry Family Papers, MdHS.

26. Ibid. Phillips, *Freedom's Port*, 41.

27. Margaret McHenry to James McHenry, April 14, 1796, McHenry Family Papers, MdHS. Curry, *The Free Black in Urban America*, 127.

28. Margaret McHenry to James McHenry, March 27, 1796, McHenry Family Papers, MdHS.

29. Margaret McHenry's Will, Jan. 22, 1830, Maryland State Archives, Annapolis, BA Wills, 1933–1834, 402–3. Phillips, *Freedom's Port*, chap. 2.

CHAPTER 12   "A Prudent, Firm, Frugal Officer"

1. M. McHenry to James McHenry, February 7, 1796, MS 647, MdHS. James McHenry's oath of office, February 8, 1796, McHenry Papers, reel 2, container 5, LC. James McHenry to John Bleakley, February 9, 1796, McHenry Family Papers, Ms. 647, box 2 of 5, MdHS.

2. Wood, *Empire of Liberty*, 92. Gibbs, *Memoirs of the Administrations of Washington and John Adams*, 1:287. *Historical Statistics of the United States* lists the War Department's expenses as $1,260,000 in 1796, $1,039,000 one year later, and $2,010,000 in 1798, the year the Quasi-War began. But it gives no comparable statistics for the Treasury Department. Steiner, *Life and Correspondence*, 422. Upham, *The Life of Timothy Pickering*, 3:254. Coffman, *The Old Army*, 401. White, *The Federalists*, 155. Leyden, "The Fourth Regiment of Infantry," in *The Army of the United States Historical Sketches*," by Rodenbough and Haskin, 452, http://www.history.army.mil/books/R&H/R&H-4IN.htm, accessed February 6, 2013.

3. Steiner, *Life and Correspondence*, 164.

4. Mattsson-Bozé, "James McHenry, Secretary of War, 1796–1800," 23–24. March 14, 1796, *American State Papers: Military Affairs*, 1:114.

5. March 14, 1796, McHenry Papers, reel 2, container 5, LC.

6. Mattsson-Bozé, "James McHenry," 23; and Washington to Hamilton, October 29, 1795, in Fitzpatrick, *Writings of Washington*, 34:352. Timothy Pickering to the Commit-

tee on the Military Establishment, February 3, 1796, *American State Papers, Military Affairs* 1:112–13. Clarfield, *Timothy Pickering and the American Republic*, argues that Pickering really wanted the added prestige that came with being secretary of state, 163–64.

7. Prucha, *The Sword of the Republic*, 30. Kohn, *Eagle*, 124, 182–86.

8. Ibid., 186–89.

9. Carroll and Ashworth, *George Washington: First in Peace*, 7:323.

10. McHenry to Washington, February 13, 1796, McHenry Papers, reel 2, container 5, LC.

11. Elkins and McKitrick, *Age of Federalism*, 439–40. Miller, *The Federalist Era*, 189. Also see chap. 12, "Pinckney's Treaty," by Bemis, in *Pinckney's Treaty*.

12. Elkins and McKitrick, *Age of Federalism*, 442–44.

13. White, *The Federalists*, 40.

14. McHenry to Attorney General Lee, March 10, 1796, McHenry Papers, reel 3, container 11, LC.

15. McHenry's response to Washington's queries concerning the Jay Treaty, March 26, 1796, McHenry Papers, reel 1, WLC. *George Washington, First in Peace*, 354, is incorrect, for it states McHenry *opposed* sending the papers, but both the copy in the Washington Papers, series 4, reel 109, LC, dated March 26, 1796, and the WLC McHenry Papers draft in McHenry's handwriting say he *favored* sending them.

16. Elkins and McKitrick, *Age of Federalism*, 445. Berger agrees with Washington and McHenry in *Executive Privilege*, 171–79.

17. Miller, *Federalist Era*, 173. Also see Stagg, "Jay's Treaty," March 10, 1796, *The Papers of James Madison*, 16:255–63. Carroll and Ashworth, *George Washington: First in Peace*, 7:365.

18. Elkins and McKitrick, in *Age of Federalism*, 446–47. DeConde, *Entangling Alliance*, 116–17. James McHenry to Robert Oliver, April 7, 1796, McHenry Papers, reel 1, WLC. McHenry to Robert Oliver, April 12, 1796, McHenry Papers, reel 3, container 11, LC.

19. Carroll and Ashworth, *George Washington: First in Peace*, 367. Elkins and McKitrick, *Age of Federalism*, 447.

20. Carroll and Ashworth, *George Washington: First in Peace*, 373. Ames, *The Works of Fisher Ames*, 2:37–71. Bernhard, *Fisher Ames*, 268–71.

21. Elkins and McKitrick, *Age of Federalism*, 448–49. Carroll and Ashworth, *George Washington: First in Peace*, 375.

22. Elkins and McKitrick, *Age of Federalism*, chap. 9, "America and Great Britain," esp. section 2.

23. Charles Lee to James McHenry, March 10, 1796, McHenry Papers, reel 1, WLC. Carrol and Ashworth, *George Washington: First in Peace*, 7:346–47. Mattsson-Bozé, *McHenry*, 124–26. James McHenry to George Washington, July 7, 1796, McHenry Papers, reel 1, WLC. George Washington to the Secretary of War, July 13, 1796, in Fitzpatrick, *Writings of Washington*, 35:136–38.

24. George Washington to the Secretary of War (Pickering), December 11, 1795, and July 16, 1796, in Fitzpatrick, *Writings of Washington*, 34:393. McHenry to Washington, July 7, 1796, McHenry Papers, reel 1, WLC.

25. Miller, *Federalist Era*, 192–96. Gibbs, *Memoirs*, 1:350–70. Perkins, *Creation of a Republican Empire*, in Cohen, *Cambridge History of American Foreign Relations*, 1:101–5. DeConde, *Entangling Alliance*, 109. Bowman, *Struggle for Neutrality*, 241.

26. Bowman, *Struggle for Neutrality*, 261. DeConde, *Entangling Alliance*, 380–83. Ammon, *James Monroe*, 135–37.

27. Hamilton to Wolcott, June 15, 1796, Syrett, *Hamilton Papers*, 20:223–24.

28. Knopf, *Anthony Wayne*, 481–84, 517–18.

29. Kohn, *Eagle and Sword*, 178. Jacobs, *Tarnished Warrior*, esp. chap. 6, "Baiting a General and Hoodwinking a Baron." Linklater, *An Artist in Treason*, chap. 5, "Death of a Rival."

30. Kohn, *Eagle*, 178–89.

31. McHenry's notes of Wilkinson's grievances against Wayne, starting January 31, 1796, McHenry Papers, GW, series 4, reel 108, LC.

32. Charles Lee to James McHenry, November 20, 1796, McHenry Papers, HL.

33. Knopf, *Anthony Wayne*, 481. Jacobs, *The Beginning of the U.S. Army*, 291.

34. Kohn, Eagle and Sword, 186.

35. Mattsson-Bozé, "James McHenry," chap. 2.

36. Ibid., 30–34. Pound, *Benjamin Hawkins*, 91.

37. McHenry to Washington, August 24, 1796, Washington Papers, series 4, reel 109, LC. Sheehan, *Seeds of Extinction*.

38. Mattsson-Bozé, "James McHenry," 33, 40–41.

39. Clarfield, *Timothy Pickering*, 161. Pickering and Upham, *The Life of Timothy Pickering*, 3:262–66. Washington's Papers, reel 109, LC. Mattsson-Bozé, "James McHenry," 43.

40. Wood, *Empire of Liberty*, 211.

41. Ibid. Dauer, *Adams Federalists*, 94–111. Freeman, "The Presidential Election of 1796," in Ryerson, *John Adams and the Founding of the Republic*, 142–67.

42. Steiner, *Life and Correspondence*, 201–2. William Vans Murray to James McHenry, November 2, 1796, McHenry Papers, HL.

43. Wood, *Empire of Liberty*, 212. Ferling, *John Adams: A Life*, 332.

CHAPTER 13   "Are We Forever to Be Overawed and Directed by Party Passions?"

1. Hamilton to Washington, January 25–31, 1797, in Syrett, *Hamilton Papers*, 20: 480–82.

2. Madison to Jefferson, January 15, 1797, in Hutchinson, *Papers of James Madison*, 16:455–56. Adams, *The Works of John Adams*, 9:282–97.

3. Oliver Wolcott to Alexander Hamilton, March 31, 1797, in Syrett, *Hamilton Papers*, 20:569–70, n. 1. Grant, *John Adams*, 385.

4. McHenry to Adams, April 13, 1797, Adams Papers, reel 384. All references to the Adams Papers are to the microfilm edition published by the MHS, Boston, which owns the originals.

5. Stinchcombe, The XYZ Affair, 17. Elkins and McKitrick, *Age of Federalism*, 531–37.

6. Clarfield, *Timothy Pickering*, 181. Ferling, *John Adams*, 333. Grant, *Adams: Party of One*, 383. Brown, *Presidency of John Adams*, 27.

7. Wolcott to Hamilton, March 31, 1797, in Syrett, *Hamilton Papers*, 20:569–74.

8. In this case, there is evidence to corroborate Wolcott's use of the term. Later, when they were both out of the cabinet, McHenry and Pickering referred to a time early in the Adams administration when they had considered resigning. Dauer, *The Adams Federalists*. Miller, *The Federalist Era*.

9. Perkins, *The Creation of a Republican Empire*, 101–3.

10. Stinchcombe, *The XYZ Affair*, 19; see "To the Heads of Department," April 14, 1797, Adams, *Works of John Adams*, 9:540; and Syrett, *Hamilton Papers*, 21:52, n. 1.

11. McHenry to Hamilton, April 14, 1797, ibid., 21:48–49.

12. Syrett, *Hamilton Papers*, Pickering to Hamilton, April 5, 1797, March 25, 1798, 21:16–20 or 21:370–77; Wolcott to Hamilton, May 18, 1798, 21:465–66; Hamilton to Wolcott, June 6, 1797, 21:98–101. McHenry to William Vans Murray, November 25, 1797, McHenry papers, reel 1, WLC. I disagree with Dauer, *The Adams Federalists*, 126, who says that McHenry, Pickering, and Wolcott all opposed the proposed mission. Clarfield, *Timothy Pickering*, 155–56. A more careful and sensitive reading of the McHenry documents indicates this is not so. Hamilton to McHenry, no date, but presumed to be March 22, 1797, in Syrett, *Hamilton Papers*, 20:574–75.

13. McHenry to Hamilton, April 14, 1797, ibid., 21:48–49.

14. McHenry's answer for Adams's Speech, April 1797, McHenry Papers, reel 3, LC.

15. See Hamilton to McHenry, April 29, 1797, in Syrett, Hamilton Papers, 21:61–68. McHenry to Adams, April 29, 1797, Adams Papers, reel 384, MHS.

16. Hamilton to Wolcott, March 30, 1797, Wolcott to Hamilton, March 31, 1797, in Syrett, *Hamilton Papers*, 20:567–74. Pickering to Hamilton, March 26, 1797, ibid., 20:548–49. Pickering to Adams, May 1, 1797, Adams Papers, reel 384, MHS.

17. McHenry to Hamilton, March 14, 1797, and "Copy of Paper Delivered to Adams April 8, 1797," McHenry Papers, reel 3, LC. "Propositions of Defense; given to Wm. Smith, 24 May 1797," McHenry Papers, reel 1, WLC. For cabinet discussion see *Gibbs, Memoirs of the Administrations of Washington and Adams*, 1:496. "Copy of Paper Delivered to Adams April 8, 1797," McHenry Papers, reel 3, LC.

18. "Special Session Message" of John Adams to Congress, May 15, 1797, in Richardson, *A Compilation of the Messages and Papers of the Presidents*, 1:236.

19. Steiner, *Life and Correspondence*, 224. *Works of Adams*, 9:286–87. Billias, *Elbridge Gerry*, chap. 17, "Nonpartisan Politics and Diplomacy: Origins of the XYZ Affair." Grant, *Adams: Party of One*, 384–87.

20. Steiner, *Life and Correspondence*, 225–26.

21. Mattsson-Bozé, "James McHenry," 72–73.

22. McHenry to Washington, July 9, 1797, in Twohig, *Papers of Washington: Retirement*, 1:243–44.

23. McHenry Family Papers, MdHS, April–June, 1797. Cominges to General, June 11, 1797, McHenry Papers, MdHS. Translated from the French.

24. Elkins and McKitrick, *Age of Federalism*, 568–70.

25. Whitaker, *The Mississippi Question*, 101–15. Carter, *Territorial Papers*, part five. Melton, *The First Impeachment*, 81–95.

26. Miller, *Federalist Era*, 191. Melton, *The First Impeachment*, 234. Van Tassel and Finkelman, "Senator William Blount," in *Impeachable Offenses*, 86–90.

27. Mattsson-Bozé, "James McHenry," 80–107.

28. Ibid. McHenry to McKee, July 25, 1797, McHenry Papers, MdHS.

29. Mattsson-Bozé, "James McHenry," 85.

30. Whitaker, *Mississippi Question*, 64.

31. Mattsson-Bozé, "James McHenry," 98–100. "Thoughts on the Policy of France Should It Obtain the Floridas," McHenry Papers, reel 6, LC.

32. Pernick, "Politics, Parties, and Pestilence," 559–86. Gragg, "'A Most Critical Time,'" 80–87.

33. Hamilton to McHenry, March 1797, Hamilton to Wolcott, March 30, 1797, Syrett, *Hamilton Papers*, 20:567–68, 574–75. White, *The Federalists*, 39, 42–43.

34. Gragg, "'A Most Critical Time,'" 80–87. McHenry to Benjamin Rush, August 22, 1797, McHenry Papers, reel 1, WLC, and McHenry to Adams, August 25, 1797, McHenry Papers, reel 3, LC.

35. McHenry to Pickering, September 24, 1797, McHenry Papers, reel 1, WLC.

36. McHenry to Pickering, September 7 and October 22, 1797, and McHenry to Wolcott, October 13, 1797, McHenry Papers, reel 1, WLC.

37. Adams to McHenry, October 27, 1797, "Letterbook of John Adams," Adams Papers, reel 19, MHS.

38. Here see Mattsson-Bozé's "James McHenry," 108–9, or Steiner's *Life and Correspondence*, 258–59.

39. White, *The Federalists*, 195–96.

40. American State Papers, 1:816 (December 28, 1797). The best "account" of this is in White, *The Federalists*, 338–40. Kohn, in *Eagle and Sword*, 188, considers this a minor victory.

41. Jones to McHenry, November 13, 1797, McHenry Papers, reel 3, container 11, LC and Lewis to McHenry, November 15, 1797, McHenry Papers, reel 2, LC. McHenry to N. Jones, November 28, 1797, McHenry Papers, reel 1, WLC.

42. McHenry to Adams, December 30, 1797, McHenry Papers, reel 3, container 11, LC. White, *The Federalists*, 283.

43. *The Debates and Proceedings in the Congress of the United States*, 7:804.

44. Adams to Secretaries and Attorney General, January 24, 1798, in Gibbs, *Memoirs of the Administrations of Washington and Adams*, 2:10–11.

45. Steiner, *Life and Correspondence*, 291.

46. Ibid.

47. Mattsson-Bozé, "James McHenry," 116.

48. Ibid., 115–16.

49. Mattsson-Bozé gives a detailed accounting of this in his chapter "Naval Affairs" in "James McHenry." Toll, *Six Frigates*, 88–89.

CHAPTER 14   "Mitigated Hostilities"

1. DeConde, *The Quasi-War*, chap. 2, "The XYZ Affair." Williams, *A Founding Family*, 316–18. Wood, *Empire of Liberty*, 241–44. Grant, *Adams: Party of One*, 388–92. Toll, *Six Frigates*, 89–92. Perkins, *Cambridge History of American Foreign Relations*, 1:104–7. Herring, *From Colony to Superpower*, 204–33.

2. Miller's *The Federalist Era*, 210–12. Stinchcombe and Cullen, *The Papers of John Marshall*, "Response to Talleyrand," 3:428–59. Elkins and McKitrick, *Age of Federalism*, 565–69. Stinchcombe, *The XYZ Affair*, esp. chaps. 3 and 6.

3. Ferling, *John Adams: A Life*, 352–53. Smith, *John Adams*, 2:953–54.

4. McHenry to Adams, March 14, 1798, "Adams Papers," reel 387, MHS. Steiner, *Life and Correspondence*, 295. Lycan, *Alexander Hamilton and American Foreign Policy*, 302–6. Smith, *John Adams*, 2:955.

5. Smith, *John Adams*, 2:955. Ferling, *John Adams: A Life*, 353–54.

6. Smith, *John Adams*, 2:955.

7. Miller, *The Federalist Era*, 213.

8. Mattsson-Bozé, "James McHenry," 130–32.

9. Ibid., 122–23.

10. McHenry to Hamilton, May 12, 1798, in Syrett, *Hamilton Papers*, 21:459–60. McHenry to Lee, and McHenry to Lee, February 24, 1797, George Washington Papers, reel 110, LC.

11. Hamilton to McHenry, May 17, 1798, in Syrett, *Hamilton Papers*, 21:461–62. One note that seems to go with these instructions indicates that Pickering wrote the first

draft—so McHenry may have enlisted help from all quarters. "Draft of General Instructions to Commanders of Armed Vessels in the Service of the United States," May 19, 1798, McHenry Papers, reel 1, WLC. The final version is McHenry to Adams, May 18, 1798, Adams Papers, reel 388, MHS.

12. See "Introductory Note" to Hamilton to McHenry, June 1, 1798, in Syrett, *Hamilton Papers*, 21:474–78, 484, 491–92.

13. McHenry to Adams, June 13, 1798, McHenry Papers, reel 3, container 11, LC.

14. See Hamilton to McHenry, June 1, 1798, McHenry to Hamilton, June 4 and 6, 1798, in Syrett, *Hamilton Papers*, 21:474–78, 484, 491–92. For information on Stoddert and the navy, see Robert G. Albion, "The First Days of the American Navy," *Military Affairs*, 12:1–11.

15. Beveridge, *The Life of John Marshall*, 2:348–49. Smith, *John Marshall*, 235–36.

16. Smith, *John Adams*, 2:971. Brown, *The Presidency of John Adams*, 57. Ferling, *John Adams: A Life*, 372–74. Baker, *John Marshall: A Life in Law*, 287–88. Smith, *John Marshall*, 235.

17. Page Smith writes, "But for Adams sentiment and reason combined to make a strong navy the *desideratum*. A war between France and America must be fought primarily on the sea. A large regular army would be expensive and dangerous. At every point Adams was dilatory about mustering up the army but pressed the establishment of an adequate navy as vigorous as possible." *John Adams*, 2:973. Ferling, *John Adams: A Life*, 357.

18. Levy, *Emergence of a Free Press*, chap. 7, "From the Revolution to the First Amendment." Michael Durey, "Thomas Paine's Apostles," 44:661–88. Smith, *Freedom's Fetters*, 94. Pasley, *The Tyranny of Printers*, 119. Smith, *Printers and Press Freedom*, 84.

19. Steiner, *Life and Correspondence*, 308.

20. Pickering to Washington, September 13, 1798, Twohig, *Papers of Washington: Retirement*, 2:608–9.

21. Smith, *John Adams*, 2:972. John Adams to Abigail Adams, January 9, 1797, Adams Papers, reel 383, MHS.

22. Steiner, *Life and Correspondence*, 309.

23. Adams to McHenry, July 6, 1798, in Charles Francis Adams, *Works of John Adams*, 8:573–74.

CHAPTER 15.   "I Must Be Allowed to Chuse"

1. Steiner, *Life and Correspondence*, 311n4. Wilbur, "Crisis in Leadership," 75 and chaps. 7 and 8. Clarfield, *Timothy Pickering*, 162. Tachau, "George Washington and the Reputation of Edmund Randolph," *Journal of American History* 73 (1986): 15–34. Pickering to Washington, July 6, 1798, *Life of Timothy Pickering*, by Pickering and Upham, 3:419–23.

2. Washington to Pickering, July 11, 1798, in Twohig, *Papers of Washington: Retirement*, 2:397–99.

3. Hamilton to Washington, June 2, 1798, in Syrett, *Hamilton Papers*, 21:479–80.

4. Hamilton to Washington, July 8, 1798, ibid., 21:534–35.

5. Adams to Washington, July 7, 1798, Adams, *Works of Adams*, 8:575.

6. Washington to McHenry, July 4, 1798, Twohig, *Papers of Washington: Retirement*, 2:368–70, 382–84.

7. Pickering later wrote Jay that Washington had never shown McHenry the letter the secretary of state had sent the ex-president. See Steiner, *Life and Correspondence*, 311n4. Also McHenry to Adams, July 12, 1798, Washington Papers, series 4, reel 112, LC.

8. Washington to Adams, September 25, 1798, in Twohig, *Papers of Washington: Retirement*, 3:36–43.

9. Washington to Hamilton, July 14 and Washington to Knox, July 16, 1798, in Twohig, *Papers of Washington: Retirement*, 2:407–9, 423–25.

10. Ferling, *John Adams: A Life*, 360–61. Smith, *John Adams*, 2:973–74 and 978–79.

11. Ibid., 2:973–79.

12. Ibid.

13. Steiner, *Life and Correspondence*, 313.

14. Freeman, *Affairs of Honor*, 222. Elkins and McKitrick, *Age of Federalism*, 524.

15. McHenry to Washington, September 19, 1798, Crackel, *Papers of Washington: Retirement*, Digital Edition, http://rotunda.upress.virginia.edu/founders/default .xqy?keys=GEWN-search-2-9&expandNote=on#match, accessed February 8, 2013.

16. Nagel, *The Adams Women*, 123–30. Furthermore, Pickering had previously initiated a private correspondence with Hamilton, again concerting without McHenry's knowledge. The secretary of state had informed Hamilton (despite Washington's requested confidentiality) that the general intended placing Pinckney over the New Yorker. This Hamilton would not take; he could understand being ranked below Knox but not Pinckney, who had barely outranked him during the Revolution, and whose subsequent public service did not match the New Yorker's. Since Pickering chose not to communicate this to McHenry and Adams, we will never know what might have passed had the president and secretary of war known Hamilton's willingness to serve under Knox. After all he, Pickering, did not want Hamilton below Knox. Pickering to Hamilton, July 16, 1798. Hamilton to Pickering, July 17, 1798, in Syrett, *Hamilton Papers*, 22:22–24.

17. McHenry to Washington, August 6, 1798, in Twohig, *Papers of Washington: Retirement*, 2:494.

18. Mattsson-Bozé, "James McHenry," 151.

19. McHenry to Hamilton, July 20, 1798, and Hamilton to McHenry, July 22, 1798, in Syrett, *Hamilton Papers*, 22:26–68.

20. Wood, *Empire of Liberty*, 204. Miller, *The Federalist Era*, 84–85. Mattsson-Bozé, "James McHenry," chap. 8.

21. McHenry to Hamilton, July 25, 1798 and Hamilton to McHenry, July 30, 1798, in Syrett, *Hamilton Papers*, 22:29–31 and 41–42.

22. In November 1796 Hamilton had used a similar tactic against Pickering. Hamilton had disliked a written response Pickering had published against the French foreign minister Adet. Hamilton thought it too harsh and the situation too delicate. So he wrote both Washington and Wolcott expressing his displeasure. To Washington he urged a vigilant watchful eye and to Wolcott he wrote a detailed conception describing what he thought our foreign policy toward France ought to be. The point is that Hamilton was going behind Pickering's back to influence him through others. Because he, Hamilton, was not so intimately involved, his letters opposing Pickering did not become truly derisive as they did against McHenry. One Pickering scholar insists that Hamilton wished Pickering to be replaced, but he overstates the case. See Guidorizzi, "Timothy Pickering: Opposition Politics," 47. For this correspondence between Hamilton, Washington, and Wolcott see November 1796, in Syrett, *Hamilton Papers*, vol. 20.

23. Hamilton to McHenry, July 30, 1798, ibid., 22:41–42.

24. Hamilton to Washington, July 29–August 1, 1798, ibid., 22:36–40.

25. Hamilton to Washington, July 29–August 1, 1798, in Syrett, *Hamilton Papers*, 22:36–40.

26. Ibid.

27. Ibid.

28. Steiner, *Life and Correspondence*, 314. McHenry to Washington, August 1, 1798, Washington Papers, series 4, reel 112, LC.

29. Smith, *John Adams*, 2:1007, Steiner, *Life and Correspondence*, 316–17. Washington to Hamilton, August 9, 1798, in Fitzpatrick, *Writings of Washington*, 36:393–95.

30. Ibid.

31. Hamilton to Wolcott, August 6, 1798, in Syrett, *Hamilton Papers*, 22:58–59.

32. McHenry to Hamilton, August 10, 1798, in Syrett, *Hamilton Papers*, 22:66–68. McHenry to Washington, August 6, 8, 13, in Twohig, *Papers of Washington: Retirement*, 2:494, 496–97, 522.

33. Steiner, *Life and Correspondence*, 324. Washington to McHenry, August 13, 1798, in Twohig, *Papers of Washington: Retirement*, 2:520–51.

34. Wolcott to Hamilton, August 9, 1798, in *Syrett, Hamilton Papers*, 22:64–65.

35. Knox to McHenry, August 5, 1798, in Adams, *Works of Adams*, 8:578–79.

36. McHenry to Hamilton, August 11 and 13, 1798, in Syrett, *Hamilton Papers*, 22:68–71, 77.

37. Ibid., Hamilton to McHenry, August 19, 1798, 22:81–85.

38. Adams to McHenry, August 14, 1798, in Adams, *Works of Adams*, 8:580.

39. McHenry to Adams, August 22, 1798, in Steiner, *Life*, 325–26.

40. White, *The Federalists*, 39.

41. Pickering to Hamilton, August 21–22, in Syrett, *Hamilton Papers*, 22:147–49.

42. Pickering to Hamilton, August 23, 1798, ibid., 22:159–61.

43. Adams to McHenry, August 29, 1798, in Adams, *Works of Adams*, 8:587–89.

44. McHenry to Adams, September 6, 1798, ibid., 8:593. Gibbs, *Memoirs of the Administration of Washington and Adams*, 2:92; and Steiner, *Life and Correspondence*, 338.

45. Adams to McHenry, September 13, 1798, in Adams, *Works of Adams*, 8:593–94.

46. McHenry to Hamilton, September 6, 1798, in Syrett, *Hamilton Papers*, 22:176.

47. McHenry to Hamilton, September 10, 1798, ibid., 22:179.

48. Wolcott to Adams, September 13, 1798, in Syrett, *Hamilton Papers*, 22:10–14 or Gibbs, *Memoirs*, 2:93–99.

49. Washington to McHenry, August 10, 1798, in Twohig, *Papers of Washington: Retirement*, 2:508–10. Hamilton to Washington, July 29–August 1, 1798, in Syrett, *Hamilton Papers* 22:36–40. Hamilton to McHenry, August 25, 1798, ibid., 22:163. McHenry to Washington, August 25, 1798, in Twohig, *Papers of Washington: Retirement*, 2:559–61.

50. McHenry to Washington, August 25 and September 10, 1798, ibid., 2:559–61, 600–601. Pickering to Washington, September 13, 1798, ibid., 2:608–10.

51. Washington to McHenry, September 14 and 16, 1798, ibid., 2:610–12, 3:4–5. McHenry to Washington, September 19, 1798, ibid., 3:14–25. Washington to Adams, September 25, 1798, ibid., 3:36–43. Washington to McHenry, October 1, 1798, ibid., 3:65–66.

52. Adams to Wolcott, in Syrett, *Hamilton Papers*, September 24, 1798, 22:16. Adams to McHenry, September 30, 1798, John Adams Letterbook, reel 119, Adams Papers, MHS.

53. Gibbs, *Memoirs*, 2:102–3. McHenry to Hamilton, October 15, 1798, in Syrett, *Hamilton Papers*, 22:199.

54. Zahniser, *Charles Cotesworth Pinckney*, 196–97.

55. Adams to Washington, October 9, 1798, in Adams, *Works of Adams*, 8:600–601. McHenry to Hamilton, October 16, 1798, in Syrett, *Hamilton Papers*, 22:199–200.

56. Adams to McHenry, October 22, 1798, in Adams, *Works of Adams*, 8:612–13. Page Smith, *John Adams*, 2:980–83.

CHAPTER 16   "Referred to the General Officers"

1. MacDonald, *Alexander Hamilton*, 343. U.S. Army Quartermaster Foundation, http://www.qmfound.com/Samuel_Hodgdon.htm, accessed February 8, 2013.

2. Washington to McHenry, July 5, 1798, in Twohig, *Papers of Washington: Retirement*, 2:382–84.

3. Washington to McHenry, July 27, 1798, ibid., 2:457–58.

4. Adams to McHenry, October 22, 1798, in Adams, *Works of Adams*, 8:612–13. Also see Ferling, *Adams*, 368–69.McHenry to Washington, October 30, 1798, in Twohig, *Papers of Washington: Retirement*, 3:157–58.

5. Hamilton to Washington, October 29, 1798, in Syrett, *Hamilton Papers*, 22:221–22.

6. McHenry to Washington, November 9, 1798, in Twohig, *Papers of Washington: Retirement*, 3:189–90. Hamilton to Eliza Hamilton, November 10, 1798, in Syrett, *Hamilton Papers*, 22:323–24.

7. "Queries Propounded by the Commander in Chief to Majors Genl. Hamilton & Pinckney," November 10, 1798, ibid., 22:244–46.

8. Washington to McHenry, November 13, 1798, in Syrett, *Hamilton Papers*, 22:247–48. McHenry to Washington, November 14, 1798, ibid., 249n5. McHenry to Adams, November 25, 1798, McHenry Papers, reel 4, container 11, LC.

9. See correspondence from November 10 to December 16, 1798, in Syrett, *Hamilton Papers*.

10. Washington to McHenry, September 30, 1798, McHenry to Washington, October 5, 1798, in Twohig, *Papers of Washington: Retirement*, 3:59, 81. Hamilton to McHenry, February 6, 1799, in Syrett, *Hamilton Papers*, 22:466–67.

11. Kohn, *Eagle and Sword*, 249–52.

12. Wood, "Conspiracy and the Paranoid Style," *WMQ*, 39:401–41. Smelser, "The Jacobin Phrenzy," 13:457–82; and Smelser's "The Federalist Period as an Age of Passion," *American Quarterly* 10 (1958): 391–419. Howe, "Republican Thought and the Political Violence of the 1790s," *American Quarterly* 19: 147–65. McHenry Papers, Miscellaneous, Unidentified and Assorted Writings, reel 5, LC.

13. McHenry to Adams, November 25, 1798, McHenry Papers, reel 4, container 11, LC.

14. Smelser, "The Federalist Period as an Age of Passion," 19:403. Schama, *Patriots and Liberators*.

15. Smith, *John Adams*, 2:989. Clarfield, *Timothy Pickering*, 188–89.

16. Gibbs, *Memoirs*, 2:168–71.

17. "Second Annual Address," James Richardson, *Messages and Papers of the Presidents*, 1:271–5.

18. Washington to McHenry, December 13, 1798, in Syrett, *Hamilton Papers*, 22:341–53.

19. Ibid.

20. Ibid., 22:353–54.

21. Peterson, *Book of the Continental Soldier*, chap. 11.

22. Risch, *Quartermaster Support of the Army*, 13–15 and 49–52.

23. White, *The Federalists*, 121, 360–63. Elkins and McKitrick, *Age of Federalism*, chap. 4. Bowling, *The Creation of Washington, D.C.*, chap. 8. Washington to McHenry, October 1, 1798, in Fitzpatrick, *Writings of Washington*, 36:477–79; and McHenry to

Washington, October 5, 1798, Washington Papers, series 4, reel 113, LC. Wolcott to Hamilton, October 10, 1798, in Syrett, *Hamilton Papers*, 22:196–97. Bland, "The Oliver Wolcotts of Connecticut," 231, 235–38, 252, 330–34.

24. Mollo, *Military Fashion*, 32, 73.

25. Risch, *Quartermaster Support*, 120.

CHAPTER 17   "A Paltry Insurrection"

1. Steiner, *Life and Correspondence*, 362. McHenry to Hamilton, January 5, 10, 11, 1799, in Syrett, *Hamilton Papers*, 22:403, 409, 410, Hamilton to McHenry, January 14, 16, 21, ibid., 22:416–17, 421, 431–32. Kohn, *Eagle and Sword*, 229.

2. Ibid., 252.

3. Washington to McHenry, January 6, 27, 28, in Twohig, *Papers of Washington: Retirement*, 3:306–7, 342–46.

4. Smith, *John Adams*, 2:1007. McHenry to Washington, March 31, 1799, in Twohig, *Papers of Washington: Retirement*, 3:453–57.

5. Hamilton to Washington, February 16, 1799, in Syrett, *Hamilton Papers*, 22:483–84. Mattsson-Bozé, "James McHenry," 216–17.

6. Ferling, *John Adams: A Life*, 374–79. Also see Hill, *William Vans Murray*, chaps. 9 and 10.

7. Ferling, *John Adams: A Life*, 374–79.

8. Ibid., 179.

9. John Adams, "To the Printers of the Boston Patriot," Letter X, 1809, in Adams, *Works of Adams*, 9:269–73.

10. Ferling, *John Adams: A Life*, 379–80.

11. Mattsson-Bozé, "James McHenry", 246–47.

12. *Annals*, Fifth Congress, Appendix, 3777–3785 and 3789–90. Coakley, *The Role of Federal Military Forces in Domestic Disorders*, 69–70. Elkins and McKitrick, *Age of Federalism*, 695–96. Nobles, *Divisions throughout the Whole*, 10–11. Taylor, *Liberty Men and Great Proprietors*, 1–10. Newman, *Fries's Rebellion*, 1, 5–6, 114, 116, 118–19.

13. Ferling, *John Adams: A Life*, 273. Mattsson-Bozé, "James McHenry," chap. 9. Davis, *The Fries Rebellion*, 1798–99. Newman, *Fries's Rebellion*, 5–6.

14. Mattsson-Bozé, "James McHenry," chap. 9. Newman, *Fries's Rebellion*, 134–41.

15. Ferling, *John Adams: A Life*, 312, 373. Richardson, *A Compilation of the Messages and Papers of the Presidents*, 1:286–87. Elkins and McKitrick, *Age of Federalism*, 697. Newman, *Fries's Rebellion*, 143.

16. McHenry to Hamilton, March 15, 1798, in Syrett, *Hamilton Papers*, 22:539–41. Newman, *Fries's Rebellion*, 148.

17. Hamilton to McHenry, March 18, 1799, and Macpherson to Hamilton, March 25, 1799, ibid., 22:552–55. Steiner, *Life and Correspondence*, 433–44. Newman, *Fries's Rebellion*, 148–49.

18. McHenry to Hamilton, March 29, 1799, in Syrett, *Hamilton Papers*, 22:591–92.

19. Gibbs, *Memoirs*, 2:230, Wolcott to Hamilton, April 1, 1799, in Syrett, *Hamilton Papers*, 23:1–2. Bland, "The Oliver Wolcotts of Connecticut," 312.

20. McHenry to Adams, April 5, 1799, McHenry Papers, reel 4, container 12, LC, Adams to McHenry, April 13, 1799, Adams, *Works of Adams*, 8:631–32. Newman, *Fries's Rebellion*, 157–58.

21. Newman, *Fries's Rebellion*, 118, 155.

CHAPTER 18 "I Have Always . . . Considered You as a Man of Understanding and of the Strictest Integrity"

1. Creveld, *Supplying War*. Carp, *To Starve the Army at Pleasure*, 219. Hamilton to McHenry, April 8, 1799, and McHenry to Hamilton, February 4, 1799, in Syrett, *Hamilton Papers*, 23:15–19 and 22:455–65. Also see Mattsson-Bozé, "James McHenry," 220.

2. Kreidberg and Henry, *History of Military Mobilization in the United States Army*, 20–21. Hamilton to McHenry, June 14, 1799, ibid., 23:186–87. Hamilton to McHenry, April 8, 1799, in Syrett, *Hamilton Papers*, 23:15–19, Hamilton to Wolcott, April 8, 1799, ibid., 23:25. McHenry to Hamilton, April 17, 1799, ibid., 23:38–39. Mattsson-Bozé, "James McHenry," 221–30.

3. Hamilton to McHenry, March 5, 1799, in Syrett, *Hamilton Papers*, 22:519–20. McHenry to Hamilton, March 8, March 13, Hamilton to McHenry, March 10, 1799, ibid., 22:522–23, 529–31, 526–27. McHenry to Hamilton, March 21 and 30, 1799, ibid., 22:560–66, 593–94.

4. Hamilton to McHenry, April 17 and 22, 1799, ibid., 23:52 and 23:58–59. Mattsson-Bozé, "James McHenry", 225–26.

5. Smith, *Harpers Ferry Armory and the New Technology*, chap. 1.

6. Hamilton to McHenry, September 2, 1799, in Syrett, *Hamilton Papers*, 23:370–73.

7. Mattsson-Bozé, "James McHenry," 233. Steiner, *Life and Correspondence*, chap. 15.

8. Correspondence between Robert Gilmer and McHenry, McHenry Papers, reel 5, container 14, series D, LC. Lessum and Mackenzie, *Fort McHenry*, 1–3.

9. Adams to Pickering, August 6, 1799, in Adams, *Works of Adams*, 9:10–12.

10. Ferling, *John Adams: A Life*, 383. Stoddert to Adams, August 29, 1799, in Adams, *Works of Adams*, 9:18–19.

11. Adams to Stoddert, September 4, 1799, ibid., 9:19–20.

12. Stoddert to Adams, September 13, 1799, ibid., 9:25–29, Adams to Stoddert, September 21, 1799, ibid., 9:33–34.

13. Smith, *John Adams*, 2:1015–16.

14. Mattsson-Bozé, "James McHenry," 249. McHenry to William S. Dana, September 16, 1799, McHenry Papers, WLC.

15. Elkins and McKitrick, *Age of Federalism*, 607. Dauer, *Adams Federalists*, 230. White, *The Federalists*, 250. Ferling, *John Adams: A Life*, on 382, 397. Miller, *The Federalist Era*, 245, 264. Smith, *John Adams*, 1001, 1047. Wood, "Conspiracy and the Paranoid Style," *WMQ*, 39:401–41. Clarfield, *Timothy Pickering*, 181. Bland, "The Oliver Wolcotts of Connecticut," 231, 235–38, 252, 330–34.

16. William Pinkney to James McHenry, February 26, 1798, in Steiner, *Life and Correspondence*, 295–99. McHenry to Adams, November 25, 1798, McHenry Papers, reel 4, container 11, LC. Howe, "Republican Thought and the Political Violence of the 1790s," *American Quarterly* 19:147–65.

17. Hofstadter, *The Idea of a Party System*, 4. Shaw, *The Character of John Adams*, 247. Freeman, *Affairs of Honor*, passim.

18. Mattsson-Bozé, "James McHenry," 253–54. McHenry to Washington, November 10, 1799, in Twohig, *Papers of Washington, Retirement*, 4:397–402.

19. McHenry to Washington, November 10, 1799, ibid.

20. Kohn, *Eagle and Sword*, 259.

21. Murray to McHenry, June 9, 1797, 227; June 22, 1797, 227–30; July 14, 1797, 230–42; July 18, 1797, 243–45; September 22, 197, 275–85; August 20 and 30, 1798, 341, in Steiner,

Life and Correspondence. Hill, *William Vans Murray*, 15, 35, 44, 46, 51, 53–54, 124, 133, 143, 151, 161, 179.

22. *American State Papers*, Class V: *Military Affairs*, 1:132. *Annals*, Fifth Congress, Appendix, 1438.

23. Mattsson-Bozé, "James McHenry," 256–57. Steiner, *Life and Correspondence*, 422–23.

24. Gibbs, *Memoirs*, 2:340.

25. James McHenry to John McHenry, ibid., 2:346–48.

26. See McHenry to Adams, May 31, 1800, Adams Papers, reel 397. Mattsson-Bozé, "James McHenry," chap. 12. James McHenry to John McHenry, May 20, 1800, Gibbs, *Memoirs*, 2:346–48.

27. James McHenry to John McHenry, ibid., 2:346–48.

28. Shaw, *The Character of John Adams*, 126.

29. McHenry to Adams, May 31, 1800, Adams Papers, reel 397. Wolcott to McHenry, Gibbs, *Memoirs*, 2:410–11. Kohn, *Eagle and Sword*. Kurtz, *Presidency of John Adams*.

30. Ferling, *John Adams: A Life*, 394.

31. Kurtz, *Presidency of John Adams*, 393.

32. McHenry to John McHenry Jr., May 20, 1799, in Steiner, *Life and Correspondence*, 453.

33. McHenry to Hamilton, May 13, 1800, in Syrett, *Hamilton Papers*, 23:478. McHenry to Bishop John Carroll, in John B. Boles's "Politics, Intrigue, and the Presidency: James McHenry to Bishop Carroll, May 16, 1800," *Maryland Historical Magazine* 69: 64–85, esp. 76–77.

34. Hamilton to McHenry, May 23, 1800, in Syrett, *Hamilton Papers*, 23:520. McHenry to John McHenry Jr., May 20, 1799, in Steiner, *Life and Correspondence*, 453.

35. McHenry to Hamilton, June 2, 1800, ibid., 23:550.

36. Kohn, *Eagle and Sword*, 267.

CHAPTER 19   "To Retire to the Shades of Tranquility"

1. Theodore Sedgwick to Hamilton, May 13, 1800, in Syrett, *Hamilton Papers*, 24:483n2. McHenry to Wolcott, January 22, 1801, in Gibbs, *Memoirs*, 2:468–69. Freeman, *Affairs of Honor*, points out the importance of letters among these men, 36.

2. Elkins and McKitrick, *Age of Federalism*, 732–34. Wood, *Empire of Liberty*, 274. Freeman, *Affairs of Honor*, discusses the election of 1796, 214–27, and the election of 1800, 227–61. Also see her essay "Corruption and Compromise in the Election of 1800: The Process of Politics on the National Stage," in Horn, Lewis, and Onuf, *The Revolution of 1800*, 87–120.

3. McHenry to Wolcott, July 22, 1800, in Gibbs, *Memoirs*, 2:384–86. For a good and more detailed account of this election in Maryland, see Brown, "Party Battles," chap. 7.

4. McHenry to Wolcott, in Gibbs, *Memoirs*, 2:384–86.

5. Ibid. For more on the role such methods played in the founding era, see Freeman, *Affairs of Honor*, chap. 2, "Slander, Poison, Whispers, and Fame: The Art of Political Gossip."

6. Hamilton to McHenry, August 27, 1800, in Syrett, *Hamilton Papers*, 25:97.

7. McHenry to Hamilton, September 4, 1800, ibid., 25:111. Hamilton to McHenry, November 22, 1800, ibid., 25:246–47. "Letter from Alexander Hamilton, Concerning the Public Character of John Adams, Esq., President of the United States," October 24, 1800,

ibid., 25:169–234. McHenry to Hamilton, November 19, 1800 and December 1, 1800, ibid., 25:242–44, 25:252–53.

8. McHenry to Wolcott, October 12, 1800, ibid., 25:158n1.

9. McHenry to Hamilton, December 31, 1800, ibid., 25:282–83. Hamilton to McHenry, January 4, 1801, ibid., 25:292–93.

10. Miller, *Federalist Era*, 271. Elkins and McKitrick, *Age of Federalism*, 749–50. Freeman, *Affairs of Honor*, 245–53.

11. Steiner, *Life and Correspondence*, 512–19.

12. *Annals*, Seventh Congress, 1255–61. Griswold, ibid., 1261.

13. McHenry, *A Letter to the Honourable the Speaker of the House of Representatives of the United States.*

14. Steiner, *Life and Correspondence*, 527.

15. Hill, *William Vans Murray*, 219. Steiner, *Life and Correspondence*, 530–32. For more on "Duelling as Politics," see chap. 4 of Freeman, *Affairs of Honor.*

CHAPTER 20   "At the Twilight's Last Gleaming"

1. The McHenry Family, January 12, 1805, "Domestic Bagatelles," McHenry Family Papers, MS 647, box 9, Maryland Historical Society, Baltimore. For a more complete treatment of the McHenry family as revealed in these papers, see Karen Robbins, "'Domestic Bagatelles': Servants, Generations and Gender in the McHenry Family of the Early Republic," *Maryland Historical Magazine* 104 (Spring 2009): 31–51.

2. *The American Heritage Dictionary. The Cambridge History of English and American Literature*, vol. 15, "Colonial and Revolutionary Literature; Early National Literature, Part I," vol. 6, "Franklin," section 10, 14. Benjamin Franklin to Madame Brillon: "The Ephemera," *Benjamin Franklin Papers*, http://www.franklinpapers.org, accessed February 6, 2013. Benjamin Franklin, *Dialogue between Franklin and the Gout*, http://www.4literature.net, accessed February 6, 2013. Medlin, "Benjamin Franklin's Bagatelles for Madame Helvétius," *Early American Literature* 15:45.

3. Mintz and Kellogg, *Domestic Revolutions.*

4. January 12, 1805, "Domestic Bagatelles."

5. Ibid. Wood, *Radicalism of the American Revolution*, 145–47. Appleby, *Inheriting the Revolution*, 130–33. January 12, 1805, "Domestic Bagatelles."

6. Kahana, "Master and Servant in the Early Republic, 1780–1830," *Journal of the Early Republic* 20:57.

7. February 16, 1805, "Domestic Bagatelles."

8. Ibid.

9. Newman, *Fries' Rebellion*, 152.

10. February 16, 1805, "Domestic Bagatelles."

11. Ibid.

12. Ibid.

13. Ibid.

14. Ibid.

15. February 2 to April 20, 1805, ibid.

16. April 27, 1805, ibid.

17. June 8, July 6, 1805, ibid.

18. July 6, 1805, ibid. Mintz and Kellogg, *Domestic Revolutions*, 9–11. Nagel, *The Adams Women*, 76. Norton, *Liberty's Daughters*, chap. 9. Woloch, *Women and the American Ex-*

perience, 116–25. Cott, *The Bonds of Womanhood*, chap. 3. Kerber, *Women of the Republic*, chap. 4. Shammas, "Anglo-American Household Government in Comparative Perspective," WMQ 52:104–44, esp. 128–29. Lewis, "The Blessings of Domestic Society," in Onuf, *Jeffersonian Legacies*, 109–46. Ryan, *Cradle of the Middle Class*, 31–33.

19. June 8, July 13, 1805, "Domestic Bagatelles."

20. January 19, August 10, November 11, December 7 and 21, 1805, ibid.

21. February 16, 1805, ibid.

22. Steiner, *Life and Correspondence*, 535, 556.

23. Ibid., 558.

24. For a more complete account, see Ellis, *Passionate Sage*, chap. 2. Ellis does a marvelous job of explaining Adams's eccentricities and "irascibility," as well as his sometimes changing political views. Freeman, *Affairs of Honor*, chap. 3, "The Art of Paper War."

25. Steiner, *Life and Correspondence*, 552–53, 569. Freeman, *Affairs of Honor*, 156.

26. Steiner, *Life and Correspondence*, 552–53, 569.

27. Smelser, *The Democratic Republic*, 196. The background to this general account can also be found in Smelser. Tucker and Hendrickson, in *Empire of Liberty*, chaps. 19–22, describe this in detail. While they grant Jefferson's accomplishments, such as the Louisiana Purchase, they are quite clearly critical of the morality of the center of Jefferson's foreign policy, arguing that his morality blinded him to the possibility of compromise. Since war was also unacceptable, economic sanctions remained the only alternative. Anyone wishing more information regarding foreign policy under Jefferson should see Spivak, *Jefferson's English Crisis*. Spivak argues that the embargo was initially intended to be only defensive and short-lived, and not a long-term effort at economic coercion. But Jefferson's continuing political and psychological frustrations led him to forget that embargoes must be short because so total (x–xi).

28. Steiner, *Life and Correspondence*, 572.

29. Steiner, *Life and Correspondence*, 587–88. McHenry to Robert Oliver, December 29, 1812, McHenry Papers, box 4/5, MdHS.

30. Coad, "James McHenry: A Minor American Poet," 58–60.

31. Ibid., 58. For a full description of this event, see Royster, *Light-Horse Harry Lee*, 156–68. Stagg, *Mr. Madison's War*, chap. 2, "The Politics of War." Transcription of pamphlet by Leache, "An Exact and Authentic Narrative, of the Events which took place in Baltimore, on the 27th and 28th of July last," http://penelope.uchicago.edu/Thayer/E/Gazetteer/Topics/history/American_and_Military/1812_Baltimore_Riot/Sep1_1812_pamphlet/home.html, accessed February 6, 2013.

32. Coad, "A Signer Writes a Letter in Verse," 33–36.

33. Muller, *The Darkest Day*, 8–10. Much of this account of the Chesapeake campaign is drawn from Muller's book.

34. Steiner, *Life and Correspondence*, 590–95.

35. Ibid., 607, 603–4.

36. Ibid., 610.

37. Coad, "McHenry: A Minor American Poet," 62–63.

38. Muller, *Darkest Day*, 71, 126, chap. 5.

39. Ibid., 194. For the correspondence between Robert Gilmor and McHenry, see the McHenry Papers, reel 5, container 14, series D, LC. Unfortunately, about half of the documents are illegible, but the general story does emerge. Also see Lessum and Mackenzie, *Fort McHenry*, 1–3. Also see Muller, *Darkest Day*, 194–95.

40. Muller, *Darkest Day*, 179–83.

41. Ibid., 55–58. Steiner, *Life and Correspondence*, 610–11.

42. Coles, *The War of 1812*, 184–86. Muller, *Darkest Day*, chap. 6. Stagg, *Mr. Madison's War*, 427–28.

43. Steiner, *Life and Correspondence*, 610–11.

44. Muller, *Darkest Day*, 203–4.

45. John McHenry (James's son) to a Friend, 1816, McHenry Family Papers, Ms. 647, Box 5/5, MdHS.

46. Ibid.

47. Steiner, *Life and Correspondence*, 615.

48. Ibid. Peggy died at seventy-one, outliving all but one of her children. John had become an attorney, married, had one son, and died at the age of thirty-two. Anna would outlive her by four years, having married and borne four children of her own.

Bibliography

MANUSCRIPTS

Adams Papers. Massachusetts Historical Society. Microfilm copy in University of
Pittsburgh Library.
Ferdinand J. Dreer Autograph Collection. Historical Society of Pennsylvania. McHenry
Correspondence.
Gratz Collection. Historical Society of Pennsylvania.
James McHenry Papers. "Domestic Bagatelles." Maryland Historical Society.
James McHenry Papers. Duke University Library.
James McHenry Papers. Henry E. Huntington Library.
James McHenry Papers. Library of Congress. Microfilm copy.
James McHenry Papers. Maryland Historical Society.
James McHenry Papers. Members of Congress Collection. William L. Clements
Library.
James McHenry Collection. New York Historical Society.
McHenry Family Papers. Maryland Historical Society.
"Records, First Presbyterian Church, Philadelphia, Pennsylvania, 1747–72." Vol. 1A.
"A Register of Marriages, Baptisms and Communicants Kept by and for the Use of
the First Presbyterian Church in the City to the Year 1806." Presbyterian Historical
Society, Philadelphia.
Wayne Mss. Historical Society of Pennsylvania.
Wills Books, Book M, 1762, #209, Philadelphia County, Pennsylvania, Historical
Society of Pennsylvania, Philadelphia.

PRINTED AND ONLINE PRIMARY SOURCES

Adams, John. *The Works of John Adams, Second President of the United States: With a
Life of the Author, Notes and Illustrations*. Edited by Charles Francis Adams. 10 vols.
Boston: Little, Brown, 1850–1856.
Alexander, James Dallas. *Laws of the Commonwealth of Pennsylvania*. Philadelphia:
N.p., 1797.
The American Museum. Philadelphia: N.p., 1788.
American State Papers: Documents, Legislative and Executive. 38 vols. Washington,
D.C.: Gales and Seaton, 1832–1861.
Ames, Seth, ed. *The Works of Fisher Ames*. 2 vols. Boston: 1854.

Baltimore Daily Intelligencer.

Burnett, Edmund Cody. *The Continental Congress.* New York: Macmillan, 1941.

Caldwell, David. "Will of David Caldwell." Philadelphia Historical Society of Pennsylvania, Philadelphia County.

Carter, Clarence Edwin, ed. *The Territorial Papers of the United States.* Washington, D.C.: U.S. Government Printing Office, 1936.

A Compilation of the Messages and Papers of the Presidents, 1789–1908. Edited by James D. Richardson. 11 vols. Published by the authority of Congress.

Debates and Proceedings in the Congress of the United States, 1789–1824. [Annals of Congress.] 42 vols. Washington, D.C.: Gales and Seaton, 1834–1856.

Den Boer, Gordon, ed. *Documentary History of the First Federal Elections, 1788–1790.* 4 vols. Madison: University of Wisconsin Press, 1984.

Douglass, Frederick. *Narrative of the Life of Frederick Douglass, An American Slave, Written by Himself.* Edited by David W. Blight. Boston: Bedford Books of St. Martin's Press, 1993.

Elliot, Jonathan, ed. *The Debates in the Several State Conventions on the Adoption of the Federal Constitution.* 5 vols. 2nd ed. New York: Burt Franklin, 1888.

Farrand, Max, ed. *The Records of the Federal Convention of 1787.* 4 vols. Rev. ed. New Haven, Conn., and London: Yale University Press, 1937.

Fitzpatrick, James C., ed. *The Writings of George Washington.* 39 vols. Washington, D.C.: Government Printing Office, 1933.

Ford, Worthington C., ed. *Journals of the Continental Congress.* 34 vols. Washington, D.C.: Government Printing Office, 1906.

Franklin, Benjamin. *Benjamin Franklin Papers,* http://www.franklinpapers.org.

Franklin, Benjamin. *Dialogue between Franklin and the Gout.* http://www.4literature.net.

Gibbs, George, ed. *Memoirs of the Administrations of Washington and John Adams, Edited from the Papers of Oliver Wolcott.* 2 vols. New York: Printed for the Subscribers, 1846.

Historical Statistics of the United States, Colonial Times to 1957. Washington, D.C.: U.S. Government Printing Office, 1960.

Hutchinson, William T., ed. *The Papers of James Madison.* Chicago: University of Chicago Press, 1962–1956.

Idzerda, Stanley J., ed. *Lafayette in the Age of the American Revolution, Selected Letters and Papers, 1776–1790.* Ithaca and London: Cornell University Press, 1980.

Jenkins, William Sumner. *Records of the States of the United States of America: A Microfilm Compilation.* Washington, D.C.: Library of Congress Photoduplication Service, 1949.

Knopf, Richard C., ed. *Anthony Wayne, A Name in Arms: Soldier, Diplomat, Defender of Expansion Westward of a Nation; the Wayne-Knox-Pickering-McHenry Correspondence.* Pittsburgh: University of Pittsburgh Press, 1959.

Leache, Eugene H. "An Exact and Authentic Narrative, of the Events which took place in Baltimore, on the 27th and 28th of July last, Carefully Collected from Some of the Sufferers and Eye-witnesses, to which is added a Narrative of Mr. John Thomson, One of the Unfortunate Sufferens, &c." Printed for the Subscribers, 1812. http://penelope.uchicago.edu/Thayer/E/Gazetteer/Topics/history/American_and _Military/1812_Baltimore_Riot/Sep1_1812_pamphlet/home.html.

McHenry, James. *A Letter to the Honourable the Speaker of the House of Representatives of the United States.* Baltimore: Printed by John W. Butler, 1803.

McHenry, James. *A Sidelight on History, Being the Letters of James McHenry, aide-de-camp of the Marquis De La Fayette to Thomas Sim Lee, Governor of Maryland, Written During the Yorktown Campaign, 1781.* Privately printed, 1931; reprint ed. New York: New York Times and Arno Press, 1971.

Marshall, John. *The Papers of John Marshall.* William C. Stinchcombe and Charles T. Cullen, eds. 7 vols. to date. Chapel Hill: University of North Carolina Press, 1974–2006.

Maryland Journal and Baltimore Advertiser.

Murray, William Vans. "Letters of William Vans Murray to John Quincy Adams, 1797–1803." American Historical Association *Annual Report* for 1912. 2 vols. Washington, D.C.: Government Printing Office, 1914. Vol. 2.

Pennsylvania Packet and General Advertiser.

Pennsylvania, Wills Books, Book M, 1762, #209.

"Records, First Presbyterian Church, Philadelphia, Pennsylvania, 1747–72." Vol. 1A.

"A Register of Marriages, Baptisms and Communicants kept by and for the use of the First Presbyterian Church in the City to the Year 1806." Philadelphia, Presbyterian Historical Society.

Rush, Benjamin. "An Address to the Inhabitants of the British Settlements on the Slavery of the Negroes in America. The 2nd. ed. To Which is added A Vindication of the Address in answer to a Pamphlet entitled, 'Slavery not forbidden in Scripture, or a Defence of the West Indian Planters,' By a Pennsylvanian." Philadelphia: John Dunlap, 1773.

Rush, Benjamin. *Autobiography of Benjamin Rush.* Princeton, N.J.: Princeton University Press, 1948.

Rush, Benjamin. *Letters of Benjamin Rush.* L. H. Butterfield, ed. 2 vols. Princeton, N.J.: Published for the American Philosophical Society by Princeton University Press, 1951.

Showman, Richard K., ed. *The Papers of General Nathanael Greene.* 3 vols. Chapel Hill: University of North Carolina Press, 1976.

Steiner, Bernard C. *Archives.* Vol. 47, *Red Book.* Miscellaneous McHenry Papers.

Steiner, Bernard C. *Archives of Maryland, XLV, Journal and Correspondence of the State Council of Maryland, 1780–1781.* Baltimore: Maryland Historical Society, 1927.

Syrett, Harold C. *The Papers of Alexander Hamilton.* 27 vols. New York and London: Columbia University Press, 1961.

"Taxables in the City of Philadelphia, 1756." *Pennsylvania Genealogical Magazine* 22, no. 1: 1961–1962.

Washington, George. *The Papers of George Washington.* Edited by W. W. Abbot et al. Charlottesville: University of Virginia, 1987.

Washington, George. *The Papers of George Washington Digital Edition.* Confederation Series. Theodore J. Crackel, editor in chief. 6 vols.

Washington, George. *The Writings of George Washington.* Jared Sparks, ed. New York: Harper, 1848.

Washington, George. *The Writings of George Washington.* James C. Fitzpatrick, ed. 39 vols. Washington, D.C.: Government Printing Office, 1933.

SECONDARY SOURCES

Albion, Robert G. "The First Days of the American Navy." *Military Affairs* 12: 1–11.

Ammon, Harry. *James Monroe: The Quest for National Identity.* New York: McGraw-Hill, 1971.

Appleby, Joyce. *Inheriting the Revolution: The First Generation of Americans.* Cambridge, Mass.: Belknap Press, 2000.

Applegate, Howard Lewis. "The Forgotten Men of the Revolution." *Picket Post* 71 (February 1961): 24–29.

Applegate, Howard Lewis. "Preventive Medicine in the American Revolutionary Army." *Military Medicine* (May 1961): 379–81.

Applegate, Howard Lewis. "Remedial Medicine in the American Revolutionary Army." *Military Medicine* (June 1961): 450–53.

Bailyn, Bernard. *The Ideological Origins of the American Revolution.* Cambridge, Mass.: Belknap Press of Harvard University Press, 1967.

Bailyn, Bernard. *Voyagers to the West: A Passage in the Peopling of America on the Eve of the Revolution.* New York: Vintage, 1988.

Baker, John. *John Marshall: A Life in Law.* New York: Macmillan, 1974.

Bales, Robert F. "Role and Role Conflict, Task Roles and Social Roles in Problem-Solving Groups." *Readings in Social Psychology.* 3rd ed. Edited by Eleanor E. Maccoby, Theodore M. Newcomb, and Eugene L. Hartley. New York: Henry Holt, 1958.

Barker, F., and Cheyne, J., eds. *An Account of the Rise, Progress, and Decline of the Fever Lately Epidemical in Ireland, Together with Communications from Physicians in the Provinces, and Various Official Documents.* London: Printed for Baldwin, Cradock and Joy; and Dublin: P. Hodges and M'Arthur, 1821.

Barkley, John M. "The Presbyterian Church in Ireland." *Journal of Presbyterian History* 44 (1966):244–65.

Beckett, James C. *A Short History of Ireland.* London: Hutchinson University Library, 1952. Reprint ed., 1964.

Bedini, Silvio. *The Life of Benjamin Banneker.* New York: Charles Scribner's Sons, 1972.

Beeman, Richard. *Plain, Honest Men: The Making of the American Constitution.* New York: Random House, 2009.

Bemis, Samuel Flagg. *The Diplomacy of the American Revolution.* Bloomington: Indiana University Press, 1935.

Bemis, Samuel Flagg. *Pinckney's Treaty: America's Advantage from Europe's Distress, 1783–1800.* New Haven, Conn.: Yale University Press, 1960.

Berger, Raoul. *Executive Privilege: A Constitutional Myth.* Cambridge, Mass.: Harvard University Press, 1974.

Berkin, Carol. *Revolutionary Mothers: Women in the Struggle for America's Independence.* New York: Vintage, 2005.

Berlin, Ira. *Many Thousands Gone: The First Two Centuries of Slavery in North America.* Cambridge, Mass. and London: Belknap Press of Harvard University Press, 1998.

Bernhard, Winfred E. A. *Fisher Ames: Federalist and Statesman.* Chapel Hill: University of North Carolina Press, 1965.

Beveridge, Albert J. *The Life of John Marshall.* 4 vols. Boston and New York: Houghton Mifflin, 1919.

Billias, George A. *Elbridge Gerry: Founding Father and Republican Statesman.* New York: McGraw-Hill, 1976.

Blackmar, Elizabeth. *Manhattan for Rent, 1785–1850.* Ithaca: Cornell University Press, 1989.

Bland, James Edward. "The Oliver Wolcotts of Connecticut, The National Experience, 1775–1800." Ph.D. dissertation, Harvard University, 1969.

Boles, John B. "Politics, Intrigue, and the Presidency: James McHenry to Bishop Carroll, May 16, 1800." *Maryland Historical Magazine* 69, no. 1 (1974): 64–85.

Bowling, Kenneth R. *The Creation of Washington, D.C.: The Idea and Location of the American Capital.* Fairfax, Va.: George Mason University Press, 1991.

Bowman, Albert Hall. *The Struggle for Neutrality: Franco-American Diplomacy during the Federalist Era.* Knoxville: University of Tennessee Press, 1974.

Bridenbaugh, Carl. *Cities in Revolt, Urban Life in America, 1743–1776.* New York: Capricorn, 1964.

Bridenbaugh, Carl, and Jessica. *Rebels and Gentlemen: Philadelphia in the Age of Franklin.* New York: Reynal & Hitchcock, 1942.

Brodsky, Alyn. *Benjamin Rush: Patriot and Physician.* New York: Truman Talley, St. Martin's Press, 2004.

Brown, Dorothy M. "Party Battles and Beginnings in Maryland: 1786–1812." Ph.D. dissertation, Georgetown University, 1961.

Brown, Dorothy M. "Politics of Crisis: The Maryland Elections of 1788–1789." *Maryland Historical Magazine* 57 (1962): 195–209.

Brown, Harvey E. *The Medical Department of the United States Army from 1775 to 1873.* Washington, D.C.: Surgeon General's Office, 1873.

Brown, Ralph Adams. *The Presidency of John Adams.* Lawrence: University Press of Kansas, 1975.

Brown, Roger H. *Redeeming the Republic: Federalists, Taxation, and the Origins of the Constitution.* Baltimore: Johns Hopkins University Press, 1993.

Burg, David F. *An Eyewitness History: The American Revolution.* New York: Facts on File, 2001.

Burnett, Edmund Cody. *The Continental Congress.* New York: Macmillan, 1941.

Calloway, Colin G. *The American Revolution in Indian Country: Crisis and Diversity in Native American Communities.* Cambridge, U.K., and New York: Cambridge University Press, 1995.

Carp, Benjamin L. *Defiance of the Patriots: The Boston Tea Party & the Making of America.* New Haven, Conn., and London: Yale University Press, 2010.

Carp, E. Wayne. *To Starve the Army at Pleasure: Continental Army Administration and American Political Culture, 1775–1783.* Chapel Hill: University of North Carolina Press, 1984.

Carroll, John A., and Mary A. Ashworth, eds. *George Washington, First in Peace.* New York: Charles Scribner's Sons, 1957.

Carter, Clarence Edwin, ed. *The Territorial Papers of the United States.* Washington, D.C.: U.S. Government Printing Office, 1936.

Clarfield, Gerard H. *Timothy Pickering and the American Republic.* Pittsburgh: University of Pittsburgh Press, 1980.

Clinton, Catherine. *The Plantation Mistress: Woman's World in the Old South.* New York: Pantheon, 1982.

Coad, Oral Sumner. "James McHenry: A Minor American Poet." *Journal of the Rutgers University Library* 28 (1945):33–64.

Coad, Oral Sumner. "A Signer Writes a Letter in Verse." *Journal of the Rutgers University Library* 32, no. 1 (1968): 33–36.

Coakley, Robert W. *The Role of Federal Military Forces in Domestic Disorder, 1789–1878.* Army Historical Series. Washington, D.C.: U.S. Government Printing Office, for the Center of Military History, 1988.

Coles, Harry L. *The War of 1812.* Chicago: University of Chicago Press, 1965.

Cooke, Jacob. "Country above Party: John Adams and the 1799 Mission to France." In *Fame and the Founding Fathers.* Edited by Edmund P. Willis. Bethlehem, Pa.: Moravian College, 1967, 53–79.

Cooke, Jacob E. *Tench Coxe and the Early Republic.* Chapel Hill: University of North Carolina Press, 1978.

Cott, Nancy F. *The Bonds of Womanhood: "Woman's Sphere" in New England, 1780–1835.* New Haven, Conn.: Yale University Press, 1977.

Cronin, Mike. *A History of Ireland.* New York: Palgrave Macmillan, 2001.

Crowl, Philip. *Maryland during and after the Revolution: A Political and Economic Study.* Baltimore: Johns Hopkins University Press, 1943.

Cullen, Charles T., ed. *The Papers of John Marshall.* Chapel Hill: University of North Carolina Press, in association with the Institute of Early American History and Culture, Williamsburg, Virginia, 1973.

Curry, Leonard P. *The Free Black in Urban America, 1800–1850: The Shadow of the Dream.* Chicago: University of Chicago Press, 1981.

Dauer, Manning J. *The Adams Federalists.* Baltimore: Johns Hopkins University Press, 1953, 1968.

Davis, W. W. H. *The Fries Rebellion: 1798–99: An Armed Resistance to the House Tax Law, Passed by Congress, July 9, 1798, in Bucks and Northampton Counties, Pennsylvania.* Doylestown, Pa.: Doylestown Publishing, 1899.

DeConde, Alexander. *Entangling Alliance: Politics and Diplomacy under George Washington.* Durham, N.C.: Duke University Press, 1958.

DeConde, Alexander. *The Quasi-War: The Politics and Diplomacy of the Undeclared War with France, 1797–1801.* New York: Charles Scribner's Sons, 1966.

D'Elia, Donald J. *Benjamin Rush: Philosopher of the American Revolution.* Philadelphia: American Philosophical Society, 1974.

Dickson, R. J. *Ulster Emigration to Colonial America, 1718–1775.* London: Routledge & Kegan Paul, 1966.

Doerflinger, Thomas M. *A Vigorous Spirit of Enterprise: Merchants and Economic Development in Revolutionary Philadelphia.* Chapel Hill, N.C., and London: Published for the Institute of Early American History and Culture, Williamsburg, Virginia, 1986.

Duffy, Christopher. *The Military Experience in the Age of Reason.* New York: Atheneum, 1988.

Dull, Jonathan R. *A Diplomatic History of the American Revolution.* New Haven, Conn., and London: Yale University Press, 1985.

Dull, Jonathan R. "Franklin the Diplomat: the French Mission." In *Transactions of the American Philosophical Society Held at Philadelphia for Promoting Useful Knowledge.* Philadelphia: American Philosophical Society, 1982.

Dupuy, Cols. R. Ernest and Trevor N., retired. *The Compact History of the Revolutionary War.* New York: Hawthorn, 1963.

Durey, Michael. "Thomas Paine's Apostles: Radical Emigres and the Triumph of Jeffersonian Republicanism." *William and Mary Quarterly* 44 (1987): 661–88.

Elkins, Stanley, and Eric L. McKitrick. *The Age of Federalism: The Early American Republic, 1788–1800*. New York: Oxford University Press, 1993.

Ellis, Joseph J. *Passionate Sage: The Character and Legacy of John Adams*. New York: W. W. Norton, 1993.

Ellis, Richard J. *Presidential Travel: The Journey from George Washington to George W. Bush*. Lawrence: University Press of Kansas, 2008.

Fehrenbacher, Don E. *Slavery, Law & Politics: The Dred Scott Case in Historical Perspective*. Oxford: Oxford University Press, 1981.

Fenwick, Marshall. *Springlore in Virginia*. Bowling Green, Ohio: Bowling Green State University Press, 1978.

Ferguson, E. James. *The Power of the Purse: A History of American Public Finance, 1776–1790*. Chapel Hill: University of North Carolina Press, 1961.

Ferling, John E. *Almost a Miracle: The American Victory in the War of Independence*. Oxford: Oxford University Press, 2007.

Ferling, John E. *John Adams: A Life*. Knoxville: University of Tennessee Press, 1992.

Finkelman, Paul. *An Imperfect Union: Slavery, Federalism, and Comity*. Chapel Hill: University of North Carolina Press, 1981.

Finkelman, Paul. "Jefferson and Slavery: 'Treason Against the Hopes of the World.'" In *Jeffersonian Legacies*. Edited by Peter S. Onuf. Charlottesville: University Press of Virginia, 1993.

Finkelman, Paul. "John McLean: Moderate Abolitionist and Supreme Court Politician." *Vanderbilt Law Review* 62, no. 2 (2009): 519–65.

Finkelman, Paul. "Slavery and the Constitution: Making a Covenant with Death." In *Beyond Confederation: Origins of the Constitution and American National Identity*. Edited by Richard Beeman et al. Chapel Hill: Published for the Institute of Early American History and Culture, Williamsburg, Virginia, by the University of North Carolina Press, 1987.

Finkelman, Paul. *Slavery and the Founders: Race and Liberty in the Age of Jefferson*. Armonk, N.Y., and London: M. E. Sharpe, 1996.

Fischer, David Hackett. *Albion's Seed: Four British Folkways in America*. New York: Oxford University Press, 1989.

Fischer, David Hackett. *Paul Revere's Ride*. New York and Oxford: Oxford University Press, 1994.

Fischer, David Hackett. *Washington's Crossing*. Oxford: Oxford University Press, 2004.

Fitzpatrick, John C. "The Aides-de-Camp of General George Washington." *DAR Magazine* 57 (January 1923): 1–15.

Fleming, Thomas. *Washington's Secret War: The Hidden History of Valley Forge*. New York: Smithsonian, 2005.

Flexner, James Thomas. *George Washington, Anguish and Farewell, 1793–1799*. Boston: Little, Brown, 1969, 1972.

Flexner, James Thomas. *The Traitor and the Spy: Benedict Arnold and John André*. Boston and Toronto: Little, Brown, 1953.

Foner, Eric. *Thomas Paine and Revolutionary America*. New York: Oxford University Press, 1976.

Foster, Roy F. *Modern Ireland, 1600–1972*. New York: Penguin, 1988.

Foster, Thomas. *Sex and the Eighteenth-Century Man: Massachusetts and the History of Sexuality in America*. Boston: Beacon Press, 2007.

Fox-Genovese, Elizabeth. *Within the Plantation Household: Black and White Women of the Old South*. Chapel Hill and London: University of North Carolina Press, 1988.

Freeman, Joanne B. *Affairs of Honor: National Politics in the New Republic*. New Haven, Conn., and London: Yale University Press, 2001.

Freeman, Joanne B. "Corruption and Compromise in the Election of 1800: The Process of Politics on the National Stage." In *The Revolution of 1800: Democracy, Race and the New Republic*. Edited by James Horn, Jan Ellen Lewis, and Peter S. Onuf. Charlottesville: University of Virginia Press, 2002.

Frey, Sylvia R. *Water from the Rock: Black Resistance in a Revolutionary Age*. Princeton, N.J.: Princeton University Press, 1991.

Furstenberg, François. *In the Name of the Father: Washington's Legacy, Slavery, and the Making of a Nation*. New York: Penguin, 2006.

Gaines, James R. *For Liberty and Glory: Washington, Lafayette and Their Revolutions*. New York and Oxford: W. W. Norton, 2007.

Gibson, James E. "Benjamin Rush's Apprenticed Students." *Transactions and Studies of the College of Physicians of Philadelphia* 14 (1946): 127–32.

Gibson, James E. *Doctor Bodo Otto and the Medical Background of the American Revolution*. Menasha, Wisc.: George Banta, 1937.

Gillespie, Michael Allen, and Michael Lienesch, eds. *Ratifying the Constitution*. Lawrence: University Press of Kansas, 1989.

Gillett, Ezra Hall. *History of the Presbyterian Church in the United States of America*. Philadelphia: Presbyterian Board of Publication and Sabbath School Work, 1864.

Glasgow, Maude. *Scotch-Irish in Northern Ireland and American Colonies*. New York: G. P. Putnam's Sons, 1936.

Goebel, Julius, Jr. *Antecedents and Beginnings to 1801*. Vol. 1. In *The Oliver Wendell Holmes Devise: History of the Supreme Court of the United States*. Edited by Paul A. Freund. New York: Macmillan, 1971.

Goerlitz, Walter. *History of the German General Staff, 1657–1945*. English ed. New York: Frederick A. Praeger, 1953.

Goldman, Sheldon. *Constitutional Law: Cases and Essays*. 2nd ed. New York: Langman, 1991.

Gordon-Reed, Annette. *The Hemingses of Monticello: An American Family*. New York: W. W. Norton, 2008.

Gragg, Larry. "'A Most Critical Time': Philadelphia in 1973." *History Today* 29 (February 1979): 80–87.

Grant, James. *John Adams: A Party of One*. New York: Farrar, Straus, & Giroux, 2005.

Graymont, Barbara. *The Iroquois*. In *Indians of North America*. Edited by Marjorie P. K. Weiser. New York and Philadelphia: Chelsea House, 1988.

Gregory, Dr. John. *A Father's Legacy to His Daughters*. London, 1774.

Greene, Jack P., ed. *The Ambiguity of the American Revolution*. New York: Harper & Row, 1968.

Gross, Robert A., ed. *In Debt to Shays: The Bicentennial of an Agrarian Rebellion*. Charlottesville and London: University Press of Virginia, 1993.

Guidorizzi, Richard Peter. "Timothy Pickering: Opposition Politics in the Early Years of the Republic." Ph.D. dissertation, St. John's University, 1968.

Harvey, Robert. *"A Few Bloody Noses": The Realities and Mythologies of the American Revolution*. Woodstock and New York: Overlook, 2001.

Haw, James, et al. *Stormy Patriot: The Life of Samuel Chase*. Baltimore: Maryland Historical Society, 1980.

Hawke, David F. *Benjamin Rush: Revolutionary Gadfly*. Indianapolis: Bobbs-Merrill, 1971.

Henderson, H. James. *Party Politics In the Continental Congress*. New York: University Press of America, 1974.

Herring, George C. *From Colony to Superpower: U.S. Foreign Relations since 1776*. Oxford: Oxford University Press, 2008.

Higginbotham, A. Leon. *In the Matter of Color, Race and the American Legal Process: The Colonial Period*. Oxford: Oxford University Press, 1978.

Higginbotham, Don. *The War of American Independence: Military Attitudes, Policies and Practice, 1763–1789*. Bloomington: Indiana University Press, 1977.

Hill, Peter P. *William Vans Murray, Federalist Diplomat: The Shaping of Peace with France, 1797–1801*. Syracuse, N.Y.: Syracuse University Press, 1971.

Hodges, Graham Russell. *Root & Branch: African-Americans in New York and East Jersey, 1613–1863*. Chapel Hill and London: University of North Carolina Press, 1999.

Hoffman, Daniel N. *Governmental Secrecy and the Founding Fathers: A Study in Constitutional Controls*. London: Greenwood, 1981.

Hoffman, Ronald. *A Spirit of Dissension: Economics, Politics, and the Revolution in Maryland*. Baltimore and London: Johns Hopkins University Press, 1973.

Hoffman, Ronald, and Sally D. Mason. *Princes of Maryland, Planters of Maryland: A Carroll Saga, 1500–1782*. Chapel Hill and London: University of North Carolina Press, 2000.

Hofstadter, Richard. *The Idea of a Party System*. Berkeley and Los Angeles: University of California Press, 1969.

Holmes, Finlay. *The Presbyterian Church in Ireland: A Popular History*. Dublin: Columba, 2000.

Hooper, Glenn. *Travel Writing and Ireland, 1760–1860*. New York: Palgrave Macmillan, 2005.

Horton, James Oliver, and Lois E. Horton. *Black Bostonians: Family Life and Community Struggle in the Antebellum North*. New York and London: Holmes & Meier, 1999.

Howe, John R., Jr. "Republican Thought and Political Violence of the 1790s." *American Quarterly* 19 (Summer 1967): 147–65. http://www.stmarys.edu/about_first.htm

Jabour, Anya. *Marriage in the Early Republic: Elizabeth and William Wirt and the Companionate Ideal*. Baltimore and London: Johns Hopkins University Press, 1998.

Jacobs, Clyde E. *The Eleventh Amendment and Sovereign Immunity*. Westport, Conn.: Greenwood, 1972.

Jacobs, James Ripley. *The Beginning of the U.S. Army, 1783–1812*. Princeton, N.J.: Princeton University Press, 1947.

Jacobs, James Ripley. *Tarnished Warrior: Major-General James Wilkinson*. New York: Macmillan, 1938.

Jensen, Merrill, ed. *The Documentary History of the Ratification of the Constitution*. Madison: State Historical Society of Wisconsin, 1976.

Jensen, Merrill. *The New Nation: A History of the United States during the Confederation, 1781–1789*. New York: Vintage, 1950.

Jensen, Merrill. *The Origins of the Federal Republic: Jurisdictional Controversies in the United States, 1775–1787*. Philadelphia: University of Pennsylvania Press, 1983.

Kahana, Jeffrey S. "Master and Servant in the Early Republic, 1780–1830." *Journal of the Early Republic* 20 (Spring 2000): 57.

Kaminski, John P., and Jill Adair McCaughan, eds. *A Great and Good Man: George Washington in the Eyes of His Contemporaries.* Madison, Wisc.: Madison House, 1989.

Kann, Mark. *On the Man Question: Gender and Civic Virtue in America.* Pennsylvania: Temple University Press, 1991.

Kerber, Linda. *Women of the Republic: Intellect and Ideology in Revolutionary America.* Chapel Hill: Institute of Early American History and Culture, Williamsburg, Virginia by the University of North Carolina Press, 1980.

Kilbride, Daniel. "Philadelphia and the Southern Elite: Class, Kinship, and Culture in Antebellum America." Ph.D. dissertation, University of Florida, 1997.

Knopf, Richard C. *Anthony Wayne: A Name in Arms: Soldier, Diplomat, Defender of Expansion Westward of a Nation, The Wayne-Knox-Pickering-McHenry Correspondence.* Pittsburgh: University of Pittsburgh Press, 1959, 1960; reprint ed., Westport, Conn.: Greenwood, 1975.

Knox, Captain Dudley W., U.S. Navy, (Ret.), supervisor. *Naval Documents Related to the Quasi-War Between the United States and France.* Washington, D.C.: U.S. Government Printing Office, 1935.

Kohn, Richard H. *Eagle and Sword: The Federalists and the Creation of the Military Establishment in America, 1783–1802.* New York: Free Press, 1975.

Kreidberg, Lt. Col. Marvin A., and First Lt. Merton G. Henry. *History of Military Mobilization in the United States Army, 1775–1945.* Washington, D.C.: Department of the Army, 1955.

Kurtz, Stephen G. *The Presidency of John Adams: The Collapse of Federalism, 1795–1800.* Philadelphia: University of Pennsylvania Press, 1957.

Langer, William L., ed. *An Encyclopedia of World History: Ancient, Medieval, and Modern, Chronologically Arranged.* 5th ed. Boston: Houghton Mifflin, 1972.

Laver, Harry S. *Citizens More than Soldiers: The Kentucky Militia and Society in the Early Republic.* Lincoln: University of Nebraska Press, 2007.

Lefebvre, Georges. *The French Revolution From 1793 to 1799.* 2 vols. New York: Columbia University Press, 1964.

Lengel, Edward G. *General George Washington: A Military Life.* New York: Random House, 2007.

Lessum, Harold I., and George C. Mackenzie. *Fort McHenry: National Monument and Historic Shrine, Maryland.* Washington, D.C.: U.S. Government Printing Office, 1954; reprint ed., 1961.

Levesque, George A. *Black Boston: African-American Life and Culture in Urban America, 1750–1860.* New York and London: Garland, 1994.

Levy, Leonard. *Legacy of Suppression: Freedom of Speech and Press in Early American History.* Cambridge, Mass.: Belknap Press of Harvard University Press, 1964.

Lewis, Jan. "The Blessings of Domestic Society: Thomas Jefferson's Family and the Transformation of American Politics." In *Jeffersonian Legacies.* Edited by Peter S. Onuf. Charlottesville: University Press of Virginia, 1993, 109–46.

Lewis, Jan. "The Republican Wife: Virtue and Seduction in the Early Republic." *William and Mary Quarterly* 44 (1987): 689–721.

Lewis, W. D. "The University of Delaware and Its Predecessors; a Bibliography." *Delaware Notes,* 1944, series 17.

Leyden, Lieutenant James A. Adjutant 4th U.S. Infantry. "The Fourth Regiment of Infantry." In *The Army of the United States Historical Sketches of Staff and Line with Portraits of Generals-in-Chief.* Edited by Theophilus Francis Rodenbough, Bvt. Brigadier General U.S.A., and William L. Haskin, Major, First Artillery. New York: Maynard Merrill, 1896, 452. http://www.history.army.mil/books/R&H/R&H-4IN .htm

Linklater, Andro. *An Artist in Treason: The Extraordinary Double Life of General James Wilkinson.* New York: Walker, 2009.

Lycan, Gilbert. *Alexander Hamilton and American Foreign Policy.* Norman: University of Oklahoma Press, 1970.

MacDonald, Forrest. *Alexander Hamilton: A Biography.* New York: W. W. Norton, 1979.

MacDonald, Forrest. *Novus Ordo Seclorum: The Intellectual Origins of the Constitution.* Lawrence: University Press of Kansas, 1985.

McDowell, Robert B. *Ireland in the Age of Imperialism and Revolution, 1760–1801.* New York: Oxford University Press, 1979.

McDowell, Robert B. *Irish Public Opinion, 1750–1800.* London: Faber & Faber, 1944.

McKitrick, Eric L., and Stanley Elkins. "The Founding Fathers: Young Men of the Revolution." *Political Science Quarterly* 76 (1961): 180–216.

Mackesy, Piers. *The War for America, 1775–1783.* Cambridge, Mass.: Harvard University Press, 1965.

Maier, Pauline. *American Scripture: Making the Declaration of Independence.* New York: Vintage, 1997.

Maier, Pauline. *From Resistance to Revolution: Colonial Radicals and the Development of American Opposition to Britain, 1765–1776.* New York: Vintage, 1972.

Malone, Dumas. *Jefferson and the Rights of Man.* Boston: Little, Brown, 1951.

Mattsson-Bozé, Howard. "James McHenry, Secretary of War, 1796–1800." Ph.D. dissertation, University of Minnesota, 1965.

Medlin, Dorothy. "Benjamin Franklin's Bagatelles for Madame Helvétius: Some Biographical and Stylistic Considerations." *Early American Literature* 15 (1980): 45.

Meier, Louis Alois, M.D., C.M. *Early Pennsylvania Medicine.* Philadelphia: Gilbert, 1976.

Melton, Buckner F., Jr. *The First Impeachment: The Constitution's Framers and the Case of Senator William Blount.* Macon, Ga.: Mercer University Press, 1998.

Middlekauff, Robert. *The Glorious Cause: The American Revolution, 1763–1789.* New York and Oxford: Oxford University Press, 1982.

Miller, Guy Howard. "A Contracting Community: American Presbyterians, Social Conflict, and Higher Education, 1730–1830." Ph.D. dissertation, University of Michigan, 1970.

Miller, John C. *The Federalist Era, 1789–1801.* New York: Harper & Row, 1963.

Mintz, Steven, and Susan Kellogg. *Domestic Revolutions: A Social History of American Family Life.* New York: Free Press, 1988.

Mitchell, Broadus. *Alexander Hamilton: Youth to Maturity, 1755 to 1788.* New York: Macmillan, 1957.

Mollo, John. *Military Fashion: A Comparative History of the Uniforms of the Great Armies from the 17th Century to the First World War.* New York: G. P. Putnam's Sons, 1972.

Morris, Richard B. *Encyclopedia of American History.* Bicentennial ed. New York: Harper & Row, 1976.

Morris, Richard B. *The Forging of the Union, 1781–1789*. New York: Harper & Row, 1987.

Morris, Thomas D. *Free Men All: The Personal Liberty Laws of the North, 1780–1861*. Baltimore and London: Johns Hopkins University Press, 1974.

Muller, Charles G. *The Darkest Day: The Washington-Baltimore Campaign During the War of 1812*. Philadelphia: University of Pennsylvania Press, 1963, 2003.

Munroe, John A. *The University of Delaware: A History*. Newark: University of Delaware Press, 1986.

Nagel, Paul C. *The Adams Women: Abigail and Louisa Adams, Their Sisters and Daughters*. Oxford and New York: Oxford University Press, 1987.

Nash, Gary. "Forging Freedom: The Emancipation Experience in the Northern Seaport Cities." In *Slavery and Freedom in the Age of the American Revolution*. Edited by Ira Berlin and Ronald Hoffman. Charlottesville: United States Capitol Historical Society by the University Press of Virginia, 1983.

Nash, Gary. *The Unknown American Revolution: The Unruly Birth of Democracy and the Struggle to Create America*. New York: Penguin, 2005.

Nash, Gary. *Urban Crucible: The Northern Seaports and the Origins of the American Revolution*. Abridged ed. Cambridge, Mass.: Harvard University Press, 1986.

Nash, Gary. *Urban Crucible: Social Change, Political Consciousness, and the Origins of the American Revolution*. Cambridge, Mass., and London: Harvard University Press, 1979.

Nash, Gary H. *The Unknown American Revolution: The Unruly Birth of Democracy and the Struggle to Create America*. New York: Penguin, 2005.

Nash, Gary B., and Jean R. Soderlund. *Freedom by Degrees: Emancipation in Pennsylvania and Its Aftermath*. New York: Oxford University Press, 1991.

Newman, Paul Douglas. *Fries's Rebellion: The Enduring Struggle for the American Revolution*. Philadelphia: University of Pennsylvania Press, 2004.

Nobles, Gregory H. *Divisions throughout the Whole: Politics and Society in Hampshire County, Massachusetts, 1740–1775*. Cambridge, U.K.: Cambridge University Press, 1983.

Norton, Mary Beth. *Liberty's Daughters: The Revolutionary Experience of American Women, 1750–1800*. Ithaca, N.Y., and London: Cornell University Press, 1980.

Nybakken, Elizabeth I. "New Light on the Old Side: Irish Influences on Colonial Presbyterianism." *Journal of American History* 68, no. 4: 813–32.

Onuf, Peter S. "Liberty, Development, and Union: Visions of the West in the 1780s." In *Congress and the Confederation, The New American Nation 1775–1820* series. Edited by Peter S. Onuf. New York: Garland, 1991.

Onuf, Peter S. "Maryland: The Small Republic and the New Nation." In *Ratifying the Constitution*. Edited by Michael Allen Gillespie and Michael Lienesch. Lawrence: University Press of Kansas, 1989.

Onuf, Peter S. *The Origins of the Federal Republic: Jurisdictional Controversies in the United States, 1775–1787*. Philadelphia: University of Pennsylvania Press, 1983.

Orth, John V. *The Judicial Power of the United States: The Eleventh Amendment in American History*. Oxford: Oxford University Press, 1987.

Paul, Joel Richard. *Unlikely Allies: How a Merchant, a Playwright and a Spy Saved the American Revolution*. New York: Riverhead, 2009.

Pears, Thomas C., Jr. "Colonial Education among Presbyterians (Concluded)." *Journal of Presbyterian History* 30 (1952): 165–74.

Pennypacker, Morton. *General Washington's Spies on Long Island and in New York*. Brooklyn, N.Y.: Long Island Historical Society, 1939.

Perkins, Bradford. *The Creation of a Republican Empire, 1776–1865*. Vol. 1 of *The Cambridge History of American Foreign Relations*. Edited by Warren I. Cohen. Cambridge, U.K.: Cambridge University Press, 1993.

Pernick, Martin. "Politics, Parties, and Pestilence: Epidemic Yellow Fever in Philadelphia and the Rise of the First Party System." *William and Mary Quarterly* 29 (October 1972): 559–86.

Peterson, Harold Leslie. *The Book of the Continental Soldier: Uniforms, Weapons, and Equipment with Which He Lived and Fought*. Harrisburg, Pa.: Stackpole, 1968.

Phillips, Christopher. *Freedom's Port: The African-American Community of Baltimore, 1790–1860*. Urbana and Chicago: University of Illinois Press, 1997.

Porter, Roy. *The Cambridge Illustrated History of Medicine*. Cambridge, U.K.: Cambridge University Press, 1996.

Porter, Roy. *The Greatest Benefit to Mankind: A Medical History of Humanity*. New York and London: W. W. Norton, 1997.

Pound, Merritt B. *Benjamin Hawkins—Indian Agent*. Athens: University of Georgia Press, 1951.

Powell, Jonathan. "Presbyterian Loyalists: A Chain of Interest in Philadelphia." *Journal of Presbyterian History* 57 (1979): 135–71.

Powell, Martyn J. *Britain and Ireland in the Eighteenth-Century Crisis of Empire*. Hampshire, U.K., and New York: Palgrave Macmillan, 2003.

Prince, Carl. *The Federalists and the Origins of the U.S. Civil Service*. New York: New York University Press, 1977.

Prucha, Francis Paul. *The Sword of the Republic: The United States Army on the Frontier, 1783–1846*. Toronto: Macmillan, 1969.

Rakove, Jack N. *The Beginnings of National Politics: An Interpretive History of the Continental Congress*. New York: Alfred A. Knopf, 1979.

Rakove, Jack N. *Original Meanings: Politics and Ideas in the Making of the Constitution*. New York: Alfred A. Knopf, 1997.

Rappleye, Charles. *Robert Morris: Financier of the American Revolution*. New York: Simon & Schuster, 2010.

Reid, John Phillip. *Constitutional History of the American Revolution*. Madison: University of Wisconsin Press, 1987.

Reiss, Oscar. *Medicine in Colonial America*. New York: Oxford: University Press, 2000.

Renzulli, L. Marx, Jr. *Maryland: The Federalist Years*. Rutherford, N.J.: Fairleigh Dickinson University Press, 1972.

Ridgway, Whitman H. *Community Leadership in Maryland, 1790–1840*. Chapel Hill: University of North Carolina Press, 1979.

Risch, Erna. *Quartermaster Support of the Army: A History of the Corps, 1775–1939*. Washington, D.C.: U.S. Government Printing Office for the Center of Military History United States Army, 1989.

Risjord, Norman K. *Chesapeake Politics, 1781–1800*. New York: Columbia University Press, 1978.

Robbins, Karen. "Ambition Rewarded: James McHenry's Entry into Post-Revolutionary Maryland Politics," *Maryland Historical Magazine* 93 (Summer 1998): 191–214.

Robbins, Karen. "'Domestic Bagatelles': Servants, Generations and Gender in the McHenry Family of the Early Republic." *Maryland Historical Magazine* 104 (Spring 2009): 31–51.

Robbins, Karen. "Power among the Powerless: Domestic Resistance by Free and Slave Women in the McHenry Family of the New Republic." *Journal of the Early Republic* 23 (Spring 2003): 47–68.

Robinson, Donald L. *Slavery in the Structure of American Politics, 1765–1820.* New York: Harcourt Brace Jovanovich, 1971.

Rossiter, Clinton. *1787: The Grand Convention.* New York: Macmillan, 1966.

Royster, Charles. *Light-Horse Harry Lee and the Legacy of the American Revolution.* New York: Alfred A. Knopf, 1981.

Royster, Charles. *A Revolutionary People at War: The Continental Army and American Character, 1775–1783.* Published for the Institute of Early American History and Culture, Williamsburg, Virginia. Chapel Hill: University of North Carolina Press, 1979.

Ryan, Mary. *Cradle of the Middle Class: The Family in Oneida County, New York, 1790–1865.* Cambridge, U.K.: Cambridge University Press, 1991, 31–33.

Ryden, George H. "The Newark Academy of Delaware in Colonial Days." *Pennsylvania History* 2 (1935): 205–24.

Ryerson, Richard Alan. *The Revolution Is Now Begun—The Radical Committees of Philadelphia, 1765–1776.* Philadelphia: University of Pennsylvania Press, 1978.

Schama, Simon. *Patriots and Liberators: Revolution in the Netherlands, 1780–1813.* New York: Alfred A. Knopf, 1977.

Scharf, John Thomas. *Chronicles of Baltimore: Being a Complete History of Baltimore Town and Baltimore City from the Earliest Period to the Present Time.* Berwyn Heights, Md.: Heritage, reprint edition, 1989.

Scharf, John Thomas. *History of Maryland, from the Earliest Period to the Present Day.* 2 vols. Baltimore: J. B. Piet, 1879.

Schachner, Nathan. *Alexander Hamilton.* New York and London: D. Appleton-Century, 1946.

Shammas, Carole. "Anglo-American Household Government in Comparative Perspective." *William and Mary Quarterly* 52 (1995): 104–44.

Shaw, Peter. *The Character of John Adams.* Chapel Hill: University of North Carolina Press, 1976.

Sheehan, Bernard H. *Seeds of Extinction: Jeffersonian Philanthropy and the American Indian.* Chapel Hill: Published for the Institute of Early American History and Culture at Williamsburg, Virginia by the University of North Carolina Press, 1973.

Sloan, Douglas. *The Scottish Enlightenment and the American College Ideal.* New York: Teacher's College Press, Teacher's College, Columbia University, 1971.

Smelser, Marshall. *The Democratic Republic, 1801–1815.* New York: Harper & Row, 1968.

Smelser, Marshall. "The Federalist Period as an Age of Passion." *American Quarterly* 10 (Winter 1958): 391–419.

Smelser, Marshall. "The Jacobin Phrenzy: Federalism and the Menace of Liberty, Equality, and Fraternity." *Review of Politics* 13 (October 1951): 457–82.

Smith, James Morton. *Freedom's Fetters: The Alien and Sedition Laws and American Civil Liberties.* Ithaca, N.Y.: Cornell University Press, 1956.

Smith, Jean Edward. *John Marshall: Definer of a Nation.* New York: Henry Holt, 1996.

Smith, Merritt Roe. *Harpers Ferry Armory and the New Technology: The Challenge of Change.* Ithaca, N.Y.: Cornell University Press, 1977.

Smith, Page. *John Adams.* 2 vols. Garden City, N.Y.: Doubleday, 1962.

Smith, Paul H., ed. *Letters of Delegates to Congress, 1774–1789*. 26 vols. Washington, D.C.: Library of Congress, 1976–2000.

Spivak, Burton. *Jefferson's English Crisis: Commerce, Embargo, and the Republican Revolution*. Charlottesville: University Press of Virginia, 1979.

Stagg, J. C. A. *Mr. Madison's War: Politics, Diplomacy and Warfare in the Early American Republic*. Princeton, N.J.: Princeton University Press, 1983.

Starkey, Armstrong. "Paoli to Stony Point: Military Ethics and Weaponry During the American Revolution." *Journal of Military History* (January 1994): 7–27.

Starr, Paul. *The Social Transformation of American Medicine: The Rise of a Sovereign Profession and the Making of a Vast Industry*. New York: Basic, 1982.

Steffen, Charles G. *The Mechanics of Baltimore: Workers and Politics in the Age of Revolution, 1763–1812*. Urbana and Chicago: University of Illinois Press, 1984.

Steiner, Bernard C. *The Life and Correspondence of James McHenry, Secretary of War under Washington and Adams*. Cleveland: Burrows, 1907.

Steiner, Bernard C. "Maryland's Adoption of the Federal Constitution." *American Historical Review* 5 (October 1899): 22–44.

Steirer, William Frank, Jr. "Philadelphia Newspapers: Years of Revolution and Transition, 1764, 1795." Ph.D. dissertation, University of Pennsylvania, 1972.

Stinchcombe, William. *The XYZ Affair*. Westport, Conn.: Greenwood, 1980.

Stiverson, Gregory. "Necessity, the Mother of Union: Maryland and the Constitution, 1785–1789." In *The Constitution and the States: The Role of the Original Thirteen in the Framing and Adoption of the Federal Constitution*. Edited by Patrick T. Conley and John P. Kaminski. Madison, Wisc.: Madison House, 1988.

Tachau, Mary K. Bonsteel. "George Washington and the Reputation of Edmund Randolph." *Journal of American History* 73 (1986): 15–34.

Taylor, Alan. *Liberty Men and Great Proprietors: The Revolutionary Settlement on the Maine Frontier, 1760–1820*. Chapel Hill: Published for the Institute of Early American History and Culture by the University of North Carolina Press, 1990.

Tinkcom, Harry Marlin. *The Republicans and Federalists in Pennsylvania, 1790–1801: A Study in National Stimulus and Local Response*. Harrisburg: Pennsylvania Historical and Museum Commission, 1950.

Toll, Ian W. *Six Frigates: The Epic History of the Founding of the U.S. Navy*. New York: W. W. Norton, 2006.

Tucker, Robert W., and David C. Hendrickson. *Empire of Liberty: The Statecraft of Thomas Jefferson*. New York: Oxford University Press, 1990.

Ulrich, Laurel Thatcher. *Good Wives: Image and Reality in the Lives of Women in Northern New England, 1650–1750*. New York: Vintage, 1980; reprint ed. 1991.

Unger, Howard Giles. *American Tempest: How the Boston Tea Party Sparked a Revolution*. Cambridge, Mass.: DaCapo Press, 2011.

Upham, Charles W. *The Life of Timothy Pickering*. 4 vols. Boston: Little, Brown, 1873.

U.S. Army Quartermaster Foundation. http://www.qmfound.com/Samuel_Hodgdon .htm.

Van Creveld, Martin. *Supplying War: Logistics from Wallenstein to Patton*. Cambridge, U.K.: Cambridge University Press, 1977.

Van Tassel, Emily, and Paul Finkelman. "Senator William Blount." In *Impeachable Offenses: A Documentary History from 1787 to the Present*. Washington, D.C.: Congressional Quarterly, 1999, 86–90.

Warren, Charles. *The Making of the Constitution.* New York: Barnes & Noble, 1967 reprint.

Watson, Mark Skinner. *Chief of Staff: Prewar Plans and Preparations.* Volume 1 of the subseries *The War Department* and volume 6 of *The United States Army in World War II.* Kent Roberts Greenfield, general ed. Washington, D.C.: U.S. Government Printing Office, 1950.

Wickwire, Franklin, and Mary. *Cornwallis: the American Adventure.* Boston: Houghton Mifflin, 1970.

Wiecek, William M. *The Sources of Antislavery Constitutionalism in America, 1760–1848.* Ithaca and London: Cornell University Press, 1977.

Wiencek, Henry. *An Imperfect God: George Washington, His Slaves, and the Creation of America.* New York: Farrar, Straus & Giroux, 2003.

White, Deborah Gray. *Ar'n't I A Woman? Female Slaves in the Plantation South.* New York: W. W. Norton, 1985.

White, Leonard D. *The Federalists: A Study in Administrative History, 1789–1801.* New York: Free Press, 1965.

White, Shane. *Somewhat More Independent: The End of Slavery in New York City, 1770–1810.* Athens and London: University of Georgia Press, 1991.

Whitaker, Preston. *The Mississippi Question, 1795–1803: A Study in Trade, Politics and Diplomacy.* New York: D. Appleton-Century, 1934.

Whitman, T. Stephen. *The Price of Freedom: Slavery and Freedom in Baltimore and Early National Maryland.* New York and London: Routledge, 1999.

Whitten, Dolphus, Jr. "The State Delegations in the Philadelphia Convention of 1787." Ph.D. dissertation, University of Texas, 1961.

Wilbur, William Allan. "Crisis in Leadership: Alexander Hamilton, Timothy Pickering the Politics of Federalism, 1795, 1804." Ph.D. dissertation, Syracuse University, 1969.

Wills, Garry. *Cincinnatus: George Washington and the Enlightenment.* New York: Doubleday, 1984.

Wilson, Charles H., Jr. "The Supreme Court's Bill of Attainder Doctrine: A Need for Clarification." *California Law Review* 54 (March 1966): 212–51.

Wingo, Barbara Christine Gray. "Politics, Society, and Religion: The Presbyterian Clergy of Pennsylvania, New Jersey, and New York, and the Formation of the Nation, 1775–1808." Ph.D. dissertation, Tulane University, 1976.

Woloch, Nancy. *Women and the American Experience,* 4th ed. Boston: McGraw-Hill, 2006.

Wood, Gordon S. "Conspiracy and the Paranoid Style: Causality and Deceit in the Eighteenth Century." *William and Mary Quarterly* 39 (July 1982): 401–41.

Wood, Gordon S. *Empire of Liberty: A History of the Early Republic, 1789–1815.* Oxford: Oxford University Press, 2009.

Wood, Gordon S. *The Radicalism of the American Revolution.* New York: A. A. Knopf, 1992; paperback ed., New York: Vintage, 1993.

Zagarri, Rosemarie. *A Woman's Dilemma: Mercy Otis Warren and the American Revolution.* Wheeling, Ill.: Harlan Davidson, 1995.

Zahniser, Marvin R. *Charles Cotesworth Pinckney, Founding Father.* Chapel Hill: University of North Carolina Press, 1967.

Zilversmit, Arthur. *The First Emancipation: The Abolition of Slavery in the North.* Chicago and London: University of Chicago Press, 1967.

Index